Annual Editions: The Family, Forty-First Edition

Patricia Hrusa Williams

http://create.mheducation.com

ISBN-10: 1259181758   ISBN-13: 9781259181757

Contents

Unit 4 139

Unit 5 227

Preface

The purpose of *Annual Editions: The Family*, 41/e is to bring to the reader the latest thoughts and trends in our understanding of the family, to identify current concerns as well as problems and potential solutions, and to present alternative views on family processes. The intent of this anthology is to explore family relationships and to reflect the family's evolving function and importance. The articles in this volume are taken from professional journals as well as other professionally-oriented publications and popular lay publications aimed at both special populations and a general readership. The selections are carefully reviewed for their currency and accuracy.

In the current edition, a number of new articles have been added to reflect reviewers' comments on the previous edition. As the reader, you will note the tremendous range in tone and focus of these articles, from first-person accounts to reports of scientific discoveries as well as philosophical and theoretical writings. Some are more practical and applications-oriented, while others are more conceptual and research-oriented. Together they highlight the multidisciplinary nature of the study of the family and the myriad influences that shape the family as a social structure and unit of socialization.

This anthology is organized to address many of the important aspects of family and family relationships. The first unit takes an overview perspective and looks at varied perspectives on the family. The second unit examines the beginnings of relationships as individuals go through the process of exploring and establishing connections. In the third unit is an examination of family communication, relationships, and interactions in various types of relationships including marital, parent–child, sibling, and intergenerational relationships. The fourth unit is concerned with crises and ways in which these can act as challenges and opportunities for families and their members. Finally, the fifth unit takes an affirming tone as it looks at family strengths and rituals, ways of empowering families, and emerging trends within families and their formation.

Annual Editions: The Family, 41/e is intended to be used as a supplemental text for lower-level, introductory marriage, family, or sociology of the family classes, particularly when they tie the content of the readings to essential information on marriages and families, however they are defined. As a supplement, this book can also be used to update or emphasize certain aspects of standard marriage and family textbooks. Because of the provocative nature of many of the essays in this anthology, it works well as a basis for class discussion, debate, and critical thinking exercises about various aspects of marriages and family relationships. This edition of *Annual Editions: The Family* contains websites noted after each article that can be used to further explore topics addressed in the readings.

Patricia Hrusa Williams
Editor

Editor

Patricia Hrusa Williams is an Assistant Professor in the Department of Early Childhood and Elementary Education at the University of Maine at Farmington. She received her BA in Health & Society and Psychology from the University of Rochester. Her PhD is in Applied Child Development from Tufts University. Dr. Williams' primary areas of interest are family support programs, parental involvement in early childhood education, infant–toddler development, service learning, and the development of writing and critical thinking skills in college students. She has authored, co-authored, or edited over 15 published articles in books, academic journals, and the popular press. Dr. Williams lives with her husband and three children in the mountains of western Maine.

Academic Advisory Board

Correlation Guide

The *Annual Editions* series provides students with convenient, inexpensive access to current, carefully selected articles from the public press. **Annual Editions: The Family, 41/e** is an easy-to-use reader that presents articles on important topics such as *family evolution, love, sex, and relationships, family challenges and opportunities,* and many more. For more information on other McGraw-Hill Create™ titles and collections, visit www.mcgrawhillcreate.com.

This convenient guide matches the articles in **Annual Editions: The Family, 41/e** with the corresponding chapters in **Marriages and Families: Intimacy, Diversity, and Strengths, 8/e** by Olson et al.

Marriages and Families: Intimacy, Diversity, and Strengths, 8/e by Olson et al.	Annual Editions: The Family, 41/e
Chapter 1: Perspectives on Intimate Relationships	Matches Made on Earth: Why Family Values Are Human Values The Changing American Family
Chapter 2: Cultural Diversity and Diversity in Family Structure: Family Strengths and Challenges	Bridging Cultural Divides: The Role and Impact of Binational Families Family Matters Goy Meets Girl The Changing Face of the American Family
Chapter 3: Understanding Marriage and Family Dynamics	Are You with the Right Mate? How to Stay Married Sibling Rivalry Grows Up: Adult Brothers and Sisters Are Masters at Digs; Finding a Way to a Truce Truth or Dare Why Do Marriages Fail?
Chapter 4: Communication and Intimacy	Secret Histories: In an Age of Lessening Privacy, Some Family Secrets Persist Truth or Dare What Kids Learn from Hearing Family Stories
Chapter 5: Conflict and Conflict Resolution	Family Members' Informal Roles in End-of-Life Decision Making in Adult Intensive Care Units Sibling Rivalry Grows Up: Adult Brothers and Sisters Are Masters at Digs; Finding a Way to a Truce Terrorism in the Home: Eleven myths and facts about domestic violence
Chapter 6: Sexual Intimacy	12 Rude Revelations About Sex From Promise to Promiscuity The State of Extramarital Affairs
Chapter 7: Gender Roles and Power in the Family	Behind Every Great Woman Boys on the Side The Changing Face of the American Family
Chapter 8: Managing Economic Resources	Exploring the Lived Experiences of Homeless Families with Young Children International Perspectives on Work-Family Policies: Lessons from the World's Most Competitive Economies
Chapter 9: Friendship, Intimacy, and Singlehood	Boys on the Side The End of Courtship?
Chapter 10: Dating, Mate Selection, and Living Together	Boys on the Side The Expectations Trap There's No Such Thing as Everlasting Love (According to Science) Waiting to Wed
Chapter 11: Marriage: Building a Strong Foundation	Are You with the Right Mate? From Promise to Promiscuity Goy Meets Girl How to Stay Married The Gay Guide to Wedded Bliss The State of Extramarital Affairs There's No Such Thing as Everlasting Love (According to Science)

Marriages and Families: Intimacy, Diversity, and Strengths, 8/e by Olson et al.	Annual Editions: The Family, 41/e
Chapter 12: Parenthood: Joys and Challenges	Getting It Right From the Start My Rules for My Kids: Eat Your Vegetables; Don't Blame the Teacher Not Wanting Kids Is Entirely Normal Parenting Wars Teen Spirit The Child's Advocate in Donor Conceptions: The Telling of the Story The Coming Special Needs Care Crisis You Got Your Sperm Where?
Chapter 13: Midlife and Older Couples	Baby Boomers Care for Grandchildren as Daughters Pursue Careers Daddy Issues: Why Caring For My Aging Father Has Me Wishing He Would Die Family Members' Informal Roles in End-of-Life Decision Making in Adult Intensive Care Units How to Stay Married The Accordion Family
Chapter 14: Stress, Abuse, and Family Problems	A Guide in the Darkness Alcohol and Drug Misuse: A Family Affair Anguish of the Abandoned Child Keeping the Promise: Maintaining the Health of Military and Veteran Families and Children Supporting Siblings of Children with Autism Spectrum Disorders Support Needs of Siblings of People with Developmental Disabilities Terrorism in the Home: Eleven myths and Facts about Domestic violence The Coming Special Needs Care Crisis We Are Family: When Elder Abuse, Neglect, and Financial Exploitation Hit Home
Chapter 15: Divorce, Single-Parent Families, and Stepfamilies	Helping Children Endure Divorce The Changing Face of the American Family The Effects of Co-Parenting Relationships with Ex-Spouses on Couples in Step-Families Why Do Marriages Fail?
Chapter 16: Strengthening Marriages and Families Worldwide	Family Unplugged International Perspectives on Work-Family Policies: Lessons from the World's Most Competitive Economies What Kids Learn from Hearing Family Stories

This convenient guide matches the articles in **Annual Editions: The Family, 41/e** with the corresponding chapters in **Intimate Relationships, 7/e** by Miller.

Intimate Relationships, 7/e by Miller	Annual Editions: The Family, 41/e
Chapter 1: The Building Blocks of Relationships	Bridging Cultural Divides: The Role and Impact of Binational Families Matches Made on Earth: Why Family Values Are Human Values
Chapter 2: Research Methods	Family Matters The Changing Face of the American Family
Chapter 3: Attraction	A Million First Dates: How Online Romance Is Threatening Monogamy The End of Courtship? The Expectations Trap
Chapter 4: Social Cognition	A Million First Dates: How Online Romance Is Threatening Monogamy The End of Courtship? The Expectations Trap
Chapter 5: Communication	Secret Histories: In an Age of Lessening Privacy, Some Family Secrets Persist Truth or Dare
Chapter 6: Interdependency	Behind Every Great Woman The Changing Face of the American Family Waiting to Wed You Got Your Sperm Where?

Intimate Relationships, 7/e by Miller	Annual Editions: The Family, 41/e
Chapter 7: Friendship	Sibling Rivalry Grows Up: Adult Brothers and Sisters Are Masters at Digs; Finding a Way to a Truce Truth or Dare
Chapter 8: Love	Are You with the Right Mate? How to Stay Married There's No Such Thing as Everlasting Love (According to Science)
Chapter 9: Sexuality	12 Rude Revelations About Sex Boys on the Side From Promise to Promiscuity The State of Extramarital Affairs
Chapter 10: Stresses and Strains	A Guide in the Darkness Alcohol and Drug Misuse: A Family Affair Keeping the Promise: Maintaining the Health of Military and Veteran Families and Children Secret Histories: In an Age of Lessening Privacy, Some Family Secrets Persist
Chapter 11: Conflict	Goy Meets Girl Secret Histories: In an Age of Lessening Privacy, Some Family Secrets Persist
Chapter 12: Power and Violence	Terrorism in the Home: Eleven myths and facts about domestic violence We Are Family: When Elder Abuse, Neglect, and Financial Exploitation Hit Home
Chapter 13: The Dissolution and Loss of Relationships	Helping Children Endure Divorce The Effects of Co-Parenting Relationships with Ex-Spouses on Couples in Step-Families Why Do Marriages Fail?
Chapter 14: Maintaining and Repairing Relationships	Are You with the Right Mate? How to Stay Married The Gay Guide to Wedded Bliss

Topic Guide

Unit 1

UNIT

Prepared by: Patricia Hrusa Williams, *University of Maine at Farmington*

Evolving Perspectives on the Family

Our image of what family is and what it should be is a powerful combination of personal experience, family forms we encounter or observe, and attitudes we hold. Once formed, this image informs decision making and interpersonal interaction throughout our lives and has far-reaching effects. On an intimate level, it influences individual and family development as well as the relationships we create and maintain both inside and outside the family. On a broader level, it affects legislation, social policy, and programmatic supports developed and offered to couples, parents, and families. In many ways, the images we build and hold can be positive. They can act to clarify our thinking and facilitate interaction with like-minded individuals. They can also be negative, narrowing our thinking and limiting our ability to see how we can learn from others and appreciate how other ways of carrying out family functions have value. Interaction with others can be impeded because of contrasting views.

This unit is intended to meet several goals in exploring the evolving family including: (1) to sensitize the reader to sources of beliefs about the "shoulds" of the family—what the family should be and the ways in which family roles and communication should be carried out, (2) to show how different views of the family can influence attitudes toward community responsibility and family policy, and (3) to show how changes in society are changing the nature of family life. Among the issues to be considered in this unit are how historical, demographic, social, and philosophical changes are influencing families and the nature of family life in the United States and abroad.

Prepared by: Patricia Hrusa Williams,
University of Maine at Farmington

Article

The Changing Face of the American Family

Tim Stanley

Learning Outcomes

After reading this article, you will be able to:

- Explain the meaning and origins of the term "nuclear family."
- Describe shifts in family structure from 1900 to the present.
- Recognize differences in the ways the media have portrayed families from 1950 to the present.

On September 20th, 1984 a new sitcom aired on NBC. *The Cosby Show* starred Bill Cosby as Heathcliff 'Cliff' Huxtable, a middle-class, black obstetrician living with his wife and five children in Brooklyn, New York. It kicked off with a situation that millions of parents could identify with: Cliff's son, Theo, had come home with a report card covered in Ds. Theo's mother was deeply upset and Cliff was furious. But Theo said that his bad grades didn't bother him because he didn't want to go to college. His goal was to grow up to be like 'regular people' and, if Cliff loves his son, won't he accept him for what he is? The audience applauded. This was what TV had been teaching them for over a decade, that love and understanding were more important than competition and success. But, to their shock, Cosby's character didn't agree. 'Theo,' he said, 'that is the dumbest thing I ever heard! No wonder you get Ds in everything! . . . I'm telling you, you are going to try as hard as you can. And you're going to do it because I said so. I am your father. I brought you into this world, and I will take you out!' The audience's laughter was nervous at first, but by the end of the scene they were clapping wildly. Bill Cosby had just turned the liberal logic of TV Land on its head. 'Father knows best' parenting was back.

This scene is discussed in the PBS documentary *America in Primetime*, shortly to be shown by the BBC.

The programme makes the point that because the Cosbys are African-Americans, we might presume that the politics of the show are liberal—sitcoms in the 1970s had tended to use black characters to explore poverty and racism. Yet Cliff Huxtable's old fashioned parenting had much more in common with the optimistic conservatism of the 1980s presidency of Republican Ronald Reagan. The Huxtables were wealthy, professional, churchgoers, dominated by a stern father. Alas, among black families their traditional structure increasingly made them the exception rather than the rule. In the America of the 1980s divorce and illegitimacy were rising fast. By 1992, when the show ended, 68 per cent of African-American babies were born out of wedlock. The last episode of *Cosby* coincided with riots in Los Angeles, the product of economic segregation and black fury at a brutal police force. The show might have started out as a healthy antidote to touchy-feely liberalism, but it ended as escapist fantasy.

The Cosby Show's huge viewing figures—among both blacks and whites—tell a confusing story. On the one hand divorce and illegitimacy were changing the character of the American family for good. Un-wed co-habitation was more likely; partners were more inclined to abandon an unhappy relationship; sex outside marriage was common. On the other hand Americans still held heterosexual marriage in high regard and wanted to watch shows that affirmed it. The big TV hits of the 1980s were all centred around traditional families— *Mr Belvedere, Who's The Boss?, Growing Pains*. Ronald Reagan's favourite show was *Family Ties,* which starred Michael J. Fox as a teenager who rebelled against his liberal parents by campaigning for Ronald Reagan.

The answer to this paradox lay in the enduring appeal of the nuclear family. America's nuclear unit wasn't around very long. It was forged by the unique economic and political circumstances of the 1950s, was undermined by social revolution in the 1960s and was revived as an ideal in the 1970s by a conservative movement with a deceptively rosy view of the past. But, while the nuclear family was only representative of how a number of people lived for a few years, its myth has hardened into an ideology. For many Americans it remains synonymous with the hallowed promise of the American dream.

Sitcom Suburbia

In 1957 CBS premiered a TV show called *Leave it to Beaver.* It starred Jerry Mathers as Theodore 'The Beaver' Cleaver, an inquisitive boy who lived with his parents June and Ward in a leafy suburb. The plot of every episode was the same: Beaver got in trouble, his parents reprimanded him and our hero would learn something about the realities of life.

In one storyline Beaver met the son of divorced parents and was jealous of all the presents he got from his estranged dad. But he quickly discovered that divorce also leads to insecurity and depression, so the episode ended with Beaver begging his parents never to part. Divorce wasn't the only model of social dysfunction that the show explored: spinsters like prim Aunt Martha were sexless harpies, while bachelors, like Andy the alcoholic handyman, were layabout bums. It was a world of conservative certainty, held together by a terror of nonconformity.

Today *Leave it to Beaver* is shorthand for the calm and luxury of American life before the storm of the 1960s. In fact the world that it depicted was a historical aberration; before 1950 things had been very different. In 1900 the vast majority of women went out to work and the US had the highest divorce rate in the world. Roughly one in ten children grew up in a single-parent household, hundreds of thousands of offspring were abandoned due to shortages of money and families were plagued with disease and death. Between 35 and 40 per cent of children lost a parent or a sibling before their 20s.

It wasn't until the 1950s that life began to get sweeter and more stable for the average American. The decade was characterised by a rising birth rate, a stable divorce rate and a declining age of marriage. In 1950 most married women walked down the aisle aged just 20. Only 16 per cent of them got a job outside the home and a majority of brides were pregnant within seven months of their wedding. They didn't stop at one child: from 1940 to 1960 the number of families with three children doubled and the number of families having a fourth child quadrupled.

Contemporary anthropologists dubbed this the 'nuclear family'. They meant nuclear as in a unit built around the nucleus of the father and mother, but the name also resonates with the politics of the Cold War. The family was on the front line of an existential conflict between communism and capitalism. On the communist side, the propagandists said, were collectivism, atheism and poverty. On the capitalist side was self-reliance, freedom of religion and a degree of material comfort unparalleled in US history. Science was eradicating disease, salaries were rising, household goods were alleviating drudgery and the nuclear family had a friend in big business.

The advertising agencies tried to create the model of the perfect housewife. A famous article in *Housekeeping Monthly* of May 13th, 1955 explained what perfection entailed:

> *Your goal: To try and make sure your home is a place of peace, order, and tranquility where your husband can renew himself in body and spirit. . . . Make him comfortable. Have him lean back in a comfortable chair or have him lie down in the bedroom. . . . Arrange his pillow and offer to take off his shoes. Speak in a low, soothing and pleasant voice. . . . Remember, he is the master of the house and as such will always exercise his will with fairness and truthfulness. You have no right to question him. A good wife always knows her place.*

Having popularised the ideal of a 'good wife', the advertisers recommended products that would put perfection within her reach. 'Christmas Morning, She'll Be Happier With a Hoover!' claimed one ad, which featured a housewife excitedly examining her new vacuum cleaner. Spending on advertising rose from $6 billion in 1950 to over $13 billion in 1963.

The efforts of advertising's Mad Men were central to the 1950s boom. Robert Sarnoff, president of the National Broadcasting Company, said in 1956: 'The reason we have such a high standard of living is because advertising has created an American frame of mind that makes people want more things, better things, and newer things.' He was probably right. Private debt doubled during the 1950s, driving up profit and productivity and returning much of it to the male wage earner. The economy grew by roughly 37 per cent, with low rates of inflation and unemployment. By 1960 the average family had 30 per cent more purchasing power than it had had in 1950. The nuclear unit was the engine of America's growth and the main beneficiary of its economic greatness.

The Sixties Swing Out of Control

But was everyone really as happy as the ads implied? In 1963 a book hit the shelves that claimed to expose all the oppression and misery that lay behind *Leave it to Beaver*'s white picket fences. Its author, Betty Friedan, described herself as a housewife and mother from the New York suburbs. In 1957 Friedan had been asked to conduct a survey of former Smith College classmates. The results depressed her. Girls who had studied and excelled at the arts and sciences were expected to surrender their minds and personalities to their roles as wives: 89 per cent of the Smith alumni who answered her survey were now homemakers. Intellectually repressed and lacking anyway to express themselves beyond cooking or sex, the housewife of the 1960s was suffocated by what Friedan called the feminine mystique. 'Each suburban wife struggles with it alone' she wrote. 'As she made the beds, shopped for groceries, matched slipcover material, ate peanut butter sandwiches with her children, chauffeured Cub Scouts and Brownies, lay beside her husband at night—she was afraid to ask even of herself the silent question—"Is this all?" '

The Feminine Mystique stayed on *The New York Times* bestseller list for six weeks and laid the groundwork for a feminist revolution that would redefine the nuclear unit forever. Friedan wanted women to take control of their lives and the shortcuts to liberation were contraception and employment. But the book wasn't quite the impartial account that its author claimed. Although she was technically a homemaker, Friedan was not an apolitical housewife who spent her evenings arranging her husband's pillow. She was active in socialist politics and had worked as a journalist for the United Electrical Workers union for a number of years after her marriage. Friedan probably hid all these details because she wanted to divorce feminism from radicalism and so make it more palatable to the average woman. More troublingly, she exaggerated the degree to which the women of Smith College were the passive victims of patriarchy. In fact most of the housewives who answered her survey said they were the happiest they had ever been—a majority expressed no desire to return to the world of work. But they did not buy the advertisers' myth of suburban fulfilment and many said that they felt frustrated that they could not use their intellect in more demanding ways. Instead they were channelling those energies into voluntary work and party political activism. Contemporary women were already finding ways to overcome the feminine mystique, while retaining their identities as wives and mothers.

Although Friedan and the women's liberation movement sometimes imagined that they masterminded the 1960s cultural revolution their role was actually to politicise social changes that were already happening. Just as science helped to forge the nuclear family, with better nutrition and disease control, so it created the conditions for its destruction. In 1960 the US Food and Drug Administration officially licensed the sale of the oral contraceptive known as the Pill. By 1962 an estimated 1,187,000 women were using it. Policy makers thought the Pill would strengthen the nuclear family by increasing disposable income via reduced pregnancies. What it did in practice was to weaken the links between sexual pleasure, childbirth and marriage. Sex before and outside marriage increased, while women who had married became more likely to seek work or stay in it.

The effects of such subtle changes in sexual practice were startling. Between 1960 and 1980 the divorce rate almost doubled. In 1962 only half of all respondents disagreed with a statement suggesting that parents who don't get along should stay together for the children; by 1977 over 80 per cent disagreed. In the early 1960s roughly half of women told pollsters that they had engaged in premarital sex. By the late 1980s the figure was five out of six. In the early 1960s approximately three quarters of Americans said premarital sex was wrong. By the 1980s that view was held by only one third of the nation. The most obvious legacy of shifting attitudes was the rocketing rate of births out of wedlock. In 1960 only five per cent of births were attributed to single mothers. By 1980 the figure was 18 per cent and by 1990 it was 28 per cent.

Both Left and Right were worried that America was coming apart. Although the 1960s were dominated by the struggles over Vietnam and Civil Rights, an equally big policy challenge was how to save the nuclear family unit. The Left concluded that the answer was greater government support. In 1965 the liberal sociologist Daniel Patrick Moynihan published *The Negro Family: The Case For National Action*. A study of poverty in the African-American ghetto, the so-called *Moynihan Report* argued that the underlying cause of inequality between black and white was not economics or race but family structure. Moynihan believed that the growing incidence of single motherhood was raising a generation of African-American males who lacked a model of self-reliance, discipline and authority. He advised Democratic President Lyndon Johnson that the solution was job training and education programmes that would empower black fathers to raise their family on a single salary. The welfare state would have to grow.

Johnson declared a 'War on Poverty' that created a plethora of entitlements to individuals. The use of government subsidies to buy meals (which had been around since the 1930s) increased dramatically under both Democrat and Republican administrations: the number of individuals using food stamps jumped from 500,000 in 1965 to 10 million in 1971. The overall effect was a fall in the proportion of Americans living in poverty from 19 per cent in 1964 to 11.1 per cent in 1973. But government generosity did nothing to stop the decline of the nuclear unit. Conservatives argued that it actually undermined the family by subsidising absentee fathers, educational underachievement, crime, drugs and a new, somewhat racialised, form of segregation between those in work and those on the dole. Moynihan's ambition to rescue the black family failed. While the median black family income rose 53 per cent in the 1960s, the rate of single parenthood also increased by over 50 per cent. Conservatives began to argue that the welfare state was not the solution but part of the problem. They claimed that the real goal of liberals like Friedan and Johnson was to create a world in which the nuclear family no longer existed.

Lost Age of Innocence

In 1976 America went to the polls to elect a new president. Its choice was Jimmy Carter, a former peanut farmer and one-term governor of Georgia. With his photogenic family and foursquare humility, the Baptist Carter felt like a throwback to the *Leave it to Beaver* spirit. In the mid-1970s America was experiencing a wave of nostalgia for the 1950s; movies like *Grease* and *American Graffiti* celebrated a lost age of innocence and certainty. Carter said that if he won the election he would hold a White House 'Conference on the Family' to discuss the best way of reviving some of those old values. It was exactly the kind of consensus-building, moral politics that Carter loved.

But after Carter's inauguration the White House announced a name change. The Conference on the Family would become the Conference on Families, reflecting the growing diversity of American family structures. Presidential aides pointed out that roughly a third of families no longer adhered to what they described as the 'nostalgic family'—their rather patronising term for the nuclear unit. One person who welcomed the rebranding was delegate Betty Friedan. In her 1981 book *The Second Stage* she wrote that she was pleased the conference recognised the most important shift in American life that had occurred in the last 20 years: 'women now work'. Indeed they did. In 1950 the proportion of married women under 45 who worked was just 26 per cent; by 1985 it would hit 67 per cent. The growing expectation—and need—for women to enter the labour market had a dramatic impact upon gender roles, child-rearing and patterns of cohabitation. Life for the Seventies woman was more independent and more complex.

Friedan hoped that the conference would continue the work of the Johnson administration in expanding government aid to individuals struggling to get by in the new social order. Recession made the task all the more important: 'With men being laid off in both blue-collar and white-collar jobs, with inflation showing no let-up, women's opportunity needed [legal] underpinning to insure the survival of the family.'

Friedan's manifesto was something that many European nations would enthusiastically embrace in the 1980s: accept that the family is no longer nuclear and build the welfare and employment opportunities necessary to strengthen its new incarnation. But this wasn't Europe and many Americans responded to social change with either resistance or denial. When the conference was finally held in 1980 it was dominated by polarising minorities of feminists and social conservatives.

America was undergoing a religious revival and the cultural Right was evolving into a well-oiled political machine. Its delegates to the Conference on Families believed that women's best hope of 'liberation' was found in marriage, where their compassionate instinct for motherhood formed a perfect union with their husbands' authority. To the feminists at the conference such views were the last gasp of an old, patriarchal order that was out of step with the unstoppable march of progress. Boasting superior numbers of delegates, the feminists were able to push through platforms endorsing abortion on demand and gay rights. Their success gave them the illusion of political momentum.

But the press and the public were rather more interested in the rhetoric of the conservative delegates, who staged a colourful walkout. Outside the conference, the anti-feminist activist Connie Marshner told the media that 'families consist of people related by heterosexual marriage, blood and adoption. Families are not religious cults, families are not Manson families, families are not heterosexual or homosexual liaisons outside of marriage.' Marshner's simple language articulated the feelings of millions of Americans that the sexual revolution was not just replacing the nuclear unit with something more complex—it was destroying the very concept of family itself.

Recognising that this view was gaining currency Carter tried to charm several televangelists at a White House breakfast in January 1980. The meeting was a disaster. When it was over, the preacher Tim LaHaye prayed 'God we have got to get this man out of the White House and get someone in here who will be aggressive about bringing back traditional moral values'. The religious Right decided that its best shot was Republican Ronald Reagan. When Reagan beat Carter by a landslide in November 1980 he captured two thirds of the white evangelical vote. Politics for the next 30 years would be dominated by the conservatism of Marshner, not the progressive ambitions of Friedan.

The Paradox of the American Family

Since the 1980s the American family has continued its inexorable evolution towards greater diversity and complexity. Yet America's popular culture, just like *The Cosby Show,* continues to celebrate a 1950s' vision of 'living right, living free'.

It is tempting to accuse conservatives of promoting paradoxical politics that are out of step with the modern world. In 2012 an estimated 19 per cent of gay people are raising a child in the US, yet every referendum on gay marriage has resulted in its ban. States like Texas offer abstinence promotions in place of sex education, yet people who take a chastity pledge are

statistically more likely to get pregnant outside marriage than those who do not. And despite feminism's supposed grip upon the American imagination, voters are more anti-abortion than at any point since the 1980s. Against the European trend toward social liberalism the United States looks even more conservative today than it was when Bill Cosby first told his son to quit griping and start revising.

But the nuclear family endures as an ideal for good reason. For many middle-class whites the 1950s really were the Golden Age. At home families were large and stable and often kept by a single, generous wage. America was the workshop of the world, producing a flood of consumer goods that improved the lives of millions. Abroad the USA established itself as a model of the good life. The American Dream—meritocratic and capable of reaping great rewards—set an international standard for democratic capitalism. Never again would Americans tell pollsters that they were as content in their own lives or as confident about their country's direction. It was an age of innocence and sometimes that innocence blinded people to the realities of patriarchy and racism. But it will remain the yardstick by which Americans judge their country for a very long time.

Further Reading

David Allyn, *Make Love, Not War. The Sexual Revolution: An Unfettered History* (Little, Brown, 2000).

Mary Dalton and Laura Linder (eds.), *The Sitcom Reader: America Viewed and Skewed* (SUNY Press, 2005).

Daniel Horowitz, *Betty Friedan and the Making of The Feminine Mystique: The American Left, The Cold War, and Modern Feminism* (University of Massachusetts Press, 1998).

Dominic Sandbrook, *Mad as Hell: The Crisis of the 1970s and the Rise of the Populist Right* (Knopf, 2011).

Critical Thinking

1. Explain what the term "nuclear family" means and its origins.

2. There has been much debate about what kind of family structure is best for U.S. families. What structure do you view as most adaptive and why?

3. How have social, political, economic, and religious forces and scientific changes affected the structure, functioning, and expectations we have for families in the United States?

4. Do you feel that the media have portrayed the American family fairly and honestly? Why or why not?

5. How should we define what a family is in the United States today?

Create Central

www.mhhe.com/createcentral

Internet References

World Family Map
http://worldfamilymap.org/2013

Australian Institute of Family Studies
www.aifs.gov.au

Feminist Perspectives on Reproduction and the Family
http://plato.stanford.edu/entries/feminism-family

Kearl's Guide to the Sociology of the Family
www.trinity.edu/MKEARL/family.html

TIM STANLEY is associate fellow of the Rothermere American Institute, Oxford University. His documentary *Sitcom USA* will be broadcast on BBC2 on October 27th 2012 at 9 pm.

Article   Prepared by: Patricia Hrusa Williams, *University of Maine at Farmington*

Family Matters

What's the most important factor blocking social mobility? Single parents, suggests a new study.

W. Bradford Wilcox

Learning Outcomes

After reading this article, you will be able to:

- Identify community and family factors associated with social mobility in the United States.

- Describe how single parenthood may be linked with other factors that limit children's later economic outcomes.

Next week, in his State of the Union address, President Obama is expected to return to a theme he and many progressives have been hitting hard in recent months: namely, that the American Dream is in trouble and that growing economic inequality is largely to blame. In a speech to the Center for American Progress last month, Obama said: "The combined trends of increased inequality and decreasing mobility pose a fundamental threat to the American Dream." Likewise, [The] *New York Times* columnist Paul Krugman recently wrote that the nation "claims to reward the best and brightest regardless of family background" but in practice shuts out "children of the middle and working classes."

Progressives like Obama and Krugman are clearly right to argue that the American Dream is in trouble. Today, poor children have a limited shot at moving up the economic ladder into the middle or upper class. One study found that the nation leaves 70 percent of poor children below the middle class as adults. Equally telling, poor children growing up in countries like Canada and Denmark have a greater chance of moving up the economic ladder than do poor children from the United States. As Obama noted, these trends call into question the "American story" that our nation is exceptionally successful in delivering equal opportunity to its citizens.

But the more difficult question is: Why? What are the factors preventing poor children from getting ahead? An important new Harvard study that looks at the best community data on mobility in America—released this past weekend—suggests a cause progressives may find discomforting, especially if they are interested in reviving the American Dream for the 21st century.

The study, "Where is the Land of Opportunity?: The Geography of Intergenerational Mobility in the United States," authored by Harvard economist Raj Chetty and colleagues from Harvard and Berkeley, explores the community characteristics most likely to predict mobility for lower-income children. The study specifically focuses on two outcomes: absolute mobility for lower-income children—that is, how far up the income ladder they move as adults; and relative mobility—that is, how far apart children who grew up rich and poor in the same community end up on the economic ladder as adults. When it comes to these measures of upward mobility in America, the new Harvard study asks: Which "factors are the strongest predictors of upward mobility in multiple variable regressions"?

1) Family structure. Of all the factors most predictive of economic mobility in America, one factor clearly stands out in their study: family structure. By their reckoning, when it comes to mobility, "the strongest and most robust predictor is the fraction of children with single parents." They find that children raised in communities with high percentages of single mothers are significantly less likely to experience absolute and relative mobility. Moreover, "[c]hildren of married parents also have higher rates of upward mobility if they live in communities with fewer single parents." In other words, as Figure 1 indicates, it looks like a married village is more likely to raise the economic prospects of a poor child.

What makes this finding particularly significant is that this is the first major study showing that rates of single parenthood

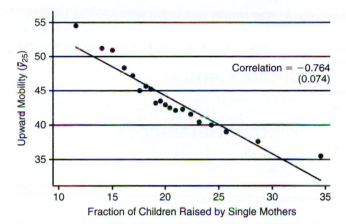

Figure 1   Upward Mobility by Share of Single Mothers in a Community   A. Upward Mobility vs. Fraction Single Mothers in CZ

Source: Chetty et al. 2014

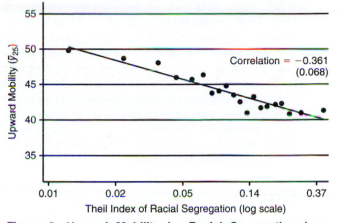

Figure 2   Upward Mobility by Racial Segregation in a Community   A. Upward Mobility vs. Theil Index of Racial Segregation

Source: Chetty et al. 2014

at the community level are linked to children's economic opportunities over the course of their lives. A lot of research—including new research from the Brookings Institution—has shown us that kids are more likely to climb the income ladder when they are raised by two, married parents. But this is the first study to show that lower-income kids from both single- and married-parent families are more likely to succeed if they hail from a community with lots of two-parent families.

2) Racial and economic segregation. According to this new study, economic and racial segregation are also important characteristics of communities that do not foster economic mobility. Children growing up in communities that are racially segregated, or cluster lots of poor kids together, do not have a great shot at the American Dream. In fact, in their study, racial segregation is one of only two key factors—the other is family structure—that is consistently associated with both absolute and relative mobility in America. Figure 2 illustrates the bivariate association between racial segregation and economic mobility.

3) School quality. Another powerful predictor of absolute mobility for lower-income children is the quality of schools in their communities. Chetty et al. measure this in the study by looking at high-school dropout rates. Their takeaway: Poor kids are more likely to make it in America when they have access to schools that do a good job of educating them.

4) Social capital. In a finding that is bound to warm the heart of their colleague, Harvard political scientist Robert Putnam, Chetty and his team find that communities with more social capital enjoy significantly higher levels of absolute mobility for poor children. That is, communities across America that have high levels of religiosity, civic engagement, and voter involvement are more likely to lift the fortunes of their poorest members.

5) Income inequality. Finally, consistent with the diagnosis of Messrs. Obama and Krugman, Chetty and his team note that income inequality within communities is correlated with lower levels of mobility. However, its predictive power—measured in their study by a Gini coefficient—is comparatively weak: According to their results, in statistical models with all of the five factors they designated as most important, economic inequality was *not* a statistically significant predictor of absolute or relative mobility.

Chetty, who recently won the John Bates Clark Medal for his achievements as an economist under the age of 40, has been careful to stress that this research cannot prove causation—that removing or adding these factors will cause mobility in America. The study also acknowledges that many of these key factors are correlated with one another, such as income inequality and the share of single mothers in a community. This means that economic inequality may degrade the two-parent family *or* that increases in single parenthood may increase economic inequality. But what does seem clear from this study of the "land[s] of opportunity" in America is that communities characterized by a thriving middle class, racial and economic integration, better schools, a vibrant civil society, and, especially, strong two-parent families are more likely to foster the kind of equality of opportunity that has recently drawn the attention of Democrats and Republicans alike.

Throughout his presidency, Barack Obama has stressed his commitment to data-driven decision-making, not ideology. Similarly, progressives like Krugman have stressed their scientific bona fides, as against the "anti-science" right. If progressives like the president and the Nobel laureate are serious about reviving the fortunes of the American Dream in the 21st century in light of the data, this new study suggests they will need to take pages from *both* left and right playbooks on matters ranging from zoning to education reform. More fundamentally, these new data indicate that any effort to revive opportunity in America must run through two arenas where government has only limited power—civil society and the American family. This is a tall order, to be sure, but unless President Obama, and progressives more generally, can enlist a range of political, civic, business, and cultural leaders—not to mention parents— in this undertaking, this new study suggests they will not succeed in achieving one of their most cherished goals: reviving America as a "land of opportunity."

Critical Thinking

1. How do you think growing up in a community with many single-parent families influences children's development, experiences, and future aspirations?

2. Why can't we say single parenthood causes children to remain mired in the cycle of poverty and unable to achieve social mobility?

3. What types of interventions and supports are needed to assist the children of single-parent families and those who reside in communities where single parents predominate?

Create Central

www.mhhe.com/createcentral

Internet References

Child Trends
    http://www.childtrends.org

Fragile Families and Child Wellbeing Study, Princeton and Columbia Universities
    http://www.fragilefamilies.princeton.edu

World Family Map
    http://worldfamilymap.org/2014/about

W. BRADFORD WILCOX is director of the National Marriage Project and a visiting scholar at the American Enterprise Institute. Follow him on Twitter.

Article Prepared by: Patricia Hrusa Williams, *University of Maine at Farmington*

Bridging Cultural Divides: The Role and Impact of Binational Families

SAMANTHA N.N. CROSS AND MARY C. GILLY

Learning Outcomes

After reading this article, you will be able to:

- Define the term "binational family."

- Explain trends and changes in the demographic composition of U.S. families.

- Understand how immigration, culture, and intermarriage influences family decision making.

The press has given considerable attention recently to what unites diverse groups within or between countries—groups separated by culture, ideology, race, religion, or economic status. Much of this talk has stemmed from the unique background of President Barack Obama (the product of a binational relationship), often presented as the rare candidate who could bridge barriers of race, culture, ideology, and party. However, the discourse is primarily at a macro level. In politics, as in marketing, it is often overlooked that for barriers to truly be breached, change and exchange also must occur at more micro levels. This essay argues that binational families (with partners from different countries) provide an important micro-setting for appreciating marketplace diversity and inclusion and the bridging of cultural divides.

Mélange, hotch-potch, a bit of this and a bit of that is how newness enters the world.

—Rushdie (1990)

Brown (1979) contends that two important changes have happened, at both micro and macro levels, that require a major reorientation in researchers' thinking: the change in the composition and structure of the American family and market globalization. Andreasen (1990, p. 848) also notes that accelerating rates of immigration have a considerable effect on the level of "intranational and international cultural interpenetration." He argues that it is the responsibility of consumer researchers to describe and explain both the nature of cultural interpenetration and the consequences for both the immigrant and the penetrated cultural groups (Andreasen 1990). This is important for both advancement of knowledge and societal benefit.

The foreign-born population in countries worldwide has increased; for example, the United States saw an increase of 85% between 1990 and 2009, from 19.8 million to 36.7 million (U.S. Census Bureau 2010). Similarly, in the United Kingdom, the foreign-born population almost doubled between 1993 and 2011, from 3.8 million to approximately 7.0 million (Rienzo and Vargas-Silva 2012). This growth in the number of immigrants inevitably has an impact on the growth of intermarriages (Bean and Stevens 2003). Yet marketing research studies that examine this notion of cultural interpenetration, though growing, remain limited. More work is needed to explore the nature and consequences of cultural interpenetration, within both the family and society.

In this essay, the driving questions are as follows: What is the role of the binational family and what are the implications for marketplace diversity, inclusion, and creativity? We begin with a brief overview of studies in family decision making and cultural interpenetration. This is followed by a discussion of the role of the binational family as a familial and societal force. We end with implications for marketing, public policy, and society.

Studies in Family Decision Making

Over the past 50 years, research in household decision making has predominantly focused on gender roles in the purchase or consumption of a particular product or service. The emphasis has been on which partner has the most influence, the factors contributing to the differing levels of influence, and how that influence has changed over time (e.g., Belch and Willis 2002; Blood and Wolfe 1960; Commuri and Gentry 2005; Davis and Rigaux 1974; Ford, LaTour, and Henthorne 1995; Qualls 1987; Spiro 1983; Wolfe 1959).

Several theories have evolved to explain the bases of power and influence in the home. Blood and Wolfe's (1960) resource theory proposes that as women became more educated and contributed more income, decision-making processes became more egalitarian. Raven, Centers, and Rodrigues (1975) later applied social power theory, developed by French and Raven (1959), to the family decision-making process. Qualls (1987) concludes that family decision making should be viewed as a network of household relationships rather than as a series of static independent actions. Webster (2000) notes that the particular cultural characteristics of the society determine individual behavior and the type of decision making prevalent in households.

Nevertheless, Commuri and Gentry (2000) insist that the definition of the family must be enlarged, with more studies examining family composition, nontraditional family structures, and cross-cultural comparisons. They note a tendency to emphasize family member characteristics and the effect on relative household influence rather than the characteristics and identity of the household itself. Epp and Price (2008) offer insights into family identity and consumption practices and consider nontraditional family forms, including divorced couples and their children. However, they do not consider binational families, in which members face challenges from the outset with defining and reconciling their disparate identities (Cross and Gilly 2012).

We also argue that it is important to understand how the family functions as a unit or group. While an important foundational knowledge has been developed, the family decision-making literature to date and the critiques of it (Commuri and Gentry 2000; Olsen and Cromwell 1975) have taken a predominantly inward focus. The emphasis has been on the internal impact of influence strategies, decision processes, and identity on household purchase choices. Yet given the importance of the family as a key social and consumption unit (Davis 1970), researchers also must appreciate the wider role of evolving nontraditional family units within diverse societies. We address this gap by examining the role and influence of the binational family.

In addition, in studies of the family or household, researchers draw parallels between the family and other social or structured groups. The family is often described as an institution (Laslett 1973): a collective entity with members who participate and contribute within and outside its social structure or system. Researchers discuss issues of household production, family dynamics, decision-making roles, responsibilities and tasks, housework, conflict, management of domestic labor, expertise, resource allocation, and influence strategies (Commuri and Gentry 2000, 2005). Researchers tend to view spousal relations as partnerships and the family as a unit whose members engage in family planning. The family as an entity also goes through different stages, described as the family life cycle (Gilly and Enis 1982; Murphy and Staples 1979; Wagner and Hanna 1983). These parallels allow additional analogies between the inclusive role of binational families and diversity inclusion in other settings.

Studies in Cultural Interpenetration

While the family decision-making literature has considered culture (Davis and Rigaux 1974; Ford, LaTour, and Henthorne 1995; Green et al. 1983; Wallendorf and Reilly 1983; Webster 1994, 2000), it mainly makes comparisons of culturally homogeneous households in one country with culturally homogeneous households in another country. This research indicates that culture affects family decision-making styles, but it offers little insight into cultural differences *within* families (Cross 2007). Research on immigrants bringing their own culture to another country is also fairly common in consumer behavior, marketing, anthropology, and sociology research. However, this cultural interpenetration research focuses on the individual and/or group experience rather than the experience of two cultures within one household.

Stewart (1999, pp. 40–41) argues that anthropology researchers' increased interest in cultural interpenetration has resulted in critiques of earlier views of " 'culture' that cast it as too stable, bounded, and homogeneous to be useful in a world characterized by migrations (voluntary or forced), cheap travel, international marketing, and telecommunications." He suggests that cultural interpenetration and borrowing are now viewed as "part of the very nature of cultures" because of their porousness. Although the studies he cites involve subgroups navigating the majority culture (e.g., Anglo-Indians in Madras), his conclusion that syncretism (mixing of different beliefs) is not eliminated as assimilation occurs suggests that cultural mixing occurs at the binational household level. Craig and Douglas (2006) go further to advocate that cultural mixing enriches both cultures. Thus, we infer that families also benefit from cultural mixing.

Appadurai (1990) identifies five global "flows" that affect cultural interpenetration. One, ethnoscapes, is relevant here. He argues that the flow of people (including immigrants, students, and tourists) helps transmit cultural content. Several empirical studies of immigrant groups support this idea. For example, Peñaloza and Gilly (1999) find that Mexican immigrants' consumption behavior is affected by living in the United States and that the marketers serving them alter product offerings and ways of doing business.

Immigrants must adopt products and practices in their country of residence, but research indicates that they are not wholly assimilated and keep some of their own cultural traditions, adopt some traditions of the host culture, and combine cultures in creative ways (Oswald 1999). While studies of immigrants reveal that most intend to return to their native country (Oswald 1999; Peñaloza 1994), intermarriage makes such a return much less likely. Thus, while immigrants in binational relationships may share some attributes with other immigrants, if they live in their partner's country, they are expected to establish deeper roots within that culture.

The Role of Binational Families

In this essay, the term "binational family" refers to a family with partners born and raised in different countries of origin. Several other terms are also prevalent in the literature (e.g., "bicultural," "biethnic," "interethnic"). "Bicultural" often refers to a person's ability to comfortably navigate life in two different cultures and implies familiarity with the language and customs in two different cultural contexts (e.g., Lau-Gesk 2003; Luna, Ringberg, and Peracchio 2008). In a binational family, at least one of the partners is an immigrant to the country of residence and is considered bicultural. Similarly, "biethnic" or "interethnic" specifically refer to familiarity within, or a combination of, two different ethnic groups (i.e., a crossing of ethnic lines), even for participants born and reared in the same country (Alba and Nee 2003; Freeman 1955). Binational families may also be biethnic or biracial, which refers to the crossing of racial boundaries. We focus on the dynamics within the binational family—dynamics that often encompass the nuances of other mixed families, whether bicultural, biethnic, or biracial.

As a unit comprising family members with ties both within and outside their country of residence, the binational family, and the individual partners within the family, play an intermediary role. They provide a conjugal and communal link between different cultural norms and perspectives. Through that link, each partner also gains access and exposure to the history, traditions, social norms, and consumption experiences of the country from which his or her partner originated. When the family resides in the native country of one of the spouses, this connection is particularly important for the immigrant spouse trying to navigate the vagaries of an unfamiliar host culture. Meng and Gregory (2005) argue that the immigrant spouse gains an economic labor advantage through intermarriage—an "intermarriage premium." Cross and Gilly (2012) also posit that the native spouse functions as a cultural intermediary and navigator for the immigrant spouse. Although Wamwara-Mbugua (2007) did not study binationals, she finds that Kenyan immigrant couples delegated initial decision making to the spouse who had been in the United States longer, even when it conflicted with traditional Kenyan gender roles. Lauth Bacas (2002) notes that cross-border marriage partners perform the role of gatekeeper to each cultural context. This gatekeeping role moves beyond that of the "kinkeeper"—the role ascribed to the individual family member responsible for maintaining kinship ties (Leach and Brathwaite 1996; Rosenthal 1985). Although not explored in this essay, the kin-keeping role in binational families should be inherently more complex, given the cross-cultural dynamics.

However, the influence goes beyond the household. The binational family unit is often viewed as atypical or novel, inciting curiosity and drawing attention from the wider community in which the family resides. This, and other nontraditional family structures, may initially exacerbate cultural and societal divides, leading to negative consequences such as prejudice, stigmatization, and even threat. Yet we argue that, over time, the increased presence of binational and other culturally heterogeneous families eventually provides a starting point for greater tolerance and appreciation of voluntarily formed diverse unions. These families allow people with disparate backgrounds to meet and exchange perspectives. This cultural exchange provides opportunities for growth in knowledge and understanding, to enhance the range of experiences, and to create new customs and novel consumption relationships.

The Binational Family as Bridge, Broker, and Boundary Spanner

The exposure gained through the marriage of people with differing cultural backgrounds affects the entire unit—the partners, children, and members of family and social networks, as well as the surrounding community. In the management innovation literature, several terms have been used to describe people who provide a link between different individuals, groups, and experiences.

Wasserman and Faust (1994, p. 114) describe one of these terms, "bridge," as a "critical tie" and note that "the removal of a bridge leaves more [disparate] components than when the bridge is included." Lin (1999) highlights the importance and usefulness of accessing and extending bridges in networks to obtain missing resources and facilitate information and influence flows. Another metaphor is that of a "broker." Hargadon and Sutton (1997, p. 716) note that the product design firm IDEO acts as a technology broker by introducing unknown solutions and creating new products "that are original combinations of existing knowledge from disparate industries." The authors also distinguish the firm acting as technology broker and the engineers within IDEO, who themselves act as "individual technology brokers." Williams (2002) uses the term "boundary spanner" to describe people who manage across divides. He believes that more focus is needed on the nature and behavior of these boundary spanners, also described as "diversity seekers" (Brumbaugh and Grier 2013), constructs that should be explored within different institutional and contextual situations.

These terms ("bridge," "broker," "boundary spanner," and "diversity seeker") refer to the person who is able to link otherwise disconnected groups. Individual members of binational families *do* play key parts in maintaining harmonious and continuous links between family members in the different cultures. However, we argue that *both* the binational family unit and its members play a similar structural and symbolic role in binding disparate families, networks, cultures, and communities. In the binational family structure, the union itself, not just a single person, functions as "a bridge between cultures," allowing cultural exchange between the partners, who are themselves cultural bridges (Lauth Bacas 2002). This unconventional union of culturally dissimilar partners unifies the two cultures and support structures of the partners in different countries. Prior existence of this link is slim to unlikely, given the geographical, cultural, and other boundaries between the partners. Thus, in the early stages of the household, this central position is unifying. As time passes and the partnership and families evolve, the link persists, even if the binational household dissolves. This is a bridge that binds and is practically irrevocable, particularly when children result. Thus, the impact of the binational union is pervasive and inclusive as social and family networks become interconnected.

The Binational Family as a Venue for Creative Consumption

Foner (1997, p. 961) notes that first-generation immigrants who relocate from one county to another "fuse . . . the old and the new to create a new kind of family life." Foner, a sociologist, points out that for these immigrants, the family is a place where "creative culture-building takes place." In the linguistics literature, Baron and Cara (2003, pp. 6–7) describe a similar process as the "creative response" of people encountering one another and new situations. They refer to this as a creolization process that can occur whenever members of different cultures meet in "expressive interaction . . . [allowing] us to see cultural

encounters as a process of continuous creative exchange." This process is often central to the maintenance and evolution of society.

As a unit in which cultural encounters occur daily, the binational family can also be viewed as a unique setting for creative culture building. It can even be argued that this creative process is vital to the maintenance of harmonious relations within the household and the very longevity of the family unit. Ultimately, the binational family lies at the intersection of the cultures of the two spouses. At this intersection, cross-cultural interactions, unique blending processes, and creative consumption experiences thrive. This cross-fertilization process between the different cultures occurs through conflict and compromise and through simultaneous fusion and diffusion. It eventually leads to a merging of meaning systems, to create new variations that transcend the individual preferences of the spouses. As a deviation from the traditional family structure, in this kind of family, deviation from norms and "inventive combination" (Hargadon and Sutton 1997) most likely occur. This process inevitably extends beyond the binational family unit and has an impact on the diversity of marketplace offerings, societal tolerance for difference, and the cultural flexibility of the surrounding communities.

Implications for Marketing and Public Policy

Binational families are a growing and inevitable phenomenon. This familial structure accommodates diversity and shapes the preferences, choices, experiences, and perspectives of the family members and those whom they encounter. We advocate that the existence of these families offers several societal and public policy implications.

Research suggests that for immigrant spouses, social and economic adaptation is enhanced when immigrants and natives intermarry (Cross and Gilly 2012; Meng and Gregory 2005). This enhanced participation and contribution strengthens the family and the immigrant partner's commitment to and identification with the new home country, which leads to greater engagement in prosocial behaviors. Immigrants who intermarry are also less likely to segregate in immigrant enclaves. Their inclusion in the wider, dominant community has a positive influence on public perception of immigrants, providing an alternate community perspective to national political sensationalism about immigration. Binational families also include same-sex couples. Yet in countries in which same-sex unions are not legally recognized, exclusionary immigration policies continue to be a threat that policy makers must acknowledge.

In communities in which binational and immigrant families co-reside with native families, immigrant spouses may seek marketplace offerings from their home countries. The acquisition of less accessible, preferred items is influenced by and affects export/import laws and customs restrictions. When natives and immigrants intermarry, members of their social networks are also exposed to these items. Norms slowly change about the acceptability and co-consumption of initially novel products with more familiar items. Vendors in these communities can capitalize on increased opportunities to meet changing marketplace expectations with creative product combinations and service experiences. Both partners in binational families also tend to take an active role in food shopping, to meet their differing cultural preferences (Cross and Gilly 2012). This has implications for grocery store vendors, who typically focus their marketing efforts on females and mono-national families, rather than on both genders and culturally mixed families.

Members of binational families, particularly the children, acquire a level of intercultural competence (Demangeot et al. 2013) and flexibility through the ongoing cross-cultural interactions within the home. They thus provide a potential recruitment pool for public and private employers seeking employees to participate in cross-cultural teams, who can lead an increasingly diverse workforce and serve a multicultural domestic and global population.

Conjugal tolerance eventually leads to societal tolerance. The insights gained from studying the processes and interactions within binational families move beyond prior notions of the "melting pot" or "salad bowl" concepts of assimilation, toward more fluid alternatives for harmonious cross-cultural coexistence and the resolution of intercultural conflict. In the United States, policies on individual self-classification on the census and elsewhere have changed. As the presence of binational families expands, so too will other perceptions of normalcy (Baker 2006) evolve, leading to a more dynamic, innovative, inclusive marketplace and global society.

References

Alba, Richard and Victor Nee (2003), *Remaking the American Mainstream*. Cambridge, MA: Harvard University Press.

Andreasen, Alan R. (1990), "Cultural Interpenetration: A Critical Consumer Research Issue for the 1990s," in *Advances in Consumer Research*, Vol. 17, Marvin E. Goldberg, Gerald Gorn, and Richard W. Pollay, eds. Provo, UT: Association for Consumer Research, 847–49.

Appadurai, Arjun (1990), "Disjuncture and Difference in the Global Cultural Economy," in *Media and Cultural Studies*, Meenakshi Gigi Durham and Douglas M. Kellner, eds. Malden, MA: Blackwell.

Baker, Stacy M. (2006), "Consumer Normalcy: Understanding the Value of Shopping Through Narratives of Consumers with Visual Impairments," *Journal of Retailing*, 82 (1), 37–50.

Baron, Robert and Ana C. Cara (2003), "Introduction: Creolization and Folklore—Cultural Creativity in Process," *Journal of American Folklore*, 116 (459), 4–8.

Bean, Frank D. and Gillian Stevens (2003), *America's Newcomers and the Dynamics of Diversity*. New York: Russell Sage Foundation.

Belch, Michael A. and Laura A. Willis (2002), "Family Decision at the Turn of the Century: Has the Changing Structure of Households Impacted the Family Decision-Making Process?" *Journal of Consumer Behaviour*, 2 (2), 111–24.

Blood, Robert O. and Donald Wolfe (1960), *Husbands and Wives*. New York: The Free Press.

Brown, Wilson (1979), "The Family and Consumer Decision Making: A Cultural View," *Journal of the Academy of Marketing Science*, 7 (4), 335–45.

Brumbaugh, Anne M. and Sonya A. Grier (2013), "Agents of Change: A Scale to Identify Diversity Seekers," *Journal of Public Policy & Marketing*, 32 (Special Issue), 144–55.

Commuri, Suraj and James W. Gentry (2000), "Opportunities for Family Research in Marketing," *Academy of Marketing Science Review*, 8 (accessed October 15, 2012), [available at http://www.amsreview.org/articles/commuri08-2000.pdf].

——— and ——— (2005), "Resource Allocation in Households with Women as Chief Wage Earners," *Journal of Consumer Research*, 32 (September), 185–95.

Craig, C. Samuel and Susan P. Douglas (2006), "Beyond National Culture: Implications of Cultural Dynamics for Consumer Research," *International Marketing Review*, 23 (3), 322–42.

Cross, Samantha N.N. (2007), "For Better or for Worse: The Intersection of Cultures in Binational Homes," in *Advances in Consumer Research*, Vol. 35, A.Y. Lee and D. Soman, eds. Duluth, MN: Association for Consumer Research, 162–65.

——— and Mary C. Gilly (2012), "Cultural Competence, Cultural Capital and Cultural Compensatory Mechanisms in Binational Households," working paper, Iowa State University.

Davis, Harry L. (1970), "Dimensions of Marital Roles in Consumer Decision Making," *Journal of Marketing Research*, 7 (May), 168–77.

——— and Benny P. Rigaux (1974), "Perception of Marital Roles in Decision Processes," *Journal of Consumer Research*, 1 (1), 51–62.

Demangeot, Catherine, Natalie Ross Adkins, Rene Dentiste Mueller, Geraldine Rosa Henderson, Nakeisha S. Ferguson, James M. Mandiberg, et al. (2013), "Toward Intercultural Competency in Multicultural Marketplaces," *Journal of Public Policy & Marketing*, 32 (Special Issue), 156–64.

Epp, Amber M. and Linda L. Price (2008), "Family Identity: A Framework of Identity Interplay in Consumption Practices," *Journal of Consumer Research*, 35 (June), 50–70.

Foner, Nancy (1997), "The Immigrant Family: Cultural Legacies and Cultural Changes," *International Migration Review*, 31 (4, Special Issue: Immigrant Adaptation and Native-Born Responses in the Making of Americans), 961–74.

Ford, John B., Michael S. LaTour, and Tony L. Henthorne (1995), "Perception of Marital Roles in Purchase Decision Processes: A Cross-Cultural Study," *Journal of the Academy of Marketing Science*, 23 (2), 120–31.

Freeman, Linton (1955), "Homogamy in Interethnic Mate Selection," *Sociology and Social Research*, 39, 369–77.

French, John R.P., Jr., and Bertram Raven (1959), "The Bases of Social Power," in *Studies in Social Power*, Dorwin Cartwright, ed. Ann Arbor, MI: Research Center for Group Dynamics, Institute for Social Research, University of Michigan, 150–67.

Gilly, Mary C. and Ben M. Enis (1982), "Recycling the Family Life Cycle: A Proposal for Redefinition," *Advances in Consumer Research*, Vol. 9, Andrew Mitchell, ed. Ann Arbor: Association for Consumer Research, 271–76.

Green, Robert T., Jean-Paul Leonardi, Jena-Louis Chandon, Isabella C.M. Cunningham, Bronis Verhage, and Alain Strazzieri (1983), "Societal Development and Family Purchasing Roles: A Cross-National Study," *Journal of Consumer Research*, 9 (March), 436–42.

Hargadon, Andrew and Robert I. Sutton (1997), "Technology Brokering and Innovation in a Product Development Firm," *Administrative Science Quarterly*, 42 (4), 716–49.

Laslett, Barbara (1973), "The Family as a Public and Private Institution: An Historical Perspective," *Journal of Marriage and the Family*, 35 (3, Special Section: New Social History of the Family), 480–92.

Lau-Gesk, Loraine G. (2003), "Activating Culture Through Persuasion Appeals: An Examination of the Bicultural Consumer," *Journal of Consumer Psychology*, 13 (3), 301–315.

Lauth Bacas, Jutta (2002), "Cross-Border Marriages and the Formation of Transnational Families: A Case Study of Greek–German Couples in Athens," Transnational Communities Programme Working Paper Series (accessed October 15, 2012), [available at www.transcomm.ox.ac.uk/working%20papers/WPTC-02-10%20Bacas.pdf].

Leach, Margaret S. and Dawn O. Brathwaite (1996), "A Binding Tie: Supportive Communication of Family Kinkeepers," *Journal of Applied Communication Research*, 24 (3), 200–216.

Lin, Nan (1999), "Building a Network Theory of Social Capital," *Connections*, 22 (1), 28–51.

Luna, David, Torsten Ringberg, and Laura A. Peracchio (2008), "One Individual, Two Identities: Frame Switching Among Biculturals," *Journal of Consumer Research*, 35 (2), 279–93.

Meng, Xin and Robert G. Gregory (2005), "Intermarriage and the Economic Assimilation of Immigrants," *Journal of Labor Economics*, 23 (1), 135–75.

Murphy, Patrick E. and William A. Staples (1979), "A Modernized Family Life Cycle," *Journal of Consumer Research*, 6 (1), 12–22.

Olson, David H. and Ronald E. Cromwell (1975), "Methodological Issues in Family Power," in *Power in Families*, Ronald E. Cromwell and David H. Olson, eds. New York: Sage Publications, 131–50.

Oswald, Laura R. (1999), "Culture Swapping: Consumption and the Ethnogenesis of Middle-Class Haitian Immigrants," *Journal of Consumer Research*, 25 (March), 303–318.

Peñaloza, Lisa N. (1994), "Atravesando Fronteras/Border Crossings: A Critical Ethnographic Exploration of the Consumer Acculturation of Mexican Immigrants," *Journal of Consumer Research*, 21 (June), 32–54.

——— and Mary C. Gilly (1999), "Marketer Acculturation: The Changer and the Changed," *Journal of Marketing*, 63 (July), 84–104.

Qualls, William J. (1987), "Household Decision Behavior: The Impact of Husbands' and Wives' Sex Role Orientation," *Journal of Consumer Research*, 14 (2), 264–79.

Raven, Bertram H., Richard Centers, and Aroldo Rodrigues (1975), "The Bases of Conjugal Power," in *Power in Families*, Ronald E. Cromwell and David H. Olson, eds. New York: Sage Publications, 217–32.

Rienzo, Cinzia and Carlos Vargas-Silva (2012), "Migrants in the UK: An Overview," *The Migration Observatory*, (May 15), (accessed June 30, 2012), [available at http://migrationobservatory.ox.ac.uk/briefings/migrants-uk-overview].

Rosenthal, Carolyn J. (1985), "Kinkeeping in the Familial Division of Labor," *Journal of Marriage and Family*, 47 (4), 965–74.

Rushdie, Salman (1990), *In Good Faith.* London: Granta.

Spiro, Rosann L. (1983), "Persuasion in Family Decision-Making," *Journal of Consumer Research*, 9 (4), 393–402.

Stewart, Charles (1999), "Syncretism and Its Synonyms: Reflections on Cultural Mixture," *Diacritics*, 29 (Autumn), 40–62.

U.S. Census Bureau (2010), "2010 Census Data," [available at http://www.census.gov/2010census/data].

Wagner, Janet and Sherman Hanna (1983), "The Effectiveness of Family Life Cycle Variables in Consumer Expenditure Research," *Journal of Consumer Research*, 10 (3), 281–91.

Wallendorf, Melanie and Michael D. Reilly (1983), "Ethnic Migration, Assimilation, and Consumption," *Journal of Consumer Research*, 10 (3), 292–302.

Wamwara-Mbugua, L. Wakiuru (2007), "An Investigation of Household Decision Making Among Immigrants," in *Advances in Consumer Research*, Vol. 34, Gavan Fitzsimons and Vicki Morwitz, eds. Valdosta, GA: Association for Consumer Research, 180–86.

Wasserman, Stanley and Katherine Faust (1994), *Social Network Analysis.* Cambridge, UK: Cambridge University Press.

Webster, Cynthia (1994), "Effects of Hispanic Ethnic Identification on Marital Roles in the Purchase Decision-Process," *Journal of Consumer Research*, 21 (2), 319–31.

——— (2000), "Is Spousal Decision Making a Culturally Situated Phenomenon?" *Psychology & Marketing*, 17 (12), 1035–58.

Williams, Paul (2002), "The Competent Boundary Spanner," *Public Administration*, 80 (1), 103–124.

Wolfe, Donald M. (1959), "Power and Authority in the Family," in *Studies in Social Power*, Dorwin Cartwright, ed. Ann Arbor, MI: Research Center for Group Dynamics, Institute for Social Research, University of Michigan, 99–117.

Critical Thinking

1. Why do you think the authors have chosen to use the term "binational family" instead of referring to these families using some other terms mentioned in the article such as bicultural, biethnic, or interethnic?

2. How do you think being a binational family influences family dynamics and interactions between couples and family members?

3. What are special considerations and things to keep in mind when working with binational families?

Create Central

www.mhhe.com/createcentral

Internet References

Family and Culture
http://familyandculture.com/index.html

World Fact Book
https://www.cia.gov/library/publications/the-world-factbook

World Family Map
http://worldfamilymap.org/2014/about

SAMANTHA N.N. CROSS is Assistant Professor of Marketing, College of Business, Iowa State University. MARY C. GILLY is Professor of Marketing, Paul Merage School of Business, University of California, Irvine. Financial support to the first author through the Ray Watson Doctoral Fellowship at the University of California, Irvine; the Academy of Marketing Science Jane K. Fenyo Best Paper Award for Student Research; and the ACR/Sheth Foundation Dissertation Grant is gratefully acknowledged.

Cross, Samantha N.N.; Gilly, Mary C. "Bridging Cultural Divides: The Role and Impact of Binational Families." From *Journal of Public Policy and Marketing,* vol. 32, May 2013, pp. 106–111. Copyright © 2013 American Marketing Association. Reprinted by permission.

Prepared by: Patricia Hrusa Williams,
University of Maine at Farmington

Article

Matches Made on Earth
Why Family Values Are Human Values

Nancie L. Gonzalez

Learning Outcomes

After reading this article, you will be able to:

- Recognize the social construction of "family values" in families and society.

- Identify the impact of religion in how family values are constructed.

- Illustrate the diversity of family values.

The term "family values," the importance of which fundamentalist Christians have been preaching for decades, continues to permeate religious and political printed matter and discussions in the United States today. The conservatives' concept of family values is generally characterized by abstinence from sex until marriage, which is then entered into with a like-minded individual of the opposite sex and is thereafter permanent and free from adultery. It is also expected that children will ensue, either through birth or adoption. In line with these prescriptions, proponents of traditional family values foment prejudice and activism against divorce, abortion, homosexuality, single-parent families, and even the choice not to have children. The fact that their efforts have become more intensive and intrusive lately can be explained, I believe, by the increasingly tolerant and diverse sexual, racial, and religious views and behavior of the American public at large.

The problem isn't that some people espouse conservative ideals of family, but that they promulgate them as the only way to live, looking down upon and often demonizing those with other values. Indeed, the family values crowd often refers to any who oppose its agenda as having no values at all. They support their ideals as based upon divine "truth" by quoting the Bible and rejecting scientific evidence that supports a different set of explanations for the existence and history of humankind. They repeatedly argue that more general social acceptance of other ways to live will endanger their own. This fear has inspired efforts for decades to influence our school boards and our local, state, and national governments to change text books, curricula, and the law to reflect socially conservative views. When these fail, parents turn to private schools or home schooling, and later enroll their offspring in one of the several conservative Christian colleges whose faculties and administrative personnel are vetted to make sure their values are religiously and politically "correct." The fact that some of these schools are admittedly training their graduates to seek public office or employment in state and national venues is further evidence of their intolerance, and their misunderstanding of the nature of society and culture.

Most of the idealistic family values held by conservative Christians today are not now nor have they ever been characteristic of the world at large. Statistics, as well as more informal evidence suggest that the so-called nontraditional behaviors they condemn are now common throughout the United States and much of the industrialized world, often despite laws forbidding them. Furthermore, such behaviors have existed in many parts of the world for centuries. The problem I see for humanists is to convince much of the conservative American public that these prejudices and fears are unwarranted on at least two grounds: 1) family values are the products of human sociocultural conditions, and cannot be attributed to either divine or biological imperatives, and 2) pluralism in marriage and family values should be expected in any large twenty-first century society as a result of technological advances that have made globalization both possible and perhaps inevitable.

If neither a deity nor our genes are wholly determinative, we must ask our conservative counterparts: what accounts for the vast panorama of intimate human bonding practices, either in the past, or today?

It may be useful to consider what social and biological scientists have concluded about the origin and nature of marriage and the family. All animals must struggle for self and species survival, which demands food, defense, reproduction, and care of newborns until they can care for themselves. Both genetics and learning are involved for all species, but only humans have created *social institutions* to help themselves in these endeavors. By social, I mean any kind of bonding with other humans to share in the food quest; to ward off environmental and other dangers; to reproduce, nurture, and educate the young; and to provide physical and psychological well-being for themselves, their children, and their neighbors. The specific characteristics of these institutions vary with the society; trial and error must have occurred over time, and some societies failed to persist. But those institutions that worked well became customary, "traditional," and thus value-laden. Children would be taught by example and by experience. But traditions change as cultural evolution occurs and as societies grow, develop new technologies, and increasingly influence each other. The young and the most pragmatically minded are likely to change with the times, yet there are always some who cling to the older ways—not that this is, in itself, dysfunctional, for the "old ways" still serve some purposes, and sometimes are reinstated or reinterpreted by succeeding generations.

Although marriage and the family have existed in all human societies and form the primary roots of all the particulars of family values everywhere, different societies have constructed their own definitions of incest; permissible marriage partners; appropriate sexual behavior before, during, and after marriage; "normal" and alternate sexual orientations; ideal post-marital residence; and composition of the ideal family and household, including what to do if too many children "appear," or if conception occurs at an inconvenient time. For example, marriages that we likely consider incestuous but others don't include marriage between first cousins, especially patrilateral parallel cousin marriage (where the children of two brothers marry) seen in some parts of the Middle East and Africa. Among some Bedouin cultures, there was even a stated preference for such a marriage. Similarly, cross-cousin marriage is widespread in many "tribal" societies, including the Yanomamo in South America.

Different societies have constructed their own definitions of incest appropriate sexual behavior, "normal" and alternate sexual orientations, and ideal post-marital residence.

Formal bonding or marriage rituals probably developed in very early human societies, since it was important then as now to confer legitimacy of the children in relation to membership in whatever social unit was pertinent (tribe, clan, patrilineage, matrilineage, nation-state, religious group, and so forth). Formal marriage also establishes rights of inheritance of property, as well as social position. In many societies, including our own, women, and to a lesser extent, men, are treated like adolescents until they marry.

Neither religious nor biological explanations for conservative family values take into account the fact that even the notion of two sexes is not, and probably never has been, biologically correct. We have no way to know whether prehistoric societies recognized inborn sexual variations, what the frequency of such variations might have been, or whether "different" newborns would even have been allowed to live. However, colonial travelers to America noted that some native cultures recognized the existence of some among them whose bodies, psyches, or both weren't comfortable living in either of the two primary gender roles of male or female. They called these people "two spirits" and provided a socially acceptable niche for them.

Homosexuality of different types has been documented throughout Western civilization since at least the ancient Greeks. However, only in the current century has the recognition developed in Western societies that sexual orientation is not merely a matter of differences in genitalia, and that it isn't a mere matter of choice. The growing acceptance of the idea that sexuality and sexual identity should not alter one's basic humanity and civil rights has led to changes in the laws in many countries, including the decriminalization of certain sex practices and the legalization of same-sex marriage. At the time of this writing, five U.S. states as well as the District of Columbia now allow gay and lesbian couples to marry, and in three more states same-sex marriages are recognized but not performed legally. Nine other states recognize certain legal rights of same-sex couples through civil unions, domestic partnerships, or reciprocal beneficiary laws. Still, these arrangements are only gradually becoming acceptable to the general public, and since same-sex marriage hasn't been documented as legal in any society in history, we shouldn't be surprised that it is and will remain controversial for some time. Nevertheless, it should now be added to the evidence we have for different kinds of marriage and family institutions.

S tudies of pre-agricultural and pre-industrial societies, as well as continuing historical research over the past century have documented such a variety of marriage customs and rules that a God hypothesis would almost have to suggest an anthropological deity who understood that no single practice should be imposed upon all. However, the following discussion focuses not on the supernatural, but the natural ways in which human pair bonding and family formation have occurred. These include *monogamy* as the permanent or lifetime union of two persons, usually, but not always, of opposite sex. This was probably the most common marriage form for Paleolithic foragers, as was the nuclear family. However, that small unit had affinal relatives (we call them in-laws), some of whom lived together in what anthropologists call a band. As the noted nineteenth-century anthropologist Edward B. Tylor suggested, early societies had to "marry out or die out." Institutions promoting reproduction and care of the young were crucial to social survival.

Polygamy is often confused with *polygyny—the* union of one man with several wives—but polygamy also includes *polyandry—one* woman with several husbands. All of these forms, especially polygyny, were more typical of larger, more advanced societies based upon pastoralism, agriculture, or both. The advantages were to enlarge the family unit by drawing in more nubile and fertile women, while at the same time providing care for those who might no longer have been able to bear children. If the sex ratio, for whatever reason, was unbalanced, as it was among early converts to the Church of the Latter Day Saints, polygyny also was a way for new single young women to be immediately drawn in to an existing family. The custom was formally abolished by the Mormons in the early part of the twentieth century, but the family values created more than one hundred years earlier have held on for some.

Polyandry has been fairly rare, practiced primarily in the Himalayan regions of Nepal, Tibet, India, and Bhutan. It has also occurred in the Canadian Arctic, Nigeria, and Sri Lanka, and is known to have been present in some pre-contact Polynesian societies, though probably only among higher caste women. Some forms of polyandry appear to be associated with a perceived need to retain aristocratic titles or agricultural lands within kin groups, and/or because of the frequent absence, for long periods, of a man from the household. In Tibet the practice is particularly popular among the priestly Skye class but also among poor small farmers who can ill afford to divide their small holdings. As to the latter variety, as some males return to the household, others leave for a long time, so that there is usually one husband present. Fraternal polyandry occurs when multiple brothers share a common wife. This occurs in the pastoral Toda community in Southern India. Similarly, among the Tibetan Nyinba, anthropologist Nancy Levine described the strong bond between brothers as essential in creating a strong sense of family unity and keeping land holdings intact, thus preserving socioeconomic standing.

Group marriage involving multiple members of both sexes has sometimes been averred to have existed; however, there appears to be no reputable description of it in the anthropological or historical literature. In recent years a movement has arisen that produces something very similar to the idea of group marriage; the term *polyamory* has been offered to describe plural simultaneous attachments between and among people, including lesbian, gay, bisexual, and transgendered individuals (LGBTs). From the perspective of this writing, this may or may not be new under the sun, but it doesn't (yet?) constitute marriage.

Serial monogamy is perhaps the most common type of marriage known in much of the world today. Individuals in such unions may have only one spouse but, shedding that one, they may contract any number later—again, usually only one at a time, except in those societies that still accept and approve polygyny. Serial monogamy depends on the existence of easy divorce laws or more informal practices, such as what is generally called "living together." *Domestic partnerships* by law may or may not be considered marriages. In the United States persons of both the same and opposite sex have for some time entered into such unions, but those of opposite sex partners have generally received greater social acceptance, even without the legal protections, status, or financial benefits society offers to married couples.

Why do some people choose not to abide by the marriage rules of their own society? Obviously, reasons vary. Some think a trial marriage to be a good idea; others simply don't care about rules of any kind. A few may be prohibited from marrying because one or the other is already bound by a previous, legitimate union which can't be formally dissolved. And while others have simply adopted a more individualized lifestyle, some are still convinced of the values of marriage in a previous age (as in polygyny). In short, the choice of whether and whom to marry has increasingly been seen as a personal, individual decision, and it is no longer important to the functioning of the modern industrial state that all persons marry, unless they wish the state to adjudicate property or child custody rights.

Co-residence of the partners and the creation of a household are usually, but not always, typical in any kind of marriage. Yet households vary enormously in both size and composition, and usually, but not always, include some kind of family. In societies in which men must find work through short or long term emigration, *consanguineal households* have arisen that contain no married pair. Such a household is most often headed by an elderly woman, together with some of her sons and daughters and their children. The marital partners of these co-residential adults live elsewhere—often with their own mothers. The United States today is also seeing an increase in extended families moving in together due to economic constraints, as well as "single" parents who live with a partner.

A study by the Pew Research Center released in November, titled, "The Decline of Marriage and Rise of New Families," revealed changing attitudes about what constitutes a family. Among survey respondents, 86 percent said a single parent and child constitute a family; 80 percent considered an unmarried couple living together with a child a family; and 63 percent said a gay or lesbian couple raising a child is a family.

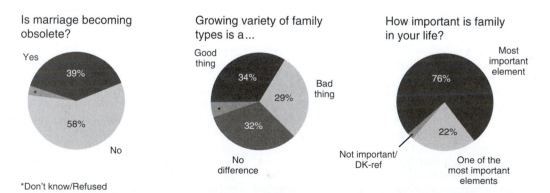

Is marriage becoming obsolete?
Yes 39%
No 58%
*

Growing variety of family types is a...
Good thing 34%
Bad thing 29%
No difference 32%
*

How important is family in your life?
Most important element 76%
One of the most important elements 22%
Not important/ DK-ref

*Don't know/Refused

Data from the Pew Research Center's 2010 survey, "The Decline of Marriage and Rise of New Families"

Obviously, the "traditional family" so highly valued by the religious right can't be considered as the typical American household today. Instead, the term "family" has taken on a much broader meaning to incorporate various combinations of persons of different genders, sexual orientations, and familial or non-familial relationships living together, as in the refrigerator magnet that proclaims, "Friends Are the Family You Choose for Yourself."

We still, and always will, value the need to bond with others. Kinship remains one major way to do so, but social and geographical mobility have lessened its role as the most important tie that binds. Today it may be similar age groups, vocations, or philosophical views on the nature of the universe or of the hereafter that form the basis of relationships. People will continue to find or invent ways to get together, live together, and share what is important in life with others.

Does this mean that marriage and the family as we know it will likely disappear in the near future as Focus on the Family fears? Does the fact that many young people of various genders and sexual identities choose not to marry or stay married, nor to form traditional households augur the demise, or even the diminution in value of these institutions in our society? Should the legal sanctioning of same-sex marriage in any way affect the dignity of opposite-sex couples joined by similar ceremonies? I think not. Society has, for the most part, already accepted the newer bonding patterns described above—at least for persons of opposite sex.

Taking away any social stigma, LGBT couples will likely experience the same joys and struggles in marriage as straight couples do, thus proving that sexual orientation is irrelevant when it comes to pair-bonding. Although the ethnographic and historical evidence doesn't confirm that true marriages were ever legally sanctioned between persons thought to be of the same sex, present-day reminiscences and folklore suggest that love, sex, and companionship were known and accepted among them, and that untold numbers of people have lived in happy unions with persons perceived to be of the same sex for perhaps hundreds of years.

Finally, what about love and companionship? It is only in modern Western society that these have become the very most important components of marriage. There is no evidence that these occur only between spouses of opposing sex or gender. The idea that sexual activity is only appropriate between members of the opposite sex is a product of our cultural conditioning, born of the thousands of years when it was important to keep people focused on finding a mate of the opposite sex to ensure continued reproduction. The need for population control, rather than survival of the species or of any specific society, makes this value irrelevant today, as it does for the idea that all marriages should produce children. Also, the extended family of yore is no longer functional in industrial society—today one does indeed marry the individual, not the whole family.

Sex is no longer seen as a major reward for contracting marriage, regardless of one's sexual orientation. Tests of virginity

have disappeared as premarital sex with more than one partner has become more common and seems to be a largely irrelevant factor for many marriages, including the first. Yet, the fact that homosexual and lesbian partners engage in sexual activities without marriage is always seen as a disgrace, even for many of them who may share the traditional religious notion that unmarried sex is a sin.

As we continue to consider the nature and causes of the diversity of family values in the post-industrial, individualistic, global society in which we now live, I hope that the single set of specific rules of behavior promulgated by Focus on the Family and other such organizations comes to be seen as outmoded, even by the so-called moral majority. As the U.S. Constitution has always insisted, all citizens should have equal rights, so for those who find the "old ways" to their taste, we should wish them well, but plead with them not to damage the lives of those who choose to live or even to think differently, nor to forget that our nation was founded by outsiders and has continually accepted those from other cultures, and that we have, in fact, valued and profited by our diversity.

Critical Thinking

1. What are some of your family values? Where do your family values come from?

2. Do you feel that family values are a naturally occurring phenomenon or are they learned from society and culture?

3. After reading this article, are there some family values from your family of origin that differ now that you are in college?

4. What do you think about the author's question about "marriage and the family as we know it" disappearing?

Create Central

www.mhhe.com/createcentral

Internet References

World Family Map
http://worldfamilymap.org/2013

Australian Institute of Family Studies
www.aifs.gov.au

Feminist Perspectives on Reproduction and the Family
http://plato.stanford.edu/entries/feminism-family

Kearl's Guide to the Sociology of the Family
www.trinity.edu/MKEARL/family.html

NANCIE L. GONZALEZ is Professor Emeritus of Anthropology at the University of Maryland. She has conducted ethnographic and ethnohistorical research on marriage and family patterns in a number of societies, including the American Southwest, the Caribbean, Central America, China, and the West Bank and has published widely since the 1960s. She is presently working on a memoir dealing with changes in marriage and family patterns as revealed in letters and diaries from five generations of her own family. She lives in Richmond, Virginia.

Gonzalez, Nancie L. From *The Humanist*, January/February 2011, pp. 14-17. Copyright © 2011 by Nancie L. Gonzalez. Reprinted by permission of the author.

Unit 2

Exploring and Establishing Relationships

UNIT

Prepared by: Patricia Hrusa Williams, *University of Maine at Farmington*

Exploring and Establishing Relationships

By and large, we are social animals, and as such, we seek out meaningful connections with other humans. John Bowlby, Mary Ainsworth, and others have proposed that this drive toward deep connections is biologically-based and is at the core of what it means to be human. However it plays out in childhood and adulthood, the need for connection, to love and be loved, is a powerful force moving us to establish and maintain close relationships. As we explore various possibilities, we engage in the complex business of relationship building. In doing this, many processes occur simultaneously. Messages are sent and received; differences are negotiated; assumptions and expectations are or are not met. The ultimate goals are closeness and continuity. How we feel about others

and what we see as essential in our dealings with other people play important roles as we work to establish and maintain relationships.

In this unit, we look at factors that underlie the establishment and beginning stages of relationships. Among the topics to be covered in this unit are an exploration of factors that influence how and why connections are built including biology, emotion, sex, personality, and the context in which relationships are established and developed. Changing views and practices in dating, mating, marriage, commitment, family formation, procreation, and early family development are explored in an effort to understand the changing nature of intimate and family relationships in modern society.

Prepared by: Patricia Hrusa Williams,
University of Maine at Farmington

Article

12 Rude Revelations about Sex

ALAIN DE BOTTON

Learning Outcomes

After reading this article, you will be able to:

- Explain the science behind sex, sexual desire, and sexual behavior.
- Examine some of the major themes in the study of sex and intimate relationships.
- Understand sexual terms such as erotic and intimacy.
- Recognize the emotional and physical manifestations of sexual desire and behavior.

We have been led to believe, is as natural as breathing. But in fact, contends British philosopher Alain de Botton, it is "close to rocket science in complexity." It's not only a powerful force, it's often contrary to many other things we care about. Sex inherently sets up conflicts within us. We crave sex with people we don't know or love. It makes us want to do things that seem immoral or degrading, like slapping someone or being tied up. We feel awkward asking the people we love for the sex acts we really want.

There's no denying that sex has its sweaty charms, and in its most exquisite moments dissolves the isolation that embodied life imposes on us. But those moments are rare, the exception rather than the rule, says de Botton, founder of London's School of Life. "Sex is always going to cause us headaches; it's not something we can miraculously grow relaxed about." We suffer privately, feeling "painfully strange about the sex we are either longing to have or struggling to avoid."

If we turn to sex books to help us work out this central experience of our lives, we are typically assured that most problems are mechanical, a matter of method. In his own new book, *How to Think More About Sex,* de Botton makes the case that our difficulties stem more from the multiplicity of things we want out of life, or the accrual of everyday resentments, or the weirdness of the sex drive itself. Here are some of the most basic questions it answers.

Why do most people lie about their true desires?

It is rare to go through life without feeling that we are somehow a bit odd about sex. It is an area in which most of us have a painful impression, in our heart of hearts, that we are quite unusual. Despite being one of the most private activities, sex is nevertheless surrounded by a range of powerfully socially sanctioned ideas that codify how normal people are meant to feel about and deal with the matter. In truth, however, few of us are remotely normal sexually. We are almost all haunted by guilt and neuroses, by phobias and disruptive desires, by indifference and disgust. We are universally deviant—but only in relation to some highly distorted ideals of normality.

Most of what we are sexually remains impossible to communicate with anyone whom we would want to think well of us. Men and women in love instinctively hold back from sharing more than a fraction of their desires out of a fear, usually accurate, of generating intolerable disgust in their partners.

Nothing is erotic that isn't also, with the wrong person, revolting, which is precisely what makes erotic moments so intense: At the precise juncture where disgust could be at its height, we find only welcome and permission. Think of two tongues exploring the deeply private realm of the mouth—that dark, moist cavity that no one but our dentist usually enters. The privileged nature of the union between two people is sealed by an act that, with someone else, would horrify them both.

What unfolds between a couple in the bedroom is an act of mutual reconciliation between two secret sexual selves emerging at last from sinful solitude. Their behavior is starkly at odds with the behavior expected of them by the civilized world. At last, in the semi-darkness a couple can confess to the many wondrous and demented things that having a body drives them to want.

Why is sex more difficult to talk about in this era, not less?

Whatever discomfort we feel around sex is commonly aggravated by the idea that we belong to a liberated age—and ought by now to be finding sex a straightforward and untroubling matter, a little like tennis, something that everyone should have as often as possible to relieve the stresses of modern life.

The narrative of enlightenment and progress skirts an unbudging fact: Sex is not something we can ever expect to feel easily liberated from. It is a fundamentally disruptive and overwhelming force, at odds with the majority of our ambitions and all but incapable of being discreetly integrated within civilized society. Sex is not fundamentally democratic or kind. It refuses to sit neatly on top of love. Tame it though we might try, it tends to wreak havoc across our lives; it leads us to destroy our relationships, threatens our productivity, and compels us to stay up too late in nightclubs talking to people whom we don't like but whose exposed midriffs we wish to touch. Our best hope should be for a respectful accommodation with an anarchic and reckless power.

How is sex a great lie detector?

Involuntary physiological reactions such as the wetness of a vagina and the stiffness of a penis are emotionally so satisfying (which means, simultaneously, so erotic) because they signal a kind of approval that lies utterly beyond rational manipulation. Erections and lubrication simply cannot be effected by will-power and are therefore particularly true and honest indices of interest. In a world in which fake enthusiasms are rife, in which it is often hard to tell whether people really like us or whether they are being kind to us merely out of a sense of duty, the wet vagina and the stiff penis function as unambiguous agents of sincerity.

A kiss is pleasurable because of the sensory receptivity of our lips, but a good deal of our excitement has nothing to do with the physical dimension of the act: It stems from the simple realization that someone else likes us quite a lot.

What is the lure of sex in the back of an airplane?

Most of the people we come in contact with in daily life hardly notice us. Their businesslike indifference can be painful and humiliating for us—hence, the peculiar power of the fantasy that life could be turned upside down and the normal priorities reversed. The eroticism of nurses' uniforms, for example, stems from the gap between the rational control they symbolize and the unbridled sexual passion that can for a while, if only in fantasy, gain the upper hand over it.

Just as uniforms can inspire lust by their evocation of rule-breaking, so can it be exciting to imagine sex in an unobserved corner of the university library, in a restaurant's cloakroom, or in a train car. Our defiant transgression can give us a feeling of power that goes beyond the merely sexual. To have sex in the back of an airplane full of business travelers is to have a go at upending the usual hierarchy of things, introducing desire into an atmosphere in which cold-hearted discipline generally dominates over personal wishes. At 35,000 feet up, just as in an office cubicle, the victory of intimacy seems sweeter and our pleasure increases accordingly. Eroticism is most clearly manifest at the intersection between the formal and the intimate.

Is pornography a betrayal of humanity?

Pornography is often accused of being comfortingly "fake" and therefore unthreatening to the conduct of any sensible existence. But it is deeply contrary to the rest of our plans and inclinations,

rerouting rational priorities. Most pornography is humiliating and vulgar. Nobility has surely been left far behind when an anonymous woman is forced onto a bed, three penises are roughly inserted into her orifices, and the ensuing scene is recorded. Yet this poison is not easy to resist. Thousands of content providers have exploited a design flaw of the male—a mind designed to cope with little more tempting than the occasional sight of a tribeswoman across the savannah. There is nothing robust enough in our psyche to compensate for developments in technology. Pornography, like alcohol and drugs, reduces our capacity to tolerate ambiguous moods of free-floating worry and boredom. Internet pornography assists our escape from ourselves, helping us to destroy our present and our future with depressing ease. Yet it's possible to conceive of a pornography in which sexual desire would be invited to support, rather than undermine, our higher values. It could be touching and playful. It could show people having sex who like one another, or people like those we know from the rest of life rather than aberrations. No longer would we have to choose between being human and being sexual.

Why is "Not tonight, Dear" so destructive?

Logic might suggest that being married or in a long-term relationship must guarantee an end to the anxiety that otherwise dogs attempts by one person to induce another to have sex. But while either kind of union may make sex a constant theoretical option, it will neither legitimate the act nor ease the path toward it. Moreover, against a background of permanent possibility, an unwillingness to have sex may be seen as a far graver violation of the ground rules than a similar impasse in other contexts. Being turned down by someone we have just met in a bar is not so surprising or wounding. Suffering sexual rejection by the person with whom we have pledged to share our life is much odder and more humiliating.

Why is impotence an achievement?

There are few greater sources of shame for a man, or feelings of rejection for his partner. The real problem with impotence is the blow to the self-esteem of both parties.

We are grievously mistaken in our interpretation. Impotence is the strangely troublesome fruit of reason and kindness intruding on the free flow of animal impulses, of our new inclination to wonder what another might be feeling and then to identify with his or her potential objections to our invasive or unsatisfactory demands.

All but the least self-aware among us will sometimes be struck by how distasteful our desire for sex can seem to someone else, how peculiar and physically off-putting our flesh may be, and how unwanted our caresses. An advanced capacity for love and tenderness can ironically render us too sensitive to try to pester anyone else into having sex with us, although now and then we may cross paths with individuals who are not appalled by our longing for urgent and forceful sexual congress, and who see nothing disgusting in even the farthest erotic extremes.

Impotence is at base, then, a symptom of respect, a fear of causing displeasure through the imposition of our own desires or the inability to satisfy our partner's needs—a civilized worry that we will disappoint or upset others. It is an asset that should be valued as evidence of an achievement of the ethical imagination.

What do religions know about sex that we don't?

Only religions still take sex seriously, in the sense of properly respecting its power to turn us away from our priorities. Only religions see it as something potentially dangerous and needing to be guarded against. Perhaps only after killing many hours online at youporn.com can we appreciate that on this one point religions have got it right: Sex and sexual images can overwhelm our higher rational faculties with depressing ease. Religions are often mocked for being prudish, but they wouldn't judge sex to be quite so bad if they didn't also understand that it could be rather wonderful.

Does marriage ruin sex?

A gradual decline in the intensity and frequency of sex between a married couple is an inevitable fact of biological life, and as such, evidence of deep normality—although the sex-therapy industry has focused most of its efforts on assuring us that marriage should be enlivened by constant desire.

Most innocently, the paucity of sex within established relationships has to do with the difficulty of shifting registers between the everyday and the erotic. The qualities demanded of us when we have sex stand in sharp opposition to those we employ in conducting the majority of our other, daily activities. Marriage tends to involve—if not immediately, then within a few years—the running of a household and the raising of children, tasks that often feel akin to the administration of a small business and call on many of the same skills.

Sex, with its contrary emphases on expansiveness, imagination, playfulness, and a loss of control, must by its very nature interrupt this routine of regulation and self-restraint. We avoid sex not because it isn't fun but because its pleasures erode our subsequent capacity to endure the strenuous demands that our domestic arrangements place on us.

Sex also has a way of altering and unbalancing our relationship with our household co-manager. Its initiation requires one partner or the other to become vulnerable by revealing what may feel like humiliating sexual needs. We must shift from debating what sort of household appliance to acquire to making the more challenging request, for example, that our spouse should turn over and take on the attitude of a submissive nurse or put on a pair of boots and start calling us names.

The satisfaction of our needs may force us to ask for things that are, from a distance, open to being judged both ridiculous and contemptible so that we may prefer, in the end, not to

entrust them to someone on whom we must rely for so much else in the course of our ordinary upstanding life. We may in fact find it easier to put on a rubber mask or pretend to be a predatory, incestuous relative with someone we're not also going to have to eat breakfast with for the next three decades.

Why are bread crumbs in the kitchen bad for sex?

The common conception of anger posits red faces, raised voices, and slammed doors, but only too often it just curdles into numbness. We tend to forget we are angry with our partner, and hence become anaesthetized, melancholic, and unable to have sex with him or her because the specific incidents that anger us happen so quickly and so invisibly, in such chaotic settings (at the breakfast table, before the school run) that we can't recognize the offense well enough to mount a coherent protest against it. And we frequently don't articulate our anger, even when we do understand it, because the things that offend us can seem so trivial or odd that they would sound ridiculous if spoken aloud: "I am angry with you because you cut the bread in the wrong way." But once we are involved in a relationship, there is no longer any such thing as a minor detail.

In an average week, each partner may be hit by, and in turn fire, dozens of tiny arrows without even realizing it, with the only surface legacies of these wounds being a near imperceptible cooling between the pair and, crucially, the disinclination of one or both to have sex with the other. Sex is a gift that is not easy to hand over once we are annoyed.

We are unable to rise above the fray and shift the focus from recrimination towards identification of the true sources of hurt and fear. Couples need to appreciate that their hostilities were shaped by the flow of their individual personalities through the distorting emotional canyons of their particular childhoods. We think we already know everything necessary about how to be with another person, without having bothered to learn anything at all. We are unprepared for the effort we must legitimately expend to make even a very decent adult relationship successful.

Why are hotels metaphysically important?

The walls, beds, comfortably upholstered chairs, room service menus, televisions, and tightly wrapped soaps can do more than answer a taste for luxury. Checking into a hotel room for a night is a solution to long-term sexual stagnation: We can see the erotic side of our partner, which is often closely related to the unchanging environment in which we lead our daily lives. We can blame the stable presence of the carpet and the living room chairs at home for our failure to have more sex: The physical backdrop prevents us from evolving. The furniture insists that we can't change—because it never does.

In a hotel room, we may make love joyfully again because we have rediscovered, behind the roles we are forced to play by our domestic circumstances, the sexual identities that first drew us together—an act of aesthetic perception that will have been critically assisted by a pair of terry cloth bathrobes, a complimentary fruit basket, and a view onto an unfamiliar harbor. We can see our lover as if we had never laid eyes on him before.

Why is adultery overrated?

Contrary to all public verdicts on adultery, the lack of any wish whatsoever to stray is irrational and against nature, a heedless disregard for the fleshly reality of our bodies, a denial of the power wielded over our more rational selves by such erotic triggers as high-heeled shoes and crisp shirts, by smooth thighs and muscular calves.

But a spouse who gets angry at having been betrayed is evading a basic, tragic truth: No one can be everything to another person. The real fault lies in the ethos of modern marriage, with its insane ambitions and its insistence that our most pressing needs might be solved with the help of only one other person.

If seeing marriage as the perfect answer to all our hopes for love, sex, and family is naive and misguided, so too is believing that adultery can be an effective antidote to the disappointments of marriage. It is impossible to sleep with someone outside of marriage and not spoil the things we care about inside it. There is no answer to the tensions of marriage.

When a person with whom we have been having an erotic exchange in an Internet chat room suggests a meeting at an airport hotel, we may be tempted to blow up our life for a few hours' pleasure. The defenders of feeling-based marriage venerate emotions for their authenticity only because they avoid looking closely at what actually floats through most people's emotional kaleidoscopes, all the contradictory, sentimental, and hormonal forces that pull us in a hundred often crazed and inconclusive directions.

We could not be fulfilled if we weren't inauthentic some of the time—inauthentic, that is, in relation to such things as our passing desires to throttle our children, poison our spouse, or end our marriage over a dispute about changing a lightbulb. A degree of repression is necessary for both the mental health of our species and the adequate functioning of a decently ordered society. We are chaotic chemical propositions. We should feel grateful for, and protected by, the knowledge that our external circumstances are often out of line with what we feel; it is a sign that we are probably on the right course.

Critical Thinking

1. The author states "few of us are remotely normal sexually." Do you agree or disagree? Why?

2. Describe some practical challenges sexual desires and impulses present in our daily lives.

3. Is sex more physical or emotional? Why?

4. What is a question about sex that has not been addressed in this article?

Create Central

www.mhhe.com/createcentral

Internet References

Go Ask Alice!
www.goaskalice.columbia.edu

The Kinsey Institute for Research in Sex, Gender, and Reproduction
www.kinseyinstitute.org

The Society for the Scientific Study of Sexuality
www.sexscience.org

The Electronic Journal of Human Sexuality
www.ejhs.org/index.htm

ALAIN DE BOTTON is founder of The School of Life, based in London.

de Botton, Alain. From *Psychology Today,* January/February 2013, pp. 54–61. Copyright © 2013 by Sussex Publishers, LLC. Reprinted by permission.

Article

Prepared by: Patricia Hrusa Williams, *University of Maine at Farmington*

Boys on the Side

The hookup culture that has largely replaced dating on college campuses has been viewed, in many quarters, as socially corrosive and ultimately toxic to women, who seemingly have little choice but to participate. Actually, it is an engine of female progress—one being harnessed and driven by women themselves.

HANNA ROSIN

Learning Outcomes

After reading this article, you will be able to:

- Define the term hookup culture.

- Recognize differences in the meaning of sexual liberation to men and women in modern society.

- Identify changes in our society leading to the development of the hookup culture and changes in women's sexual behavior.

The porn pic being passed around on the students' cellphones at an Ivy League business-school party last fall was more prank than smut: a woman in a wool pom-pom hat giving a snowman with a snow penis a blow job. *Snow-blowing*, it's called, or *snowman fellatio,* terms everyone at this midweek happy hour seemed to know (except me). The men at the party flashed the snapshot at the women, and the women barely bothered to roll their eyes. These were not women's-studies types, for sure; they were already several years out of college and proud veterans of the much maligned hookup culture that, over the past 15 years or so, has largely replaced dating on college campuses and beyond.

One of the women had already seen the photo five times before her boyfriend showed it to her, so she just moved her pitcher of beer in front of his phone and kept on talking. He'd already suggested twice that night that they go to a strip club, and when their mutual friend asked if the two of them were getting married, he gave the friend the finger and made sure his girlfriend could see it, so she wouldn't get any ideas about a forthcoming ring. She remained unfazed. She was used to his "juvenile thing," she told me.

I had gone to visit the business school because a friend had described the women there as the most sexually aggressive he had ever met. Many of them had been molded on trading floors or in investment banks with male–female ratios as terrifying as 50-to-1, so they had learned to keep pace with the boys. Women told me stories of being hit on at work by "FDBs" (finance douche bags) who hadn't even bothered to take off their wedding rings, or sitting through Monday-morning meetings that started with stories about who had banged whom (or what) that weekend. In their decade or so of working, they had been routinely hazed by male colleagues showing them ever more baroque porn downloaded on cellphones. Snowblowing was nothing to them.

In fact, I found barely anyone who even *noticed* the vulgarity anymore, until I came across a new student. She had arrived two weeks earlier, from Argentina. She and I stood by the bar at one point and watched a woman put her hand on a guy's inner thigh, shortly before they disappeared together. In another corner of the room, a beautiful Asian woman in her second year at school was entertaining the six guys around her with her best imitation of an Asian prostitute—"Oooo, you so big. Me love you long time"—winning the Tucker Max showdown before any of the guys had even tried to make a move on her. (She eventually chose the shortest guy in the group to go home with, because, she later told me, he seemed like he'd be the best in bed.)

"Here in America, the girls, they give up their mouth, their ass, their tits," the Argentinean said to me, punctuating each with the appropriate hand motion, "before they even know the guy. It's like, 'Hello.' 'Hello.' 'You wanna hook up?' 'Sure.' They are so aggressive! Do they have hearts of steel or something? In my country, a girl like this would be desperate. Or a prostitute."

So there we have it. America has unseated the Scandinavian countries for the title of Easiest Lay. We are, in the world's estimation, a nation of prostitutes. And not even prostitutes with hearts of gold.

Is that so bad? Or is there, maybe, a different way to analyze the scene that had just unfolded? Admittedly, what the Argentinean and I had just witnessed fills the nightmares of those who lament the evil hookup culture: ubiquitous porn, young women so inured to ubiquitous porn that they don't bother to protest, young women behaving exactly like frat boys, and no one guarding the virtues of honor, chivalry, or even lasting love. It's a sexual culture lamented by, among others, Caitlin Flanagan, [. . .] in her nostalgia-drenched new book, *Girl Land.* Like many other critics, Flanagan pines for an earlier time, when fathers protected "innocent" girls from "punks" and predators, and when girls understood it was their role to also protect themselves.

Girl Land, like so much writing about young women and sexuality, concentrates on what has been lost. The central argument holds that women have effectively been duped by a sexual revolution that persuaded them to trade away the protections of (and from) young men. In return, they were left even more vulnerable and exploited than before. Sexual liberation, goes the argument, primarily liberated men—to act as cads, using women for their own pleasures and taking no responsibility for the emotional wreckage that their behavior created. The men hold all the cards, and the women put up with it because now it's too late to zip it back up, so they don't have a choice.

But this analysis downplays the unbelievable gains women have lately made, and, more important, it forgets how much those gains depend on sexual liberation. Single young women in their sexual prime—that is, their 20s and early 30s, the same age as the women at the business-school party—are for the first time in history more successful, on average, than the single young men around them. They are more likely to have a college degree and, in aggregate, they make more money. What makes this remarkable development possible is not just the pill or legal abortion but the whole new landscape of sexual freedom—the ability to delay marriage and have temporary relationships that don't derail education or career. To put it crudely, feminist progress right now largely depends on the existence of the hookup culture. And to a surprising degree, it is women—not men—who are perpetuating the culture, especially in school, cannily manipulating it to make space for their success, always keeping their own ends in mind. For college girls these days, an overly serious suitor fills the same role an accidental pregnancy did in the 19th century: a danger to be avoided at all costs, lest it get in the way of a promising future.

The business-school women I met were in an extreme situation. Wall Street culture had socialized them to tolerate high degrees of sexual crudeness, and they were also a decade past the tentative explorations of their freshman year. But they are merely the most purified sample of a much larger group of empowered college-age women. Even freshmen and sophomores are not nearly as vulnerable as we imagine them to be.

On a mild fall afternoon in 2011, I sat in a courtyard with some undergraduates at Yale to ask about their romantic lives. A few months earlier, a group of mostly feminist-minded students had filed a Title IX complaint against the university for tolerating a "hostile sexual environment on campus." The students specifically cited a 2010 incident when members of the Delta Kappa Epsilon fraternity stood outside freshman dorms chanting "No means yes! Yes means anal!" I'd heard this phrase before, from the business-school students, of course: on spring break, they had played a game called "dirty rounds"—something like charades, except instead of acting out movie or book titles, they acted out sex slogans like the one above, or terms like *pink sock* (what your anus looks like after too much anal sex). But the Yale undergraduates had not reached that level of blitheness. They were incensed. The week before I arrived, an unrelated group of students ran a letter in the campus paper complaining that the heart of the problem was "Yale's sexual culture" itself, that the "hookup culture is fertile ground for acts of sexual selfishness, insensitivity, cruelty and malice."

At Yale I heard stories like the ones I had read in many journalistic accounts of the hookup culture. One sorority girl, a junior with a beautiful tan, long dark hair, and a great figure, whom I'll call Tali, told me that freshman year she, like many of her peers, was high on her first taste of the hookup culture and didn't want a boyfriend. "It was empowering, to have that kind of control," she recalls. "Guys were texting and calling me all the time, and I was turning them down. I really enjoyed it! I had these options to hook up if I wanted them, and no one would judge me for it." But then, sometime during sophomore year, her feelings changed. She got tired of relationships that just faded away, "no end, no beginning." Like many of the other college women I talked with, Tali and her friends seemed much more sexually experienced and knowing than my friends at college. They were as blasé about blow jobs and anal sex as the one girl I remember from my junior year whom we all considered destined for a tragic early marriage or an asylum. But they were also more innocent. When I asked Tali what she really wanted, she didn't say anything about commitment or marriage or a return to a more chivalrous age. "Some guy to ask me out on a date to the frozen-yogurt place," she said. That's it. A $3 date.

But the soda-fountain nostalgia of this answer quickly dissipated when I asked Tali and her peers a related question: Did they want the hookup culture to go away—might they prefer the mores of an earlier age, with formal dating and slightly more obvious rules? This question, each time, prompted a look of horror. Reform the culture, maybe, teach women to "advocate for themselves"—a phrase I heard many times—but end it? Never. Even one of the women who had initiated the Title IX complaint, Alexandra Brodsky, felt this way. "I would never come down on the hookup culture," she said. "Plenty of women enjoy having casual sex."

Books about the hookup culture tend to emphasize the frustration that results from transient sexual encounters, stripped of true intimacy: "A lot of [boys] just want to hook up with you and then never talk to you again . . . and they don't care!" one woman complains to Kathleen Bogle in *Hooking Up: Sex, Dating, and Relationships on Campus.* "That might not stop you [from hooking up,] because you think: 'This time it might be different.' " From her interviews with 76 college students, Bogle also deduces that the double standard is alive and well. Men tally "fuck points" on their frat-house bulletin boards. Women who sleep with "too many" men are called "houserats" or "laxtitutes" (a term of art denoting women who sleep with several guys on the lacrosse team) or are deemed "HFH," meaning "hot for a hookup" but definitely not for anything more. The hookup culture, writes Bogle, is a "battle of the sexes" in which women want relationships and men want "no strings attached."

But it turns out that these sorts of spotlight interviews can be misleading. Talk to an individual 19-year-old woman such as Tali on a given day, and she may give you an earful of girl trouble. But as her girlfriend might tell her after a teary night, you have to get some perspective. Zoom out, and you see that for most women, the hookup culture is like an island they visit, mostly during their college years and even then only when they are bored or experimenting or don't know any better. But it is not a place where they drown. The sexual culture may be more coarse these days, but young women are more than adequately equipped to handle it, because unlike the women in earlier ages, they have more important things on their minds, such as good grades and internships and job interviews and a financial future of their own. The most patient and thorough research about the hookup culture shows that over the long run, women benefit greatly from living in a world where they can have sexual adventure without commitment or all that much shame, and where they can enter into temporary relationships that don't get in the way of future success.

In 2004, Elizabeth Armstrong, then a sociologist at Indiana University, and Laura Hamilton, a young graduate student, set out to do a study on sexual abuse in college students' relationships. They applied for permission to interview women on a single floor of what was known as a "party dorm" at a state university in the Midwest. About two-thirds of the students came from what they called "more privileged" backgrounds, meaning they had financial support from their parents, who were probably college-educated themselves. A third came from less

privileged families; they supported themselves and were probably the first in their family to go to college. The researchers found their first day of interviewing so enlightening that they decided to ask the administration if they could stay on campus for four years and track the 53 women's romantic lives.

Women in the dorm complained to the researchers about the double standard, about being called sluts, about not being treated with respect. But what emerged from four years of research was the sense that hooking up was part of a larger romantic strategy, part of what Armstrong came to think of as a "sexual career." For an upwardly mobile, ambitious young woman, hookups were a way to dip into relationships without disrupting her self-development or schoolwork. Hookups functioned as a "delay tactic," Armstrong writes, because the immediate priority, for the privileged women at least, was setting themselves up for a career. "If I want to maintain the lifestyle that I've grown up with," one woman told Armstrong, "I have to work. I just don't see myself being someone who marries young and lives off of some boy's money." Or from another woman: "I want to get secure in a city and in a job . . . I'm not in any hurry at all. As long as I'm married by 30, I'm good."

The women still had to deal with the old-fashioned burden of protecting their personal reputations, but in the long view, what they really wanted to protect was their future professional reputations. "Rather than struggling to get into relationships," Armstrong reported, women "had to work to avoid them." (One woman lied to an interested guy, portraying herself as "extremely conservative" to avoid dating him.) Many did not want a relationship to steal time away from their friendships or studying.

Armstrong and Hamilton had come looking for sexual victims. Instead, at this university, and even more so at other, more prestigious universities they studied, they found the opposite: women who were managing their romantic lives like savvy headhunters. "The ambitious women calculate that having a relationship would be like a four-credit class, and they don't always have time for it, so instead they opt for a lighter hookup," Armstrong told me.

The women described boyfriends as "too greedy" and relationships as "too involved." One woman "with no shortage of admirers" explained, "I know this sounds really pathetic and you probably think I am lying, but there are so many other things going on right now that it's really not something high up on my list . . . I know that's such a lame-ass excuse, but it's true." The women wanted to study or hang out with friends or just be "100 percent selfish," as one said. "I have the rest of my life to devote to a husband or kids or my job." Some even purposely had what one might think of as fake boyfriends, whom they considered sub-marriage quality, and weren't genuinely attached to. "He fits my needs now, because I don't want to get married now," one said. "I don't want anyone else to influence what I do after I graduate."

The most revealing parts of the study emerge from the interviews with the less privileged women. They came to college mostly with boyfriends back home and the expectation of living a life similar to their parents', piloting toward an early marriage. They were still fairly conservative and found the hookup culture initially alienating ("Those rich bitches are way slutty" is how Armstrong summarizes their attitude). They felt trapped between the choice of marrying the kind of disastrous hometown guy who never gets off the couch, and will steal their credit card—or joining a sexual culture that made them uncomfortable. The ones who chose the first option were considered the dorm tragedies, women who had succumbed to some Victorian-style delusion. "She would always talk about how she couldn't wait to get married and have babies," one woman said about her working-class friend. "It was just like, *Whoa. I'm 18. . . . Slow down.* You know? Then she just crazy dropped out of school and wouldn't contact any of us. . . . The way I see it is that she's from a really small town, and that's what everyone in her town does . . . [they] get married and have babies."

Most of the women considered success stories by their dormmates had a revelation and revised their plan, setting themselves on what was universally considered the path to success. "Now I'm like, *I don't even need to be getting married yet [or] have kids,*" one of the less privileged women told the researchers in her senior year. "All of [my brother's] friends, 17-to-20-year-old girls, have their . . . babies, and I'm like, *Oh my God. . . .* Now I'll be able to do something else for a couple years before I settle down . . . before I worry about kids." The hookup culture opened her horizons. She could study and work and date, and live on temporary intimacy. She could find her way to professional success, and then get married.

Does this mean that in the interim years, women are living a depraved, libertine existence, contributing to the breakdown of social order? Hardly. In fact, women have vastly more control over their actions and appetites than we have been led to believe. You could even say that what defines this era is an unusual amount of sexual control and planning. Since 2005, Paula England, a sociologist at New York University, has been collecting data from an online survey about hookups. She is up to about 20,000 responses—the largest sample to date. In her survey, college seniors report an average of 7.9 hookups over four years, but a median of only five. ("Hookups" do not necessarily involve sex; students are instructed to use whatever definition their friends use.) This confirms what other surveys have found: people at either end of the scale are skewing the numbers. Researchers guess that about a quarter of college kids skip out on the hookup culture altogether, while a similar number participate with gusto—about 10 hookups or more (the

laxtitutes?). For the majority in the middle, the hookup culture is a place to visit freshman year, or whenever you feel like it, or after you've been through a breakup, says England. Most important, hookups haven't wrecked the capacity for intimacy. In England's survey, 74 percent of women and about an equal number of men say they've had a relationship in college that lasted at least six months.

When they do hook up, the weepy-woman stereotype doesn't hold. Equal numbers of men and women—about half—report to England that they enjoyed their latest hookup "very much." About 66 percent of women say they wanted their most recent hookup to turn into something more, but 58 percent of men say the same—not a vast difference, considering the cultural panic about the demise of chivalry and its consequences for women. And in fact, the broad inference that young people are having more sex—and not just coarser sex—is just wrong; teenagers today, for instance, are far less likely than their parents were to have sex or get pregnant. Between 1988 and 2010, the percentage of teenage girls having sex dropped from 37 to 27, according to the latest data from the Centers for Disease Control and Prevention. By many measures, the behavior of young people can even look like a return to a more innocent age.

Almost all of the college women Armstrong and Hamilton interviewed assumed they would get married, and were looking forward to it. In England's survey, about 90 percent of the college kids, male and female, have said they want to get married.

One of the great crime stories of the past 20 years, meanwhile, is the dramatic decline of rape and sexual assault. Between 1993 and 2008, the rate of those crimes against females dropped by 70 percent nationally. When women were financially dependent on men, leaving an abusive situation was much harder for them. But now women who in earlier eras might have stayed in such relationships can leave or, more often, kick men out of the house. Women, argues Mike Males, a criminologist at the Center on Juvenile and Criminal Justice, "have achieved a great deal more power. And that makes them a lot harder to victimize."

We've landed in an era that has produced a new breed of female sexual creature, one who acknowledges the eternal vulnerability of women but, rather than cave in or trap herself in the bell jar, instead looks that vulnerability square in the face and then manipulates it in unexpected, and sometimes hilarious, ways. In the fall of 2010, Karen Owen, a recent graduate of Duke University, became momentarily famous when her friends leaked her pornographic PowerPoint presentation cataloging her sexual exploits with 13 Duke athletes, whom she identified by name, skill, and penis size ("While he had girth on his side, the subject was severely lacking in length"). In Owen's hands, scenes of potential humiliation were transformed into punch lines. ("Mmm tell me about how much you like big, black cocks," Subject 6, a baseball player, told her. "But, I've never even hooked up with a black man!" she told him. "Oh . . . well, just pretend like you have," he responded. "Umm ok . . . I like big, black . . . cocks?")

The 2012 successor to the iconic single-girl show of a decade ago, *Sex and the City,* is *Girls,* a new HBO series created by the indie actress/filmmaker Lena Dunham, who plays the main character, Hannah. When Hannah has sex, she is not wearing a Carrie Bradshaw–style $200 couture bra and rolling in silk sheets, but hiking her shirt up over belly flesh loose enough that her boyfriend, Adam, can grab it by the fistful. In one scene, they attempt anal sex: "That feels awful." In another, Adam spins a ridiculously degrading fantasy about Hannah as an 11-year-old hooker with a "fucking Cabbage Patch lunch box." Hannah plays along, reluctantly. But when they're done, she doesn't feel deep remorse or have to detox with her girlfriends or call the police. She makes a joke about the 11-year-old, which he doesn't get, and then goes home to rock out with her roommate to Swedish pop star Robyn's *"Dancing on My Own."*

In Hannah's charmed but falling-apart life, her encounters with Adam count as "experience," fodder for the memoir she half-jokingly tells her parents will make her "the voice of [her] generation." She is our era's Portnoy, entitled and narcissistic enough to obsess about precisely how she gets off. (Adam, meanwhile, plays the role of the Pumpkin, or the Pilgrim, or the Monkey, the love or lust objects from Philip Roth's *Portnoy's Complaint*—all merely props in Portnoy's long and comical sexual journey.) The suspense in the series is not driven by the usual rom-com mystery—will she or won't she get her man?—because she snags him pretty early in the series. Instead it's driven by the uncertainty of Hannah's career—will she or won't she fulfill her potential and become a great writer? When, in the season finale, Adam asks to move in, she rejects him. We're left to believe that one reason is because she's afraid he might get in the way of her bigger plans to be a writer.

There is no retreating from the hookup culture to an earlier age, when a young man showed up at the front door with a box of chocolates for his sweetheart, and her father eyed him warily. Even the women most frustrated by the hookup culture don't really want that. The hookup culture is too bound up with everything that's fabulous about being a young woman in 2012—the freedom, the confidence, the knowledge that you can always depend on yourself. The only option is what Hannah's friends always tell her—stop doing what feels awful, and figure out what doesn't.

Young men and women have discovered a sexual freedom unbridled by the conventions of marriage, or any conventions. But that's not how the story ends. They will need time, as one young woman at Yale told me, to figure out what they want and how to ask for it. Ultimately, the desire for a deeper human connection always wins out, for both men and women. Even for those business-school women, their hookup years are likely to end up as a series of photographs, buried somewhere on their Facebook page, that they do or don't share with their husband—a memory that they recall fondly or sourly, but that hardly defines them.

Critical Thinking

1. Do you think men and women have different reasons for pursuing hookups? If so, what are they?

2. Do you think there is a sexual double standard in judging the behavior of men versus women who participate in hook-ups? If so, why do you think this double standard exists?

3. Why do you think the hookup culture can be more prevalent on some college campuses? What are some cautions you might provide to other students about the changes in sexual behaviors and norms on college campuses?

Create Central

www.mhhe.com/createcentral

Internet References

Go Ask Alice!
www.goaskalice.columbia.edu

The Electronic Journal of Human Sexuality
www.ejhs.org/index.htm

The Kinsey Institute for Research in Sex, Gender, and Reproduction
www.kinseyinstitute.org

The Society for the Scientific Study of Sexuality
www.sexscience.org

Article

Prepared by: Patricia Hrusa Williams,
University of Maine at Farmington

There's No Such Thing as Everlasting Love (According to Science)

EMILY ESFAHANI SMITH

Learning Outcomes

After reading this article, you will be able to:

- Understand differences in theoretical, practical, and scientific definitions of love.
- Explain the science, biochemistry, and physiological components behind love.

In her new book *Love 2.0: How Our Supreme Emotion Affects Everything We Feel, Think, Do, and Become,* the psychologist Barbara Fredrickson offers a radically new conception of love.

Fredrickson, a leading researcher of positive emotions at the University of North Carolina at Chapel Hill, presents scientific evidence to argue that love is not what we think it is. It is not a long-lasting, continually present emotion that sustains a marriage; it is not the yearning and passion that characterizes young love; and it is not the blood-tie of kinship.

Rather, it is what she calls a "micro-moment of positivity resonance." She means that love is a connection, characterized by a flood of positive emotions, which you share with another person—*any* other person—whom you happen to connect with in the course of your day. You can experience these micro-moments with your romantic partner, child, or close friend. But you can also fall in love, however momentarily, with less likely candidates, like a stranger on the street, a colleague at work, or an attendant at a grocery store. Louis Armstrong put it best in "It's a Wonderful World" when he sang, "I see friends shaking hands, sayin' 'how do you do?' / They're really sayin', 'I love you.'"

Fredrickson's unconventional ideas are important to think about at this time of year. With Valentine's Day around the corner, many Americans are facing a grim reality: They are love-starved. Rates of loneliness are on the rise as social supports are disintegrating. In 1985, when the General Social Survey polled Americans on the number of confidants they have in their lives, the most common response was three. In 2004, when the survey was given again, the most common response was zero.

According to the University of Chicago's John Cacioppo, an expert on loneliness, and his co-author William Patrick, "at any given time, roughly 20 percent of individuals—that would be 60 million people in the U.S. alone—feel sufficiently isolated for it to be a major source of unhappiness in their lives." For older Americans, that number is closer to 35 percent. At the same time, rates of depression have been on the rise. In his 2011 book *Flourish,* the psychologist Martin Seligman notes that according to some estimates, depression is 10 times more prevalent now than it was five decades ago. Depression affects about 10 percent of the American population, according to the Centers for Disease Control.

A global poll taken last Valentine's Day showed that most married people—or those with a significant other—list their romantic partner as the greatest source of happiness in their lives. According to the same poll, nearly half of all single people are looking for a romantic partner, saying that finding a special person to love would contribute greatly to their happiness.

But to Fredrickson, these numbers reveal a "worldwide collapse of imagination," as she writes in her book. "Thinking of love purely as romance or commitment that you share with one special person—as it appears most on earth do—surely limits the health and happiness you derive" from love.

"My conception of love," she tells me, "gives hope to people who are single or divorced or widowed this Valentine's Day to find smaller ways to experience love."

You have to physically be with the person to experience the micro-moment. For example, if you and your significant other are not physically together—if you are reading this at work alone in your office—then you two are not in love. You may feel connected or bonded to your partner—you may long to be in his company—but your body is completely loveless.

To understand why, it's important to see how love works biologically. Like all emotions, love has a biochemical and physiological component. But unlike some of the other positive emotions, like joy or happiness, love cannot be kindled individually—it only exists in the physical connection between two people. Specifically, there are three players in the biological love system—mirror neurons, oxytocin, and vagal tone. Each involves connection and each contributes to those micro-moments of positivity resonance that Fredrickson calls love.

When you experience love, your brain mirrors the person's you are connecting with in a special way. Pioneering research by Princeton University's Uri Hasson shows what happens inside the brains of two people who connect in conversation. Because brains are scanned inside of noisy fMRI machines, where carrying on a conversation is nearly impossible, Hasson's team had his subjects mimic a natural conversation in an ingenious way. They recorded a young woman telling a lively, long, and circuitous story about her high school prom. Then, they played the recording for the participants in the study, who were listening to it as their brains were being scanned. Next, the researchers asked each participant to re-create the story so they, the researchers, could determine who was listening well and who was not. Good listeners, the logic goes, would probably be the ones who clicked in a natural conversation with the story-teller.

What they found was remarkable. In some cases, the brain patterns of the listener mirrored those of the storyteller after a short time gap. The listener needed time to process the story after all. In other cases, the brain activity was almost perfectly synchronized; there was no time lag at all between the speaker and the listener. But in some rare cases, if the listener was particularly tuned in to the story—if he was hanging on to every word of the story and really got it—his brain activity actually *anticipated* the story-teller's in some cortical areas.

The mutual understanding and shared emotions, especially in that third category of listener, generated a micro-moment of love, which "is a single act, performed by two brains," as Fredrickson writes in her book.

Oxytocin, the so-called love and cuddle hormone, facilitates these moments of shared intimacy and is part of the mammalian "calm-and-connect" system (as opposed to the more stressful "fight-or-flight" system that closes us off to others). The hormone, which is released in huge quantities during sex, and in lesser amounts during other moments of intimate connection, works by making people feel more trusting and open to connection. This is the hormone of attachment and bonding that spikes during micro-moments of love. Researchers have found, for instance, that when a parent acts affectionately with his or her infant—through micro-moments of love like making eye contact, smiling, hugging, and playing—oxytocin levels in both the parent and the child rise in sync.

The final player is the vagus nerve, which connects your brain to your heart and subtly but sophisticatedly allows you to meaningfully experience love. As Fredrickson explains in her book, "Your vagus nerve stimulates tiny facial muscles that better enable you to make eye contact and synchronize your facial expressions with another person. It even adjusts the miniscule muscles of your middle ear so you can better track her voice against any background noise."

The vagus nerve's potential for love can actually be measured by examining a person's heart rate in association with his breathing rate, what's called "vagal tone." Having a high vagal tone is good: People who have a high "vagal tone" can regulate their biological processes like their glucose levels better; they have more control over their emotions, behavior, and attention; they are socially adept and can kindle more positive connections with others; and, most importantly, they are more loving.

In research from her lab, Fredrickson found that people with high vagal tone report more experiences of love in their days than those with a lower vagal tone.

Historically, vagal tone was considered stable from person to person. You either had a high one or you didn't; you either had a high potential for love or you didn't. Fredrickson's recent research has debunked that notion.

In a 2010 study from her lab, Fredrickson randomly assigned half of her participants to a "love" condition and half to a control condition. In the love condition, participants devoted about one hour of their weeks for several months to the ancient Buddhist practice of loving-kindness meditation. In loving-kindness meditation, you sit in silence for a period of time and cultivate feelings of tenderness, warmth, and compassion for another person by repeating a series of phrases to yourself wishing them love, peace, strength, and general well-being. Ultimately, the practice helps people step outside of themselves and become more aware of other people and their needs, desires, and struggles—something that can be difficult to do in our hyper individualistic culture.

Fredrickson measured the participants' vagal tone before and after the intervention. The results were so powerful that she was invited to present them before the Dalai Lama himself in 2010. Fredrickson and her team found that, contrary to the conventional wisdom, people could significantly increase their vagal tone by self-generating love through loving-kindness meditation. Since vagal tone mediates social connections and bonds, people whose vagal tones increased were suddenly capable of experiencing more micro-moments of love in their days. Beyond that, their growing capacity to love more will translate into health benefits given that high vagal tone is associated with lowered risk of inflammation, cardiovascular disease, diabetes, and stroke.

Fredrickson likes to call love a nutrient. If you are getting enough of the nutrient, then the health benefits of love can dramatically alter your biochemistry in ways that perpetuate more micro-moments of love in your life, and which ultimately contribute to your health, well-being, and longevity.

Fredrickson's ideas about love are not exactly the stuff of romantic comedies. Describing love as a "micro-moment of positivity resonance" seems like a buzz-kill. But if love now seems less glamorous and mysterious than you thought it was, then good. Part of Fredrickson's project is to lower cultural expectations about love—expectations that are so misguidedly high today that they have inflated love into something that it isn't, and into something that no sane person could actually experience.

Jonathan Haidt, another psychologist, calls these unrealistic expectations "the love myth" in his 2006 book *The Happiness Hypothesis:*

> True love is passionate love that never fades; if you are in true love, you should marry that person; if love ends, you should leave that person because it was not true love; and if you can find the right person, you will have true love forever. You might not believe this myth yourself, particularly if you are older than thirty; but many young people in Western nations are raised on it, and it acts as

an ideal that they unconsciously carry with them even if they scoff at it. . . . But if true love is defined as eternal passion, it is biologically impossible.

Love 2.0 is, by contrast, far humbler. Fredrickson tells me, "I love the idea that it lowers the bar of love. If you don't have a Valentine, that doesn't mean that you don't have love. It puts love much more in our reach everyday regardless of our relationship status."

Lonely people who are looking for love are making a mistake if they are sitting around and waiting for love in the form of the "love myth" to take hold of them. If they instead sought out love in little moments of connection that we all experience many times a day, perhaps their loneliness would begin to subside.

Critical Thinking

1. What is your definition of love? What are some similarities and differences between your definition and the ones presented in the article?

2. Explain the love myth.

3. Do you believe that people can be trained to be more loving, as the article implies? Why or why not?

4. What are some advantages and disadvantages of defining love as "micro-moments" of positive feelings and emotions?

Create Central

www.mhhe.com/createcentral

Internet References

Go Ask Alice!
www.goaskalice.columbia.edu

The Kinsey Institute for Research in Sex, Gender, and Reproduction
www.kinseyinstitute.org

The Society for the Scientific Study of Sexuality
www.sexscience.org

The Electronic Journal of Human Sexuality
www.ejhs.org/index.htm

Article

Prepared by: Patricia Hrusa Williams,
University of Maine at Farmington

The Expectations Trap

Much of the discontent couples encounter today is really culturally inflicted, although we're conditioned to blame our partners for our unhappiness. Yet research points to ways couples can immunize themselves against unseen pressures now pulling them apart.

HARA ESTROFF MARANO

Learning Outcomes

After reading this article, you will be able to:

- Recognize cultural aspects of love and marriage.

- Identify personality characteristics which are important to dating success.

- Describe how culture impacts happiness within relationships.

Six years, ten months, and eight days into their marriage, Sam and Melissa blew apart. Everyone was stunned, most of all the couple themselves. One day she was your basic stressed-out professional woman (and mother of a 3-year-old) carrying the major financial burden of their household. The next day she was a betrayed wife. The affair Sam disclosed detonated a caterwaul of hurt heard by every couple in their circle and her large coterie of friends and family. With speed verging on inevitability, the public knowledge of their private life commandeered the driver's seat of their own destiny. A surge of support for Melissa as the wronged woman swiftly isolated Sam emotionally and precluded deep discussion of the conditions that had long alienated him. Out of respect for the pain that his mere presence now caused, Sam decamped within days. He never moved back in.

It's not clear that the couple could have salvaged the relationship if they had tried. It wasn't just the infidelity. "We had so many background and stylistic differences," says Sam. "It was like we came from two separate cultures. We couldn't take out the garbage without a Geneva Accord." Constant negotiation was necessary, but if there was time, there was also usually too much accumulated irritation for Melissa to tolerate. And then, opening a public window on the relationship seemed to close the door on the possibility of working through the disappointments, the frustrations, the betrayal.

Within weeks, the couple was indeed in discussions—for a divorce. At least they both insisted on mediation, not litigation, and their lawyers complied. A couple of months, and some time and determination later, they had a settlement. Only now that Sam and Melissa have settled into their mostly separate lives, and their daughter appears to be doing well with abundant care from both her parents, are they catching their respective breaths—two years later.

Americans value marriage more than people do in any other culture, and it holds a central place in our dreams. Over 90 percent of young adults aspire to marriage—although fewer are actually choosing it, many opting instead for cohabitation. But no matter how you count it, Americans have the highest rate of romantic breakup in the world, says Andrew J. Cherlin, professor of sociology and public policy at Johns Hopkins. As with Sam and Melissa, marriages are discarded often before the partners know what hit them.

"By age 35, 10 percent of American women have lived with three or more husbands or domestic partners," Cherlin reports in his recent book, *The Marriage-Go-Round: The State of Marriage and the Family in America Today.* "Children of married parents in America face a higher risk of seeing them break up than children born of unmarried parents in Sweden."

With general affluence has come a plethora of choices, including constant choices about our personal and family life. Even marriage itself is now a choice. "The result is an ongoing self-appraisal of how your personal life is going, like having a continual readout of your emotional heart rate," says Cherlin. You get used to the idea of always making choices to improve your happiness.

The constant appraisal of personal life to improve happiness creates a heightened sensitivity to problems that arise in intimate relationships.

The heightened focus on options "creates a heightened sensitivity to problems that arise in intimate relationships." And negative emotions get priority processing in our brains. "There are so many opportunities to decide that it's unsatisfactory," says Cherlin.

It would be one thing if we were living more satisfied lives than ever. But just gauging by the number of relationships wrecked every year, we're less satisfied, says Cherlin. "We're carrying over into our personal lives the fast pace of decisions and actions we have everywhere else, and that may not be for the best." More than ever, we're paying attention to the most volatile parts of our emotional makeup—the parts that are too reactive to momentary events to give meaning to life.

> **More than ever, we're paying attention to the most volatile parts of our emotional makeup—parts that are too reactive to momentary events to give meaning to life.**

Because our intimate relationships are now almost wholly vehicles for meeting our emotional needs, and with almost all our emotions invested in one relationship, we tend to look upon any unhappiness we experience—whatever the source—as a failure of a partner to satisfy our longings. Disappointment inevitably feels so *personal* we see no other possibility but to hunt for individual psychological reasons—that is, to blame our partners for our own unhappiness.

But much—perhaps most—of the discontent we now encounter in close relationships is culturally inflicted, although we rarely interpret our experience that way. Culture—the pressure to constantly monitor our happiness, the plethora of choices surreptitiously creating an expectation of perfection, the speed of everyday life—always climbs into bed with us. An accumulation of forces has made the cultural climate hostile to long-term relationships today.

Attuned to disappointment and confused about its source, we wind up discarding perfectly good relationships. People work themselves up over "the ordinary problems of marriage, for which, by the way, they usually fail to see their own contributions," says William Doherty, professor of family sciences at the University of Minnesota. "They badger their partners to change, convince themselves nothing will budge, and so work their way out of really good relationships." Doherty believes it's possible to stop the careering disappointment even when people believe a relationship is over.

It's not going to happen by putting the genie back in the bottle. It's not possible to curb the excess of options life now offers. And speed is a fixture of the ongoing technological revolution, no matter how much friction it creates in personal lives. Yet new research points to ways that actually render them irrelevant. We are, after all, the architects of our own passions.

The Purpose of Marriage

Marriage probably evolved as the best way to pool the labor of men and women to enable families to subsist and assure that children survive to independence—and data indicate it still is. But beyond the basics, the purpose of marriage has shifted constantly, says Stephanie Coontz, a historian at Washington's Evergreen State College. It helps to remember that marriage

---

Case Study
Stephen and Christina

Five years into his marriage, not long after the birth of his first son, most of Stephen G.'s interactions with his wife were not pleasant. "I thought the difficulties would pass," he recalls. "My wife, Christina, got fed up faster and wanted me to leave." He was traveling frequently and finances were thin; she'd gone back to school full-time after having worked until the baby was born. "Very few needs were being met for either of us. We were either yelling or in a cold war."

They entered counseling to learn how to co-parent if they indeed separated. "It helped restore our friendship: At least we could talk civilly. That led to deeper communication—we could actually listen to each other without getting defensive. We heard that we were both hurting, both feeling the stress of new parenthood without a support system of either parents or friends. We could talk about the ways we weren't there for each other without feeling attacked. It took a lot longer for the romance to return."

Stephen, now 37, a sales representative for a pharmaceutical company in San Francisco, says it was a time of "growing up. I had to accept that I had new responsibilities. And I had to accept that my partner, now 38, is not ideal in every way although she is ideal in many ways. But her short temper is not enough of a reason to leave the relationship and our two kids. When I wish she'd be different, I have to remind myself of all the ways she is the person I want to be with. It's not something you 'get over.' You accept it."

---

evolved in an atmosphere of scarcity, the conditions that prevailed for almost all of human history. "The earliest purpose of marriage was to make strategic alliances with other people, to turn strangers into relatives," says Coontz. "As society became more differentiated, marriage became a major mechanism for adjusting your position."

It wasn't until the 18th century that anyone thought that love might have anything to do with marriage, but love was held in check by a sense of duty. Even through the 19th century, the belief prevailed that females and males had different natures and couldn't be expected to understand each other well. Only in the 20th century did the idea take hold that men and women should be companions, that they should be passionate, and that both should get sexual and personal fulfillment from marriage.

We're still trying to figure out how to do that—and get the laundry done, too. The hassles of a negotiated and constantly renegotiated relationship—few wish a return to inequality—assure a ready source of stress or disappointment or both.

From We to Me

Our mind-set has further shifted over the past few decades, experts suggest. Today, the minute one partner is faced with dissatisfaction—feeling stressed-out or neglected, having

Case Study
Susan and Tim

Susan Pohlman, now 50, reluctantly accompanied her workaholic husband on a business trip to Italy believing it would be their last together. Back home in Los Angeles were their two teenagers, their luxurious home, their overfurnished lives—and the divorce lawyer she had contacted to end their 18-year marriage.

They were leading such parallel lives that collaboration had turned to competition, with fights over things like who spent more time with the kids and who spent more time working. But knocked off balance by the beauty of the coast near Genoa toward the end of the trip, Tim asked, out of the blue, "What if we lived here?" "The spirit of this odd day overtook me," recalls Susan. At 6 P.M. on the evening before departure, they were shown a beautiful apartment overlooking the water. Despite knowing no Italian, they signed a lease on the spot. Two months later, with their house sold, they moved with their kids to Italy for a year.

"In L.A. we were four people going in four directions. In Italy, we became completely dependent on each other. How to get a phone? How to shop for food? Also, we had no belongings. The simplicity forced us to notice the experiences of life. Often, we had no idea what we were doing. There was lots of laughing at and with each other." Susan says she "became aware of the power of adventure and of doing things together, and how they became a natural bridge to intimacy."

Both Pohlmans found Italy offered "a more appreciative lifestyle." Says Susan: "I realized the American Dream was pulling us apart. We followed the formula of owning, having, pushing each other. You have all this stuff but you're miserable because what you're really craving is interaction." Too, she says, American life is exhausting, and "exhaustion distorts your ability to judge problems."

Now back in the U.S. and living in Arizona, the Pohimans believe they needed to remove themselves from the culture to see its distorting effects. "And we needed to participate in a paradigm shift: 'I'm not perfect, you're not perfect; let's not get hung up on our imperfections.'" But the most powerful element of their move could be reproduced anywhere, she says: "The simplicity was liberating."

consumer mind-set is a major portal through which destructive forces gain entry and undermine conjoint life.

"Marriage is for *me*" is the way Austin, Texas, family therapist Pat Love puts it. "It's for meeting *my* needs." It's not about what *I do*, but how it makes me *feel*.

Such beliefs lead to a sense of entitlement: "I deserve better than I'm getting." Doherty sees that as the basic message of almost every advertisement in the consumer culture. You deserve more and we can provide it. You begin to think: This isn't the deal I signed up for. Or you begin to feel that you're putting into this a lot more than you're getting out. "We believe in our inalienable right to the intimate relationships of our choice," says Doherty.

In allowing such free-market values to seep into our private lives, we come to believe that a partner's job is, above all, to provide pleasure. "People do not go into relationships because they want to learn how to negotiate and master difficulties," observes Brown University psychiatrist Scott Haltzman. "They want the other person to provide pleasure." It's partner as service provider. The pleasure bond, unfortunately, is as volatile as the emotions that underlie it and as hollow and fragile as the hedonic sense of happiness.

The Expectations Trap: Perfection, Please

If there's one thing that most explicitly detracts from the enjoyment of relationships today, it's an abundance of choice. Psychologist Barry Schwartz would call it an *excess* of choice—the tyranny of abundance. We see it as a measure of our autonomy and we firmly believe that freedom of choice will lead to fulfillment. Our antennae are always up for better opportunities, finds Schwartz, professor of psychology at Swarthmore College.

Just as only the best pair of jeans will do, so will only the best partner—whatever that is. "People walk starry-eyed looking not into the eyes of their romantic partner but over their romantic partner's shoulder, in case there might be somebody better walking by. This is not the road to successful long-term relationships." It does not stop with marriage. And it undermines commitment by encouraging people to keep their options open.

Like Doherty, Schwartz sees it as a consequence of a consumer society. He also sees it as a self-fulfilling phenomenon. "If you think there might be something better around the next corner, then there will be, because you're not fully committed to the relationship you've got."

It's naïve to expect relationships to feel good every minute. Every relationship has its bumps. How big a bump does it have to be before you do something about it? As Hopkins's Cherlin says, if you're constantly asking yourself whether you should leave, "there may be a day when the answer is yes. In any marriage there may be a day when the answer is yes."

One of the problems with unrestrained choice, explains Schwartz, is that it raises expectations to the breaking point. A sense of multiple alternatives, of unlimited possibility, breeds in us the illusion that perfection exists out there, somewhere, if

a partner who isn't overly expressive or who works too hard or doesn't initiate sex very often—then the communal ideal we bring to relationships is jettisoned and an individualistic mentality asserts itself. We revert to a stingier self that has been programmed into us by the consumer culture, which has only become increasingly pervasive, the current recession notwithstanding.

Psychologically, the goal of life becomes *my* happiness. "The minute your needs are not being met then you appropriate the individualistic norm," says Doherty. This accelerating only we could find it. This one's sense of humor, that one's looks, another one's charisma—we come to imagine that there will be a package in which all these desirable features coexist. We search for perfection because we believe we are entitled to the best—even if perfection is an illusion foisted on us by an abundance of possibilities.

If perfection is what you expect, you will always be disappointed, says Schwartz. We become picky and unhappy. The cruel joke our psychology plays on us, of course, is that we are terrible at knowing what will satisfy us or at knowing how any experience will make us feel.

A sense of multiple alternatives, of unlimited possibility, breeds in us the illusion that the perfect person is out there waiting to be found.

If the search through all possibilities weren't exhausting (and futile) enough, thinking about attractive features of the alternatives not chosen—what economists call opportunity costs—reduces the potential pleasure in whatever choice we finally do make. The more possibilities, the more opportunity costs—and the more we think about them, the more we come to regret any choice. "So, once again," says Schwartz, "a greater variety of choices actually makes us feel worse."

Ultimately, our excess of choice leads to lack of intimacy. "How is anyone going to stack up against this perfect person who's out there somewhere just waiting to be found?" asks Schwartz. "It creates doubt about this person, who seems like a good person, someone I might even be in love with—but who knows what's possible *out* there? Intimacy takes time to develop. You need to have some reason to put in the time. If you're full of doubt at the start, you're not going to put in the time."

Moreover, a focus on one's own preferences can come at the expense of those of others. As Schwartz said in his 2004 book, *The Paradox of Choice: Why More Is Less,* "most people find it extremely challenging to balance the conflicting impulses of freedom of choice on the one hand and loyalty and commitment on the other."

And yet, throughout, we are focused on the partner we want to have, not on the one we want—or need—to be. That may be the worst choice of all.

Disappointment—or Tragedy?

The heightened sensitivity to relationship problems that follows from constantly appraising our happiness encourages couples to turn disappointment into tragedy, Doherty contends.

Inevitably, images of the perfect relationship dancing in our heads collide with our sense of entitlement; "I'm entitled to the best possible marriage." The reality of disappointment becomes intolerable. "It's part of a cultural belief system that says we are entitled to everything we feel we need."

Through the alchemy of desire, wants become needs, and unfulfilled needs become personal tragedies. "A husband who isn't very expressive of his feelings can be a disappointment or a tragedy, depending on whether it's an entitlement," says Doherty. "And that's very much a cultural phenomenon." We take the everyday disappointments of relationships and treat them as intolerable, see them as demeaning—the equivalent of alcoholism, say, or abuse. "People work their way into 'I'm a tragic figure' around the ordinary problems of marriage." Such stories are so widespread, Doherty is no longer inclined to see them as reflecting an individual psychological problem, although that is how he was trained—and how he practiced for many years as an eminent family therapist. "I see it first now as a cultural phenomenon."

First Lady Michelle Obama is no stranger to the disappointment that pervades relationships today. In *Barack and Michelle: Portrait of an American Marriage,* by Christopher Anderson, she confides how she reached a "state of desperation" while working full-time, bringing in the majority of the family income, raising two daughters, and rarely seeing her husband, who was then spending most of his week away from their Chicago home as an Illinois state senator, a job she thought would lead nowhere while it paid little. "She's killing me with this constant criticism," Barack complained. "She just seems so bitter, so angry all the time." She was annoyed that he "seems to think he can just go out there and pursue his dream and leave all the heavy lifting to me."

But then she had an epiphany: She remembered the guy she fell in love with. "I figured out that I was pushing to make Barack be something I wanted him to be for me. I was depending on him to make me happy. Except it didn't have anything to do with him. I needed support. I didn't necessarily need it from Barack."

Certainly, commitment narrows choice. But it is the ability to remember you really do love someone—even though you may not be feeling it at the moment.

Commitment is the ability to sustain an investment, to honor values over momentary feelings. The irony, of course, is that while we want happiness, it isn't a moment-by-moment experience; the deepest, most enduring form of happiness is the result of sustained emotional investments in other people.

Architects of the Heart

One of the most noteworthy findings emerging from relationship research is that desire isn't just something we passively feel when everything's going right; it develops in direct response to what we do. Simply having fun together, for example, is crucial to keeping the sex drive alive.

But in the churn of daily life, we tend to give short shrift to creating positive experiences. Over time, we typically become more oriented to dampening threats and insecurities—to resolving conflict, to eliminating jealousy, to banishing problems. But the brain is wired with both a positive and negative motivational system, and satisfaction and desire demand keeping the brain's positive system well-stoked.

Even for long-term couples, spending time together in novel, interesting, or challenging activities—games, dancing, even conversation—enhances feelings of closeness, passionate love, and satisfaction with the relationship. Couples recapture the excitement of the early days of being in love. Such passion naturally feeds commitment.

From Michelle to Michelangelo

Important as it is to choose the right partner, it's probably more important to *be* the right partner. Most people are focused on changing the wrong person in the relationship; if anyone has to change in a relationship, it's you—although preferably with the help of your partner.

> **Important as it is to choose the right partner, it's probably more important to *be* the right partner. We focus on changing the wrong person.**

Ultimately, "marriage is an inside job," Pat Love told the 2009 Smart Marriages Conference. "It's internal to the person. You have to let it do its work." And its biggest job is helping individuals grow up. "Marriage is about getting over yourself. Happiness is not about focusing on yourself." Happiness is about holding onto your values, deciding who you are and being that person, using your particular talent, and investing in others.

Unfortunately, says Margin family therapist and *PT* blogger Susan Pease Gadoua, not enough people today are willing to do the hard work of becoming a more mature person. "They think they have a lot more choices. And they think life will be easier in another relationship. What they don't realize is that it will be the same relationship—just with a different name."

The question is not how you want your partner to change but what kind of partner and person you want to be. In the best relationships, not only are you thinking about who you want to be, but your partner is willing to help you get there. Psychologist Caryl E. Rusbult calls it the Michelangelo phenomenon. Just as Michelangelo felt the figures he created were already "in" the stones, "slumbering within the actual self is an ideal form," explains Eli Finkel, associate professor of psychology at Northwestern University and frequent Rusbult collaborator. Your partner becomes an ally in sculpting your ideal self, in bringing out the person you dream of becoming, leading you to a deep form of personal growth as well as long-term satisfaction with life and with the relationship.

It takes a partner who supports your dreams, the traits and qualities you want to develop—whether or not you've articulated them clearly or simply expressed vague yearnings. "People come to reflect what their partners see in them and elicit from them," Finkel and Rusbult report in *Current Directions in Psychological Science.*

Case Study
Patty and Rod

Patty Newbold had married "a really great guy," but by the time their 13th anniversary rolled around, she had a long list of things he needed to change to make the marriage work. At 34, she felt depressed, frantic—and guilty, as Rod was fighting a chronic disease. But she had reached a breaking point, "I read my husband my list of unmet needs and suggested a divorce," even though what she really wanted was her marriage back. "I wanted to feel loved again. But it didn't seem possible."

Newbold has had a long time to think about that list. Her husband died the next day, a freak side effect of his medications. "He was gone, but the list remained. Out of perhaps 30 needs, only one was eased by losing him. I was free now to move the drinking glasses next to the sink."

As she read through the list the morning after he died, she realized that "marriage isn't about my needs or his needs or about how well we communicate about our needs. It's about loving and being loved. *Life* is about meeting (or letting go of) my own *needs. Marriage* is about loving another person and receiving love in return. It suddenly became oh so clear that receiving love is something I make happen, not him." And then she was flooded with memories of all the times "I'd been offered love by this wonderful man and rejected it because I was too wrapped up in whatever need I was facing at the time."

Revitalized is "a funny word to describe a relationship in which one party is dead," she reports, "but ours was revitalized. I was completely changed, too." Everything she learned that awful day has gone into a second marriage, now well into its second decade.

Such affirmation promotes trust in the partner and strengthens commitment. And commitment, Rusbult has found, is a key predictor of relationship durability. "It creates positive bias towards each other," says Finkel. "It feels good to achieve our goals. It's deeply satisfying and meaningful." In addition, it immunizes the relationship against potential distractions—all those "perfect" others. Finkel explains, "It motivates the derogation of alternative partners." It creates the perception—the illusion—that even the most attractive alternative partners are unappealing. Attention to them gets turned off—one of the many cognitive gymnastics we engage in to ward off doubts.

Like growth, commitment is an inside job. It's not a simple vow. Partners see each other in ways that enhance their connection and fend off threats. It fosters the perception that the relationship you're in is better than that of others. It breeds the inclination to react constructively—by accommodation—rather than destructively when a partner does something inconsiderate. It even motivates that most difficult of tasks, forgiveness for the ultimate harm of betrayal, Rusbult has shown.

It is a willingness—stemming in part from an understanding that your well-being and your partner's are linked over the long term—to depart from direct self-interest, such as erecting a grudge when you feel hurt.

The Michelangelo phenomenon gives the lie to the soul mate search. You can't find the perfect person; there is no such thing. And even if you think you could, the person he or she is today is, hopefully, not quite the person he or she wants to be 10 years down the road. You and your partner help each other become a more perfect person—perfect, that is, according to your own inner ideals. You are both, with mutual help, constantly evolving.

Critical Thinking

1. Describe some of the influences that culture has on happiness within marriages.

2. In the case study of Stephen and Christina, what do you think were some of the causes of the friction in their relationship?

3. What are some ways that couples can keep their relationships from becoming strained?

4. List some of the expectations that you have or had in a relationship. Did you see any in the reading?

5. Do you think that there is a trend in today's society that marriage should be perfect? Why or why not?

Create Central

www.mhhe.com/createcentral

Internet References

Love Is Respect
www.loveisrespect.org
Relationships Australia
www.relationships.org.au

Article

Prepared by: Patricia Hrusa Williams,
University of Maine at Farmington

Waiting to Wed

MARK REGNERUS AND JEREMY UECKER

Learning Outcomes

After reading this article, you will be able to:

- Explain trends in coupling and the development of long-term committed relationships in young adults.

- Understand factors important to mate selection.

- Recognize the effects of commitment on sexual and emotional selves.

Some outside observers look at the relationship scene among young adults and consider that it is entirely about short-term hookups and that the majority of emerging adults are avoiding lasting and meaningful intimate relationships in favor of random sex. While sexual norms have certainly changed, there's no evidence to suggest that emerging adults are uninterested in relationships that last, including marriage. In fact, they want to marry. Lots of studies show that nearly all young women and men say they would like to get married someday. We're not talking half or even 80 percent, but more like 93 to 96 percent. Most just don't want to marry now or anytime soon. They feel no rush.

The slow but steady increase in average age at first marriage—to its present-day 26 for women and 28 for men—suggests that the purpose of dating or romantic relationships is changing or has changed. Most sexual relationships among emerging adults neither begin with marital intentions nor end in marriage or even cohabitation. They just begin and end.

Reasons for their termination are numerous, of course, but one overlooked possibility is that many of them don't know how to get or stay married to the kind of person they'd like to find. For not a few, their parents provided them with a glimpse into married life, and what they saw at the dinner table—if they dined with their parents much at all—didn't look very inviting. They hold the institution of marriage in high regard, and they put considerable pressure—probably too much—on what their own eventual marriage ought to look like. And yet it seems that there is little effort from any institutional source aimed at helping emerging adults consider how their present social, romantic and sexual experiences shape or war against their vision of marriage—or even how marriage might fit in with their other life goals.

In fact, talk of career goals seems increasingly divorced from the relational context in which many emerging adults may eventually find themselves. They speak of the MDs, JDs and PhDs they intend to acquire with far more confidence than they speak of committed relationships or marriage. The former seem attainable, the latter unclear or unreliable. To complicate matters, many educated emerging adults are concerned about possible relational constraints on their career goals.

Since emerging adults esteem the idea of marriage and yet set it apart as inappropriate for their age, waiting until marriage for a fulfilling sex life is considered not just quaint and outdated but quite possibly foolish. Sex outside relationships might still be disparaged by many, but not sex before marriage. And yet creating successful sexual relationships—ones that last a very long time or even into marriage—seems only a modest priority among many in this demographic group. Jeffrey Arnett, a developmental psychologist who focuses on emerging adulthood, notes the absence of relationship permanence as a value in the minds of emerging adults:

> Finding a love partner in your teens and continuing in a relationship with that person through your early twenties, culminating in marriage, is now viewed as unhealthy, a mistake, a path likely to lead to disaster. Those who do not experiment with different partners are warned that they will eventually wonder what they are missing, to the detriment of their marriage.

Arnett's right. The majority of young adults in America not only think they should explore different relationships, they believe it may be foolish and wrong not to.

Instead, they place value upon flexibility, autonomy, change and the potential for upgrading. Allison, an 18-year-old from Illinois, characterizes this value when she describes switching from an older, long-term boyfriend (and sexual partner) to a younger one: "I really liked having a steady boyfriend for a long time, but then it just got to the point where it was like, 'OK, I need something different.' It wasn't that I liked him any less or loved or cared about him any less, I just needed a change." Many emerging adults—especially men—conduct their relationships with a nagging sense that there may still be someone better out there.

Despite the emphasis on flexibility and freedom, most emerging adults wish to fall in love, commit and marry someday. And some already have (more about them shortly). The vast majority of those who haven't married believe themselves to be too young to "settle down." They are definitely not in a hurry. In a recent nationwide survey of young men, 62 percent of unmarried 25- to 29-year-olds (and 51 percent of 30- to 34-year-olds) said they were "not interested in getting married any time soon."

While their reticence could be for good reasons, their widespread use of this phrase suggests a tacitly antagonistic perspective about marriage. "Settling down" is something people do when it's time to stop having fun and get serious—when it's time to get married and have children, two ideas that occur together in the emerging-adult mind. In the same national survey of men we just noted, 81 percent of unmarried men age 25 to 29 agreed that "at this stage in your life, you want to have fun and freedom." (Even 74 percent of single 30- to 34-year-olds agreed.) That figure would have been even higher had men in their early twenties been interviewed.

Trevor, a 19-year-old virgin from North Carolina, agrees wholeheartedly with this sentiment. He would like to marry someday. When asked if there were certain things that people should accomplish before they're ready to marry, he lists the standard economic criteria. But he also conveys a clear understanding that his best days would be behind him: "I'd say before you're married, make sure you have a place to live. Don't have a child before marriage. . . . Have a decent paying job because, I mean, it's only going to get worse."

A distinctive fissure exists in the minds of young Americans between the carefree single life and the married life of economic pressures and family responsibilities. The one is sexy, the other is sexless. In the minds of many, sex is for the young and single, while marriage is for the old. Marriage is quaint, adorable.

Thus a key developmental task for Juan, a 19-year-old from Southern California, is to have his fill of sex before being content with a fixed diet. His advice would be to "get a lot of stuff out of your system, like messing around with girls and stuff, or partying."

Likewise, Megan, 22, from Texas, doesn't conceive of parenthood as a sexual life stage, the irony of it aside. She captures what very many young men and women believe to be a liability of marriage: the end of good sex. The last omnibus sex study of Americans—issued in 1994—disputes Megan's conclusion, but the power of surveys and statistics is nothing compared to the strength of a compelling story in the minds of many people.

We asked Megan whether married life would be less sexual than her single life:

Probably. [*Because?*] Just, as you age, your sex drive goes down. [*OK.*] I mean not because you want to be less sexual, that could be the case, but I won't know till I'm older. [*So some people say when you get married, you settle down, like it's literally a settling down. Do you look at marriage and married sex as being like, "That's off in the future; it might be a disappointment. Now I'm having a better time"?*] Yeah. [*Do you?*] Yes. [*Why?*] Why do I think it might be a disappointment? [*Sure.*] Um, just because of the horror stories of getting married. Nobody wants to have sex anymore. [*Where do you hear these stories?*] Movies, other people. . . . [*Like what? Can you think of one?*] Um, there's plenty. Like the movie that just came out—*License to Wed*—there's this one scene where the guy is sitting on top of a roof with his best friend talking about how his wife doesn't want to have sex anymore.

Although Megan enjoys sex for its own sake and predicts a declining sex life in her future marriage, it's not the presumed death of sex that frightens her about marriage: "It's living with a guy that freaks me out." Author Laura Sessions Stepp claims that today's young adults are so self-centered that they don't have time for "we," only for "me." They begrudge the energy that real relationships require. If that's true—and we suspect that's a journalistic overgeneralization—Megan should get together with Patrick. While so far he's slept with six women, Patrick informed us that he cannot imagine being married, and yet he too plans to do exactly that someday:

Well, I don't want to get married now. I guess, like, I do want to find a girl, but I just can't see myself being married. . . . [*And you can't see yourself getting married or being married because?*] I guess I just don't like the idea of being real tied down.

Patrick's current girlfriend is someone to hang out with, have sex with and generally enjoy the company of. Imagining more than that frightens him: "You sacrifice like so much stuff to be in a relationship that I guess I'm just not ready to make that huge sacrifice yet." Nor is 23-year-old Gabriela from Texas:

Once you get married, your responsibilities change. It's no longer, "Oh, I want to go to China next year. I have to save up money." No. Now you have to pay for the house—or you have a job and you can't just leave, because your husband can't get that day off. And things like that. It isn't just you, it becomes you and another person. [*So what do you think of that?*] I think that it's fine when I'm older. [*Which will be when?*] At least 30.

Devon, a 19-year-old from Washington, does most of his peers one better. Getting married—which he too eventually plans to do—is not just about "settling down" from the vibrant sex life of his late teen years. It signifies a death, albeit a scripted and necessary one. When asked what he wanted out of marriage, he said, "Just to have a good ending to my life, basically." Chen, a 20-year-old from Illinois, agrees: "I don't really plan on getting married for a while, or settling down for a while. I'd like to do all my living when I'm young. Like, save all the rest of life—falling in love and having a family—for later."

Such perspectives fly in the face of much empirical evidence about the satisfactions of marriage. That is, marriage tends to be good for emotional as well as sexual intimacy. Married people have access to more regular, long-term sex than do serially monogamous single adults. But that doesn't feel true to many emerging adults. Many perceive their parents as having modest or poor sex lives, and movie sex largely features singles.

Not every emerging adult pictures marriage as a necessary but noble death, of course. Elizabeth from New York likewise sees her twenties as about having fun. But her thirties (and marriage) would not be simply about settling down; they would be the time "when your life is really gonna kick into gear." We suspect that contemporary male and female perspectives on marriage, sexuality and fertility are indeed different, on average—that many men anticipate the institution as necessary and good for them, but with less enthusiasm for it than women express. For emerging-adult men, the single life is great and married life could be good. For women, the single life is good but married life is potentially better.

Ironically, after years of marriage, men tend to express slightly higher marital satisfaction than women. Moreover, marriage seems to be particularly important in civilizing men, turning their attention away from dangerous, antisocial or self-centered activities and toward the needs of a family. Married men drink less, fight less and are less likely to engage in criminal activity than their single peers. Married husbands and fathers are significantly more involved and affectionate with their wives and children than are men in cohabiting relationships (with or without children). The norms, status rewards and social support offered to men by marriage all combine to help them walk down the path of adult responsibility.

No wonder the idea of marriage can feel like a death to them. It is indeed the demise of unchecked self-centeredness and risk taking. Many men elect to delay it as long as seems feasible, marrying on average around age 28. That's hardly an old age, of course, but remember that age 28 is their median (or statistical middle) age at first marriage—meaning that half of all men marry then or later. Their decision to delay makes sense from a sexual economics perspective: they can access sex relatively easily outside of marriage, they can obtain many of the perceived benefits of marriage by cohabiting rather than marrying, they encounter few social pressures from peers to marry, they don't wish to marry someone who already has a child, and they want to experience the joys and freedoms of singleness as long as they can.

A good deal more is known about why people are not marrying in early adulthood than why some still do. And yet a minority marry young—and even more wish they were married-despite the fact that cohabitation and premarital sex are increasingly normative and socially acceptable. While the majority of emerging adults have no wish to be married at present, more than we expected actually harbor this desire. Just under 20 percent of unmarried young men and just under 30 percent of such women said they would like to be married now. Religious emerging adults are more apt to want to be married. And those emerging adults who are in a romantic or sexual relationship are nearly twice as likely to want to be married now than those who aren't in a relationship. Cohabiters are more than four times as likely to want to be married as those who are single. In fact, just under half of cohabiting young women and 40 percent of cohabiting young men said they'd like to be married right now.

Obviously, getting married introduces the risk of getting divorced. And that very specter remains a key mental barrier to relationship commitment among emerging adults. Six in ten unmarried men in their late twenties—who are already beginning to lag behind the median age at marriage—report that one of their biggest concerns about marriage is that it will end in divorce. Thus getting married young is increasingly frowned upon not just as unwise but as a moral mistake in which the odds of failure are perceived as too high to justify the risk.

This conventional wisdom is at work in journalist Paula Kamen's interview with a 24-year-old woman who claims she knows her boyfriend far better than her parents knew each other when they married. But would she marry him? No: "Like, are you stupid? Have you read the statistics lately?"

Emerging adults claim to be very stats-savvy about marriage. They are convinced that half of all marriages end in divorce, suggesting that the odds of anyone staying married amounts to a random flip of a coin. In reality, of course, divorce is hardly a random event. Some couples are more likely to divorce than others: people who didn't finish high school, people with little wealth or income, those who aren't religious, African Americans, couples who had children before they married, those who live in the South, those who cohabited before marrying and those who live in neighborhoods that have elevated crime and poverty rates. Lots of emerging adults have a few of these risk factors for divorce, but most don't have numerous factors.

And yet the compelling idea in the minds of many is that any given marriage's chance of success—however defined—is only 50–50, and worse if you marry early. In fact, most Americans who cite the statistics argument against considering marriage in early adulthood tend to misunderstand exactly what "early marriage" is. Most sociological evaluations of early marriage note that the link between age-at-marriage and divorce is strongest among those who marry as teenagers (in other words, before age 20). Marriages that begin at age 20, 21 or 22 are not nearly so likely to end in divorce as most Americans presume. Data from the 2002 National Study of Family Growth suggest that the probability of a marriage lasting at least ten years—hardly a long-term success, but a good benchmark of endurance—hinges not only on age-at-marriage but also on gender.

- Men and women who marry at or before age 20 are by far the worst bets for long-term success.
- The likelihood of a marriage (either a man's or a woman's) lasting ten years exceeds 60 percent beginning at age 21.
- Starting around age 23 (until at least 29), the likelihood of a woman's marriage lasting ten years improves by about 3 percent with each added year of waiting.
- However, no such linear "improvement" pattern appears among men.

The most significant leap in avoiding divorce occurs by simply waiting to marry until age 21. The difference in success between, say, marrying at 23 and marrying at 28 is just not as substantial as many emerging adults believe it to be. And among men, there are really no notable differences to speak of. While sociologist Tim Heaton finds that teenage marriage—and perhaps marriage among 20- and 21-year-olds—carries a higher risk of marital disruption, he too notes that "increasing the age at marriage from 22 to 30 would not have much effect on marital stability."

Still, to most of us, marital success is more than just managing to avoid a divorce. It's about having a good marriage. Sociologist Norval Glenn's study of marital success, in which "failure" is defined as either divorce or being in an unhappy marriage, reveals a curvilinear relationship between age at marriage and marital success. Women who marry before 20 or after 27 report lower marital success, while those marrying at ages 20–27 report higher levels of success. The pattern is a bit different for men. Men who marry before age 20 appear to have only a small chance at a successful marriage, while those who marry between ages 20 and 22 or after age 27 face less daunting but still acute challenges for a successful marriage. The best odds for men are in the middle, at ages 23–27. In a meta-analysis of five different surveys that explored marriage outcomes, researchers note that respondents who marry between ages 22 and 25 express greater marital satisfaction than do those who marry later.

In other words, the conventional wisdom about the obvious benefits to marital happiness of delayed marriage overreaches. Why it is that people who wait into their late twenties and thirties may experience less marital success rather than more is not entirely clear—and the finding itself is subject to debate. But it may be a byproduct of their greater rates of cohabitation. While relationship quality typically declines a bit over the course of marriage, the same process is believed to occur during cohabitation. If so, for many couples who marry at older ages, the "honeymoon" period of their relationship may have ended before they married, not after.

All these findings, however, are largely lost on emerging adults because of the compelling power of the popular notion in America that marriages carry a 50 percent risk of divorce. Consequently, marriage is considered off-limits to many emerging adults, especially those in the middle of college or building a career. Thus while research suggests that adults who are married and in monogamous relationships report more overall happiness and both more physical and more emotional satisfaction with sex, emerging adults don't believe it. Such claims just don't feel true. And why should they? When was the last time you watched a romantic film about a happily married 40-year-old couple?

Critical Thinking

1. What factors are important in mate selection? How have these factors changed over time?

2. Why do you think young adults are waiting to wed?

3. How do you think "settling down" affects your sex life?

4. What emotional sacrifices that come with commitment seem the most difficult to adjust to?

Create Central

www.mhhe.com/createcentral

Internet References

Love Is Respect
www.loveisrespect.org

Relationships Australia
www.relationships.org.au

MARK REGNERUS teaches at the University of Texas at Austin. **JEREMY UECKER** is a postdoctoral fellow at the Carolina Population Center at the University of North Carolina in Chapel Hill. This article is adapted from their book *Premarital Sex in America: How Young Americans Meet, Mate, and Think about Marrying,* just published by Oxford University Press. © Oxford University Press.

Prepared by: Patricia Hrusa Williams,
University of Maine at Farmington

Article

The End of Courtship?

Alex Williams

Learning Outcomes

After reading this article, you will be able to:

- Identify how dating has changed due to generational, technological, societal, and economic factors.

- Understand the term "hookup culture."

- Explore the purpose and role of dating in relationship formation.

Maybe it was because they had met on OkCupid. But when the dark-eyed musician with artfully disheveled hair asked Shani Silver, a social media and blog manager in Philadelphia, out on a "date" Friday night, she was expecting at least a drink, one on one.

"At 10 p.m., I hadn't heard from him," said Ms. Silver, 30, who wore her favorite skinny black jeans. Finally, at 10:30, he sent a text message. "Hey, I'm at Pub & Kitchen, want to meet up for a drink or whatever?" he wrote, before adding, "I'm here with a bunch of friends from college."

Turned off, she fired back a text message, politely declining. But in retrospect, she might have adjusted her expectations. "The word 'date' should almost be stricken from the dictionary," Ms. Silver said. "Dating culture has evolved to a cycle of text messages, each one requiring the code-breaking skills of a cold war spy to interpret."

"It's one step below a date, and one step above a high-five," she added. Dinner at a romantic new bistro? Forget it. Women in their 20s these days are lucky to get a last-minute text to tag along. Raised in the age of so-called "hookup culture," millennials—who are reaching an age where they are starting to think about settling down—are subverting the rules of courtship.

Instead of dinner-and-a-movie, which seems as obsolete as a rotary phone, they rendezvous over phone texts, Facebook posts, instant messages and other "non-dates" that are leaving a generation confused about how to land a boyfriend or girlfriend.

"The new date is 'hanging out,'" said Denise Hewett, 24, an associate television producer in Manhattan, who is currently developing a show about this frustrating new romantic landscape. As one male friend recently told her: "I don't like to take girls out. I like to have them join in on what I'm doing—going to an event, a concert."

For evidence, look no further than "Girls," HBO's cultural weather vane for urban 20-somethings, where none of the main characters paired off in a manner that might count as courtship even a decade ago. In Sunday's opener for Season 2, Hannah (Lena Dunham) and Adam (Adam Driver), who last season forged a relationship by texting each other nude photos, are shown lying in bed, debating whether being each other's "main hang" constitutes actual dating.

The actors in the show seem to fare no better in real life, judging by a monologue by Zosia Mamet (who plays Shoshanna, the show's token virgin, since deflowered) at a benefit last fall at Joe's Pub in the East Village. Bemoaning an anything-goes dating culture, Ms. Mamet, 24, recalled an encounter with a boyfriend whose idea of a date was lounging in a hotel room while he "Lewis and Clarked" her body, then tried to stick her father, the playwright David Mamet, with the bill, according to a Huffington Post report.

Blame the much-documented rise of the "hookup culture" among young people, characterized by spontaneous, commitment-free (and often, alcohol-fueled) romantic flings. Many students today have never been on a traditional date, said Donna Freitas, who has taught religion and gender studies at Boston University and Hofstra and is the author of the forthcoming book, *The End of Sex: How Hookup Culture is Leaving a Generation Unhappy, Sexually Unfulfilled, and Confused About Intimacy.*

Hookups may be fine for college students, but what about after, when they start to build an adult life? The problem is that "young people today don't know how to get out of hookup culture," Ms. Freitas said. In interviews with students, many graduating seniors did not know the first thing about the basic mechanics of a traditional date. "They're wondering, 'If you like someone, how would you walk up to them? What would you say? What words would you use?'" Ms. Freitas said.

That may explain why "dates" among 20-somethings resemble college hookups, only without the dorms. Lindsay, a 25-year-old online marketing manager in Manhattan, recalled a recent non-date that had all the elegance of a keg stand (her last name is not used here to avoid professional embarrassment).

After an evening when she exchanged flirtatious glances with a bouncer at a Williamsburg nightclub, the bouncer invited her and her friends back to his apartment for whiskey and boxed macaroni and cheese. When she agreed, he gamely hoisted her over his shoulders, and, she recalled, "carried me home, my girlfriends and his bros in tow, where we danced around a tiny apartment to some MGMT and Ratatat remixes."

She spent the night at the apartment, which kicked off a cycle of weekly hookups, invariably preceded by a Thursday night text message from him saying, "hey babe, what are you up to this weekend?" (It petered out after four months.)

Relationship experts point to technology as another factor in the upending of dating culture.

Traditional courtship—picking up the telephone and asking someone on a date—required courage, strategic planning and a considerable investment of ego (by telephone, rejection stings). Not so with texting, e-mail, Twitter or other forms of "asynchronous communication," as techies call it. In the context of dating, it removes much of the need for charm; it's more like dropping a line in the water and hoping for a nibble.

"I've seen men put more effort into finding a movie to watch on Netflix Instant than composing a coherent message to ask a woman out," said Anna Goldfarb, 34, an author and blogger in Moorestown, N.J. A typical, annoying query is the last-minute: "Is anything fun going on tonight?" More annoying still are the men who simply ping, "Hey" or " 'sup."

"What does he think I'm doing?" she said. "I'm going to my friend's house to drink cheap white wine and watch episodes of 'Dance Moms' on demand."

Online dating services, which have gained mainstream acceptance, reinforce the hyper-casual approach by greatly expanding the number of potential dates. Faced with a never-ending stream of singles to choose from, many feel a sense of "FOMO" (fear of missing out), so they opt for a speed-dating approach—cycle through lots of suitors quickly.

That also means that suitors need to keep dates cheap and casual. A fancy dinner? You're lucky to get a drink.

"It's like online job applications, you can target many people simultaneously—it's like darts on a dart board, eventually one will stick," said Joshua Sky, 26, a branding coordinator in Manhattan, describing the attitudes of many singles in their 20s. The mass-mailer approach necessitates "cost-cutting, going to bars, meeting for coffee the first time," he added, "because you only want to invest in a mate you're going to get more out of."

If online dating sites have accelerated that trend, they are also taking advantage of it. New services like Grouper aren't so much about matchmaking as they are about group dates, bringing together two sets of friends for informal drinks.

The Gaggle, a dating commentary and advice site, helps young women navigate what its founders call the "post-dating" landscape, by championing "non-dates," including the "group non-date" and the "networking non-date." The site's founders, Jessica Massa and Rebecca Wiegand, say that in a world where "courtship" is quickly being redefined, women must recognize a flirtatious exchange of tweets, or a lingering glance at a company softball game, as legitimate opportunities for romance, too.

"Once women begin recognizing these more ambiguous settings as opportunities for romantic possibility," Ms. Massa said, "they really start seeing their love lives as much more intriguing and vibrant than they did when they were only judging themselves by how many 'dates' they had lined up."

There's another reason Web-enabled singles are rendering traditional dates obsolete. If the purpose of the first date was to learn about someone's background, education, politics and cultural tastes, Google and Facebook have taken care of that.

"We're all Ph.D.'s in Internet stalking these days," said Andrea Lavinthal, an author of the 2005 book *The Hookup Handbook*. "Online research makes the first date feel unnecessary, because it creates a false sense of intimacy. You think you know all the important stuff, when in reality, all you know is that they watch 'Homeland.' "

Dodgy economic prospects facing millennials also help torpedo the old, formal dating rituals. Faced with a lingering recession, a stagnant job market, and mountains of student debt, many young people—particularly victims of the "mancession"—simply cannot afford to invest a fancy dinner or show in someone they may or may not click with.

Further complicating matters is the changing economic power dynamic between the genders, as reflected by a number of studies in recent years, said Hanna Rosin, author of the recent book *The End of Men*.

A much-publicized study by Reach Advisors, a Boston-based market research group, found that the median income for young, single, childless women is higher than it is for men in many of the country's biggest cities (though men still dominate the highest-income jobs, according to James Chung, the company's president). This may be one reason it is not uncommon to walk into the hottest new West Village bistro on a Saturday night and find five smartly dressed young women dining together—the nearest man the waiter. Income equality, or superiority, for women muddles the old, male-dominated dating structure.

"Maybe there's still a sense of a man taking care of a woman, but our ideology is aligning with the reality of our finances," Ms. Rosin said. As a man, you might "convince yourself that dating is passé, a relic of a paternalistic era, because you can't afford to take a woman to a restaurant."

Many young men these days have no experience in formal dating and feel the need to be faintly ironic about the process— "to 'date' in quotation marks"—because they are "worried that they might offend women by dating in an old-fashioned way," Ms. Rosin said.

"It's hard to read a woman exactly right these days," she added. "You don't know whether, say, choosing the wine without asking her opinion will meet her yearnings for old-fashioned romance or strike her as boorish and macho."

Indeed, being too formal too early can send a message that a man is ready to get serious, which few men in their 20s are ready to do, said Lex Edness, a television writer in Los Angeles.

"A lot of men in their 20s are reluctant to take the girl to the French restaurant, or buy them jewelry, because those steps tend to lead to 'eventually, we're going to get married,'" Mr. Edness, 27, said. In a tight economy, where everyone is grinding away to build a career, most men cannot fathom supporting a family until at least 30 or 35, he said.

"So it's a lot easier to meet people on an even playing field, in casual dating," he said. "The stakes are lower."

Even in an era of ingrained ambivalence about gender roles, however, some women keep the old dating traditions alive by refusing to accept anything less.

Cheryl Yeoh, a tech entrepreneur in San Francisco, said that she has been on many formal dates of late—plays, fancy restaurants. One suitor even presented her with red roses. For her, the old traditions are alive simply because she refuses to put up with anything less. She generally refuses to go on any date that is not set up a week in advance, involving a degree of forethought.

"If he really wants you," Ms. Yeoh, 29, said, "he has to put in some effort."

Critical Thinking

1. Is courtship dead as the article suggests? Why or why not?
2. What is the purpose of dating?
3. How should the term "date" be defined?
4. What are the advantages and disadvantages of the post-dating or non-date culture? Does this culture promote or undermine the development of committed relationships?

Create Central

www.mhhe.com/createcentral

Internet References

Love Is Respect
   www.loveisrespect.org
Relationships Australia
   www.relationships.org.au

Prepared by: Patricia Hrusa Williams,
University of Maine at Farmington

Article

You Got Your Sperm Where?

TONY DOKOUPIL

Learning Outcomes

After reading this article, you will be able to:

- Define reproductive terms including natural insemination and artificial insemination.

- Understand the reasons sperm donors offer sperm to individuals and couples trying to conceive.

- Recognize some of the ethical, political, social, medical, and family dilemmas created by reproductive technology and sperm donation.

For months, Beth Gardner and her wife, Nicole, had been looking for someone to help them conceive. They began with sperm banks, which have donors of almost every background, searchable by religion, ancestry, even the celebrity they most resemble. But the couple balked at the prices—at least $2,000 for the sperm alone—and the fact that most donors were anonymous; they wanted their child to have the option to one day know his or her father. So in the summer of 2010, at home with their two dogs and three cats, Beth and Nicole typed these words into a search engine: "free sperm donor."

A few clicks later, the couple slid into an online underground, a mishmash of personal ads, open forums, and members-only websites for women seeking sperm—and men giving it away. Most donors pledge to verify their health and relinquish parental rights, much like regular sperm-bank donors. But unlike their mainstream counterparts, these men don't get paid. They're also willing to reveal their identities and allow any future offspring to contact them. Many of the men say they do it out of altruism, but some also talk unabashedly of kinky sex and spreading their gene pool.

Curious, Beth and Nicole posted to a Yahoo Group, and within days they had more than a dozen suitors. "We got some weirdos," says Beth, a 35-year-old tech professional near San Diego. But most of the donors were "very nice and obviously well educated." After careful vetting—consisting of a home-made questionnaire, interviews, reference checks, and STD tests—the couple settled on a 30-something professional and arranged the donation.

Like most women in search of free sperm, Beth and Nicole asked for artificial insemination, or AI. As opposed to natural insemination (code for actual sex), AI typically involves injecting fresh sperm into the vagina, or loading it into a latex cup that fits on the cervix. Beth and Nicole had to work around three people's schedules and an ovulation calendar, so the venues at which they met their donor had a saucy impromptu feel: a hotel, the back of the couple's SUV, a camper trailer, a Starbucks bathroom. At Starbucks, the donor ejaculated in the bathroom in private, exited, and handed the sperm-filled latex cup to Nicole, who in turn entered the bathroom and attached the cup to her cervix. As nature took its course, the three sat down for coffee together. "It wasn't my highest moment," says Beth. They didn't conceive.

The couple is trying again with a new donor—and Beth has become a fervent believer in the strategy. In January, she launched the Free Sperm Donor Registry (FSDR), a sleek, user-friendly portal that works kind of like a dating site, only the women are listed as "recipients" and men as "donors." The homepage quotes Ralph Waldo Emerson: "The only gift is a portion of thyself." Six months in, FSDR has more than 2,000 members, including about 400 donors, and claims a dozen pregnancies. The first live birth is expected this fall.

Reproductive medicine is as close to miracle work as humans can muster: it has supplemented the stork with the syringe, creating thousands of new lives annually where none seemed possible. But in lifting the fog around infertility, doctors have moved nature's most intimate act deeper into the lab, and created a population of prospective parents—straight, gay, single, and married—who crave a more human connection. That need is now being met by sites like FSDR, which joins a global boom in the exchange of free, fresh sperm between strangers.

At least six Yahoo Groups, three Google sites, and about a dozen fee-based websites are dedicated to the cause. Most of them are in the United Kingdom, Canada, and Australia, where sperm banks have seen donations drop in the wake of recent laws that limit fees and, in some cases, forbid anonymity. The donor pool is still large in the U.S., where college kids can make as much as $12,000 a year from sperm banks for anonymous twice-weekly donations.

But sperm banks, though regulated by the Food and Drug Administration, carry risk. In recent years sperm with a host of serious diseases and disorders has been sold to hundreds of women, according to medical journals and other published reports. Earlier this year ABC News identified at least 24 donor-children whose father had a rare aorta defect that could potentially kill his offspring at any minute. And in September, *The New York Times* reported on sperm banks' creating 100-kid clusters around a single donor, raising questions about not only disease, but accidental incest.

Cost is also a concern. In many states, insurance won't cover donor insemination unless a woman can show that she hasn't been able to get pregnant. This makes it hard for lesbian couples and single women who don't have male partners. And all couples face insurance caps that can mean thousands of dollars in out-of-pocket pay.

Many women also believe their donor-conceived children have a right to know their fathers, something most sperm banks have resisted, fearing such openness would scare off potential donors. Even banks that do reveal dads' identities will do so only when a child turns 18.

As the first generation of donor-kids come of age, a growing number are expressing frustration at this closed-door policy. Confessions of a Cryokid and Anonymous Us are among the websites where they come to vent, airing unhappiness at feeling "half-adopted" and aching at the thought that their fathers could be anyone. "The system is severely broken," says Wendy Kramer, founder of the Donor Sibling Registry, a website that unites kids who have the same donor-fathers.

Of course, the market for free sperm raises its own set of questions. What if a donor sues for custody? What if he lies about an STD? Is he a potential threat to public health? What if his real motive is sex—and would that even matter? Just who are these guys anyway?

To find out, I registered at FSDR as a "just looking" member and spent two months following forum discussions, participating in chats, surfing through profiles, and interviewing more than a dozen donors and recipients. I also contacted donors who have set up personal websites or advertised on other sites. What I found was a universe that's often more lascivious than a Nicholson Baker novel, but somehow less bizarre and more relatable. Far from being overrun by sex-crazed "sperminators" and "desperate girls," the way British tabloids have portrayed the business, most of what I found was mundanely human.

Many of the women want to reproduce on their own terms, while they still can. Some have had miscarriages; others are widowed; still others, divorced. Some say they got pregnant when they were much younger and gave up the baby or aborted it, and now want another chance. Others have been busy with careers. Hope, a single 43-year-old zoologist, echoes most FSDR searchers when she says, "I really want to have a child, and I want to give that child the best shot at having a good life, which is why I chose this route."

As with traditional sperm banks, most of FSDR's users are lesbian couples or would-be single mothers. But the site does have an active cohort of straight pairs and married women, like a 37-year-old homemaker near Columbus, Ohio, who gave her name as Wendy. She says on a forum post that her husband—whose sperm count was diminished by a childhood case of the mumps—interviewed prospective donors with her. His

one condition: AI only. "It seems more 'our' baby if sex is not involved," she recalls him saying. Their son is due in January.

Donors on FSDR are a bawdier mix of high intentions and caveman dreams. One donor, whom Carissa, a 38-year-old divorcée in Fargo, N.D., was about to invite over for a "natural insemination" session, spooked her. "He wanted me to yell, 'Make me pregnant!'" during sex, she says.

It's a telling detail. Many donors say they are motivated not by sex so much as a desire to spawn as many children as possible. "I actually have little interest in even a stone-cold fox if she isn't going to get pregnant," says Ray, a 38-year-old who declined to give his real name. Ray, who already had two kids with his wife and claims to have two more via one-night stands, started donating sperm in 2009. He prefers to donate the natural way, which he says has a higher chance of success than AI (it doesn't), and he boasts of six births and six current pregnancies in attempts with about 40 different women. "I guess in some ways, helping lesbians, I am like an astronaut of inner space," he says, "going where no man has gone before."

One of the men who responded to Beth and Nicole, a married 29-year-old, said his IQ was in the 99.8th percentile ("note: results available") and said he would like to "propagate my genes, and help support the society of tomorrow by combating dysgenic reproductive trends." Translation: make babies as smart as he is. Down a few pegs on the pomposity scale, there's "Mongol," a 31-year-old Canadian who donates AI-style on both sides of the border. He arrives prepared, with a porn-loaded BlackBerry, headphones (to preserve the tranquility of the moment), Hitachi-brand penis massager, and likes "the whole idea of having people out there related to you."

It's a motivation that flummoxes some sex researchers. Rene Almeling, a sociologist at Yale University and the author of a new study of the fertility market, *Sex Cells*, says that among the 20 sperm-bank donors she interviewed, the most common motives were money, spreading "amazing genes," as one guy put it, and helping women conceive. University of Nevada, Las Vegas, anthropologist Peter Gray, coauthor of *Fatherhood*, about the evolution of paternal behavior, says this drive to propagate reminds him of the ancient khan men of Mongolia—and of Moulay Ismail, the 17th-century emperor of Morocco—men who fathered as many as a thousand children, parenting none of them. "I'll have to think about this a bit," he says.

As the market for free sperm grows, regulators are keeping a watchful eye. Last December, Canada's public-health department issued an "information update," noting the rise of free-sperm websites and warning that "the distribution of fresh semen [for assisted conception] is prohibited." In the U.S., the FDA recently targeted at least one donor, citing his failure to comply with a 2005 law that requires donors to undergo STD and communicable-disease tests, reviewed by doctors, within seven days of every donation. (Commercial sperm banks use frozen sperm and test donors at the beginning and end of a six-month quarantine.) The case has emerged as a legal challenge for the alternative world, potentially slowing the market, since such tests can run up to $10,000, making donations cost-prohibitive.

It began in December 2006, when Trent Arsenault, now 36 and a bachelor outside San Francisco, began offering his sperm through Trentdonor.org, a website bedecked with shots of Arsenault as a cute toddler and hunky outdoorsman. Tall and blond, Arsenault works as an engineer at a tech company and is a former Naval Academy midshipman (he dropped out to move to Silicon Valley). His qualifications might make a sperm bank drool. But he prefers to work independently, he says, having already donated to about 50 women, mostly Bay Area lesbians. Perhaps thanks in part to his twice-daily "fertility smoothies" (a blend of blueberries, almonds, and other vitamin-rich fare), he has sired at least 10 children, he says.

His prospects came to a halt in September 2010, when FDA agents knocked on the door of his 700-square-foot bachelor pad. They interviewed him in his bedroom, and collected medical records and other material related to how he "recovers and distributes semen," according to the FDA investigation. The tone was cordial, Arsenault recalls. He even wrote a thank-you letter to the agency, complimenting "the professional and courteous attitude" of its agents.

But the following month, there came another knock on the door, this time from local police delivering an FDA order to "cease manufacture" of sperm, the first such order leveled against an individual citizen, according to a search of government records. Per the order, the agency considers Arsenault to be essentially a one-man sperm bank, referring to him as a "firm," and alleging that he "does not provide adequate protections against communicable diseases." If he engages in the "recovery, processing, storage, labeling, packaging, or distribution" of sperm, he faces a $100,000 fine and a year in prison. "I saved the FDA letter" Arsenault says. "It may be worth something someday on eBay."

In some ways, Arsenault is like other guys who are giving away their sperm, "fulfilling a needed role as women realize that anonymous biological fathers often deprive their offspring [of] a needed identity," as he put it in a letter to the FDA.

But he also finds the work gratifying in its own right. His only sexual activity, he says, involves masturbating into a cup and handing off the cup. "I describe myself as donorsexual," he says, "so my sexual activity is limited to donation." He jokes that in a few years he'll be "the 40-year-old virgin with 15 kids." He's appealed the FDA ruling on the grounds that free sperm donation is a form of sex, and thus not subject to government interference. The case is under internal agency review as officials decide whether Arsenault is trying to "skirt the law," as the FDA's lawyers have argued in documents sent to Arsenault, or if free sperm donation should be protected as a private sexual matter. The FDA declined to comment on the case.

Any attempt to limit private sperm donation is "preposterous," says Beth Gardner, the FSDR founder. "If it's legal to go to a bar, get drunk, and sleep with a random stranger, then it can't possibly be illegal to provide clean, healthy sperm in a cup." Still, she's the first to admit that not all donors are professional, and not all recipients make the most informed choices. She hopes FSDR will help change that, which is why it prohibits nudity, dirty talk, cruising for casual sex, and any behavior that other members deem harassing or inappropriate. There are also testimonials, how-to articles, cost comparisons, and legal materials.

Now Gardner says she has plans for expansion, adding an egg-donor section and recruiting bloggers. She may change the name to the Known Donor Registry because it's more "expansive." "The site is at the point now where I need to take it to the next level," she says. In August, page views topped more than 2 million—and, like its users, Gardner only hopes they'll multiply.

As for Arsenault, while he waits to hear about his reproductive future, he is enjoying the fruits of his past, posting pictures of his babies, and keeping up an active relationship with the five or six families who have requested one so far. Last month he visited with Keri and Amber Pigott-Robertson, a 30-something lesbian couple in Modesto, Calif., who found Arsenault through a Google search in 2009 and now have a 1-year-old daughter via his donation.

"When he saw her for the first time, his face just lit up," says Amber, who made peach pie for the occasion. "He was a perfect match. He gave us what we had been longing for, what we felt would complete us. So there's no expressing how much gratitude I have for him. People like Trent come once in a lifetime."

Critical Thinking

1. Describe the difference between natural and artificial insemination.

2. What are some reasons that a man may have for donating his sperm for free?

3. Describe some challenges or ethical dilemmas that may be created when individuals and couples become pregnant via serial sperm donors.

4. Should men be able to offer their sperm for free to those hoping to conceive? Why or why not?

Create Central

www.mhhe.com/createcentral

Internet References

The March of Dimes
   www.marchofdimes.com

Society for Assisted Reproductive Technology
   www.sart.org

Adelaide Center for Bioethics and Culture
   www.bioethics.org.au

Article   Prepared by: Patricia Hrusa Williams, *University of Maine at Farmington*

Not Wanting Kids Is Entirely Normal

Why the ingrained expectation that women should desire to become parents is unhealthy.

JESSICA VALENTI

Learning Outcomes

After reading this article, you will be able to:

- Describe what "safe haven" laws are.

- Explain the challenges of motherhood.

- Recognize the negative effects of unintended pregnancies on families and children.

In 2008, Nebraska decriminalized child abandonment. The move was part of a "safe haven" law designed to address increased rates of infanticide in the state. Like other safe haven laws, parents in Nebraska who felt unprepared to care for their babies could drop them off at a designated location without fear of arrest and prosecution. But legislators made a major logistical error: They failed to implement an age limitation for dropped-off children.

Within just weeks of the law passing, parents started dropping off their kids. But here's the rub: None of them were infants. A couple of months in, 36 children had been left in state hospitals and police stations. Twenty-two of the children were over 13 years old. A 51-year-old grandmother dropped off a 12-year-old boy. One father dropped off his entire family—nine children from ages one to 17. Others drove from neighboring states to drop off their children once they heard that they could abandon them without repercussion.

The Nebraska state government, realizing the tremendous mistake it had made, held a special session of the legislature to rewrite the law in order to add an age limitation. Governor Dave Heineman said the change would "put the focus back on the original intent of these laws, which is saving newborn babies and exempting a parent from prosecution for child abandonment. It should also prevent those outside the state from bringing their children to Nebraska in an attempt to secure services."

On November 21, 2008, the last day that the safe haven law was in effect for children of all ages, a mother from Yolo County, California, drove over 1,200 miles to the Kimball County Hospital in Nebraska where she left her 14-year-old son.

What happened in Nebraska raises the question: If there were no consequences, how many of us would give up our kids? After all, child abandonment is nothing new and it's certainly not rare in the United States. Over 400,000 children are in the foster care system waiting to be placed in homes, thousands of parents relinquish their children every year. One woman even sent her adopted child back to his home country with an apology letter pinned like a grocery list to his chest. Whether it's because of hardship or not, many Americans are giving up on parenthood.

In February 2009, someone calling herself Ann logged onto the website Secret Confessions and wrote three sentences: "I am depressed. I hate being a mom. I also hate being a stay at home mom too!" Over three years later, the thread of comments is still going strong with thousands of responses—the site usually garners only 10 or so comments for every "confession." Our anonymous Ann had hit a nerve.

One woman who got pregnant at 42 wrote, "I hate being a mother too. Every day is the same. And to think I won't be free of it until I am like 60 and then my life will be over." Another, identifying herself only as k'smom, said, "I feel so trapped, anxious, and overwhelmed. I love my daughter and she's well taken care of but this is not the path I would have taken given a second chance."

Gianna wrote, "I love my son, but I hate being a mother. It has been a thankless, monotonous, exhausting, irritating and oppressive job. Motherhood feels like a prison sentence. I can't wait until I am paroled when my son turns 18 and hopefully goes far away to college." One D.C.-based mom even said that although she was against abortion before having her son, now she would "run to the abortion clinic" if she got pregnant again.

The responses—largely from women who identify themselves as financially stable—spell out something less explicit than well-worn reasons for parental unhappiness such as poverty and a lack of support. These women simply don't feel that motherhood is all it's cracked up to be, and if given a second chance, they wouldn't do it again.

Some cited the boredom of stay-at-home momism. Many complained of partners who didn't shoulder their share of child care responsibilities. "Like most men, my husband doesn't do much—if anything—for baby care. I have to do and plan for everything," one mother wrote. A few got pregnant accidentally and were pressured by their husbands and boyfriends to carry through with the pregnancy, or knew they never wanted children but felt it was something they "should" do.

The overwhelming sentiment, however, was the feeling of a loss of self, the terrifying reality that their lives had been subsumed into the needs of their child. DS wrote, "I feel like I have completely lost any thing that was me. I never imagined having children and putting myself aside would make me feel this bad." The expectation of total motherhood is bad enough, having to live it out every day is soul crushing. Everything that made us an individual, that made us unique, no longer matters. It's our role as a mother that defines us. Not much has changed.

"The feminine mystique permits, even encourages, women to ignore the question of their identity," wrote Betty Friedan. "The mystique says they can answer the question 'Who am I?' by saying 'Tom's wife . . . Mary's mother.' The truth is—and how long it's been true, I'm not sure, but it was true in my generation and it's true of girls growing up today—an American woman no longer has a private image to tell her who she is, or can be, or wants to be."

At the time she published *The Feminine Mystique,* Friedan argued that the public image of women was largely one of domesticity—"washing machines, cake mixes . . . detergents," all sold through commercials and magazines. Today, American women have more public images of themselves than that of a housewife. We see ourselves depicted in television, ads, movies, and magazines (not to mention relief!) as politicians, business owners, intellectuals, soldiers, and more. But that's what makes the public images of total motherhood so insidious. We see these diverse images of ourselves and believe that the oppressive standard Friedan wrote about is dead, when in fact it has simply shifted. Because no matter how many different kinds of public images women see of themselves, they're still limited. They're still largely white, straight upper-middle-class depictions, and they all still identify women as mothers or non-mothers.

American culture can't accept the reality of a woman who does not want to be a mother. It goes against everything we've been taught to think about women and how desperately they want babies. If we're to believe the media and pop culture, women—even teen girls—are forever desperate for a baby. It's our greatest desire.

The truth is, most women spend the majority of their lives trying *not* to get pregnant. According to the Guttmacher Institute, by the time a woman with two children is in her mid-40s she will have spent only five years trying to become pregnant, being pregnant, and not being at risk for getting pregnant following a birth. But to avoid getting pregnant before or after those two births, she would have had to refrain from sex or use contraception for an average of 25 years. Almost all American women (99 percent), ages 15–44, who have had sexual intercourse use some form of birth control. The second most popular form of birth control after the Pill? Sterilization. And now, more than ever, women are increasingly choosing forms of contraception that are for long-term use. Since 2005, for example, IUD use has increased by a whopping 161 percent. That's a long part of life and a lot of effort to avoid parenthood!

Now, it may be that these statistics simply indicate that modern women are just exerting more control over when and under what circumstances they become mothers. To a large degree that's true. But it doesn't jibe with an even more shocking reality: that half of pregnancies in the United States are unintended. Once you factor in the abortion rate and pregnancies that end in miscarriage, we're left with the rather surprising fact that one-third of babies born in the United States were unplanned. Not so surprising, however, is that the intention to have children definitively impacts how parents feel about their children, and how those children are treated—sometimes with terrifying results.

Jennifer Barber, a population researcher at the University of Michigan, studied more than 3,000 mothers and their close to 6,000 children from a range of socioeconomic backgrounds. Barber and her colleagues asked women who had recently given birth, "Just before you became pregnant, did you want to become pregnant when you did?" Those who answered yes were categorized as "intended"; those who answered no were then asked, "Did you want a baby but not at that time, or did you want none at all?" Depending on their answer, they were classified as "mistimed" or "unwanted." Over 60 percent of the children studied were reported as planned, almost 30 percent were unplanned ("mistimed"), and 10 percent were unequivocally "unwanted."

The results of Barber's research showed that the children who were unintended—both those who were mistimed and those who were unwanted—got fewer parental resources than those children who were intended. Basically, children who were unplanned didn't get as much emotional and cognitive support as children who were planned—as reported both by the researchers and the mothers themselves. Barber's research looked at things like the number of children's books in the home, and how often a parent read to a child or taught them skills like counting or the alphabet for the "cognitive" aspect. For the "emotional" support rating, they developed a scale measuring the "warmth" and "responsiveness" of the mother, how much time the family spent together, and how much time the father spent with the child. Across the board, children who were wanted got more from their parents than children who weren't. Children who were unplanned were also subject to harsher parenting and more punitive measures than a sibling who was intended.

Barber pointed out that this kind of pattern could be due to parental stress and a lack of patience that's "directed explicitly toward an unwanted child," and that a mistimed or unwanted birth could raise stress levels in the parents' interactions with their other children as well. She also says that in addition to benign emotional neglect, parenting unintended children is also associated with infant health problems and mortality, maternal depression, and sometimes child abuse.

[. . .]

When Torry Hansen of Shelbyville, Tennessee, sent her seven-year-old adopted son by himself on a plane back to his home country of Russia with nothing more than a note explaining she didn't want to parent him, she became one of the most reviled women in America. Russian officials were so incensed that they temporarily halted all adoption to the United States. We sometimes expect fathers to shirk their responsibility; but when mothers do it, it shakes the core of what we've been taught to believe about women and maternal instinct.

Anthropologist Sarah Blaffer Hrdy argued in a 2001 Utah lecture, for example, that being female is seen as synonymous with having and nurturing as many children as possible. So when mothers abandon their children, it's seen as unnatural. This simplistic, emotional response to parents—mothers, in particular—who give up their kids is part of the reason Americans have such a difficult time dealing with the issue. As Hrdy says, "No amount of legislation can ensure that mothers will love their babies."

That's why programs like safe haven laws—age limitations or not—will never truly get to the heart of the matter. As Mary Lee Allen, director of the Children's Defense Fund's child welfare and mental health division, has said, "These laws help women to drop their babies off but do nothing to provide support to women and children before this happens."

Unfortunately, discussing the structural issues has never been an American strong suit. Hrdy notes that legislators are too afraid to focus on sensible solutions. "Talking about the source of the problem would require policymakers to discuss sex education and contraception, not to mention abortion, and they view even nonsensical social policies as preferable to the prospect of political suicide."

If policymakers and people who care about children want to reduce the number of abandoned kids, they need to address the systemic issues: poverty, maternity leave, access to resources, and health care. We need to encourage women to demand more help from their partners, if they have them. In a way, that's the easier fix, because we know what we have to do there; the issues have been the same for years. The less-obvious hurdle is that of preparing parents emotionally and putting forward realistic images of parenthood and motherhood. There also needs to be some sort of acknowledgment that not everyone should parent—when parenting is a given, it's not fully considered or thought out, and it gives way too easily to parental ambivalence and unhappiness.

Take Trinity, one of the mothers who commented on the Secret Confessions board about hating parenthood. She wrote, "My pregnancy was totally planned and I thought it was a good idea at the time. Nobody tells you the negatives before you get pregnant—they convince you it's a wonderful idea and you will love it. I think it's a secret shared among parents . . . they're miserable so they want you to be too."

By having more honest conversations about parenting, we can avoid the kind of secret depressions so many mothers seem to be harboring. If what we want is deliberate, thought-out, planned, and expected parenthood—and parenting that is healthy and happy for children—then we have to speak out.

Critical Thinking

1. In Nebraska, why do you think parents were using the "safe haven law" to abandon older children rather than infants, as the law had originally intended?

2. In the article there is a quote by the author which states "American culture can't accept the reality of a woman who does not want to be a mother." Do you agree? Why or why not?

3. What are the challenges of being a mother in modern society? Given these challenges how can we better prepare and support those who become parents by choice or through unintended pregnancies?

Create Central

www.mhhe.com/createcentral

Internet References

Administration for Children and Families: Infant Safe Haven Laws
https://www.childwelfare.gov/systemwide/laws_policies/statutes/safehaven.cfm

Planned Parenthood
http://www.plannedparenthood.org

The March of Dimes
www.marchofdimes.com

Article

Prepared by: Patricia Hrusa Williams,
University of Maine at Farmington

Getting It Right from the Start
The Case for Early Parenthood Education

THOMAS G. STICHT

Learning Outcomes

After reading this article, you will be able to:

- List parental behaviors associated with school readiness and success.
- Identify core skills which may be taught as part of early parenting education efforts.

One hundred fifty-three thousand words per week. That's the difference between the 215,000 words per week that the average child in a privileged home hears and the 62,000 words per week that the average child in a family on welfare hears. I'll explain the research behind these numbers later; for now, just consider how staggering the difference is. And consider the implications. Hearing language is the first step in learning to read and write and make sense of the world.

The language gap that results in the achievement gap begins at home. Schools can and should do their part to close this gap, but parents, by reading to their children and interacting with them in positive and encouraging ways, need to do their part, too.

The idea that families need to provide enriching educational activities is not new. In 1908, Edmund Burke Huey, regarded as "one of the foremost leaders" in educating children with learning disabilities,[1] wrote, "The school of the future will have as one of its important duties the instruction of parents in the means of assisting the child's natural learning in the home."[2] This insight was just one of many in his classic work *The Psychology and Pedagogy of Reading*, a 500-page book so highly regarded that it was reprinted by the MIT Press in 1968 and again by the International Reading Association in 2009.

Today, a substantial body of scientific evidence supports Huey's call for the instruction of parents in the means of improving children's learning at home, and therefore their learning at school. Much of this evidence comes from the best research in early childhood education and, in particular one recurring finding: the most effective early childhood education programs include *early parenthood education.* The results of studies of major early childhood education programs suggest that some of the long-term academic and social outcomes of early childhood education result not so much from the direct education of the children, but rather from education provided to highly disadvantaged parents. Changes in parenting help explain why relatively short-term education programs for children could sustain them through school, and into adulthood. Better parenting provides a long-term educational intervention for children.

Before diving into the relevant research from effective early childhood programs, let's take a closer look at why Huey concluded that schools would need to teach many parents to facilitate learning at home. As Huey understood—and cognitive scientists have since demonstrated—literacy follows oracy, so parents who foster their young children's listening, speaking, vocabulary and knowledge are also fostering success in school.

The Intergenerational Transfer of Literacy

In *The Psychology and Pedagogy of Reading,* Huey reflected on the role of speech in reading. Drawing from the scholarly literature on reading and from teachers' observations, he concluded, "The child comes to his first reader with his habits of spoken language fairly well formed, and these habits grow more deeply set with every year. His meanings inhere in this spoken language and belong but secondarily to the printed symbols."[3]

Sixty-six years later, my colleagues and I recast Huey's statement as a simple three-part model of the development of literacy. We assert that:

1. People are born with information processing skills and the capacity for storing knowledge in memory.
2. By means of these information processing skills, when exposed to oral language people acquire the oracy skills of listening comprehension and speech, and use both to construct meaning and store knowledge.
3. With proper support in literate societies, people acquire the skills of reading and writing, which draw upon the same language and knowledge base that is used for listening and speaking.[4]

My colleagues and I call this the oracy-to-literacy transfer effect.

Of course, we developed this simple transfer model not based on Huey alone, but on a large body of studies. For example, the model is supported by research conducted in the 1960s by Walter Loban, whose longitudinal work on the development of language and literacy has been internationally recognized. He assessed children's oral language ability before they started first grade, and then tested their reading skills at grades 4 through 8. He found that those with high oral language skills before the first grade became high-ability readers and those with low oral language skills became low-ability readers.

Some 20 years later, Loban's work on the relationship of oracy to literacy was greatly expanded by researchers Betty Hart and Todd Risley.[5] Over two and a half years, they observed and recorded 42 families for an hour each month. At the beginning of the study, each family had a 7- to 9-month-old infant. Knowing that preschoolers from low-income families tended to have smaller vocabularies and overall weaker oral language than their peers from higher-income families, they wanted to see what happened before preschool—to determine the quality and quantity of language to which these children were exposed as they learned to talk. The 42 families spanned the income range, with 13 professional families, 23 working-class families, and 6 families on welfare. It took years to transcribe the tapes and analyze the data, but eventually they found extraordinary differences in the extent to which parents spoke to their children. Hart and Risley wrote, "Simply in words heard, the average child on welfare was having half as much experience per hour (616 words per hour) as the average working-class child (1,251 words per hour) and less than one-third that of the average child in a professional family (2,153 words per hour)."[6] Extrapolating these hourly findings to weekly totals (assuming 100 hours awake per week), they came up with the numbers with which I opened this article: 215,000 words heard by children in professional families and 62,000 words in welfare families. The weekly total for working class families was 125,000. Extrapolating these hourly findings across early childhood, they estimated that from birth to age 4, welfare children would experience some 13 million words of oral language, working-class children, around 26 million words; and children of professional parents, some 45 million words!

According to the oracy-to-literacy transfer effect, the children hearing the most words would develop the largest oral language vocabulary, and those hearing the fewest words would develop the smallest oral language vocabulary. Furthermore, once these children learn to decode, their oral vocabulary would determine their reading and writing vocabulary. Indeed, when Hart and Risley tested the children's oral vocabulary at age 3, the professional, working-class, and welfare children ranked highest, middle, and lowest, respectively. Six years later, 29 of the children were tested again, and their oral language skills at age 3 were highly correlated with their reading vocabulary and comprehension in third grade.

While we may hope that the early oral language gap would be closed in the first few years in school, the fact is that children spend very little time in school. The primary influence on their language development remains the home environment.

Moreover, by the time children start school—even preschool—the differences in the language experiences they have had are staggering. Huey was right: many parents need to be taught how to support learning at home.

The strong oracy-to-literacy transfer effects found by Loban and Hart and Risley (and many others) explain to a large extent the ubiquitous finding in industrialized nations that parents' educational level is a strong predictor of children's literacy level. Significantly, the oracy-to-literacy transfer effect suggests that it is not parents' education level per se that produces an intergenerational transfer of literacy, but rather what better-educated parents *do* with their children using oral language and literacy skills.

Discussing the ways children of educated parents may acquire a strong foundation for reading, Huey wrote: "The secret of it all lies in the parents' reading aloud to and with the child. . . . The child should long continue to hear far more reading than he does for himself. . . . Oral work is certain to displace much of the present written work in the school of the future, at least in the earlier years; and at home there is scarcely a more commendable and useful practice than that of reading much of good things aloud to the children."[7] Decades of research support Huey yet again: on average, children's listening comprehension surpasses their reading comprehension until seventh or eighth grade. Especially in the early years, and continuing up through middle school (and for some students, even into high school), learning through oral work is indeed essential.[8]

Listening to text read aloud is especially important: researchers have found that texts use much more advanced vocabulary and grammar than spoken language. A recent summary that research stated, "Regardless of the source or situation and without exception, the richness and complexity of the words used in the oral language samples paled in comparison with the written texts. Indeed, of all the oral language samples evaluated, the only one that exceeded even preschool books in lexical range was expert witness testimony."[9] Addressing the extraordinary differences that Hart and Risley found would not be as easy as encouraging low-income parents to read and speak with their children as much as possible—but that would be a good start.

The Intergenerational Transfer of Character

Literacy is not the only essential ability that is strongly influenced by parenting; character traits like motivation and persistence are also transferred from one generation to the next. And, like literacy, these traits have a substantial impact on student achievement. For example, researchers have found that "Parental beliefs, values, aspirations, and attitudes . . . are very important, as is parental well-being. . . . Parenting skills in terms of warmth, discipline, and educational behaviours are all major factors in the formation of school success."[10]

Hart and Risley's research provides some insights into how parents differ along these lines: not only were there large differences in the *quantity* of oral language in the 42 homes, but also in the *quality* of the language. Children in professional families heard far more encouraging comments, and far fewer discouraging ones, than children in families on welfare. Specifically, in a professional family, the average child heard 32 affirmatives and 5 prohibitions per hour; in a working-class family, the average child heard 12 affirmatives and 7 prohibitions per hour; and in a welfare family, the average child heard 5 affirmatives and 11 prohibitions per hour. Recalling the data on the quantity of language, we can see that children in professional families heard a lot of language—and much of it was positive. But children in welfare families heard relatively little language—and much of it was negative. These findings suggest that the feelings conveyed through oral language may influence the development of noncognitive traits such as motivation and persistence in learning.

While at first it may seem that intervening in the emotional aspects of parenting would be quite a challenge, numerous studies have found that the major outcome of adult basic education is improved noncognitive skills. Almost universally, studies of adult basic education report that adults feel better about themselves, overcome learned helplessness, and feel more motivated to succeed in life; importantly, these positive noncognitive skills often modify adults' behaviors with their children.[11]

In research with Wider Opportunities for Women (WOW), for example, Sandra Van Fossen (a research associate at WOW) and I found that mothers enrolled in basic-skills programs reported that they spoke with their children about school more, read to them more, took them to the library more, and so forth. In one visit to a single mother's home, the mother's second-grader said, "I do my homework just like Mommy" and thrust his homework into the researcher's hand. This type of emotional, noncognitive development in the child was obtained for free as a spinoff of an adult basic education program.[12]

Adult education focused on improving parenting can also be effective. Longitudinal research on the Prenatal/Early Infancy Project, for example, found many benefits for families in the control (nonintervention) group. This project studied two interventions, one more intensive than the other. In the more intensive (and more effective) intervention, young women were visited at home by nurses from about midway through their pregnancy until their children were 2 years old. The nurses addressed everything from prenatal care to child-rearing to employment. When the children were 15 years old, they were less likely to have been arrested, abused, or neglected. Similarly, their mothers were less likely to have been arrested, convicted, or incarcerated, and they reported many fewer episodes of impairment due to alcohol or drugs. Their mothers also had fewer subsequent pregnancies and went a longer time between births, which means they could devote greater attention to each child.[13]

Particularly strong benefits for character development have been found when child and parent education are combined. For instance, the HighScope Perry Preschool Program, a carefully studied preschool program that provided weekly home visits, mainly had character—not cognitive—benefits. Discussing Perry and similar programs, Nobel Prize-winning economist James J. Heckman downplayed their effects on children's cognitive skills, stating, "Enriched early intervention programs targeted to disadvantaged children have had their biggest effect on noncognitive skills: motivation, self-control, and time preference. . . . Noncognitive skills are powerfully predictive of a number of socioeconomic measures (crime, teenage pregnancy, education, and the like). . . . Kids in the Perry Preschool Program . . . are much more successful than similar kids without intervention even though their IQs are no higher. And the same is true of many such interventions."[14]

Parenting Power in Preschool Programs

While parent education appears to be an important part of highly effective early childhood programs, such programs have many components, and I have found no research that isolates the effects of the parent education component (or any other single component).* Yet, there are indications that some of the long-term cost-beneficial effects of early childhood programs result in part from the effects that the programs had on changing how the parents interacted with their children.

In a report for the Economic Policy Institute, Robert Lynch (an economics professor at Washington College) provided an analysis of several carefully studied early childhood education programs and concluded that they produce a considerable return on investment.[15] He found that investments in high-quality early childhood education programs consistently generated more than a $3 return for every $1 invested.

As an example of possible early parenthood education activities that may have influenced the preschool children's development, Lynch reports that in the well-known Abecedarian Early Childhood Intervention program, parents were given special educational materials to help them engage in educational activities with their children. Follow-up research showed that the mothers in the intervention achieved more education than those in the comparison group, and fewer of the intervention mothers had additional births than did the comparison mothers (which, again, means more time is available for each child).

The important role of parent education is supported by Lawrence Schweinhart, who is the president of the HighScope Educational Research Foundation and was the lead researcher on the Perry Preschool longitudinal study. Discussing what he sees as the key ingredients for achieving a good return on investment from early childhood programs, he recommended that such programs "have teachers spend substantial amounts of time with parents, educating them about their children's development and how they can extend classroom learning experiences into their homes." In addition, he noted, "All the programs in the long-term studies worked with parents. In fact, in the HighScope Perry Preschool program, teachers spent half their work time engaged in such activities."[16] This strongly suggests that some of the success of early childhood programs maybe dependent upon educational activities to improve the skills and knowledge of parents.

---

*Such research would be very helpful to program developers, but it is time consuming and expensive. To determine the effectiveness of each program component, a whole series of studies would have to be done in which one component at a time is changed.

It has been more than 100 years since Huey set forth a clear and effective path for supporting learning in the home. Educating those who are, or are about to become, parents offers the possibility of obtaining payoffs for future generations before conception occurs. And, if we focus our limited resources on reaching first-time parents, then one "dose" of parenting education could also benefit succeeding children. Given the intergenerational nature of literacy and character, that one dose could even benefit future generations. It is time that we move from thinking about education in terms of each child, to thinking about education from a multiple-lifecycles perspective. If we are really serious about attaining long-lasting increases in student achievement, we should look to both the school and the home: early parenthood education should take its place alongside early childhood education as a primary means of getting education right from the start.

Notes

1. See the "Psychological Bulletin" comment in John B. Carroll's foreword to Edmund Burke Huey, *The Psychology and Pedagogy of Reading* (Cambridge, MA: MIT Press, 1968).

2. Edmund Burke Huey, *The Psychology and Pedagogy of Reading* (Newark, DE: International Reading Association, 2009), 206.

3. Huey, *The Psychology and Pedagogy of Reading* (2009), 81.

4. Thomas G. Sticht, Lawrence J. Beck, Robert N. Hauke, Glenn M. Kleiman, and James H. James, *Auding and Reading: A Developmental Model* (Alexandria, VA: Human Resources Research Organization, 1974).

5. Betty Hart and Todd R. Risley, *Meaningful Differences in the Everyday Experiences of Young American Children* (Baltimore, MD: Paul H. Brookes Publishing, 1995).

6. Betty Hart and Todd R. Risley, "The Early Catastrophe: The 30 Million Word Gap," *American Educator* 27, no.1 (Spring 2003): 8.

7. Huey, *The Psychology and Pedagogy of Reading* (2009), 220–221.

8. Andrew Biemiller, "Oral Comprehension Sets the Ceiling on Reading Comprehension," *American Educator* 27, no. 1 (Spring 2003): 23.

9. Marilyn Jager Adams, "Advancing Our Students' Language and Literacy: The Challenge of Complex Texts," *American Educator* 34, no. 4 (Winter 2010–2011): 5.

10. Leon Feinstein, Kathryn Duckworth, and Ricardo Sabates, *A Model of the Inter-Generational Transmission of Educational Success* (London: Centre for Research on the Wider Benefits of Learning, 2004).

11. See, for example, Parkdale Project Read, *"I've Opened Up": Exploring Learners' Perspectives on Progress* (Toronto, ON:

2006), accessed April 15, 2011, www.nald.ca/library/research/openup/cover.htm; and Mary Beth Bingman and Olga Ebert, *"I've Come a Long Way": Learner-Identified Outcomes of Participation in Adult Literacy Programs* (Cambridge, MA: National Center for the Study of Adult Learning and Literacy, February 2000).

12. Sandra Van Fossen and Thomas G. Sticht, *Teach the Mother and Reach the Child: Results of the Intergenerational Literacy Action Research Project of Wider Opportunities for Women* (Washington, DC: Wider Opportunities for Women, July 1991).

13. Robert Lynch, *Exceptional Returns: Economic, Fiscal, and Social Benefits of Investment in Early Childhood Development* (Washington, DC: Economic Policy Institute, 2004).

14. James Heckman, interview by Douglas Clement, editor of *The Region,* Federal Reserve Bank of Minneapolis, June 2005.

15. Lynch, *Exceptional Returns.*

16. Lawrence J. Schweinhart, "Creating the Best Prekindergartens: Five Ingredients for Long-Term Effects and Returns on Investment," in *The Obama Education Plan: An Education Week Guide* (San Francisco: Jossey-Bass, 2009), 21–25.

Critical Thinking

1. What aspects of the home environment are important to future success in school?

2. What information do first-time parents need in order to help promote their children's literacy skills and traits important to later school success?

3. Do you think early parent education should be mandatory for all first-time parents? Why or why not?

Create Central

www.mhhe.com/createcentral

Internet References

Zero to Three
www.zerotothree.org

National Association for the Education of Young Children
www.nacyc.org

THOMAS G. STICHT is an international consultant in adult education, recipient of UNESCO's Mahatma Gandhi Medal, and author of hundreds of scholarly articles. Previously, he has served as the president of Applied Behavioral and Cognitive Sciences Inc., associate director of the National Institute of Education, visiting associate professor at the Harvard Graduate School of Education, and visiting noted scholar at the University of British Columbia in Canada.

Unit 3

UNIT

Prepared by: Patricia Hrusa Williams, *University of Maine at Farmington*

Family Relationships

And they lived happily ever after. . . . The romantic image conjured up by this well-known final line from fairy tales is not reflective of the reality of family life and relationship maintenance. The belief that somehow love alone should carry us through is pervasive. In reality, maintaining a relationship takes dedication, hard work, and commitment.

We come into relationships, regardless of their nature, with fantasies about how things ought to be. Partners, spouses, parents, children, siblings, and others—all family members, have at least some unrealistic expectations about each other. It is through the negotiation of their lives together that they come to work through these expectations and, hopefully, replace them with other more realistic ones. By recognizing and making their own contributions to the family, members can set and attain realistic family goals. Tolerance, acceptance of differences, and effective communication skills can facilitate this process. Along the way, family members need to learn new skills and develop new habits when relating to each other. This will not be easy, and, try as they may, not everything will be controllable. Factors both inside and outside the family may impede their progress.

Even before we enter a marriage or other committed relationship, attitudes, standards, and beliefs influence our choices. Increasingly, choices include whether we should commit to such a relationship in the first place. From the start of a committed relationship, the expectations both partners have of their relationship have an impact, and the need to negotiate differences is a constant factor. Adding a child to the family affects the lives of parents in ways that they could previously only imagine. Parenting is a complicated and often confusing process for which most of us have very little training or support. What is the "right" way to rear a child? How does the job of parents change as children grow and have different needs? There are a variety of different philosophies or approaches to parenting, many advocated through the popular media. We also have our own experiences of "being parented" which may influence our goals, choices, and ideals. These factors can all combine to make child rearing more difficult than it might otherwise have been. Other family relationships also evolve, and in our nuclear-family-focused culture, it is possible to forget that family relationships extend beyond those between spouses, parents, and children.

This unit explores marital, parent–child, sibling, and intergenerational relationships within families. The topics explored include the characteristics of family communication, successful marriages and same-sex relationships, childrearing philosophies, sibling relationships, and changes in parent–child relationships across the lifespan. A goal is to explore the diversity of structures and contexts in which couples, parents, children, and families develop and evolve.

Article   Prepared by: Patricia Hrusa Williams, *University of Maine at Farmington*

Secret Histories

In an Age of Lessening Privacy, Some Family Secrets Persist

BRUCE FEILER

Learning Outcomes

After reading this article, you will be able to:

- Recognize reasons why families sometimes keep secrets.

- Understand common features or characteristics of family secrets.

- Evaluate the ethical dilemmas and challenges involved in both keeping and revealing family secrets.

After Itzhak Goldberg's father died in 1995, at age 86, his mother gave him a watch in a red case. The 18-karat gold Patek Philippe was a rare indulgence for his father, a Polish Holocaust survivor who married, moved to Israel and ran a produce business.

As Mr. Goldberg wrote in the online magazine *Tablet,* when he opened the box, he was stunned to find, tucked in the folds of the guarantee booklet, a tiny, yellowing photograph of two beautiful young women he didn't recognize. His mother was startled but made no comment. For 17 years, out of deference to her, Mr. Goldberg, now a clinical professor of radiation oncology at Albert Einstein College of Medicine, did nothing. But after his mother died, he went looking for the truth.

"I knew my father wanted me to find that photograph," he told me recently. "He was saying, 'This is a part of my life, and I want you to know about it after I pass away.'"

One truism about contemporary life is that there are no more secrets. In the age of selfies, sexting, Twitter and Facebook, people are constantly spilling every intimate detail of their lives. Video cameras trace our every move; our cellphones know where we are at all times; Google tracks our innermost thoughts; the N.S.A. listens in when we dream. Everything is knowable, if you just know where to look.

But that idea is flawed. Secrets endure. Especially in families.

In the last year or so, a number of prominent people have stepped forward to share stories of how they were blindsided by jarring revelations about their loved ones after they died. Their stories share a common theme—call it secrets from the grave—that is all the more surprising when set against the recent debate about the loss of privacy in our lives.

One of those stories belongs to Michael Hainey, who was a 6-year-old in Chicago when his father died suddenly. Mr. Hainey and his 8-year-old brother were told little about the event. "I was aware from an early age that something was not right and was consumed with knowing the truth," he told me. "But at the same time, I lived in fear of asking anyone what happened out of concern that the world would crumble."

At 10, he broke the omertà and pressed his mother, who told him that his father, who worked the overnight shift at *The Chicago Sun-Times,* had suffered a heart attack in the parking lot at work. "Why didn't the police officers come and tell us?" he asked. She couldn't answer. As a teenager, Mr. Hainey retrieved his father's obituaries, all of which disagreed about the cause of death. One phrase jumped out: Robert Hainey died "while visiting friends." How come he never met those friends, his son wondered.

Like his father, Mr. Hainey became a journalist and is now the deputy editor of *GQ.* When he reached his mid-30s, around the age his father was when he died, he experienced a crisis and was determined to learn the truth. He described the quest that followed in his memoir, *After Visiting Friends,* which became a best seller when it was published last year. It ends with a shock: His father died while in bed with another woman. "While visiting friends" was the euphemism of choice.

After learning the secret, Mr. Hainey kept it from his mother for more than a year. "We all say we want the truth, but we all know what happens to the truth tellers," he said. "They usually get slain. You have to wield the truth with care." He eventually shared the story with her, and later his book. Her response: "It's the best gift you could ever have given me. It's the truth, and for 40 years I've had questions that I was afraid to ask."

Unlike Mr. Hainey, Emma Brockes knew that her mother was harboring a secret. As a girl growing up in London, Ms. Brockes listened to her mother tell elaborate, often violent tales about her upbringing in South Africa. One featured element: a pistol. Ms. Brockes said, "In an extravagantly light tone, she would say: 'I have this gun. I'm going to leave it to you.'"

Ms. Brockes, now a reporter with *The Guardian,* said she had no interest in pursuing the full story while her mother was alive. "But that predictable thing happened that the minute she died, my relationship with her changed overnight. All of the evasions and half-truths and awkwardnesses I had sensed were all the things I wanted to nail down."

Ms. Brockes visited South Africa and quickly learned the truth. Her grandfather was a convicted murderer and an active child molester whom her mother had gotten arrested and taken to court. After a lurid public trial, he escaped the charges, and her mother fled to London to escape him. As for the gun, Ms. Brockes said: "My mother, very classic, had been glib and jaunty about it. She'd not told me the real reason she had it, which was to protect herself from that maniac of a father." Ms. Brockes's mother even used the gun on one occasion to shoot him. "But she was absolutely useless at the task," her daughter recalled. "She fired it five or six times and failed to kill him." (He declined to press charges.)

Ms. Brockes, who chronicled this story in a memoir, *She Left Me the Gun,* which was also published last year, said she was grateful her mother shielded her from the truth. "I had an incredibly normal childhood," she said. "My mother's aim, always, was to keep me from incorporating any of the noxious stuff in her background into my identity." Family, she added, will always be a bastion of secrecy. "We might tell the world everything about ourselves, but we won't tell our parents or our children."

Selena Roberts learned a similar lesson recently from her mother. A former reporter and columnist with *The New York Times* and *Sports Illustrated,* Ms. Roberts had a distant relationship with her mom. "My older brother passed away when I was 5 years old, and it changed my parents' marriage," Ms. Roberts said. "My mother withdrew from everybody." After her parents divorced, Ms. Roberts and her surviving brother moved in with their father and had little contact with their mother.

"I really wasn't present in her life," she said. "The last 30 or 40 years of her life, she was anorexic. She lived a very austere, minimalist life. She did not buy much for herself and was very regimented about her spending."

After her mother died in 2010, Ms. Roberts, who was by her side the last two months, was stunned to discover that her mom had quietly been investing in the stock market for years and had amassed a portfolio worth more than a million dollars, which she left to her children.

"There was no hint to us that she had ever made anything more than the government salary she earned as a teacher," Ms. Roberts said. "But we found out after her death that she took great joy in numbers. It was the one thing she could understand and control." A fan of Warren Buffett and Suze Orman, Ms. Roberts's mother had been making safe, secure investments. She kept careful records in a spiral notebook, in which she also wrote that she had been sexually assaulted in a parking lot of a church when she was 7.

Ms. Roberts said: "I would have preferred her to experience more joy in her life, by being around us and seeing us more. I would have loved to see her happy. But I think the money was her way of saying what she had a very difficult time saying, which is, 'I love you.'"

Her children gave much of the money to causes their mother cared about, and Ms. Roberts used some to help start a new company, Roopstigo, which produces sports documentaries. She feels that the current vogue toward confessional self-expression is largely superficial. "I think many people use social media to project an idea of what they want people to see," she said. But, she added, there are things you would never and should never reveal on Twitter, Facebook or anyplace else. "Those are the soul of people," she said, "what motivates them, the pain they feel, the hurt and wounded parts of them. Those are where the secrets lie."

In Ms. Roberts's case, it's clear her mother wanted to keep certain things secret but also wanted her children to find out after she died. This seems to be a common provenance of family legacies: Some things are too painful to discuss while people are living but too important to be left unsaid after they die.

The story of Mr. Goldberg's father falls into that category. After his mother died, Mr. Goldberg wanted to track down the identities of the women in the fraying photograph. The records of Yad Vashem, the Holocaust memorial in Israel, had just been made available online, and Mr. Goldberg typed in his father's name. He found a note handwritten by his father in the early 1950s as well as a second account written by another person unknown to him that documented the death of a woman named Chaya Holzberg Goldberg and her two daughters. The woman was from the same town as Mr. Goldberg's father.

"I remembered that my father had relatives by that name," he told me, "and I contacted them. Several were still alive and living in New York City." At an emotional meeting that included Mr. Goldberg's wife, children and grandchildren, the family learned that Mr. Goldberg's father had been married to Chaya Goldberg before the war. The couple, who were cousins, had two children. Shortly after the second one's birth, Nazi officials searched the family's hiding place.

As Mr. Goldberg described it in *Tablet,* "When the newborn started to cry, a hand was placed over the baby's mouth to muffle the sound, and the baby girl was inadvertently smothered to death." Chaya Goldberg and the surviving child, 7-year-old Chava, were gassed at Majdanek concentration camp.

One of the attendees at the reunion was 87-year-old Jack Holzberg, Chaya's younger brother. He looked at the photograph that Mr. Goldberg found in the watch case and, with tears in his eyes, said, "That's my sister."

I asked Mr. Goldberg if he was angry at his father for not sharing the secret. "No," he said. "I had a huge respect for my father. He was an extremely strong person. Very quiet, very loving. It's not a weird thing for survivors to say: 'We went through so much pain. I don't want my kids to know.'"

Yet he did want his family to know in the end. He understood, as so many secret-keepers seem to do, that certain truths deserved to be shared, even if the sharer can't do it directly. Maybe that is one legacy of this age of no more secrets: Whereas once these secrets may have been buried in the grave, now they keep speaking even after the grave has been sealed.

And sometimes those secrets, long feared as too painful, bring comfort to those who learn them. After the tearful meeting with Jack Holzberg, Mr. Goldberg's daughter gave birth to a baby girl. She named her Chaya. Mr. Goldberg called Mr. Holzberg to tell him. The family secret would be secret no more.

Critical Thinking

1. Is it sometimes beneficial to keep some things secret within families? Why or why not?

2. The article discusses how all family secrets share some common characteristics—what are they?

3. There is a quote in the article which states "We all say we want the truth, but we all know what happens to the truth tellers . . . They usually get slain." Do you agree? Why or why not?

4. Is there ever a time a family secret should remain a secret? If so, why?

Create Central

www.mhhe.com/createcentral

Internet References

Families and Trauma, National Child Traumatic Stress Network
   http://www.nctsn.org/resources/topics/families-and-trauma

Oprah Show: Shocking Family Secrets
   http://www.oprah.com/own/Shocking-Family-Secrets-About-the-Show

Psychology Today: Family Secrets
   http://www.psychologytoday.com/blog/family-secrets

BRUCE FEILER is the author of *The Secrets of Happy Families,* which has just been released in paperback.

Article Prepared by: Patricia Hrusa Williams, *University of Maine at Farmington*

Truth or Dare

The secret to happiness lies in dishonesty.

PHILIP GULLEY

Learning Outcomes

After reading this article, you will be able to:

- Define open and honest communication.

- Explain what it means to be dishonest in a relationship.

- Identify the impact of stating candid, honest answers to questions from family members.

When I was little, my parents told me never to lie. It was lousy advice, which I promptly ignored by promising them I would always tell the truth. As a reward, they took me to the Dairy Queen for ice cream, which in my mind confirmed the value of dishonesty. The German philosopher Immanuel Kant believed all lying was bad. Spoken like a man who never married. Because let me tell you, anyone who has ever been married knows the secret to marital bliss is lying.

People should always be able to trust their spouse not to tell big lies, such as failing to inform your wife in Indiana that you have another wife in Illinois. That's a big lie. Or not mentioning that you're wanted for bank robbery in California. Or murdered someone in Kansas. Those lies are called whoppers and should be avoided, even though the last one is understandable. If I had to live in Kansas, I would murder people left and right.

But small lies are a different matter and should be sprinkled generously and thoughtfully throughout a marriage. When we were first married, my wife asked me if she looked nice in a dress she had purchased for a wedding. Being stupid, I told her I didn't care very much for the dress. She went ahead and wore it, but she felt self-conscious the whole evening. I had hoped attending a wedding with my wife might incline her mind toward romance. Instead, she wanted to beat me dead with a shovel, burn me to ashes, and toss my remains in a river.

You want to know how I know that? Because I asked her if she was mad at me, and she said, "I want to beat you dead with a shovel, burn you to ashes, and toss your remains in a river." That was another marital instance that could have been helped by lying.

If your spouse ever asks if you're mad at him or her, do not say "yes." Don't believe that psychobabble about the importance of open and honest communication in a marriage. Everyone who says that is divorced. Open and honest communication didn't work for them, and now they want you to be as miserable as they are.

> **If anyone ever tells you they want your honest opinion about something, what they really want is for you to lie and make them feel good.**

As a pastor, I do a fair amount of marriage counseling. Almost every marital conflict can be traced back to truthfulness. Not long ago, a couple came to me complaining that they always fought. I asked them to describe a typical day. They worked, came home, and then the husband sat down to watch TV while the wife cooked supper and helped the kids with their homework. Now, here's when things went south. One evening, the wife asked her husband if he would be willing to help, and he said "no." He was telling the truth. Dumb, dumb, dumb. He should have said, "I would love to help you, honey. Let me cook supper." Then he should have burned it beyond recognition, causing her to never want him in the kitchen again. But no, he had to be an idiot and tell the truth, and now their marriage is doomed.

Every Sunday, when we're driving home from our Quaker meetinghouse, I ask my wife if my sermon was good, and she always says it was. I've given approximately 1,400 sermons over the past 30 years. It seems likely that more than a few of them sucked. But to hear my wife tell it, they've all been excellent. I know she's lying, but I prefer dishonest flattery over candid feedback. If anyone ever tells you they want your honest opinion about something, what they really want is for you to lie and make them feel good.

Example: A boss approaches two of his employees and the following exchange takes place.

Boss: "I'm going to ask you something, and I need you to tell me the truth. Am I a good boss?"

Dumb Worker: "Well, since you asked, I'll be honest. You're hard to please, you're not very smart, and the people you think are good workers are really just sucking up to you."

Smart Worker: "I continue to be amazed by your insight, wisdom, and inspirational leadership."

The next week, the boss is told he must lay off a worker. Which one do you think will get the ax? Exactly.

My older son is getting married this month. The other evening, I overheard his fiancee say, "Honey, I'd like to dance at our reception. Do you like to dance?" He said he would love to. I know for a fact he hates to dance, so you can imagine how proud I was to hear him lie to his wife-to-be. I predict a long and happy marriage, built on a sturdy foundation of untruth and deception.

About the only people who shouldn't lie are doctors. I was waiting for a table at a restaurant recently when a family sat beside me. The mother was holding a baby, and she asked, "Isn't he beautiful?" His face was pruny, his nose disturbingly large, and his eyes bulged out. "What a handsome little guy," I answered. If I were a doctor, I would have had to suggest checking the kid's thyroid. For that reason alone, I would make a lousy physician. Can you imagine having to be honest with someone about their health?

Another example: A 350-pound person says that his knees hurt.

Me: "Oh, I'm sorry to hear that. Perhaps you injured them as a child."

Doctor: "Of course they hurt—you're morbidly obese. You need to lose some weight."

It's no wonder doctors make so much money. They have to spend all day telling people the truth. It's an impossible job.

We say we want honest politicians, but we keep electing liars—candidates who tell us that they can balance the budget without raising taxes. They know if they told us the truth (that we're broke because we want too much from our government but aren't willing to pay for it), they'd never get elected. So they lie, and we elect them because we don't want to face the facts. If we had wanted politicians who told the truth, Ron Paul would be our president, which would have worried me to no end. After all, anyone who always tells the truth has to be crazy.

Critical Thinking

1. There is a quote within the article which states "Almost every marital conflict can be traced back to truthfulness." Do you agree or disagree? Why?

2. Everyone sometimes has difficult feedback to provide to a family member or partner. What is the best way to convey this information so you are honest yet do not hurt someone's feelings or injure their sense of self?

3. Has there ever been a time that you unintentionally hurt someone's feelings by providing an honest answer to their question? Describe the incident. If you had to replay the scenario again, would you do the same thing?

Create Central

www.mhhe.com/createcentral

Internet References

Coalition for Marriage, Family, and Couples Education
www.smartmarriages.com

Love Is Respect
www.loveisrespect.org

Relationships Australia
www.relationships.org.au

Article

Prepared by: Patricia Hrusa Williams,
University of Maine at Farmington

Are You with the Right Mate?

REBECCA WEBBER

Learning Outcomes

After reading this article, you will be able to:

- Understand factors important to compatibility and marital satisfaction.

- Describe the personality characteristics associated with being a good mate or partner.

- Recognize reasons for growth and change in marital relationships over time.

Elliott Katz was stunned to find himself in the middle of a divorce after two kids and 10 years of marriage. The Torontonian, a policy analyst for the Ottawa government, blamed his wife. "She just didn't appreciate all I was doing to make her happy." He fed the babies, and he changed their diapers. He gave them their baths, he read them stories, and put them to bed. Before he left for work in the morning, he made them breakfast. He bought a bigger house and took on the financial burden, working evenings to bring in enough money so his wife could stay home full-time.

He thought the solution to the discontent was for her to change. But once on his own, missing the daily interaction with his daughters, he couldn't avoid some reflection. "I didn't want to go through this again. I asked whether there was something I could have done differently. After all, you can wait years for someone else to change."

What he decided was, indeed, there were some things he could have done differently—like not tried as hard to be so non-controlling that his wife felt he had abandoned decision-making entirely. His wife, he came to understand, felt frustrated, as if she were "a married single parent," making too many of the plans and putting out many of the fires of family life, no matter how many chores he assumed.

Ultimately, he stopped blaming his wife for their problems. "You can't change another person. You can only change yourself," he says. "Like lots of men today" he has since found, "I was very confused about my role as partner." After a few post-divorce years in the mating wilderness, Katz came to realize that framing a relationship in terms of the right or wrong mate is by itself a blind alley.

"We're given a binary model," says New York psychotherapist Ken Page. "Right or wrong. Settle or leave. We are not given the right tools to think about relationships. People need a better set of options."

Sooner or later, there comes a moment in *all* relationships when you lie in bed, roll over, look at the person next to you and think it's all a dreadful mistake, says Boston family therapist Terrence Real. It happens a few months to a few years in. "It's an open secret of American culture that disillusionment exists. I go around the country speaking about 'normal marital hatred.' Not one person has ever asked what I mean by that. It's extremely raw."

What to do when the initial attraction sours? "I call it the first day of your real marriage," Real says. It's not a sign that you've chosen the wrong partner. It is the signal to grow as an individual—to take responsibility for your own frustrations. Invariably, we yearn for perfection but are stuck with an imperfect human being. We all fall in love with people we think will deliver us from life's wounds but who wind up knowing how to rub against us.

A new view of relationships and their discontents is emerging. We alone are responsible for having the relationship we want. And to get it, we have to dig deep into ourselves while maintaining our connections. It typically takes a dose of bravery—what Page calls "enlightened audacity." Its brightest possibility exists, ironically, just when the passion seems most totally dead. If we fail to plumb ourselves and speak up for our deepest needs, which admittedly can be a scary prospect, life will never feel authentic, we will never see ourselves with any clarity, and everyone will always be the wrong partner.

The Way Things Are

Romance itself seeds the eventual belief that we have chosen the wrong partner. The early stage of a relationship, most marked by intense attraction and infatuation, is in many ways akin to cocaine intoxication, observes Christine Meinecke, a clinical psychologist in Des Moines, Iowa. It's orchestrated, in part, by the neurochemicals associated with intense pleasure. Like a cocaine high, it's not sustainable.

But for the duration—and experts give it nine months to four years—infatuation has one overwhelming effect: Research shows that it makes partners overestimate their similarities and idealize each other. We're thrilled that he loves Thai food, travel, and classic movies, just like us. And we overlook his avid interest in old cars and online poker.

Eventually, reality rears its head. "Infatuation fades for everyone," says Meinecke, author of *Everybody Marries the Wrong Person.* That's when you discover your psychological incompatibility, and disenchantment sets in. Suddenly, a switch is flipped, and now all you can see are your differences. "You're focusing on what's wrong with *them.* They need to get the message about what *they* need to change."

You conclude you've married the wrong person—but that's because you're accustomed to thinking, Cinderella-like, that there *is* only one right person. The consequences of such a pervasive belief are harsh. We engage in destructive behaviors, like blaming our partner for our unhappiness or searching for someone outside the relationship.

Along with many other researchers and clinicians, Meinecke espouses a new marital paradigm—what she calls "the self-responsible spouse." When you start focusing on what isn't so great, it's time to shift focus. "Rather than look at the other person, you need to look at yourself and ask, 'Why am I suddenly so unhappy and what do I need to do?'" It's not likely a defect in your partner.

In mature love, says Meinecke, "we do not look to our partner to provide our happiness, and we don't blame them for our unhappiness. We take responsibility for the expectations that we carry, for our own negative emotional reactions, for our own insecurities, and for our own dark moods."

But instead of looking at ourselves, or understanding the fantasies that bring us to such a pass, we engage in a thought process that makes our differences tragic and intolerable, says William Doherty, professor of psychology and head of the marriage and family therapy program at the University of Minnesota. It's one thing to say, "I wish my spouse were more into the arts, like I am." Or, "I wish my partner was not just watching TV every night but interested in getting out more with me." That's something you can fix.

It's quite another to say, "This is intolerable. I need and deserve somebody who shares my core interests." The two thought processes are likely to trigger differing actions. It's possible to ask someone to go out more. It's not going to be well received to ask someone for a personality overhaul, notes Doherty, author of *Take Back Your Marriage.*

No one is going to get all their needs met in a relationship, he insists. He urges fundamental acceptance of the person we choose and the one who chooses us. "We're all flawed. With parenting, we know that comes with the territory. With spouses, we say 'This is terrible.'"

The culture, however, pushes us in the direction of discontent. "Some disillusionment and feelings of discouragement are normal in the love-based matches in our culture," explains Doherty. "But consumer culture tells us we should not settle for anything that is not ideal for us."

As UCLA psychologist Thomas Bradbury puts it, "You don't have a line-item veto when it comes to your partner. It's a package deal; the bad comes with the good."

Further, he says, it's too simplistic an interpretation that your partner is the one who's wrong. "We tend to point our finger at the person in front of us. We're fairly crude at processing some information. We tend not to think, 'Maybe I'm not giving her what she needs.' 'Maybe he's disgruntled because I'm not opening up to him.' Or, 'Maybe he's struggling in his relationships with other people.' The more sophisticated question is, 'In what ways are we failing to make one another happy?'"

Now in a long-term relationship, Toronto's Katz has come to believe that "Marriage is not about *finding* the right person. It's about *becoming* the right person. Many people feel they married the wrong person, but I've learned that it's truly about growing to become a better husband."

Eclipsed by Expectations

What's most noticeable about Sarah and Mark Holdt of Estes Park, Colorado, is their many differences. "He's a Republican, I'm a Democrat. He's a traditional Christian, I'm an agnostic. He likes meat and potatoes, I like more adventurous food," says Sarah. So Mark heads off to church and Bible study every week, while Sarah takes a "Journeys" class that considers topics like the history of God in America. "When he comes home, I'll ask, 'What did you learn in Bible Study?'" she says. And she'll share her insights from her own class with him.

But when Sarah wants to go to a music festival and Mark wants to stay home, "I just go," says Sarah. "I don't need to have him by my side for everything." He's there when it matters most—at home, at the dinner table, in bed. "We both thrive on touch," says Sarah, "so we set our alarm a half hour early every morning and take that time to cuddle." They've been married for 14 years.

It takes a comfortable sense of self and deliberate effort to make relationships commodious enough to tolerate such differences. What's striking about the Holdts is the time they take to share what goes on in their lives—and in their heads—when they are apart. Research shows that such "turning toward" each other and efforts at information exchange, even in routine matters, are crucial to maintaining the emotional connection between partners.

Say one partner likes to travel and the other doesn't. "If you view this with a feeling of resentment, that's going to hurt, over and over again," says Doherty. If you can accept it, that's fine—provided you don't start living in two separate worlds.

"What you don't want to do," he says, "is develop a group of single travel friends who, when they are on the road, go out and flirt with others. You start doing things you're not comfortable sharing with your mate." Most often, such large differences are accompanied by so much disappointment that partners react in ways that do not support the relationship.

The available evidence suggests that women more than men bring some element of fantasy into a relationship. Women generally initiate more breakups and two-thirds of divorces, becoming more disillusioned than men. They compare their mates with their friends much more than men do, says Doherty.

He notes, "They tend to have a model or framework for what the relationship should be. They are more prone to the comparison between what they have and what they think they should have. Men tend to monitor the gap between what they have and what they think they deserve only in the sexual arena. They don't monitor the quality of their marriage on an everyday basis."

To the extent that people have an ideal partner and an ideal relationship in their head, they are setting themselves up for disaster, says family expert Michelle Givertz, assistant professor of communication studies at California State University, Chico. Relationship identities are negotiated between two individuals. Relationships are not static ideals; they are always works in progress.

To enter a relationship with an idea of what it should look like or how it should evolve is too controlling, she contends. It takes two people to make a relationship. One person doesn't get to decide what it should be. And to the extent that he or she does, the other partner is not going to be happy.

"People can spend their lives trying to make a relationship into something it isn't, based on an idealized vision of what should be, not what is," she says. She isn't sure why, but she finds that such misplaced expectations are increasing. Or, as Doherty puts it, "A lot of the thinking about being married to the wrong mate is really self-delusion."

Yes, Virginia, Some Mates Really *Are* Wrong

Sometimes, however, we really do choose the wrong person— someone ultimately not interested in or capable of meeting our needs, for any of a number of possible reasons. At the top of the list of people who are generally wrong for *anyone* are substance abusers—whether the substance is alcohol, prescription drugs, or illicit drugs—who refuse to get help for the problem.

"An addict's primary loyalty is not to the relationship, it's to the addiction," explains Ken Page. "Active addicts become cheaper versions of themselves and lose integrity or the ability to do the right thing when it's hard. Those are the very qualities in a partner you need to lean on." Gamblers fall into the same compulsive camp, with the added twist that their pursuit of the big win typically lands them, sooner or later, into deep debt that threatens the foundations of relationship life.

People who cheated in one or more previous relationships are not great mate material. They destroy the trust and intimacy basic to building a relationship. It's possible to make a case for a partner who cheats once, against his own values, but not for one who compulsively and repeatedly strays. Doherty considers such behavior among the "hard reasons" for relationship breakup, along with physical abuse and other forms of overcontrolling. "These are things that nobody should have to put up with in life," he says.

But "drifting apart," "poor communication," and "we're just not compatible anymore" are in a completely different category. Such "soft reasons," he insists, are, by contrast, always two-way streets. "Nobody gets all the soft goodies in life," he finds. "It's often better to work on subtle ways to improve the relationship."

A Critical Difference

There's a difference between fighting for what you want in your relationship and being in direct control of your partner, demanding that he or she change, says Real.

Firmly stand up for your wants and needs in a relationship. "Most people don't have the skill to speak up for and fight for what they want in a relationship," he observes. "They don't speak up, which preserves the love but builds resentment. Resentment is a choice; living resentfully means living unhappily. Or they speak up—but are not very loving." Or they just complain.

The art to speaking up, he says, is to transform a complaint into a request. Not "I don't like how you're talking to me," but "Can you please lower your voice so I can hear you better?" If you're trying to get what you want in a relationship, notes Real, it's best to keep it positive and future-focused.

In an ongoing marriage, he adds, "incompatibility is never the real reason for a divorce." It's a reason for breakup of a dating relationship. But when people say "she's a nice person but we're just not compatible," Doherty finds, something happened in which both were participants and allowed the relationship to deteriorate. It's a nice way to say you're not blaming your partner.

The real reason is likely to be that neither attended to the relationship. Perhaps one or both partners threw themselves into parenting. Or a job. They stopped doing the things that they did when dating and that couples need to do to thrive as a partnership—take time for conversation, talk about how their day went or what's on their mind. Or perhaps the real love was undermined by the inability to handle conflict.

"If you get to the point where you're delivering an ultimatum," says Bradbury, you haven't been maintaining your relationship properly. "It's like your car stopping on the side of the road and you say, 'It just isn't working anymore'—but you haven't changed the oil in 10 years." The heart of any relationship, he insists—what makes people the right mates for each other—is the willingness of both partners to be open and vulnerable; to listen and care about each other.

Although there are no guarantees, there are stable personal characteristics that are generally good and generally bad for relationships. On the good side: sense of humor; even temper; willingness to overlook your flaws; sensitivity to you and what you care about; ability to express caring. On the maladaptive side: chronic lying; chronic worrying or neuroticism; emotional over reactivity; proneness to anger; propensity to harbor grudges; low self-esteem; poor impulse control; tendency to aggression; self-orientation rather than an other-orientation. Situations, such as chronic exposure to nonmarital stress in either partner, also have the power to undermine relationships.

In addition, there are people who are specifically wrong for *you,* because they don't share the values and goals you hold most dear. Differences in core values often plague couples who marry young, before they've had enough life experience to discover who they really are. Most individuals are still developing their belief systems through their late teens and early 20s and still refining their lifestyle choices. Of course, you have to know what you hold most dear, and that can be a challenge for anyone at any age, not just the young.

One of the most common reasons we choose the wrong partner is that we do not know who we are or what we really want. It's hard to choose someone capable of understanding you and meeting your most guarded emotional needs and with whom your values are compatible when you don't know what your needs or values are or haven't developed the confidence to voice them unabashedly.

Maria Lin is a nonpracticing attorney who married a chef. "I valued character, connection, the heart," she says. "He was charming, funny, treated me amazingly well, and we got along great." But over time, intellectual differences got in the way. "He couldn't keep up with my analysis or logic in arguments or reasoning through something, or he would prove less capable at certain things, or he would misspell or misuse terms. It was never anything major, just little things."

Lin confides that she lost respect for her chef-husband. "I didn't realize how important intellectual respect for my partner would end up being to me. I think this was more about not knowing myself well enough, and not knowing how being intellectually stimulated was important to me, and (even worse) how it would tie to that critical factor of respect."

The Signal to Grow

It is a fact that like the other basic pillars of life, such as work and children, marriage is not always going to be a source of satisfaction. No one is loved perfectly; some part of our authentic self is never going to be met by a partner. Sure, you can always draw a curtain over your heart. But that is not the only or the best response.

"Sometimes marriage is going to be a source of pain and sorrow," says Givertz. "And that's necessary for personal and interpersonal growth." In fact, it's impossible to be deliriously happy in marriage every moment if you are doing anything at all challenging in life, whether raising children, starting a business, or taking care of an aging parent.

Disillusionment becomes an engine for growth because it forces us to discover our needs. Knowing oneself, recognizing one's needs, and speaking up for them in a relationship are often acts of bravery, says Page. Most of us are guarded about our needs, because they are typically our areas of greatest sensitivity and vulnerability.

"You have to discover—and be able to share—what touches you and moves you the most," he observes. "But first, of course, you have to accept that in yourself. Few of us are skilled at this essential process for creating passion and romance. We'd rather complain." Nevertheless, through this process, we clarify ourselves as we move through life.

At the same time, taking the risk to expose your inner life to your partner turns out to be the great opportunity for expanding intimacy and a sense of connection. This is the great power of relationships: Creating intimacy is the crucible for growing into a fully autonomous human being while the process of becoming a fully realized person expands the possibility for intimacy and connection. This is also the work that transforms a partner into the right partner.

Another crucial element of growth in relationships, says Givertz, is a transformation of motivation—away from self-centered preferences toward what is best for the relationship and its future. There is an intrapsychic change that sustains long-term relationships. Underlying it is a broadening process in which response patterns subtly shift. Accommodation (as opposed to retaliation) plays a role. So does sacrifice. So do willingness and ability to suppress an impulse to respond negatively to a negative provocation, no matter how personally satisfying it might feel in the moment. It requires the ability to hold in mind the long-term goals of the relationship. With motivation transformed, partners are more apt to take a moment to consider how to respond, rather than react reflexively in the heat of a moment.

In his most recent study of relationships, UCLA's Bradbury followed 136 couples for 10 years, starting within six months of their marriage. All the couples reported high levels of satisfaction at the start and four years later. What Bradbury and his colleague Justin Lavner found surprising was that some couples who were so satisfied at the four-year pass eventually divorced, despite having none of the risk factors identified in previous studies of relationship dissolution—wavering commitment, maladaptive personality traits, high levels of stress.

The only elements that identified those who eventually divorced were negative and self-protective reactions during discussions of relationship difficulties and nonsupportive reactions in discussing a personal issue. Displays of anger, contempt, or attempts to blame or invalidate a partner augured poorly, even when the partners felt their marriage was functioning well overall, the researchers report in the *Journal of Family Psychology.* So did expressions of discouragement toward a partner talking about a personality feature he or she wanted to change.

In other words, the inability or unwillingness to suppress negative emotions in the heat of the moment eliminates the possibility of a transformation of motivation to a broader perspective than one's own. Eventually, the cumulative impact of negative reactivity brings the relationship down.

"There is no such thing as two people meant for each other," says Michelle Givertz. "It's a matter of adjusting and adapting." But you have to know yourself so that you can get your needs for affection, inclusion, and control met in the ways that matter most for you. Even then, successful couples redefine their relationship many times, says Meinecke. Relationships need to continually evolve to fit ever-changing circumstances. They need to incorporate each partner's changes and find ways to meet their new needs.

"If both parties are willing to tackle the hard and vulnerable work of building love and healing conflict, they have a good chance to survive," says Page. If one party is reluctant, "you might need to say to your partner, 'I need this because I feel like we're losing each other, and I don't want that to happen.'"

In the end, says Minnesota's Doherty, "We're all difficult. Everyone who is married is a difficult spouse. We emphasize that our spouse is difficult and forget how we're difficult for them." If you want to have a mate in your life, he notes, you're going to have to go through the process of idealization and disillusionment—if not with your current partner then with the next. And the next. "You could really mess up your kids as you pursue the ideal mate." What's more, studies show that, on average, people do not make a better choice the second time around. Most often, people just trade one set of problems for another.

Boston's Real reports that he attended an anniversary party for friends who had been together 25 years. When someone commented on the longevity of the relationship, the husband replied: "Every morning I wake up, splash cold water on my face, and say out loud, 'Well, you're no prize either.'" While you're busy being disillusioned with your partner, Real suggests, you'll do better with a substantial dose of humility."

Critical Thinking

1. Is it "normal" to be discontented and disillusioned about your marriage and your partner?

2. What factors are most important to compatibility in relationships?

3. Does what bothers you about your relationship say more about you than your partner?

Create Central

www.mhhe.com/createcentral

Internet References

Coalition for Marriage, Family, and Couples Education
www.smartmarriages.com

National Council on Family Relations
www.ncfr.com

REBECCA WEBBER is a freelance writer based in New York.

Prepared by: Patricia Hrusa Williams,
University of Maine at Farmington

Article

How to Stay Married

Anne Kingston

Learning Outcomes

After reading this article, you will be able to:

- Explain how men's and women's views and expectations for relationships and marriage differ.

- Describe the reasons behind women's adulterous behavior.

- Understand factors important to marital longevity.

Cynthia is a 68-year-old woman in a 45-year "committed marriage" who has figured out how to keep it that way. Every other month or so she goes out to lunch with her college boyfriend Thomas, who is also married and has no intention of leaving his wife. Usually their outings end in a hot and heavy "petting session" in his Mercedes. Sometimes, he rubs Jean Naté lotion, the scent Cynthia wore in college, onto her legs and compliments her beautiful feet. They've never consummated their relationship, nor do they intend to. Being with Thomas is "like a balloon liftoff," Cynthia reports, one that eases some of the tensions between her and her 74-year-old physics professor husband. "I'm a nicer, more tolerant person because of this affair," she says.

Cynthia's story is one of more than 60 confessionals from long-time wives that punctuate Iris Krasnow's new book *The Secret Lives of Wives: Women Share What It Really Takes to Stay Married*. And what their stories reveal is that marital longevity requires wives to establish strong, separate identities from their husbands through creative coping mechanisms, some of them covert. Krasnow spoke with more than 200 women, married between 15 and 70 years, who report taking separate holidays, embarking on new careers, establishing a tight circle of female friends, dabbling in *Same Time, Next Year*-style liaisons and adulterous affairs, and having "boyfriends with boundaries." Yoga and white wine also feature predominately.

The 58-year-old Krasnow, an author and journalism professor at American University, writes she was "stunned by the secrets and shenanigans" in her journalistic journey through American marriages. She comes to the subject from the vantage point of her own 23-year marriage to an architect she loves but admits to "loathing" occasionally. She credits summers spent apart, separate hobbies and her close relationships with male buddies for some of their marital stability.

It's a theory that builds on her previous books, *Surrendering to Motherhood* and *Surrendering to Marriage*, which extol the virtues of sublimating the self to a higher ideal.

Krasnow embraces the modern expectation that individuals experience perpetual personal growth and reinvention but dismisses the notion that partners must share each of these stages: "The reality is that for many wives, attaining longevity requires getting growth spurts elsewhere and experimenting with alternative routes," she writes.

First, however, women must lower their expectations of what marriage can provide, she advises: "Wives who don't rely on their husbands for happiness end up having the happiest marriages." Speaking on her phone from her home in Maryland, she echoes the sentiment: "You have to be partners on the level of the soul," she says of marriage. "But you are your own soulmate. Everybody needs a source of passion and purpose within. When you have that you can make any relationship work. You're not depending on anyone else to make you happy."

Krasnow paints a rosy picture of what a long-lasting marriage can provide women—better health, a rich shared history, the comfort of having someone who has your back, and personal and economic stability amid global uncertainty. Many of her testimonials suggest marriages can be regenerated over time, like a liver, with longer-married couples reporting the greatest happiness of all. There's also practical considerations, writes Krasnow, who admits online dating or disrobing in front of someone new horrifies her.

The book is destined to strike a nerve at a time when expectations of marriage and divorce are under scrutiny. Both the marriage rate and the divorce rate are dropping, with the exception of "grey divorce" among people over 50, embodied by Al and Tipper Gore who split after 40 years of marriage. We're in the midst of a divorce backlash, fuelled by the conservative-marriage movement and books like Judith Wallerstein's *The Unexpected Legacy of Divorce*, which raised consciousness about how divorce fractures families. Krasnow rejects the popular notion that divorce offers an opportunity for reinvention, as propagated by the booming divorce memoir genre. We should call it what it is: "a failure," she writes.

Yet it's clear the old script doesn't fit at a time women are increasingly out-earning their husbands and people are living into their 80s. "Women want to redefine how they navigate marriage," Krasnow says.

And the happily-ever-after prescription she offers will resonate. Many of the women Krasnow interviewed are like her—educated, smart, with enough disposable income to spend summers painting in Italy or travelling to ashrams. Most have financial autonomy: even a woman in a traditional arranged marriage has a thriving career and a helpful husband who gives her her own "space."

The directive that couples should give each other "space" for marriages to thrive is far from new, of course. Krasnow quotes from Kahlil Gibran's *The Prophet*, "Let there be space in your togetherness," published in 1923. In 1929, Virginia Woolf famously wrote of the need for women to have "money and a room of one's own" to create art. In 1954, Anne Morrow Lindbergh, wife of Charles Lindbergh, wrote *Gift From the Sea* on a summer retreat from her husband and children, which espoused the importance of solitude and self-reflection for women. It was an instant bestseller. And Johnny Cash attributed part of the success of his 32-year union with June Carter Cash to separate bathrooms: "The lady needs her space," he said.

Yet that sentiment runs counter to a popular culture in thrall to a "happily ever after" fairy-tale narrative and the "you complete me" message espoused in the movie *Jerry Maguire*. It's precisely the disconnect between the expectation that husband and wife be everything to one another and the reality of marriage that causes women to keep secrets, says Susan Shapiro Barash, a professor of gender studies at Marymount Manhattan College whose books include *Little White Lies, Deep Dark Secrets: The Truth About Why Women Lie*.

As time goes on, she says a lot of women feel trapped and that they've grown apart. "But because the culture so endorses marriage as a means and an end—children, a family, a partner for life (at least 60 per cent of the time). When it doesn't, "it's sometimes such a rude awakening for women they cover it up. Longevity does not lend itself to living happily as a wife."

That's a problem in a society in which women over 80 are the fastest-growing demographic.

Krasnow's examples indicate the wives most likely to live happily ever after into old age are those who can carve happily ever after out for themselves. It's the next iteration of the wife script that has traditionally called for a wifely sacrifice.

"We are the caregivers, the softies, the gender programmed to take care of the needs of everybody else before we care for ourselves," writes Krasnow. As a respite, she describes going out with her female friends for freewheeling bimonthly dinners where she can let loose as the "unmom" and "unwife."

Krasnow quotes 77-year-old sex and relationship therapist Marilyn Charwat, who says the American standard of sexual morality—that you marry one person and stay sexually and emotionally true and connected to that person—is "inhumane and impossible."

Yet the book reflects a broad view that sexual secrecy in marriage is rampant, from a woman buoyed by the memory of a furtive kiss with a neighbour to long-term sexual liaisons.

Not that Krasnow is advocating infidelity, though flirting is fine: "I say ride that hormonal surge straight to your own bedroom and initiate great sex with your spouse," she writes. Charwat's advice is more practical. She recommends women use vibrators, which releases them from relationship "tyranny."

The infidelity chapter, in which Krasnow spoke to 14 women conducting affairs, is coyly titled "Naughty Girls," a sensibility reflected in the cautionary references to 19th-century fictional heroines Emma Bovary and Anna Karenina. In one cautionary story, which reinforces Krasnow's theory that women should stick with their marriages, Lucy leaves her husband for a man she met on a plane and regrets her mistake.

Unlike husbands, wives are driven to extramarital affairs not as a way of exiting their marriage but remaining in them. One woman says her husband's sexual unresponsiveness justified her cheating. Mimi, a Lilly Pulitzer-wearing, 57-year-old conservative who's a secret swinger with her husband, practises an odd form of monogamy by saying he is the only man able to bring her to orgasm.

Shapiro Barash, who explored adultery in *A Passion for More: Wives Reveal the Affairs That Make or Break Their Marriages*, agrees unrealistic expectations usually fuel adultery. "The affair is always about what's missing from a marriage. I have rarely heard a woman speak of her lover being similar to her husband."

Krasnow's husband isn't a talker, so she craves extramarital conversation, not sex, a need sated by her various "boyfriends with boundaries." But seeking male friendship can be more fraught with peril than sexual affairs, the book reveals. One woman interviewed felt compelled to lie about her intense platonic relationship with a man; when her husband found out, he created a scene and demanded she never see him again. Krasnow admits there can be "danger zones": such as when participants text each other every 20 minutes. "Any man in my life, I immediately make sure my husband meets him."

What Krasnow is providing is a much-needed middle-aged fairy tale that begins years after the prince grows a paunch. Her prescriptions are both surprisingly banal and brilliant sound bites. "The real secret to staying married is not getting divorced," Krasnow writes, in a tautology. Save abuse or serial adultery, every marriage is salvageable with a big caveat that there's "trust, respect and intimacy, both emotional and physical."

As long as there's "a spittle of love," there's hope, she writes. Shelley, a woman whose marriage survived her husband's affair with her best friend, blames the woman more than her husband in a telling statement: "There's something sacred with the bond of women."

Then there's 48-year-old Julia, locked in a marriage "bound by the endless need" of her seriously ill daughter, who craves an "equal partner" but feels her husband is giving up. Her solution is to take up painting.

The focus on personal happiness would seem at odds with the notion espoused in Krasnow's other books. It's a perspective voiced by Phil and Pat Denniston, a happily married California couple even though they live and work together 24-7. They speak about the risks of separate directions and observe that marriages in which participants speak in terms of "me" not "us" are doomed.

In order to get to the happy "us," it's up to the wife to make the right choices from the get-go, Krasnow writes. She recalls she once asked Barbara Bush senior the secret to a happy marriage: "Pick the right husband in the first place."

The author agrees. "You should marry someone who's flexible, confident and trusts you: if you can't count on your husband or wife in a crazy unstable world then you're marrying the wrong person. But if you do marry the wrong person, you can always fall back on your secret life."

Critical Thinking

1. What do we hope to gain from getting married?

2. How do men's and women's views of marriage differ?

3. In *The Secret Lives of Women: What It Really Takes to Stay Married,* Iris Krasnow suggests that women need to lower their expectations of what marriage can provide. Do you agree or disagree? Why?

4. Is it a reasonable expectation in marriage to find someone who "completes you?"

Create Central

www.mhhe.com/createcentral

Internet References

Coalition for Marriage, Family, and Couples Education
www.smartmarriages.com

National Council on Family Relations
www.ncfr.com

Article   Prepared by: Patricia Hrusa Williams, *University of Maine at Farmington*

The Gay Guide to Wedded Bliss

Research finds that same-sex unions are happier than heterosexual marriages. What can gay and lesbian couples teach straight ones about living in harmony?

LIZA MUNDY

Learning Outcomes

After reading this article, you will be able to:

- Define the Defense of Marriage Act.

- Explain trends in marriage in the United States.

- Identify and discuss the role which gender plays in couple's relationships and marital unions.

I t is more than a little ironic that gay marriage has emerged as the era's defining civil-rights struggle even as marriage itself seems more endangered every day. Americans are waiting longer to marry: according to the U.S. Census Bureau, the median age of first marriage is 28 for men and 26 for women, up from 23 and 20, respectively, in 1950. Rates of cohabitation have risen swiftly and sharply, and more people than ever are living single. Most Americans still marry at some point, but many of those marriages end in divorce. (Although the U.S. divorce rate has declined from its all-time high in the late '70s and early '80s, it has remained higher than those of most European countries.) All told, this has created an unstable system of what the UCLA sociologist Suzanne Bianchi calls "partnering and repartnering," a relentless emotional and domestic churn that sometimes results in people forgoing the institution altogether.

[. . .]

College graduates enjoy relatively stable unions, but for every other group, marriage is collapsing. Among "middle American" women (those with a high-school degree or some college), an astonishing 58 percent of first-time mothers are unmarried. The old Groucho Marx joke—"I don't care to belong to any club that will have me as a member"—applies a little differently in this context: you might well ask why gays and lesbians want to join an institution that keeps dithering about whether to admit them even as the repo men are coming for the furniture and the fire marshal is about to close down the clubhouse.

Against this backdrop, gay-marriage opponents have argued that allowing same-sex couples to wed will pretty much finish matrimony off. This point was advanced in briefs and oral arguments before the Supreme Court in March, in two major same-sex-marriage cases. One of these is a constitutional challenge to a key section of the Defense of Marriage Act, the 1996 law that defines marriage as a union between a man and a woman, and bars the federal government from recognizing same-sex marriages. The other involves California's Proposition 8, a same-sex-marriage ban passed by voters in 2008 but overturned by a federal judge in 2010. Appearing before the high court in March, Charles J. Cooper, the lawyer defending the California ban, predicted that same-sex marriage would undermine traditional marriage by eroding "marital norms."

The belief that gay marriage will harm marriage has roots in both religious beliefs about matrimony and secular conservative concerns about broader shifts in American life. One prominent line of thinking holds that men and women have distinct roles to play in family life; that children need both a mother and a father, preferably biologically related to them; and that a central purpose of marriage is abetting heterosexual procreation. During the Supreme Court arguments over Proposition 8, Justice Elena Kagan asked Cooper whether the essence of his argument against gay marriage was that opposite-sex couples can procreate while same-sex ones cannot. "That's the essential thrust of our position, yes," replied Cooper. He also warned that "redefining marriage as a genderless institution could well lead over time to harms to that institution."

Threaded through this thinking is a related conviction that mothers and fathers should treat their union as "permanent and exclusive," as the Princeton professor Robert P. George and his co-authors write in the new book *What Is Marriage? Man and Woman: A Defense.* Marriage, seen this way, is a rigid institution that exists primarily for the rearing of children and that powerfully constrains the behavior of adults (one is tempted to call this the "long slog 'til death" view of marriage), rather than an emotional union entered into for pleasure and companionship between adults. These critics of gay marriage are, quite validly, worried that too many American children are being raised in unstable homes, either by struggling single parents or by a transient succession of live-in adults. They fear that the spread of gay marriage could help finally sever the increasingly tenuous link between children and marriage, confirming that it's okay for dads, or moms, to be deleted from family life as hedonic fulfillment dictates.

In mounting their defense, advocates of same-sex marriage have argued that gays and lesbians who wish to marry are committed to family well-being; that concern for children's welfare is a chief reason many do want to marry; that gay people are being discriminated against, as a class, in being denied rights readily available to any heterosexual. And to the charge that same-sex marriage will change marriage, they tend to argue that it will not—that married gays and lesbians will blend seamlessly with the millions of married straight Americans. "The notion that this group can somehow fundamentally change the institution of marriage—I find it difficult to wrap my head around," says Gary Gates, a demographer with the Williams Institute, a research center affiliated with the UCLA School of Law.

But what if the critics are correct, just not in the way they suppose? What if same-sex marriage does change marriage, but primarily for the better? For one thing, there is reason to think that, rather than making marriage more fragile, the boom of publicity around same-sex weddings could awaken among heterosexuals a new interest in the institution, at least for a time. But the larger change might be this: by providing a new model of how two people can live together equitably, same-sex marriage could help haul matrimony more fully into the 21st century. Although marriage is in many ways fairer and more pleasurable for both men and women than it once was, it hasn't entirely thrown off old notions and habits. As a result, many men and women enter into it burdened with assumptions and stereotypes that create stress and resentment. Others, confronted with these increasingly anachronistic expectations— expectations at odds with the economic and practical realities of their own lives—don't enter into it at all.

Same-sex spouses, who cannot divide their labor based on preexisting gender norms, must approach marriage differently than their heterosexual peers. From sex to fighting, from child-rearing to chores, they must hammer out every last detail of domestic life without falling back on assumptions about who will do what. In this regard, they provide an example that can be enlightening to all couples. Critics warn of an institution rendered "genderless." But if a genderless marriage is a marriage in which the wife is not automatically expected to be responsible for school forms and child care and dinner preparation and birthday parties and midnight feedings and holiday shopping, I think it's fair to say that many heterosexual women would cry "Bring it on!"

Beyond that, gay marriage can function as a controlled experiment, helping us see which aspects of marital difficulty are truly rooted in gender and which are not. A growing body of social science has begun to compare straight and same-sex couples in an attempt to get at the question of what is female, what is male. Some of the findings are surprising. For instance: we know that heterosexual wives are more likely than husbands to initiate divorce. Social scientists have struggled to explain the discrepancy, variously attributing it to the sexual revolution; to women's financial independence; to men's failure to keep modern wives happy. Intriguingly, in Norway and Sweden, where registered partnerships for same-sex couples have been in place for about two decades (full-fledged marriage was introduced several years ago), research has found that lesbians are twice as likely as gay men to split up. If women become dissatisfied even when married to other women, maybe the problem with marriage isn't men. Maybe women are too particular. Maybe even women don't know what women want. These are the kinds of things that we will be able to tease out.

[. . .]

Whatever happens with the high court, it seems likely that gay marriage will continue its spread through the land. So what happens, then, to the institution of marriage? The impact is likely to be felt near and far, both fleetingly and more permanently, in ways confounding to partisans on both sides.

Rules for a More Perfect Union

Not all is broken within modern marriage, of course. On the contrary: the institution is far more flexible and forgiving than it used to be. In the wake of women's large-scale entry into the workplace, men are less likely than they once were to be saddled with being a family's sole breadwinner, and can carve out a life that includes the close companionship of their children. Meanwhile, women are less likely to be saddled with the sole responsibility for child care and housework, and can envision a life beyond the stove top and laundry basket.

And yet for many couples, as Bianchi, the UCLA sociologist, has pointed out, the modern ideal of egalitarianism has proved "quite difficult to realize." Though men are carrying more of a domestic workload than in the past, women still bear the brunt of the second shift. Among couples with children, when both spouses work full-time, women do 32 hours a week of housework, child care, shopping, and other family-related services, compared with the 21 hours men put in. Men do more paid work—45 hours, compared with 39 for women—but still have more free time: 31 hours, compared with 25 for women. Betsey Stevenson and Justin Wolfers, economists and professors of public policy at the University of Michigan, have shown that happiness rates among women have dropped even as women have acquired more life options. One possible cause is the lingering inequity in male-female marriage: women's at-home workload can become so burdensome that wives opt out of the paid workforce—or sit at the office making mental lists of the chores they do versus the chores their husbands do, and bang their heads on their desks in despair.

Not that everything is easy for fathers in dual-earner couples, who now feel afflicted by work-life conflict in even greater numbers than their wives (60 percent of men in such couples say they experience this conflict, versus 47 percent of women, according to a 2008 study by the Families and Work Institute). And men face a set of unfair expectations all their own: the Pew Research Center found in 2010 that 67 percent of Americans still believe it's "very important" that a man be ready to support a family before getting married, while only 33 percent believe the same about women.

This burden, exacerbated by the economic realities facing many men today, has undoubtedly contributed to marriage's recent decline. As our economy has transitioned away from manufacturing and industry, men with a high-school education can no longer expect the steady, well-paying union jobs that formerly enabled many to support their families. Outdated assumptions that men should bring something to the table, and that this something should be money, don't help. Surveying their prospects, many working-class mothers reject marriage altogether, perhaps reasoning that they can support a child, but don't want a dependent husband.

It's not that people don't want to marry. Most never-married Americans say they still aspire to marriage, but many of them see it as something grand and out of reach. Getting married is no longer something you do when you are young and foolish and starting out; prosperity is not something spouses build together. Rather, marriage has become a "marker of prestige," as the sociologist Andrew Cherlin puts it—a capstone of a successful life, rather than its cornerstone. But while many couples have concluded that they are not ready for marriage, they have things backwards. It's not that they aren't ready for marriage; it's that marriage isn't ready for the realities of 21st-century life. Particularly for less affluent, less educated Americans, changing economic and gender realities have dismantled the old institution, without constructing any sort of replacement.

As we attempt to come up with a more functional model, research on same-sex unions can provide what Gary Gates of the Williams Institute calls an "important counterfactual." Although gays and lesbians cannot solve all that ails marriage, they seem to be working certain things out in ways straight couples might do well to emulate, chief among them a back-to-the-drawing-board approach to divvying up marital duties. A growing body of scholarship on household division of labor shows that in many ways, same-sex couples do it better.

This scholarship got its start in the late 1960s, with a brilliant insight by the sociologist Pepper Schwartz. [. . .] Like many of her peers, she was keen to figure out what women were and what men were: which traits were biological and which social, and where there might be potential for transformational change. "It occurred to me," she says, that "a naturally occurring experiment" could shed light on these issues. Actually, two experiments: the rise of unmarried heterosexual cohabitation, and the growing visibility of gay and lesbian couples. If she surveyed people in three kinds of relationships—married; straight and cohabiting; and gay and cohabiting—and all showed similarity on some measures, maybe this would say something about both men and women. If the findings didn't line up, maybe this would say something about marriage.

After taking a teaching position at the University of Washington (where she remains a faculty member), Schwartz teamed up with a gay colleague, the late Philip Blumstein, to conduct just such a survey, zeroing in on the greater San Francisco, New York City, and Seattle metropolitan areas. It was a huge effort. Unmarried cohabiting couples were not yet easy to find, and gays and lesbians were so leery of being outed that when Schwartz asked a woman who belonged to a lesbian bridge group whether she could interview the other players about their relationships, the woman said, "We don't even talk about it ourselves." Schwartz and Blumstein collected responses to 12,000 questionnaires and conducted hundreds of interviews; at one point, they had 20 graduate students helping tabulate data. The project took about a decade, and resulted in a groundbreaking piece of sociology, the book *American Couples: Money, Work, Sex*.

What Schwartz and Blumstein found is that gay and lesbian couples were fairer in their dealings with one another than straight couples, both in intent and in practice. The lesbians in the study were almost painfully egalitarian—in some cases putting money in jars and splitting everything down to the penny in a way, Schwartz says, that "would have driven me crazy." Many unmarried heterosexual cohabitators were also careful about divvying things up, but lesbian couples seemed to take the practice to extremes: "It was almost like 'my kitty, your litter.'" Gay men, like lesbians, were more likely than straight couples to share cooking and chores. Many had been in heterosexual marriages, and when asked whether they had helped their wives with the housework in those prior unions, they usually said they had not. "You can imagine," Schwartz says, "how irritating I found this."

There were still some inequities: in all couples, the person with the higher income had more authority and decision-making power. This was least true for lesbians; truer for heterosexuals; and most true for gay men. Somehow, putting two men together seemed to intensify the sense that "money talks," as Schwartz and Blumstein put it. They could not hope to determine whether this tendency was innate or social—were men naturally inclined to equate resources with power, or had our culture ingrained that idea in them?—but one way or another, the finding suggested that money was a way men competed with other men, and not just a way for husbands to compete with their wives. Among lesbians, the contested terrain lay elsewhere: for instance, interacting more with the children could be, Schwartz says, a "power move."

Lesbians also tended to discuss things endlessly, achieving a degree of closeness unmatched by the other types of couples. Schwartz wondered whether this might account for another finding: over time, sex in lesbian relationships dwindled—a state of affairs she has described as "lesbian bed death." [. . .] She posits that lesbians may have had so much intimacy already that they didn't need sex to get it; by contrast, heterosexual women, whose spouses were less likely to be chatty, found that "sex is a highway to intimacy." As for men, she eventually concluded that whether they were straight or gay, they approached sex as they might a sandwich: good, bad, or mediocre, they were likely to grab it.

RULE 1: Negotiate in advance who will empty the trash and who will clean the bathroom. Other studies have since confirmed Schwartz and Blumstein's findings that same-sex couples are more egalitarian. In 2000, when Vermont became the first state to legalize same-sex civil unions, the psychologist Esther Rothblum saw an opportunity to explore how duties get sorted among a broad swath of the same-sex population. Rothblum, now at San Diego State University, is herself a lesbian and had long been interested in the relationships and mental health of lesbians. She also wanted to see how legal recognition affected couples.

As people from around the country flocked to Vermont to apply for civil-union licenses, Rothblum and two colleagues got their names and addresses from public records and asked them to complete a questionnaire. Then, they asked each of the civil-union couples to suggest friends in same-sex couples who were not in civil unions, and to identify a heterosexual sibling who was married, and wrote those people asking them to participate. This approach helped control for factors like background and upbringing among the subjects. The researchers asked people to rate, on a scale of one to nine, which partner was

more likely to do the dishes, repair things around the house, buy groceries. They asked who was more likely to deal with the landlord, punish the children, call the plumber, drive the kids to appointments, give spontaneous hugs, pay compliments. They also asked who was more likely to appreciate the other person's point of view during an argument.

They found that, even in the new millennium, married heterosexual couples were very likely to divide duties along old-fashioned gender lines. Straight women were more likely than lesbians to report that their partner paid the mortgage or the rent and the utility bills, and bought groceries, household appliances, even the women's clothing. These wives were also more likely to say they did the bulk of the cooking, vacuuming, dishes, and laundry. Compared with their husbands, they were far, far more likely to clean the bathroom. They were also more likely than their husbands to perform "relationship maintenance" such as showing affection and initiating serious conversations. When Rothblum and her colleagues held the heterosexual husbands up against the gay men, they found the same pattern. The straight guys were more likely to take care of the lawn, empty the trash, and make household repairs than their partners. They were the ones to fix drinks for company and to drive when the couple went out. They cooked breakfast reasonably often, but not dinner. On all these measures and more, the same-sex couples were far more likely to divide responsibilities evenly. This is not to say that the same-sex couples split each duty half-and-half. One partner might do the same chore regularly, but because there was no default assignment based on gender, such patterns evolved organically, based on preferences and talents.

Rothblum's observations are borne out by the couples I interviewed for this piece. "I'm a better cook, so I take on most of that responsibility," said Seth Thayer, who lives in a small coastal town in Maine. His husband, Greg Tinder, "is a better handyman." Others spoke of the perils of lopsided relationships. Chris Kast, a Maine newlywed, told me that he and his husband, Byron Bartlett, had both been married to women. In Bartlett's first marriage, it was tacitly assumed that he would take out the garbage. Now the two men divide tasks by inclination. "I'm more of a Felix Ungar—I notice when something's dirty—but we both clean," Kast said. "With Chris and I," Bartlett added, "we have to get *everything* done." Isabelle Dikland, a Washington, D.C., business consultant who is married to Amy Clement, a teacher, told me about a dinner party she recently attended with a group of mostly straight parents. Dikland and Clement, who had just had a second daughter, were extolling the virtues of having two children. The straight mother they were talking with seemed dubious, "if we had a second kid, guess who would do all the work," she told them. "I'd have to give up my career; I'm already doing everything." The woman glanced surreptitiously at her husband, at which point Dikland "dropped the subject really quickly."

RULE 2: When it comes to parenting, a 50-50 split isn't necessarily best. Charlotte J. Patterson, a psychologist at the University of Virginia, has arresting visual evidence of the same egalitarianism at work in parenting: compared with husband-and-wife pairs, she has found, same-sex parents tend to be more cooperative and mutually hands-on. Patterson and a colleague, Rachel Farr, have conducted a study of more than 100 same-sex and heterosexual adoptive parents in 11 states and the District of Columbia; it is among the first such studies to include gay fathers. As reported in an article in a forthcoming issue of the journal *Child Development*, the researchers visited families in their homes, scattered some toys on a blanket, invited the subjects to play with them any way they chose, and videotaped the interactions. "What you see is what they did with that blank slate," Patterson says. "One thing that I found riveting: the same-sex couples are far more likely to be in there together, and the opposite-sex couples show the conventional pattern—the mom more involved, the dad playing with Tinkertoys by himself." When the opposite-sex couples did parent simultaneously, they were more likely to undermine each other by talking at cross-purposes or suggesting different toys. The lesbian mothers tended to be egalitarian and warm in their dealings with one another, and showed greater pleasure in parenting than the other groups did. Same-sex dads were also more egalitarian in their division of labor than straight couples, though not as warm or interactive as lesbian moms. (Patterson says she and her colleagues may need to refine their analysis to take into account male ways of expressing warmth.)

By and large, all of the families studied, gay and straight alike, were happy, high functioning, and financially secure. Each type of partner—gay, straight; man, woman—reported satisfaction with his or her family's parenting arrangement, though the heterosexual wife was less content than the others, invariably saying that she wanted more help from her husband. "Of all the parents we've studied, she's the least satisfied with the division of labor," says Patterson, who is in a same-sex partnership and says she knows from experience that deciding who will do what isn't always easy.

Even as they are more egalitarian in their parenting styles, same-sex parents resemble their heterosexual counterparts in one somewhat old-fashioned way: a surprising number establish a division of labor whereby one spouse becomes the primary earner and the other stays home. Lee Badgett, an economist at the University of Massachusetts at Amherst, told me that, "in terms of economics," same-sex couples with children resemble heterosexual couples with children much more than they resemble childless same-sex couples. You might say that gay parents are simultaneously departing from traditional family structures and leading the way back toward them.

In his seminal book *A Treatise on the Family*, published in 1981, the Nobel Prize–winning economist Gary Becker argued that "specialization," whereby one parent stays home and the other does the earning, is the most efficient way of running a household, because the at-home spouse enables the at-work spouse to earn more. Feminists, who had been fighting for domestic parity, not specialization, deplored this theory, rightly fearing that it could be harnessed to keep women at home. Now the example of gay and lesbian parents might give us all permission to relax a little: maybe sometimes it really is easier when one parent works and the other is the supplementary or nonearning partner, either because this is the natural order of things or because the American workplace is so greedy and unforgiving that something or somebody has to give. As Martha Ertman, a University of Maryland law professor, put it to me, many families just function better when the same person is consistently "in charge of making vaccinations happen, making sure the model of the World War II monument gets done, getting the Christmas tree home or the challah bought by 6 o'clock on Friday." The good news is that the decision about which parent plays this role need not have anything to do with gender.

More surprising still, guess who is most likely to specialize. Gay dads. Using the most recent Census Bureau data, Gary Gates found that 32 percent of married heterosexual couples with children have only one parent in the labor force, compared with 33 percent of gay-male couples with children. (Lesbians also specialize, but not at such high rates, perhaps because they are so devoted to equality, or perhaps because their earnings are lower—women's median wage is 81 percent that of men—and not working is an unaffordable luxury.) While the percentage point dividing gay men from straight couples is not statistically significant, it's intriguing that gay dads are as likely as straight women to be stay-at-home parents.

Gay men's decisions about breadwinning can nonetheless be fraught, as many associate employment with power. A study published in the *Journal of GLBT Family Studies* in 2005 by Stephanie Jill Schacher and two colleagues found that when gay men do specialize, they don't have an easy time deciding who will do what: some stay-at-home dads perceived that their choice carried with it a loss in prestige and stature. As a result, gay men tended to fight not over who got to stay home, but over who didn't have to. "It's probably the biggest problem in our relationship," said one man interviewed for that study. Perhaps what Betty Friedan called "the problem that has no name" is inherent in child-rearing, and will always be with us.

RULE 3: Don't want a divorce? Don't marry a woman. Three years after they first gathered information from the couples who received licenses in Vermont, Esther Rothblum and her colleagues checked back to evaluate the condition of their relationships. Overall, the researchers found that the quality of gay and lesbian relationships was higher on many measures than that of the straight control group (the married heterosexual siblings), with more compatibility and intimacy, and less conflict.

Which is not to say same-sex couples don't have conflict. When they fight, however, they fight fairer. They can even fight funny, as researchers from the University of Washington and the University of California at Berkeley showed in an article published in 2003, based on a study of couples who were navigating potentially tense interactions. Recruiting married straight couples as well as gays and lesbians in committed relationships, the researchers orchestrated a scenario in which one partner had to bring up an area of conflict to discuss with the other. In same-sex couples, the partner with the bone to pick was rated "less belligerent and less domineering" than the straight-couple counterpart, while the person on the receiving end was less aggressive and showed less fear or tension. The same-sex "initiator" also displayed less sadness and "whining," and more affection, joy, and humor. In trying to make sense of the disparity, the researchers noted that same-sex couples valued equality more, and posited that the greater negativity of straight couples "may have to do with the standard status hierarchy between men and women." Which perhaps boils down to something like this: straight women see themselves as being less powerful than men, and this breeds hostility.

When it comes to conflict, a crucial variable separates many gay and lesbian couples from their straight counterparts: children. As Rothblum points out, for married heterosexual parents, happiness tends to be U-shaped: high at the beginning of marriage, then dipping to a low, then high again. What happens in that low middle is child-rearing. Although the proportion of gay and lesbian couples with children is increasing, same-sex couples are still less likely than straight couples to be parents. Not all research comparing same-sex and married straight couples has done an adequate job of controlling for this important difference. One that did, a 2008 study in the *Journal of Family Psychology*, looked at couples during their first 10 years of cohabitation. It found that childless lesbians had a higher "relationship quality" than their child-free gay-male and heterosexual counterparts. And yet a 2010 study in the same journal found that gay-male, lesbian, and straight couples alike experienced a "modest decline in relationship quality" in the first year of adopting a child. As same-sex couples become parents in greater numbers, they could well endure some of the same strife as their straight peers. It remains to be seen whether the different parenting styles identified by Charlotte Patterson might blunt some of the ennui of child-rearing.

As for divorce, the data are still coming in. A 2006 study of Sweden and Norway found higher dissolution rates among same-sex couples in registered partnerships than among married straight people. Yet in the United States, a study by the Williams Institute has found that gay unions have lower dissolution rates than straight ones. It is simply too soon to tell

with any certainty whether gay marriages will be more or less durable in the long run than straight ones. What the studies to date do (for the most part) suggest is this: despite—or maybe because of—their perfectionist approach to egalitarianism, lesbian couples seem to be more likely to break up than gay ones. Pepper Schwartz noted this in the early 1980s, as did the 2006 study of same-sex couples in Sweden and Norway, in which researchers speculated that women may have a "stronger general sensitivity to the quality of relationships." Meaning maybe women are just picky, and when you have two women, you have double the pickiness. So perhaps the real threat to marriage is: women.

The Contagion Effect

Whatever this string of studies may teach us about marriage and gender dynamics, the next logical question becomes this: Might such marriages do more than merely inform our understanding of straight marriage—might their attributes trickle over to straight marriage in some fashion?

In the course of my reporting this year in states that had newly legalized same-sex marriage, people in the know—wedding planners, officiants, fiancés and fiancées—told me time and again that nuptial fever had broken out around them, among gay and straight couples alike. Same-sex weddings seemed to be bestowing a new frisson on the idea of getting hitched, or maybe restoring an old one. At the Gay and Lesbian Wedding Expo in downtown Baltimore, just a few weeks after same-sex marriage became legal in Maryland, Drew Vanlandingham, who describes himself as a "wedding planner designer," was delighted at how business had picked up. Here it was, January, and many of his favorite venues were booked into late summer—much to the consternation, he said, of his straight brides. "They're like, 'I better get a move on!'" It was his view that in Maryland, both teams were now engaged in an amiable but spirited race to the altar.

Ministers told me of wedding booms in their congregations. In her years as the pastor of the Unitarian church in Rockville, Maryland, Lynn Strauss said she had grown accustomed to a thin wedding roster: some years she might perform one or two services; other years, none. But this year, "my calendar is full of weddings," she said. "Two in March, one in April, one in May, one in September, one in October—oh, and one in July." Three were same-sex weddings, but the rest were heterosexual. When I attended the church's first lesbian wedding, in early March, I spoke with Steve Greene and Ellen Rohan, who had recently been married by Strauss. It was Steve's third marriage, Ellen's second. Before he met Ellen, Steve had sworn he would never marry again. Ellen said the arrival of same-sex marriage had influenced their feelings. "Marriage," she said simply, "is on everyone's mind."

Robert M. Hardies, who is a pastor at the Unitarian All Souls Church in Washington, D.C., and who is engaged to be married to his longtime partner and co-parent, Chris Nealon, told me that he has seen "a re-enchantment of marriage" among those who attend same-sex ceremonies: "Straight folks come to [same-sex] weddings, and I watch it on their face—there's a feeling that this is really special. Suddenly marriage is sexy again." We could chalk these anecdotes up to the human desire to witness love that overcomes obstacles—the same desire behind all romantic comedies, whether Shakespeare's or Hollywood's. But could something a bit less romantic also be at work?

There is some reason to suppose that attitudes about marriage could, in fact, be catching. The phenomenon known as "social contagion" lies at the heart of an increasingly prominent line of research on how our behavior and emotions affect the people we know. One famous example dates from 2008, when James H. Fowler and Nicholas A. Christakis published a study showing that happiness "spreads" through social networks. They arrived at this conclusion via an ingenious crunching of data from a long-running medical study involving thousands of interconnected residents—and their children, and later their grandchildren—in Framingham, Massachusetts. "Emotional states can be transferred directly from one individual to another," they found, across three degrees of separation. Other studies have shown that obesity, smoking habits, and school performance may also be catching.

Most relevant, in a working paper that is under submission to a sociology journal, the Brown University political scientist Rose McDermott, along with her co-authors, Fowler and Christakis, has identified a contagion effect for divorce. Divorce, she found, can spread among friends. She told me that she also suspects that tending to the marriages of friends can help preserve your own. McDermott says she readily sees how marriage could itself be contagious. Intriguingly, some of the Scandinavian countries where same-sex unions have been legal for a decade or more have seen a rise, not a fall, in marriage rates. In response to conservative arguments that same-sex marriage had driven a stake through the heart of marriage in northern Europe, the Yale University law professor William N. Eskridge Jr. and Darren Spedale in 2006 published an analysis showing that in the decade since same-sex partnerships became legal, heterosexual marriage rates had increased 10.7 percent in Denmark, 12.7 percent in Norway, and 28.8 percent in Sweden. Divorce rates had dropped in all three countries. Although there was no way to prove cause and effect, the authors allowed, you could safely say that marriage had not been harmed.

So let's suppose for a moment that marital behavior is catching. How, exactly, might it spread? I found one possible vector of contagion inside the Washington National Cathedral, a neo-Gothic landmark that towers watchfully over the Washington, D.C., skyline. The seat of the bishop of an Episcopal diocese that includes D.C. and parts of Maryland, the cathedral is a symbol of American religious life, and strives to provide a spiritual home for the nation, frequently hosting interfaith events and programs. Presiding over it is the Very Reverend Gary Hall, an Episcopal priest and the cathedral's dean. Earlier this year, Hall announced that the cathedral would conduct same-sex weddings, a declaration that attracted more attention than he expected. Only people closely involved with the church and graduates of the private schools on its grounds can marry there. Even so, it is an influential venue, and Hall used the occasion to argue that same-sex couples offer an image of "radical" equality that straight couples can profitably emulate. He believes, moreover, that their example can be communicated through intermediaries like him: ministers and counselors gleaning insights from same-sex couples, and transmitting them, as it were, to straight ones. Hall says that counseling same-sex couples in preparation for their ceremonies has already altered the way he counsels men and women.

"I have a list of like 12 issues that people need to talk about that cause conflict," said Hall, who is lanky, with short gray hair and horn-rims, and who looks like he could be a dean of pretty much anything: American literature, political philosophy, East Asian studies. As we talked in his office one morning this spring, sunlight poured through a bank of arched windows onto an Oriental rug. Over the years, he has amassed a collection of cheesy 1970s paperbacks with names like *Open Marriage* and *Total Woman*, which he calls "books that got people into trouble." The dean grew up in Hollywood, and in the 1990s was a priest at a church in Pasadena where he did many same-sex blessings (a blessing being a ceremony that stops short of legal marriage). He is as comfortable talking about Camille Paglia and the LGBT critique of marriage as he is about Holy Week. He is also capable of saying things like "The problem with genital sex is that it involves us emotionally in a way that we're not in control of."

When Hall sees couples for premarital preparation, he gives them a list of hypothetical conflicts to take home, hash out, and report back on. Everybody fights, he tells them. The people who thrive in marriage are the ones who can handle disagreement and make their needs known. So he presents them with the prime sticking points: affection and lovemaking; how to deal with in-laws; where holidays will be spent; outside friendships. He talks to them about parenting roles, and chores, and money—who will earn it and who will make decisions about it.

Like Esther Rothblum, he has found that heterosexual couples persist in approaching these topics with stereotypical assumptions. "You start throwing out questions for men and women: 'Who's going to take care of the money?' And the guy says, 'That's me.' And you ask: 'Who's responsible for birth control?' And the guy says, 'That's her department.'" By contrast, he reports, same-sex couples "have thought really hard about how they're going to share the property, the responsibilities, the obligations in a mutual way. They've had to devote much more thought to that than straight couples, because the straight couples pretty much still fall back on old modes."

Now when Hall counsels heterosexuals, "I'm really pushing back on their patriarchal assumptions: that the woman's got to give up her career for the guy; that the guy is going to take care of the money." Every now and then, he says, he has a breakthrough, and a straight groom realizes that, say, contraception is his concern too. Hall says the same thing is happening in the offices of any number of pastors, rabbis, and therapists. "You're not going to be able to talk to heterosexual couples where there's a power imbalance and talk to a homosexual couple where there is a power mutuality," and not have the conversations impact one another. As a result, he believes there will be changes to marriage, changes that some people will find scary. "When [conservatives] say that gay marriage threatens my marriage, I used to say, 'That's ridiculous.' Now I say, 'Yeah, it does. It's asking you a crucial question about your marriage that you may not want to answer: If I'm a man, am I actually sharing the duties and responsibilities of married life equally with my wife?' Same-sex marriage gives us another image of what marriage can be."

Hall argues that same-sex marriage stands to change even the wedding service itself. For a good 1,000 years, he notes, the Christian Church stayed out of matrimony, which was primarily a way for society to regulate things like inheritance. But ever since the Church did get involved, the wedding ceremony has tended to reflect the gender mores of the time. For example, the Book of Common Prayer for years stated that a wife must love, honor, and obey her husband, treating him as her master and lord. That language is long gone, but vestiges persist: the tradition of the father giving away the bride dates from an era when marriage was a property transfer and the woman was the property. In response to the push for same-sex marriage, Hall says, the General Convention, the governing council of the entire Episcopal Church, has devised a liturgy for same-sex ceremonies (in most dioceses, these are blessings) that honors but alters this tradition so that both spouses are presented by sponsors.

"The new service does not ground marriage in a doctrine of creation and procreation," Hall says. "It grounds marriage in a kind of free coming-together of two people to live out their lives." A study group has convened to look at the Church's teachings on marriage, and in the next couple of years, Hall expects, the General Convention will adopt a new service for all Episcopal weddings. He is hopeful that the current same-sex service will serve as its basis.

The legalization of same-sex marriage is likely to affect even members of churches that have not performed such ceremonies. Delman Coates, the pastor of Mt. Ennon Baptist, a predominantly African American mega-church in southern Maryland, was active in his state's fight for marriage equality, presenting it to his parishioners as a civil-rights issue. The topic has also led to some productive, if difficult, conversations about "what the Scriptures are condemning and what they're confirming." In particular, he has challenged his flock over what he calls the "typical clobber passages": certain verses in Leviticus, Romans, and elsewhere that many people interpret as condemnations of homosexuality. These discussions are part of a long-standing effort to challenge people's thinking about other passages having to do with divorce and premarital sex—issues many parishioners have struggled with at home. Coates preaches that what the Bible is condemning is not modern divorce, but a practice, common in biblical times, whereby men cast out their wives for no good reason. Similarly, he tells them that the "fornication" invoked is something extreme—rape, incest, prostitution. He does not condone illicit behavior or familial dissolution, but he wants the members of his congregation to feel better about their own lives. In exchanges like these, he is making gay marriage part of a much larger conversation about the way we live and love now.

Gay marriage's ripples are also starting to be felt beyond churches, in schools and neighborhoods and playgroups. Which raises another question: Will gay and lesbian couples be peacemakers or combatants in the "mommy wars"—the long-simmering struggle between moms who stay at home and moms who work outside it? If you doubt that straight households are paying attention to same-sex ones, consider Danie, a woman who lives with her husband and two children in Bethesda, Maryland. (Danie asked me not to use her last name out of concern for her family's privacy.) Not long after she completed a master's degree in Spanish linguistics at Georgetown University, her first baby was born. Because her husband, Jesse, works long hours as a litigator, she decided to become a full-time parent—not an easy decision in work-obsessed Washington, D.C. For a while, she ran a photography business out of their home, partly because she loves photography but partly so she could assure people at dinner parties that she had paying work. Whenever people venture that women who work outside the home don't judge stay-at-home moms, Danie thinks: *Are you freaking kidding me?*

She takes some comfort, however, in the example of a lesbian couple with whom she is friendly. Both women are attorneys, and one stays home with their child. "Their life is exactly the same as ours," Danie told me, with a hint of vindication. If being a stay-at-home mother is "good enough for her, then what's my issue? She's a huge women's-rights activist." But while comparing herself with a lesbian couple is liberating in some ways, it also exacerbates the competitive anxiety that afflicts so many modern mothers. The other thing about these two mothers, Danie said, is that they are so relaxed, so happy, so present. Even the working spouse manages to be a super-involved parent, to a much greater extent than most of the working fathers she knows. "I'm a little bit obsessed with them," she says.

Related to this is the question of how gay fatherhood might impact heterosexual fatherhood—by, for example, encouraging the idea that men can be emotionally accessible, logistically capable parents. Will the growing presence of gay dads in some communities mean that men are more often included in the endless e-mail chains that go to parents of preschoolers and birthday-party invitees? As radically as fatherhood has changed in recent decades, a number of antiquated attitudes about dads have proved strangely enduring: Rob Hardies, the pastor at All Souls, reports that when his partner, Chris, successfully folded a stroller before getting on an airplane with their son, Nico, he was roundly congratulated by passersby, as if he had solved a difficult mathematical equation in public. So low are expectations for fathers, even now, that in Stephanie Schacher's study of gay fathers and their feelings about care-giving, her subjects reported that people would see them walking on the street with their children and say things like "Giving Mom a break?" Hardies thinks that every time he and Chris take their son to the playground or to story hour, they help disrupt this sort of thinking. He imagines moms seeing a man doing this and gently—or maybe not so gently—pointing it out to their husbands. "Two guys somehow manage to get their act together and have a household and cook dinner and raise a child, without a woman doing all the work," he says. Rather than setting an example that fathers don't matter, gay men are setting an example that fathers do matter, and that marriage matters, too.

The Sex Problem

When, in the 1970s and early 1980s, Pepper Schwartz asked couples about their sex lives, she arrived at perhaps her most explosive finding: non-monogamy was rampant among gay men, a whopping 82 percent of whom reported having had sex outside their relationship. Slightly more than one-third of gay-male couples felt that monogamy was important; the other two-thirds said that monogamy was unimportant or that they were neutral on the topic. In a funny way, Schwartz says, her findings suggested that same-sex unions (like straight ones) aren't necessarily about sex. Some gay men made a point of telling her they loved their partners but weren't physically attracted to them. Others said they wanted to be monogamous but were unsupported in that wish, by their partner, gay culture, or both.

Schwartz believes that a move toward greater monogamy was emerging among gay men even before the AIDS crisis. Decades later, gay-male couples are more monogamous than they used to be, but not nearly to the same degree as other kinds of couples. In her Vermont research, Esther Rothblum found

that 15 percent of straight husbands said they'd had sex outside their relationship, compared with 58 percent of gay men in civil unions and 61 percent of gay men who were partnered but not in civil unions. When asked whether a couple had arrived at an explicit agreement about extra-relational sex, a minuscule 4 percent of straight husbands said they'd discussed it with their partner and determined that it was okay, compared with 40 percent of gay men in civil unions and 49 percent of gay men in partnerships that were not legally recognized. Straight women and lesbians, meanwhile, were united in their commitment to monogamy, lesbians more so than straight women: 14 percent of straight wives said they had had sex outside their marriage, compared with 9 percent of lesbians in civil unions and 7 percent of lesbians who were partnered but not in civil unions.

The question of whether gays and lesbians will change marriage, or vice versa, is at its thorniest around sex and monogamy. Private behavior could well stay private: when she studied marriage in the Netherlands, Lee Badgett, the University of Massachusetts economist, found that while many same-sex couples proselytize about the egalitarianism of their relationships, they don't tend to promote non-monogamy, even if they practice it. Then again, some gay-rights advocates, like the writer and sex columnist Dan Savage, argue very publicly that insisting on monogamy can do a couple more harm than good. Savage, who questions whether most humans are cut out for decades of sex with only one person, told me that "monogamy in marriage has been a disaster for straight couples" because it has set unrealistic expectations. "Gay-male couples are much more likely to be realistic about what men are," he said. Savage's own marriage started out monogamous; the agreement was that if either partner cheated, this would be grounds for ending the relationship. But when he and his husband decided to adopt a child, Savage suggested that they relax their zero-tolerance policy on infidelity. He felt that risking family dissolution over such an incident no longer made sense. His husband later suggested they explicitly allow each other occasional dalliances, a policy Savage sees as providing a safety valve for the relationship. If society wants marriage to be more resilient, he argues, we must make it more "monagamish."

This is, to be sure, a difficult argument to win: a husband proposing non-monogamy to his wife on the grounds that it is in the best interest of a new baby would have a tough time prevailing in the court of public opinion. But while most gay-marriage advocates stop short of championing Savage's "wiggle room," some experts say that gay men are better at talking more openly about sex. Naveen Jonathan, a family therapist and a professor at Chapman University, in California, says he sees many gay partners hammer out an elaborate who-can-do-what-when sexual contract, one that says, "These are the times and the situations where it's okay to be non-monogamous, and these are the times and the situations where it is not." While some straight couples have deals of their own, he finds that for the most part, they simply presume monogamy. A possible downside of this assumption: straight couples are far less likely than gay men to frankly and routinely discuss sex, desire, and the challenges of sexual commitment.

Other experts question the idea that most gay males share a preference for non-monogamous relationships, or will in the long term. Savage's argument that non-monogamy is a safety valve is "very interesting, but it really is no more than a claim," says Justin Garcia, an evolutionary biologist at the Kinsey Institute for Research in Sex, Gender, and Reproduction. Garcia points out that not all men are relentlessly sexual beings, and not all men want an open relationship, "in some ways, same-sex couples are healthier—they tend to have these negotiations more," he says. But negotiating can be stressful: in many cases, Garcia notes, one gay partner would prefer to be monogamous, but gives in to the other partner.

So which version will prevail: non-monogamous marriage, or marriage as we conventionally understand it? It's worth pointing out that in the U.S., same-sex unions are slightly more likely between women, and non-monogamy is not a cause women tend to champion. And some evidence suggests that getting married changes behavior: William Eskridge and Darren Spedale found that in the years after Norway, Sweden, and Denmark instituted registered partnerships, many same-sex couples reported placing a greater emphasis on monogamy, while national rates of HIV infections declined.

Sex, then, may be one area where the institution of marriage pushes back against norms that have been embraced by many gay couples. Gary Hall of the National Cathedral allows that in many ways, gay relationships offer a salutary "critique" of marriage, but argues that the marriage establishment will do some critiquing back. He says he would not marry two people who intended to be non-monogamous, and believes that monogamy will be a "critical issue" in the dialogue between the gay community and the Church. Up until now, he says, progressive churches have embraced "the part of gay behavior that looks like straight behavior," but at some point, churches also have to engage gay couples whose behavior doesn't conform to monogamous ideals. He hopes that, in the course of this give-and-take, the church ends up reckoning with other ongoing cultural changes, from unmarried cohabitation to the increasing number of adults who choose to live as singles. "How do we speak credibly to people about their sexuality and their sexual relationships?" he asks. "We really need to rethink this."

So yes, marriage will change. Or rather, it will change again. The fact is, there is no such thing as traditional marriage. In various places and at various points in human history, marriage has been a means by which young children were betrothed,

uniting royal houses and sealing alliances between nations. In the Bible, it was a union that sometimes took place between a man and his dead brother's widow, or between one man and several wives. It has been a vehicle for the orderly transfer of property from one generation of males to the next; the test by which children were deemed legitimate or bastard; a privilege not available to black Americans; something parents arranged for their adult children; a contract under which women, legally, ceased to exist. Well into the 19th century, the British common-law concept of "unity of person" meant a woman *became* her husband when she married, giving up her legal standing and the right to own property or control her own wages.

Many of these strictures have already loosened. Child marriage is today seen by most people as the human-rights violation that it is. The Married Women's Property Acts guaranteed that a woman could get married and remain a legally recognized human being. The Supreme Court's decision in *Loving v. Virginia* did away with state bans on interracial marriage. By making it easier to dissolve marriage, no-fault divorce helped ensure that unions need not be lifelong. The recent surge in single parenthood, combined with an aging population, has unyoked marriage and child-rearing. History shows that marriage evolves over time. We have every reason to believe that same-sex marriage will contribute to its continued evolution.

The argument that gays and lesbians are social pioneers and bellwethers has been made before. Back in 1992, the British sociologist Anthony Giddens suggested that gays and lesbians were a harbinger of a new kind of union, one subject to constant renegotiation and expected to last only as long as both partners were happy with it. Now that these so-called harbingers are looking to commit to more-binding relationships, we will have the "counterfactual" that Gary Gates talks about: we will be better able to tell which marital stresses and pleasures are due to gender, and which are not.

In the end, it could turn out that same-sex marriage isn't all that different from straight marriage. If gay and lesbian marriages are in the long run as quarrelsome, tedious, and unbearable; as satisfying, joyous, and loving as other marriages, we'll know that a certain amount of strife is not the fault of the alleged war between men and women, but just an inevitable thing that happens when two human beings are doing the best they can to find a way to live together.

Critical Thinking

1. How do you think the legalization of same-sex marriage may change what it means to be married in the United States?

2. What are some of the differences in the gender roles, division of labor, and decision-making practices in same-sex and heterosexual couples?

3. Given the insights noted in this article, what are three ways marriage in the United States may change in the next 30 years? Why do you think these changes will occur? Do you think these changes will strengthen or weaken the institution of marriage?

Create Central

www.mhhe.com/createcentral

Internet References

Coalition for Marriage, Family, and Couples Education
www.smartmarriages.com

Council on Contemporary Families
www.contemporaryfamilies.org

National Council of State Legislatures, Defining Marriage
www.ncsl.org/issues-research/human-services/same-sex-marriage-overview.aspx

The Pew Forum on Religion and Public Life: Gay Marriage and Homosexuality
www.pewforum.org/Topics/Issues/Gay-Marriage-and-Homosexuality

Prepared by: Patricia Hrusa Williams,
University of Maine at Farmington

Article

Parenting Wars

Jane Shilling

Learning Outcomes

After reading this article, you will be able to:

- Recognize familial, societal, cultural, historical, and media influences on parenting.

- Understand child traits such as character and identity that are associated with positive developmental outcomes.

Recently I embarked on a long-overdue purge of my bookshelves. In the several dozen bin bags that made their way to the Oxfam bookshop (where the expressions of the staff slowly morphed from pleased gratitude, on my first visit, to unconcealed dread by the fifth) were two copies of the Communist Manifesto (*two?*); a formidable collection of works by Foucault, Sarraute, Perec and Queneau (I suppose I must once have read them—bookmarking postcards fell out of some of them—but if I did, no trace of the experience has remained); and all my parenting books. Penelope Leach's *Baby and Child,* Steve Biddulph's *Raising Boys* and *The Secret of Happy Children,* Kate Figes on *The Terrible Teens*—none of them, I realised, had been purchased by me: all had been acquired for some exercise in journalism—reviewing or interviewing, but never for private reading.

I don't know what made me think I could raise a child without an instruction manual, especially as I was the single mother of a boy, with no partner or brothers to consult about the mysteries of maleness. Sheer wilfulness, I suppose (and a certain bruised desire to avoid books that wrote of families as consisting of a child with two parents who were, in the days when I was doing my child-rearing, invariably assumed to be a mummy and a daddy). No doubt I should have made a better fist of it if I had been able to embrace Leach and Biddulph as my mentors, but my son is 21 now, and we are far into the territory for which no self-help books on parent/child relationships exist (unless you count D H Lawrence's *Sons and Lovers,* as a handy guide on what not to do).

As I began to inhabit my new identity as a mother and a lone parent, bringing up my child felt like an experience too personal and intimate to be trimmed to a template provided by experts. I was keen on babies and small children, and imagined that maternal instinct would cover the basics adequately. In this, I was faithfully replicating my own upbringing. My mother owned a copy of Dr Spock's *Baby and Child Care,* but it hadn't the air of a book that had been consulted frequently (though oddly enough I read it avidly as a child—so perhaps my son was, by default, a Spock baby).

My mother's maternal style must in turn have been modelled on her childhood, though my maternal grandmother was the youngest of a family of 13, so there would have been lots of people to offer advice on teething and potty training, a resource that my mother, an only child, and I, the first of my close friends to have a baby, both lacked.

I don't think that any of the women in my family took a conceptual or political view of child-rearing or parenthood. We were too absorbed by the day-to-day business of reading stories and wiping bottoms to find time to analyse what we were about. (I was the only one of us to combine work with motherhood throughout my son's childhood, and that wasn't a considered decision: as a lone parent, I had no choice.)

In my childhood—and, I think, my mother's—the visionary thinking came from my grandfather, who had spent his infancy and early childhood in the St Pancras workhouse and had, not coincidentally, strong views about the necessity for setting life goals and working towards them, preferably by getting an excellent education.

Even 20 years ago, my unprofessional attitude to bringing up a child was anachronistic; these days I suspect it would be regarded as borderline negligent. Mine was certainly the last generation in which one could allow oneself to muddle along without the assistance of the experts, treating parenthood as though it were analogous to friendship—a relationship that would grow and flourish of its own accord.

I might have done my best to ignore the fact, but as a single parent I was a fragmentary factor in what has grown into an urgent social crisis around the issues of childhood and family. If ever there was a time when one could raise children unselfconsciously, it is long past. Now every aspect of parenthood, from conception and birth to the forming of intellect and character, is the subject of anxious and often agonised scrutiny.

The crisis is both personal and political. On the one hand, as engaged parents, we feel that we are in some sense our children: their successes and failures represent us almost more vividly than our own achievements. And as the condition of youth becomes ever more extended, lasting in attenuated form until middle age and beyond, our children can help to feed our vision of ourselves as perennially young. (Whenever I hear a parent say that they are "more of a friend than a parent" to their son or daughter, I wonder what privately the child might think about that.)

The inevitable consequence of seeing our children as our alter egos and friends is the sense of dread that fills us when they become opaque to us. Children and adolescents need to have parenting from somewhere, and if it isn't offered by their parents they will seek it among their peers—a group that once might have included mainly the people in their year at school, but which now, thanks to social media and the internet, comprises a global community of "friends" and acquaintances, a world in which the most adhesive parent can find it difficult to stick with its offspring.

Beyond the family, there lies society—a construct composed, alarmingly enough, of other people and their children, many of them not as conscientiously raised as one's own. The media reports are dismaying; this is a generation disaffected and resentful, alienated from education, or unable to obtain the jobs that were promised them in return for their hard-won examination results, debarred by the lack of an income from buying their own home, the dependency of childhood uneasily protracted by having to return to living in the family home as adults after a taste of freedom at college. Despite our excellent intentions and our strenuous efforts, is this the world we have made for our children?

The confusion of western attitudes to parenting is reflected in a cacophony of contradictory images. Last year the cover of *Time* magazine featured a photograph of the 26-year-old attachment parenting advocate Jamie Lynne Grumet breastfeeding her son Aram, aged nearly four, who was dressed in military-style camouflage pants and standing on a small chair to reach the magnificently tanned breast protruding from her sexy black camisole top.

While Aram suckles in his miniature army fatigues, the infant literacy movement encourages parents to believe that it is never too early to begin learning to read, with initiatives such as Reading Bear, a free online programme for tinies whose editor-in-chief is Larry Sanger, the co-founder of Wikipedia. Not that a Tiger Mother-ish enthusiasm for prodigies of infant learning is an exclusively 21st-century phenomenon. Dr Johnson's friend Hester Thrale recorded in her Family Book of 1766 the achievements of her two-year-old daughter, Queeney, who later became the disaffected protagonist of Beryl Bainbridge's splendid novel *According to Queeney*:

> She repeats the Pater Noster, the three Christian virtues, and the signs of the Zodiac in Watts' verses; she likewise knows them on the globe perfectly well. . . . She knows her nine figures and the simplest combinations of them; but none beyond a hundred; she knows all the Heathen Deities by their Attributes and counts to 20 without missing one.

Eat your heart out, Amy Chua.

It is true that there has probably never been a time when parenting was regarded as the exclusive preserve of parents. In *Dream Babies,* her 1983 study of child-rearing advice to parents from Locke to Spock, Christina Hardyment notes that the history of childcare manuals is almost as old as that of mass publication. The original manuals were booklets written by doctors for use by nurses in foundling hospitals. "It is with great Pleasure I see at last the Preservation of Children become the Care of Men of Sense," wrote William Cadogan in his *Essay*

on Nursing (1748). "In my opinion this Business has been too long fatally left to the management of Women who cannot be supposed to have a proper Knowledge to fit them for the Task, notwithstanding they look upon it to be their own Province."

The sentiment, if not the language, is curiously familiar from the plethora of modern parenting books which, even as they reassure anxious parents, cannot help but undermine their confidence with categorical but contradictory claims to know what is best for their offspring. Baby not sleeping? Gina Ford will fix that in no time. What a relief. Unless, that is, you happen to pick up Penelope Leach's most recent tome, *The Essential First Year: What Babies Need Parents to Know* (2010), from which you learn that leaving a distressed baby to cry can produce levels of the stress hormone cortisol (in the baby, that is, rather than the parent) that are toxic to its developing brain and may have long-term emotional consequences, as the anxiety of being left to weep unanswered pursues the beleaguered infant throughout childhood and adult life.

In short, you have a choice between inflicting brain damage and emotional distress if you leave little Magenta to cry herself to sleep; or an identical result if you rush to comfort her every time she wakes in the small hours and then—in an unforgivable, if perhaps understandable, episode of insomnia-induced rage—hurl her into her cot and lie on the floor beside it sobbing inconsolably and screaming, "I wish I'd never had a baby."

Still, let's not catastrophise. Somehow you and your child have both survived the essential first year, and even the essential first decade. Now you are entering the difficult hinterland of adolescence, and there are yet more things to worry about.

If you've got sons, there is the academic underperformance of boys in the overly feminised school environment, not to mention peer pressure to engage in all kinds of highly hazardous, not to say illegal, behaviour, and the long hours they spend closeted with their computer in their dark and malodorous rooms. For the parents of girls, there are problems of early sexualisation and their fragile relationship with their body image; nor is there any room for complacency about their examination results, which are likely to be affected by their desire not to be regarded as a nerd, neek, or anything other than one of the "popular girls".

For both sexes there is, besides the universal hazards of bullying and being mugged in the park for your cool stuff, the horrible complication of the way in which emergent adolescent sexuality is formed (or deformed) by online pornography.

Here, happily, Steve Biddulph the no-nonsense Australian family therapist and childcare guru can help, with his bestselling books *Raising Boys* and (most recently) *Raising Girls*. When it comes to bringing up daughters, a mother's place is invariably in the wrong, and Biddulph's warmth and wisdom will doubtless console many. Nevertheless, there is something about the spectacle of a middle-aged male expert issuing advice on raising girls that conjures a faint echo of Cadogan's conviction that the raising of children is best left to men of sense.

The happiness of children (as opposed to their moral education, which predominated in child-rearing manuals before the mid-20th century) is something to which a prodigious amount of expertise has been devoted over the past couple of generations.

Almost two decades ago, in 1994, Penelope Leach published a premonitory tract about the treatment of children in affluent western society. *Children First,* subtitled *What Our Society Must Do—and Is Not Doing—for Our Children Today,* was a scathing anatomy of the societal approach to child-rearing which saw parenting as "a universal hobby that is awkward because it cannot be shelved during the working week, interrupts important adult business and is hard on soft furnishings".

Some of Leach's most urgent priorities for a child-friendly society have been addressed in the intervening years. Yet her sunlit vision of a world in which children's needs have equal weight with those of adults remains dismayingly far from reality. In 2007, a Unicef study that assessed the well-being of children in six categories—material; health and safety; education; peer relationships; behaviours and risks; and young people's own perceptions of their happiness—placed the US second-to-last and the UK last in a league of 21 economically advanced nations.

In the introduction to his book *The Beast in the Nursery* (1998), the psychoanalyst Adam Phillips writes, "As children take for granted, lives are only liveable if they give pleasure." Yet the Unicef study suggests that despite our obsession with raising happy, successful children, many of them are trapped in lives that are, by Phillips's measure, unliveable.

So, what has gone wrong? In *Kith,* her strange, poetic book on the relationship between childhood and the natural world (to be published in May), the writer Jay Griffiths asks the intractable question: "Why are so many children in Euro-American cultures unhappy?" and concludes that, in the affluent west, childhood has become a lost realm.

Children's books are written by grownups, so it is unwise to call them in evidence when discussing styles of parenting. Nevertheless, it is striking that the fiction best loved by children—from Captain Marryat and Mark Twain, E Nesbit and Richmal Crompton to Jacqueline Wilson and J K Rowling—describes childhood as a state unencumbered by parental interference, in which children confront all kinds of challenges and dangers and survive by their own resourcefulness.

In modern America and Europe, Griffiths notes, children may read about the adventures of Huck Finn or William Brown but they are unlikely to share their experiences: "Many kids today are effectively under house arrest. . . . If there is one word which sums up the treatment of children today, it is 'enclosure'. Today's children are enclosed in school and home . . . and rigid schedules of time". Society, she adds, "has historically contrived a school system that is half factory, half prison, and too easily ignores the very education which children crave".

In *How Children Succeed,* the Canadian-American writer Paul Tough addresses the question of childhood unhappiness from a perspective that is the precise opposite of Griffiths's: her approach is lyrical, emotional and elegiac; his is logical, analytical and didactic. Nonetheless their theories converge on a single point—that, as a preparation for life, education is failing huge numbers of children.

Tough's book, as he writes, "is about an idea that is . . . gathering momentum in classrooms and clinics and labs and lecture halls across the country and around the world. According to this new way of thinking, the conventional wisdom about child development over the past few decades has been misguided. We have been focusing on the wrong skills and abilities in our children, and using the wrong strategies to nurture and teach those skills. . . ."

There is something very satisfying about an educational theory that denounces all previous theories. It seems to offer the possibility of a miraculous redemption of past errors and the hope of a certain path to a better future. The main mistake of recent years, Tough argues, has been to focus on measurable academic attainment by our children, to the exclusion of the more nebulous personal qualities (or "character") necessary to translate examination results into the kind of stable success that makes young people good citizens.

"Character" is a term with curiously Victorian overtones; the more formidable early child-rearing volumes that Christina Hardyment discusses in *Dream Babies* are keen on this quality. Yet the interdisciplinary school of thought that Tough describes,

Gurus of the Nursery

For 52 years after it was first published in 1946, **Benjamin McLane Spock**'s *Baby and Child Care* was the second-bestselling book after the Bible. A physician by training, Spock turned to psychoanalysis to examine child-rearing. His ideas were highly influential and encouraged parents to see their children as individuals.

The psychologist **Penelope Leach**'s *Baby and Child: from Birth to Age Five,* was published in 1977 and has sold more than two million copies. Much of her writing has focused on the drawbacks of childcare, a position that has attracted significant criticism.

Gina Ford, the author of *The Contented Little Baby Book* (1999), has long divided opinion, in part because she has no children (she bases her writing and advice on having looked after "over 300" babies as a maternity nurse). Some swear by her philosophy of strict routines, whereas others deplore the rigidity of her approach.

When *Battle Hymn of the Tiger Mother* was published in 2011, readers and critics were stunned at **Amy Chua**'s candid account of raising her two daughters. Chua, a Yale law professor, writes that "this was supposed to be a story of how Chinese parents are better at raising kids than western ones. But instead, it's about a bitter clash of cultures, a fleeting taste of glory, and how I was humbled by a 13-year-old. . . ."

Paul Tough is a journalist and former editor at *The New York Times* Magazine. In *How Children Succeed* (newly published by Random House), he analyses the character traits that help a child have a secure and happy future.

An endorsement by Bill Clinton gives some indication of the praise that has greeted **Andrew Solomon**'s latest book, *Far From the Tree,* in the United States. Solomon—who is also an activist and lecturer—spent years researching the work by interviewing families with diverse and challenging experiences of child-rearing.

which is based on the theories of Martin Seligman, a professor of psychology at the University of Pennsylvania, and the late Christopher Peterson of the University of Michigan, factorises the success trait into seven separate elements: grit, self-control, zest, social intelligence, gratitude, optimism and curiosity.

Armed with these attributes, the theory goes that children from all kinds of unpromising backgrounds, from the vastly affluent with no experience of character-forming misfortune to the underprivileged with a discouraging excess of "deep and pervasive adversity at home", can achieve both the academic qualifications that are the golden ticket to the security of regular employment and the qualities that will make them useful members of society.

On this side of the Atlantic, the case for character development as an element of education has been vigorously promoted by Anthony Seldon, the Master of Wellington College. In May last year, the University of Birmingham's Jubilee Centre for Character and Values was launched, with funding from the John Templeton Foundation, established by the American philanthropist.

Tough describes how the principle of teaching—and assessing—character as well as academic attainment was initially taken up by two schools, KIPP Academy Middle School in the South Bronx, whose students are mostly from low-income families, and Riverdale Country School, situated in one of the most affluent neighbourhoods of New York City, and where pre-kindergarten fees start at $40,750 a year.

KIPP was already something of a model institution after a programme of immersive schooling produced a startling improvement in its academic results. But the instigator of that programme, David Levin, a Yale graduate, was dismayed by how many of his high-achieving students subsequently dropped out of college. Meanwhile, the headmaster of Riverdale, Dominic Randolph, had begun to feel that "the push on tests" at high-achieving schools such as his was "missing out on some serious parts of what it means to be human".

For the students, the problems at both ends of the socio-economic spectrum were oddly similar: low levels of maternal attachment, high levels of parental criticism, minimal after-school adult supervision, emotional and physical isolation from parents and—in the case of the rich children—excessive pressure to succeed, resulting in anxiety, depression and chronic academic problems.

The evolution of the character development programme diverged sharply at the two schools during the course of the trial. At KIPP it leaned towards the practical and prescriptive; at Riverdale the emphasis was more moral and philosophical, on leading a good life rather than wearing the uniform correctly and paying attention in class.

As the programme has continued, the statistics on college dropout rates among KIPP students have seemed modestly encouraging. It is harder to measure the success of the experiment among Riverdale students, as their path towards academic success was always much clearer. Tough acknowledges that what he calls the "new science of adversity . . . presents a real challenge to some deeply held political beliefs on both the left

and the right". In the UK, Seldon concedes that "character" might be seen as a synonym for "middle-class" or "public-school" values. Yet both men appear convinced that it is the only means of enabling young people to alter what might otherwise appear to be a fixed destiny of failure and unhappiness.

While Tough proposes the formal exercise of grit and optimism as the key to personal success, Andrew Solomon's new book, *Far From the Tree,* is a study of families whose ideas about what constitutes "success" for their child have had to be recalibrated, sometimes very sharply. Solomon interviewed 200 families for his epic survey of identity and difference, which was a decade in the writing. Each chapter is devoted to the experiences of children and parents living with one of a dozen forms of "otherness"—deafness, dwarfism, Down's syndrome, autism, schizophrenia, prodigies, criminal children and those born of rape.

Solomon's theme is the development of identity. He argues that children acquire identity both "vertically", in the form of inherited traits such as language and ethnicity, and "horizontally", from a peer group. The greater the differences between the child and his or her parents, the more powerful the tensions between the horizontal and vertical identities.

The germ of the book sprang from an article on deaf culture that Solomon wrote in 1993 for *The New York Times.* He found that most deaf children are born to hearing parents, who often feel compelled to help their children "succeed" in a hearing world by focusing on the ability to communicate orally, often to the detriment of other aspects of their development. For such children, the discovery of a culture that celebrates deafness, regarding it as a state of being as vibrant and creative as the hearing world, often appears a liberation, a portal to an identity that does not have to be lived out against a contrasting "normality".

But within that experience of liberation lies the seed of a painful truth: that, for all children marked by difference, whatever its nature (Solomon is gay, and writes movingly about his experience of growing up in a straight family), their first experience of their otherness is almost invariably provided by their own family. He explores the complicated nexus of "normalities" which exists within the family of a child who is in some way different, and between the family and the outside world, with a dogged forensic elegance.

Solomon's account, like Tough's, is laden with anecdote, but while Tough uses his case histories to personalise his theories, Solomon's purpose in writing is narrative and exploratory, rather than ideological or didactic. Like Griffiths, he seeks the key to a universe of familial complexity, and finds it in the most obvious place of all. Love, he concludes, is all you need.

That was pretty much my guiding principle when I began my own experience of parenthood. And on the whole I'm not persuaded that the outcome would have been very different if I had spent more time consulting the experts. Which is not the same thing as feeling that I have been a success as a parent. Raising a child involves a circuitous journey of many branching routes that may lead, if parents and children are lucky, loving and tolerant, to a destination that everyone involved finds bearable.

Twenty years ago, or ten, or even five, if you had asked me whether I thought I was a good mother, I would have answered "good enough" with a degree of self-satisfaction. I had, after all, raised a kind, sane, personable grown-up with a decent clutch of exam results, an entrenched reading habit and an unusual ability to discuss with enthusiasm both West Ham's position in the League table and the nuances of female fashion; and I felt that I had done it largely contra mundum.

More recently, as my son and I have settled into our roles as adult equals and our accounts of the past have diverged, I have begun to understand that he has grown into the person he is as much despite me as because of me. My main aim as a mother had been to try to avoid the aspects of my own upbringing that had caused me pain. I thought that would be easy, but it was not.

Sometimes my son's narratives of his childhood (still so recent and fresh in his mind) make me think that almost everything I did was wrong. It is a melancholy reflection, to put it mildly. But it makes me think that perhaps the real work of parenthood is to learn to accommodate the stories that your children tell you about their upbringing.

Critical Thinking

1. Shilling's article discusses and reviews several different philosophies of rearing children. Which is closest to the style of parenting your parents used? Which style or attributes do you want to adopt as a parent? Why?

2. Why are modern parents believed to be more fearful and protective than past generations?

3. What is the single most important thing parents can do to help promote the healthy development of their children?

4. The article suggests that parents have over-emphasized academic success in children and under-emphasized character development. Do you agree or disagree? Why?

Create Central

www.mhhe.com/createcentral

Internet Reference

Health and Parenting Center
www.webmd.com/parenting

Tufts University Child and Family Webguide
www.cfw.tufts.edu

Positive Parenting
www.positiveparenting.com

The National Association for Child Development
www.nacd.org

Child Trends
www.childtrends.org

JANE SHILLING is the author of *The Stranger in the Mirror*.

Article   Prepared by: Patricia Hrusa Williams, *University of Maine at Farmington*

My Rules for My Kids: Eat Your Vegetables; Don't Blame the Teacher

FRANCIS L. THOMPSON

Learning Outcomes

After reading this article, you will be able to:

- Identify parenting practices associated with raising competent, independent children.

- Recognize differences in family values and how they translate into disciplinary and child rearing practices.

My wife and I had 12 children over the course of 15 and a half years. Today, our oldest is 37 and our youngest is 22. I have always had a very prosperous job and enough money to give my kids almost anything. But my wife and I decided not to.

I will share with you the things that we did, but first let me tell you the results: All 12 of my children have college degrees (or are in school), and we as parents did not pay for it. Most have graduate degrees. Those who are married have wonderful spouses with the same ethics and college degrees, too. We have 18 grandchildren who are learning the same things that our kids learned—self respect, gratitude, and a desire to give back to society.

We raised our family in Utah, Florida, and California; my wife and I now live in Colorado. In March, we will have been married 40 years. I attribute the love between us as a part of our success with the children. They see a stable home life with a commitment that does not have compromises.

Here's what we did right (we got plenty wrong, too, but that's another list):

Chores

Kids had to perform chores from age 3. A 3-year-old does not clean toilets very well but by the time he is 4, it's a reasonably good job.

They got allowances based on how they did the chores for the week.

We had the children wash their own clothes by the time they turned 8. We assigned them a wash day.

When they started reading, they had to make dinner by reading a recipe. They also had to learn to double a recipe.

The boys and girls had to learn to sew.

Study Time

Education was very important in our family.

We had study time from 6 P.M. to 8 P.M. every week day. No television, computer, games, or other activities until the two hours were up. If they had no homework, then they read books. For those too young to be in school, we had someone read books to them. After the two hours, they could do whatever they wanted as long as they were in by curfew.

All the kids were required to take every Advanced Placement class there was. We did not let entrance scores be an impediment. We went to the school and demanded our kids be let in. Then we, as parents, spent the time to ensure they had the understanding to pass the class. After the first child, the school learned that we kept our promise that the kids could handle the AP classes.

If children would come home and say that a teacher hated them or was not fair, our response was that you need to find a way to get along. You need [to] find a way to learn the material because in real life, you may have a boss that does not like you. We would not enable children to "blame" the teacher for not learning, but place[d] the responsibility for learning the material back on the child. Of course, we were alongside them for two hours of study a day, for them to ask for help anytime.

Picky Eaters Not Allowed

We all ate dinner and breakfast together. Breakfast was at 5:15 A.M. and then the children had to do chores before school. Dinner was at 5:30 P.M.

More broadly, food was interesting. We wanted a balanced diet, but hated it when we were young and parents made us eat all our food. Sometimes we were full and just did not want to eat anymore. Our rule was to give the kids the food they hated most first (usually vegetables) and then they got the next type of food. They did not have to eat it and could leave the table. If later they complained they were hungry, we would get out that food they did not want to eat, warm it up in the microwave, and provide it to them. Again, they did not have to eat it. But they got no other food until the next meal unless they ate it.

Extracurriculars

All kids had to play some kind of sport. They got to choose, but choosing none was not an option. We started them in grade school. We did not care if it was swimming, football, baseball, fencing, tennis, etc. and did not care if they chose to change sports. But they had to play something.

All kids had to be in some kind of club: Boy Scouts, Girl Scouts, history, drama, etc.

They were required to provide community service. We would volunteer within our community and at church. For Eagle Scout projects, we would have the entire family help. Once we collected old clothes and took them to Mexico and passed them out. The kids saw what life was like for many families and how their collections made them so happy and made a difference.

Independence

When the kids turned 16, we bought each a car. The first one learned what that meant. As the tow truck pulled a once "new" car into the driveway, my oldest proclaimed: "Dad, it is a wreck!" I said, "Yes, but a 1965 Mustang fastback wreck. Here are the repair manuals. Tools are in the garage. I will pay for every part, but will not pay for LABOR." Eleven months later, the car had a rebuilt engine, rebuilt transmission, newly upholstered interior, a new suspension system, and a new coat of paint. My daughter (yes, it was my daughter) had one of the hottest cars at high school. And her pride that she built it was beyond imaginable. (As a side note, none of my kids ever got a ticket for speeding, even though no car had less than 450 horsepower.)

We as parents allowed kids to make mistakes. Five years before the 16th birthday and their "new" car gift, they had to help out with our family cars. Once I asked my son, Samuel, to change the oil and asked if he needed

help or instruction. "No, Dad, I can do it." An hour later, he came in and said, "Dad, does it take 18 quarts of oil to change the oil?" I asked where did he put 18 quarts of oil when normally only five were needed. His response: "That big screw on top at the front of the engine." I said "You mean the radiator?" Well, he did not get into trouble for filling the radiator with oil. He had to drain it, we bought a radiator flush, put in new radiator fluid, and then he had to change the real oil. We did not ground him or give him any punishment for doing it "wrong." We let the lesson be the teaching tool. Our children are not afraid to try something new. They were trained that if they do something wrong they will not get punished. It often cost us more money, but we were raising kids, not saving money.

The kids each got their own computer, but had to build it. I bought the processor, memory, power supply, case, keyboard, hard drive, motherboard, and mouse. They had to put it together and load the software on. This started when they were 12.

We let the children make their own choices, but limited. For example, do you want to go to bed now or clean your room? Rarely, did we give directives that were one way, unless it dealt with living the agreed-upon family rules. This let the child feel that she had some control over life.

In It Together

We required the children to help each other. When a fifth grader is required to read 30 minutes a day, and a first grader is required to be read to 30 minutes a day, have one sit next to the other and read. Those in high school calculus tutored those in algebra or grade-school math.

We assigned an older child to a younger child to teach them and help them accomplish their weekly chores.

We let the children be a part of making the family rules. For example, the kids wanted the rule that no toys were allowed in the family room. The toys had to stay either in the bedroom or playroom. In addition to their chores, they had to all clean their bedroom every day (or just keep it clean in the first place). These were rules that the children wanted. We gave them a chance each month to amend or create new rules. Mom and Dad had veto power of course.

We tried to be always consistent. If they had to study two hours every night, we did not make an exception to it. Curfew was 10 P.M. during school nights and midnight on non-school nights. There were no exceptions to the rules.

Vacation Policy

We would take family vacations every summer for two or three weeks. We could afford a hotel, or cruise, but did not choose those options. We went camping and backpacking. If it rained, then we would figure out how to backpack in the rain and survive. We would set up a base camp at a site with five or six tents, and I would take all kids age 6 or older on a three- to five-day backpack trip. My wife would stay with the little ones. Remember, for 15 years, she was either pregnant or just had a baby. My kids and I hiked across the Grand Canyon, to the top of Mount Whitney, across the Continental Divide, across Yosemite.

We would send kids via airplane to relatives in Europe or across the US for two or three weeks at a time. We started this when they were in kindergarten. It would take special treatment for the airlines to take a 5-year-old alone on the plane and required people on the other end to have special documentation. We only sent the kids if they wanted to go. However, with the younger ones seeing the older ones travel, they wanted to go. The kids learned from an early age that we, as parents, were always there for them, but would let them grow their own wings and fly.

Money and Materialism

Even though we have sufficient money, we have not helped the children buy homes, pay for education, pay for weddings (yes, we do not pay for weddings either). We have provided extensive information on how to do it or how to buy rental units and use equity to grow wealth. We do not "give" things to our children but we give them information and teach them "how" to do things. We have helped them with contacts in corporations, but they have to do the interviews and "earn" the jobs.

We give birthday and Christmas presents to the kids. We would play Santa Claus but as they got older, and would ask about it, we would not lie. We would say it is a game we play and it is fun. We did and do have lists for items that each child would like for presents. Then everyone can see what they want. With the [I]nternet, it is easy to send such lists around to the children and grandchildren. Still, homemade gifts are often the favorite of all.

The Real World

We loved the children regardless of what they did. But would not prevent consequences of any of their actions. We let them suffer consequences and would not try to mitigate the consequences because we saw them suffering. We would cry and be sad, but would not do anything to reduce the consequences of their actions.

We were and are not our kids' best friends. We were their parents.

Critical Thinking

1. How would you characterize the parenting style the author and his wife utilized with their 12 children?

2. The author feels that he and his wife have been successful in raising their children. How do they define success and what it means to be a competent adult?

3. In looking at the list of family rules used with their children, which rules do you agree with and which do you feel are harsh or inappropriate in some way? Provide a rationale for your choices and explain your reasoning.

Create Central

www.mhhe.com/createcentral

Internet References

Child Trends
www.childtrends.org

Health and Parenting Center
www.webmd.com/parenting

Tufts University Child and Family Webguide
www.cfw.tufts.edu

University of Alabama Parenting Assistance Line
http://www.pal.ua.edu/discipline/consistency.php

Article   Prepared by: Patricia Hrusa Williams, *University of Maine at Farmington*

Teen Spirit

Helicopter parenting has crippled American teenagers. Here's how to fix it.

DAN GRIFFIN

Learning Outcomes

After reading this article, you will be able to:

- Identify the developmental needs of teenagers.

- Explain the challenges experienced in raising teenagers in modern society.

- Evaluate the benefits of allowing teenagers to experience failure.

Ian was sitting at his usual place during what his parents had decreed was his nightly homework time. But he had his chair turned away from his open books and calculator, and he was removing the fourth raw hot dog from the package. He gingerly placed it sideways on the family dog Walter's muzzle and commanded him to "walk." Ian got the idea after a liberal sampling of YouTube's stupid pet trick videos.

Ian's mother, Debbie, peeked in on her son and then turned around to stare at her husband. It was a look that said: "Your turn. Get him back to his homework. I've reached my limit today."

"Ian, it's almost 8, let's get going!" Michael yelled.

Four minutes passed.

"Ian, if you don't get started now, I will not help you with your math."

Ian commenced homework but soon drifted to watching more dumb pet tricks on YouTube.

The key is figuring out how to get kids to tune into their own motivation, and to get the parents to tune out of their motivation to shield their kids from failure and disappointment.

Michael and Debbie had realized early that Ian was extremely bright but that he couldn't often work up to his capabilities. He was disorganized, easily distracted (the stupid pet tricks!), and discouraged by the slightest failure. So they did what many dedicated parents do these days: turn themselves into a rodeo tag team to keep him on track at his competitive Washington, D.C., private school. Every evening, they reviewed his homework assignments, made a list of priorities, kept track of upcoming tests, reviewed long-term projects, and made plans to get a tutor if the work was confusing. Then the next night, they did it again.

Lately, we have been schooled on the hell that is adolescence, and more specifically, the collateral damage this phase of life inflicts on parents. The recent *New York* magazine cover story includes several examples of families locked in the kinds of pointless battles I just described. The stories might leave parents who read them with a strong sense of recognition, and also hopelessness. But as a clinical psychologist specializing in family systems, my job is to help parents and kids get past the deadlock. The key, it turns out, is figuring out how to get kids like Ian to tune into their own motivation to get their work done, and to get the parents to tune out of their motivation to shield their kids from failure and disappointment.

"Ian" and his family are recent patients of mine at my private Washington, D.C., practice, and the teenager has the typical profile of many I see. They are often boys, smart but underachieving, possibly with some diagnosis—ADHD, a learning disability, or something on the autistic spectrum. Their parents work diligently to help them succeed: cajoling and pleading and threatening and occasionally employing more intrusive techniques copied from mob debt collectors. The worthy goal of these enormous efforts is to insure that these kids feel good about themselves, and failure to achieve that goal is often equated with failure as a parent. I consider it my job to teach every member of the family to succeed a little less and fail a lot more in the service of a greater goal, developing character. Teaching them to make space for failure is a monumental task and often requires begging on my part.

In my nearly 30 years as a psychologist and family therapist, I've learned that parents can only play one of two possible roles at any given time: cheerleader or Texas high-school football coach. The cheerleader's main goal is to keep the spirits up. As soon as the child is born, he is offered fun activities that are sometimes mildly challenging, so long as they leave the glow of "something positive just happened"—stimulating crib toys, managed play dates, rec sports. The cheerleader has learned to "praise the effort, not the outcome" so mom and dad ignore the score and pass out prizes to all. The coach's main job, on the other hand, is to build character. Built into that lesson is an assumption of challenge and possible, eventual failure. The aim is to develop a "character repertoire" that includes willpower and the ability to delay gratification and to accept hardship as part of life.

It won't surprise anyone to hear that we live in an era of cheerleaders. Many sociologists and parenting experts have diagnosed (and complained about) this prevalent style. In my experience the approach works well in the younger years; there is something charming about encouraging effort over just winning, about boosting self-esteem. But then in the middle-school years it often all comes crashing down. The kids are wholly unprepared for what they'll face and the parents, stuck in cheerleading mode, wind up like Michael and Debbie, like the parents Jennifer Senior profiles in the *New York* magazine cover story: desperate to "bring back that loving feeling"—the positive glow and sense of parental gratification.

Over the past decade Claudia Mueller and Carol Dweck have conducted six studies of 412 fifth graders, ages 10 through 12, comparing the goals and achievements of children praised for their intelligence with those of youngsters commended for making an effort. "Praising children's intelligence, far from boosting their self-esteem, encourages them to embrace self-defeating behaviors such as worrying about failure and avoiding risks," said Dweck, lead author of the study. Po Bronson warned about the risks of this parenting error in his 2007 story "How Not to Talk to Your Kids." Keep praising middle-school kids who are struggling and their grades might never recover, he writes, because they never learn strategies to deal with failure.

So what can parents do? Unfortunately, it's really hard to motivate parents to shift from cheerleading to coaching mode this late in the game. It's no fun, and it is not rewarding for parent nor child. It is also counterintuitive, particularly for parents who have spent more than a decade helping their child be as happy as possible and avoid pain. It requires parents to be witnesses to minor and possibly major train wrecks: getting F's for missed homework, being sucked into the black hole of online games, discovering marijuana—things that make pet tricks look like harmless fun by comparison. The phase requires parents to tolerate anxiety, self-doubt, and failure, not just in their child but—even harder in some ways—*in themselves as parents.*

But it's absolutely critical because parents and their kids construct a reality together that at this stage only the parents can

undo. As parents, we can get caught in the day-to-day unfolding "story"—the simplest sequence of events in our lives. *We find places for our child to have fun and succeed. He is happy. We are good parents. We are happy. End of story.*

What I try to do is get parents to appreciate some grander "narrative"—a system of stories, related to each other, that extends the single "story," say, a failure to prepare for a test, into a larger evolving narrative. Along with David Black, a clinician and research neuropsychologist at the National Institutes of Health, I am developing a program called "Transitions X: Working with Families to Build Autonomy" that includes many such experiments in teaching middle- and high-school parents and their at-risk kids independence. What's hard is getting the parent commandos to commit to an exit strategy of gradual, real troop withdrawal because it feels to them like neglect or even abuse. We want them to evolve from what has been referred to as "Helicopter Parents" to "U-2 Parents": observers instead of combatants—present, attentive, but largely undetected from such a distance.

So let's say Ian spends the night before an exam doing pet tricks instead of studying, but this time, his parents, Michael and Debbie, refrain from the usual exhortations. (This is a true story, names changed.) Ian fails the test, and he is demoralized. The next week he does the same thing again and still they don't intervene. This time he's also angry. "This really sucks, and it is your fault!" he yells at his parents. He is called into the dean's office and asked to account for his drop in grades. The dean tells him he has to improve his performance or he'll get placed in a lower math level.

Ian is still angry at his parents for "not caring" about him, but he really doesn't *want* to get a math demotion. This is the first time it's occurred to him that he might not get into a great college, which is what his parents have been signaling to him is his inevitable fate. It takes a lot of work to get his parents to stick with the program at this point. Michael and Debbie were really worried he would become overwhelmed or even break down. I convinced them that if they intervened now, they would only be delaying a train wreck until the first year of college. Sooner or later, he had to learn what to do when he failed.

Used to being bailed out by his parents, Ian was confused. Eventually he came up with the idea of asking his teacher for help. The teacher was willing to help but only if Ian made the appointments himself and showed up consistently. In these private meetings, Ian learned that his revered double honors math teacher had failed calculus the first time. The teacher was blunt in telling Ian that if he did not take responsibility for his own learning, he should give up on the idea of being a math or science major in college. Ian had been counting on this teacher for a strong recommendation. Once again, his sense of inevitable success was shaken, so he was scared into being responsible. Ian is still showing up for the appointments.

Motivating kids who have reached their teenage years without accruing much intrinsic motivation is a complicated affair. Some adolescents have been shown to dramatically increase their test scores with something as simple as the promise of M&M's. For some kids—the confident ones—cheerleading by laying the compliments on thick spurs them to take on challenges. For the less confident kids, overpraising is disastrous.

The hardest part of the parents' task is often the quid pro quo, insisting on getting some things from their kid up front, in return for the privilege—not the inevitability but the earned privilege—of going to college. Parents have to accept that the narratives are open-ended. One never knows which "failure" will be the tipping point for an adolescent toward more effort, self-reflection, assuming responsibility, in a word, discovering inner motivation.

The reason we need to make this shift is obvious if we think about our own lives. We can very often trace significant, unexpected growth in our adult lives as emerging out of disappointments and setbacks. Perhaps as a direct result of a failure, we encounter someone who becomes a pivotal mentor, who sees a spark in us we miss. We are denied admittance to what seems like the ticket to our early dream, only to discover our calling, more subtle but more configured to our values and strengths.

Critical Thinking

1. What are some challenges in parenting teenagers? How are they different than those experienced when children are younger?

2. Do you agree that modern parents are afraid to let their child experience failure, trying to instead boost their child's self-esteem?

3. How can parents best support their teenagers so they develop independence and a sense of personal motivation and identity?

Create Central

www.mhhe.com/createcentral

Internet References

KidsHeath: A Parent's Guide to Surviving the Teen Years
http://kidshealth.org/parent/growth/growing/adolescence.html

Positive Parenting
www.positiveparenting.com

Search Institute
http://www.search-institute.org

Tufts University Child and Family Webguide
www.cfw.tufts.edu

DAN GRIFFIN is a clinical psychologist and family therapist in the greater Washington area.

Article

Prepared by: Patricia Hrusa Williams,
University of Maine at Farmington

Sibling Rivalry Grows Up
Adult Brothers and Sisters Are Masters at Digs; Finding a Way to a Truce

ELIZABETH BERNSTEIN

Learning Outcomes

After reading this article, you will be able to:

- Identify the impact of sibling relationships on an individual.
- Identify competition between siblings.
- Describe the influence of sibling relationships on individuals during adulthood.

Marianne Walsh and her sister, Megan Putman, keep track of whose kids their mother babysits more. They also compete with each other over parenting styles (Ms. Walsh is strict, Ms. Putman is laid back) and their weight.

Even after siblings grow up, rivalry and one-upmanship continue to crop up, Elizabeth Bernstein reports on Lunch Break.

"My kids play more instruments, so I am winning in piano," says Ms. Walsh, 38, the younger of the two by 13 months. "But she won the skinny Olympics."

Adult sibling rivalry. Experts say it remains one of the most harmful and least addressed issues in a family. We know it when we see it. Often, we deeply regret it. But we have no idea what to do about it.

Ms. Walsh and Ms. Putman have been competitive since childhood—about clothes, about boyfriends, about grades. Ms. Walsh remembers how in grammar school her sister wrote an essay about their grandfather and won a writing award. She recited it at a school assembly with her grandpa standing nearby, beaming. Ms. Walsh, seething, vowed to win the award the next year and did.

Ms. Putman married first. Ms. Walsh, single at the time, clearly recalls the phone call when her sister told her she was pregnant. "I was excited because this was the first grandchild. Then I got off the phone and cried for two hours," says Ms. Walsh.

Marianne Walsh and her older sister, Megan Putman, have worked out a way to end negative conversations based on rivalry.

Ms. Putman, 39 and a stay-at-home-mom in Bolingbrook, Ill., remembers that she too felt jealous—of her sister's frequent travel and promotions in her marketing career. "The way my parents would go on and on about her really made me feel 'less than,'" Ms. Putman says.

Ms. Walsh eventually married, had a son and named him Jack. Seven weeks later, Ms. Putman gave birth to a son and named him Jack. The discussion? "That was always my boy name." "I never heard you say that."

Sibling rivalry is a normal aspect of childhood, experts say. Our siblings are our first rivals. They competed with us for the love and attention of the people we needed most, our parents, and it is understandable that we occasionally felt threatened. Much of what is written about sibling rivalry focuses on its effects during childhood.

But our sibling relationships are often the longest of our lives, lasting 80 years or more. Several research studies indicate that up to 45 percent of adults have a rivalrous or distant relationship with a sibling.

Stop Fighting, Already

What siblings say indicating a rivalry is smoldering. Responses either make the rivalrous feelings worse, or defuse the situation.

People questioned later in life often say their biggest regret is being estranged from a sister or brother.

The rivalry often persists into adulthood because in many families it goes unaddressed. "Most people who have been through years of therapy have worked out a lot of guilt with their parents. But when it comes to their siblings, they can't articulate what is wrong," says Jeanne Safer, a psychologist in Manhattan and author of *Cain's Legacy: Liberating Siblings from a Lifetime of Rage, Shame, Secrecy and Regret.*

Dr. Safer believes sibling rivals speak in a kind of dialect (she calls it "sib speak"). It sounds like this: "You were always Mom's favorite." "Mom and Dad are always at your house but they never visit me." "You never call me."

"It's not the loving language that good friends have," Dr. Safer says. "It's the language of grievance collection."

It's hard to know what to say in response. "You are afraid that what you say will be catastrophic or will reveal awful truths," Dr. Safer says. "It's a lifelong walk on eggshells."

Sibling discord has been around since the Bible. Cain killed Abel. Leah stole Rachel's intended husband, Jacob. Joseph fought bitterly with his 10 older half brothers. Parents often have a hand in fostering it. They may choose favorites, love unevenly and compare one child with the other.

Dr. Safer draws a distinction between sibling rivalry and sibling strife. Rivalry encompasses a normal range of disagreements and competition between siblings. Sibling strife, which is less common, is rivalry gone ballistic—siblings who, because of personality clashes or hatred, can't enjoy each other's company.

Al Golden, 85, chokes up when he talks about his twin brother, Elliott, who died three years ago. The brothers shared a room growing up in Brooklyn, N.Y., graduated from the SUNY Maritime College in New York and married within a month of each other in 1947.

Yet Mr. Golden still remembers how their father often compared their grades, asking one or the other, "How come you got a B and your brother got an A?" He rarely missed a chance to point out that Elliott wasn't as good as Al in swimming.

When the boys were ready to get married, he suggested a double wedding. Mr. Golden put his foot down. "I shared every birthday and my bar mitzvah with my brother," he said. "I'll be damned if I am going to share my wedding with him."

Elliott Golden became a lawyer and eventually a state Supreme Court judge. Al Golden went into the mirror business, then sold life insurance. He says he always envied his brother's status and secretly took pleasure in knowing he was a better fisherman and owned a big boat. Once, Elliott asked him, "I am a lawyer. How come you make more money than me?" Mr. Golden says. "He meant: 'How come you are making more than me when you are not as successful?' But it made me feel good."

One day, Mr. Golden says, Elliott accused him of not doing enough to take care of their ailing mother. After the conversation, Mr. Golden didn't speak to his brother for more than a year. "It might have been the build-up of jealousies over the years," he says.

His brother repeatedly reached out to him, as did his nieces and nephews, but Mr. Golden ignored them.

Then one day Mr. Golden received an email from his brother telling a story about two men who had a stream dividing their properties. One man hired a carpenter to build a fence along the stream, but the carpenter built a bridge by mistake. Mr. Golden thought about the email then wrote back, "I'd like to walk over the bridge."

"I missed him," Mr. Golden says now. "I never had the chance to miss him before."

Dr. Safer says brothers' rivalries often are overt, typically focusing on things like Dad's love, athletic prowess, career success, money. Women are less comfortable with competition, she says, so sister rivalries tend to be passive-aggressive and less direct. Whom did Mom love best, who is a better mother now.

Brothers often repair their rivalries with actions. When women reconcile, it's often through talking. Ms. Putman and Ms. Walsh have learned to stop arguments using a trick from childhood. When a discussion gets heated, one sister will call out "star," a code word they devised as kids to mean the conversation is over. The sister who ends it gets the last word. "You may still be mad, but you adhere to the rules of childhood," Ms. Walsh says.

For some years, the two didn't socialize much. But when Ms. Putman's husband died last fall, Ms. Walsh, now a stay-at-home-mom in Chicago, helped plan the wake and write the obituary. Arriving at her sister's house one day before the funeral, Ms. Walsh found her in bed, crying, and climbed in next to her. The sisters said, "I love you," and Ms. Putman says she realized she was going to be OK.

"Lying there, I felt that if I've got my sister, I've got my strength," Ms. Putman says. "She is my backbone."

Putting a Stop to Sibling Rivalry

Fix the problem by addressing it head-on, says psychologist Jeanne Safer.

- The first step is to think. Who is this person outside his or her relationship with you? What do you like about your sibling? Remember the positive memories. Identify why you think the relationship is worth fixing—if it is.
- Take the initiative to change. It could be a gesture, like an offer to help with a sick child, a conversation or a letter. Be sincere and don't ignore the obvious. Say: "These conversations between us are painful. I would like to see if we can make our relationship better."
- Gestures count. Not everyone is comfortable talking about a strained relationship, especially men. But phone calls, invitations to spend time together, attempts to help should be seen as peace offerings.
- Consider your sibling's point of view. Try not to be defensive. What did childhood look like through his or her eyes? "You have to be willing to see an unflattering portrait of yourself," Dr. Safer says.
- Tell your sibling what you respect. "I love your sense of humor." "I admire what a good parent you are."
- And, finally: "It won't kill you to apologize," Dr. Safer says.

Critical Thinking

1. What factors are important to the development of healthy sibling relationships?
2. Is rivalry an inevitable aspect of sibling relationships?
3. When sibling rivalry exists, does it ever end?
4. What does sibling rivalry look like during adulthood?
5. What are some ground rules that should be established to promote healthy sibling relationships across the lifespan?

Create Central

www.mhhe.com/createcentral

Internet References

Sibling Support Project
  www.siblingsupport.org

Tufts University Child and Family Webguide
  www.cfw.tufts.edu

National Council on Family Relations
  www.ncfr.com

Support Needs of Siblings of People with Developmental Disabilities by Catherine K. Arnold, Tamar Heller, and John Kramer

109

Article

Prepared by: Patricia Hrusa Williams,
University of Maine at Farmington

Support Needs of Siblings of People with Developmental Disabilities

CATHERINE K. ARNOLD, TAMAR HELLER, AND JOHN KRAMER

Learning Outcomes

After reading this article, you will be able to:

- Identify the challenges adult siblings of those with developmental and intellectual disabilities face.

- Understand the support needs of adult siblings and aging parents of those with developmental disabilities.

Siblings of people with disabilities have been traditionally overlooked by parents, professionals, and researchers as a group with support needs and as potential advocates for their siblings with disabilities. Although the needs of people with developmental disabilities and their parents have been the focus of extensive research within the disability field, research on the needs of siblings is lacking (Hodapp, Glidden, & Kaiser, 2005). Much of the early research pathologized the experience of growing up with a brother or sister with a disability (Stoneman, 2005). More recent research on the sibling experience finds a mix of both positive and negative outcomes (Gallagher, Powell, & Rhodes, 2006). The support needs of adult siblings of people with developmental disabilities have received little attention from researchers up to this point. This study aimed to help fill this gap and give voice to the perspective of siblings so that their needs could be addressed by professionals and policymakers.

Siblings often become the next generation of caregivers when parents are no longer able to fill this role (Heller & Kramer, 2009). Sixty percent of people with developmental disabilities live with their families, and in 25% of these homes the primary caregiver is over the age of 60 (Braddock et al., 2011). As parents age and are less able to support their child with a disability, the involvement of siblings in the lives of their brothers and sisters with disabilities becomes more necessary. A review of the adult sibling literature found that most siblings anticipated taking on a greater supportive role in the future (Heller & Arnold, 2010).

The perspective of siblings of people with disabilities has not been looked at extensively in the research on families and disabilities, and the parent perspective is often incorporated, which is not always the same as siblings' self-reporting. However, a national survey of adult siblings by Hodapp, Urbano, and Burke (2010) showed siblings have service needs related to their struggle to balance care for their sibling with disabilities, their aging parents, and their own families. A study by Rawson (2009) interviewed siblings aged 17–23 years whose brothers and sisters with disabilities lived in a residential school for people with complex needs and found that siblings needed transition information, specifically on legal and financial planning, housing, and education. Siblings requested greater communication and wanted to be engaged in the decisions related to their brothers and sisters with disabilities. Also, Heller and Kramer (2009) surveyed adult siblings and found that the major support needs of siblings include the need for information, especially on planning for the future, as well as support groups both in person and online. The present study builds on the research done with siblings of people with disabilities and goes into greater depth with the perspective of siblings through a qualitative analysis.

Although support programs and services have been developed for individuals with developmental disabilities and their parents, supports for their siblings have been limited and mostly focused on children. There has been some intervention research that looks at the supports for siblings when they are children. Targeting nondisabled siblings for interventions to teach interaction skills and strategies was found to increase sibling play, communication, and successful interaction (Celiberti & Harris, 1993; Clark, Cunningham, & Cunningham, 1989; James & Egel, 1986). Sibling support groups for children were found to improve self-esteem, increase knowledge of their sibling's disability, and enhance interactions between siblings (Evans, Jones, & Mansell, 2001). Groups such as Sibshops provide "opportunities for brothers and sisters of children with special health and developmental needs to obtain peer support and education within a recreational context" (Meyer & Vadasy, 1994, p. 1). An evaluation of Sibshops by Johnson and Sandall (2005) suggests that providing support to siblings during childhood can have an enduring positive effect throughout their lives.

As siblings become more involved in the care of their brother or sister with a disability, their own support needs may increase. By understanding the needs of nondisabled siblings, parents and professionals can better empower and encourage siblings in supporting their brothers and sisters with disabilities. This study investigates the support needs of siblings of people with a developmental disability so they can be addressed by parents, professionals, and policymakers.

Method

Sample

The sample included 139 adult siblings of people with developmental disabilities. Adult siblings of people with developmental disabilities aged 18 and older were recruited through two strategies: an online Yahoo! Group listserv called SibNet and a statewide sibling conference. First, information about the research study was posted on SibNet, a listserv for adult siblings of people with disabilities. At the time of dissemination, SibNet had 485 members with unique e-mail addresses, yet only 426 of those e-mail addresses were valid. One hundred sixteen SibNet members responded, and eight respondents were excluded who were under 18 years old and therefore below the age of consent. The total number of respondents from SibNet in this study is 108 siblings. Second, surveys were handed out at a statewide sibling conference to 57 people. The survey was completed by 31 siblings who attended the conference. Combining the respondents from SibNet and the sibling conference, the overall corrected sample consisted of 139 respondents out of 483 for a response rate of 31%.

Demographics of respondents and their sibling with disabilities are shown in Table 1. The average age of all respondents is 37 years old with ages ranging from 18 to 62 years. The vast majority of respondents (92%) were female with no minority status (87%). Most respondents had an education level of some college or more (93%). Over half the sample was married, and 37% had between one and eight children. Sixty-nine percent of the respondents had family incomes over $40,000. For individuals with developmental disabilities, the average age was 34 years (range = 10–72 years). Sixty percent of siblings with disabilities were brothers. About 75% of siblings had an intellectual disability with the remainder having other developmental disabilities. The living situation of siblings varied, with 41% living at home with parents, 8% living with their nondisabled siblings, 24% living in a residential facility, 7% living with other family members, and 11% living with a spouse or independently.

Survey

The Supporting Siblings Survey included 59 questions that focused on respondents' sibling with a disability, their parents, their relationship to their siblings, and their family's future plans. Feedback on the survey was gathered from people with developmental disabilities, parents, and siblings. Pilot testing was done to help strengthen and finalize the survey. Most of the questions were close-ended with only the last four questions being open-ended. The open-ended questions captured descriptive information about the concerns and the support needs of siblings. For the focus of the research in this study, the two specific questions used to explore the support needs of siblings included: "What programs would you like to see targeted

Table 1   Demographics

Variable	n	%
Sibling respondent		
Gender		
Male	10	8
Female	120	92
Ethnic minority status		
Yes	19	13
No	128	87
Educational level		
High school or GED	8	6
Trade/vocational school	1	1
Some college	20	15
College	43	33
Some graduate school	14	11
Graduate school	45	34
Marital status		
Married	70	53
Not married	62	47
Children		
Yes	49	37
No	83	63
Income		
< $20,000	15	12
$20,001–40,000	24	19
$40,001–60,000	31	24
$60,001–80,000	25	20
$80,001–100,000	12	9
< $100,000	21	16
Sibling with a disability		
Gender		
Male	80	60
Female	54	40
Living situation		
Home with parents	55	41
In your home	11	8
Residential placement	32	24
Other family members	9	7
Living with spouse	2	2
Independently	12	9
Other	12	9

towards *families* of people with disabilities?" and "What programs would you like to see targeted towards *siblings* of people with disabilities?" These two questions provided space for siblings to write any thoughts and ideas that were relevant to their support needs.

Analysis

The responses to the open-ended questions were transferred from SPSS to a Word document with no identifiers. Two coders, both family members of people with developmental

Table 2 Support Needs of Siblings

Theme	Core variable	Definition
Include me	Sibling support	Sibling support services to connect siblings, share information, and provide support.
Include me	Inclusive family	A more inclusive definition of family that includes siblings and not just parents.
Start spreading the news	Education	Education and training opportunities such as conferences, workshops, and seminars.
Start spreading the news	Future planning	Information and support on planning for the future, such as financial and legal planning, guardianship transition, and estate planning.
Start spreading the news	System navigation	Information on how to navigate the system.
Start spreading the news	Disability awareness	Education of the public about people with disabilities.
Fix the mess	System improvement	Improvement of the support system such as shorter waiting lists, better service coordination, transportation, supported living services, better pay and career advancement for direct support professionals, and more.
Fix the mess	Funding	More funding sources or financial support.
Fix the mess	Respite	In-home and out-of-home respite services.
N/A	Anything	Anything at all.
N/A	Do not know	Do not know.

disabilities in the disability field, independently read through all the responses identifying overarching patterns and themes. The finalized coding frame (see Table 2) consisted of 11 core variables for sibling support needs. All coded responses were compared and showed 80% agreement. Any discrepancies were addressed until 100% agreement was reached for the coding of core variables to each response. A description of the support needs of siblings is highlighted in the results using quotes from siblings.

Results

The results of the present research captured the perspective of siblings and described the support needs of siblings. Of the 139 survey respondents, 120 shared their ideas for support needs. Quotations from the participants' open-ended responses highlighted the experience of siblings. The overarching themes that emerged from the data provided the framework for the support needs of siblings. Three overarching themes emerged that included 11 core variables. Table 2 shows the support needs of siblings. "Include me" emerged as a theme that encompassed two variables: *sibling support,* indicating the need for more sibling support services to connect siblings, share information, and provide support; and *inclusive family,* regarding the need for a more inclusive definition of family that includes siblings and not just parents. "Start spreading the news" was another primary theme related to siblings' need for information. Four core variables were captured within this theme: (a) education, indicating the need for education and training opportunities such as conferences, workshops, and seminars; (b) future planning, indicating the need for information and support on planning for the future, such as financial and legal planning, guardianship transition, and estate planning; (c) system navigation, regarding information on how to navigate the system;

and (d) disability awareness, for more education of the public about people with disabilities. "Fix the mess" was another major theme that included three variables: (a) system improvement, regarding the need for improvement in the support system, such as shorter waiting lists, better service coordination, transportation, supported living services, better pay and career advancement for direct support professionals, and more; (b) funding, for more funding sources or financial support; and (c) respite, for in-home and out-of-home respite services. Table 3 shows the frequency of sibling support needs. The top five support needs included sibling support (53%), education (35%), inclusive family (34%), future planning (31%), and system improvement (23%).

Table 3 Frequency of Sibling Support Needs

Core variables	N	%
Sibling support	63	53
Education	42	35
Inclusive family	41	34
Future planning	37	31
System improvement	28	23
System navigation	22	18
Funding	20	17
Respite	12	10
Disability awareness	5	4
Do not know	5	4
Anything	2	2

Note: The total number of respondents was 120.
Some numbers were rounded.

Include Me

The overarching theme of "include me" highlighted siblings' yearning to be included in supports and services. Two core variables included sibling support and inclusive family.

Sibling support. Respondents were emphatic that they wanted more sibling support, making comments such as, "Group support with other siblings to enable open conversation about the many issues involved." They clearly wanted support "just like their parents!" as one respondent exclaimed. Numerous respondents shared the importance of targeting siblings as a group with support needs because they have felt neglected and desperately wanted to be included. One sibling wrote:

> More support for siblings. It felt like a guilty secret when I was a child and knew nobody in the same situation as myself. Also the professional people who spoke to my brother over the years never thought to ask me how I was.

Another sibling shared, "I think that a sibling support group would be appropriate. Sometimes, we as siblings tend to feel alone and isolated from others when we spend a lot of time caring for our sibling." And, another sibling said, "I think there need to be more groups for adult siblings. People tend to forget about the siblings anyway especially after they are adults." The need for sibling support was distinguished as an important way for siblings to "talk about their concerns" and get "advice/support with other adult sibs in my same situation." Sibling support can provide a space where siblings "can become empowered before crisis occurs." One sibling shared how an Internet sibling group "was my first introduction to feeling 'normal.'" Another sibling wrote how she had begun advocating for the creation of an adult sibling group with her local Arc.

Inclusive family. Another area of need is the notion of a more inclusive definition of family that includes siblings and not just parents. Siblings expressed their desire to be part of the services that are offered to families in general. Respondents wanted supports that included "the whole family—not just parents." They wanted to have their voice heard and be treated as people with a valuable role and perspective. One sibling shared, "I want to see more adult siblings being included in the 'Family' theory. I want us to be invited to meetings, and our thoughts and ideas respected." Another sibling wrote:

> I think there needs to be a focus on the family as a whole and creating programs that provide the opportunity for all family members to participate. There is not any consideration or emphasis on siblings being a valued part of the family and being included.

Start Spreading the News

The overarching theme of "start spreading the news" represented the respondents' need for information and education. The four core variables that made up this theme consisted of the following types of information gathering: (a) education and

training opportunities, (b) future planning, (c) how to navigate the system, and (d) disability awareness education of the general public.

Education and training opportunities. Education was the second highest support need, with 42 siblings indicating the need for education and training opportunities such as conferences, workshops, and seminars. "I think siblings need information around many of the same issues as parents," stated one respondent. The siblings felt it was important to make "access to information more open" since much of their current experience is that "[w]e have to seek everything out for ourselves." Specific information topics were on "how to advocate for the rights of their siblings" and information "for sibling caregivers as their family member [with disabilities] and parents age."

Future planning. Siblings wanted "[f]amily programs so parents and siblings go through future family plans together." The primary aspect of future planning noted was to "[e]ncourag[e] families to talk about and plan for the future." Getting the dialogue started was a key aspect of future planning that helped to get families talking about their concerns and taking concrete steps to address those concerns and prepare for the future. The worry about what will happen when parents die could then be discussed, and families could begin the process of "making the transition of guardianship from parents to siblings."

System navigation. Siblings indicated a need for information on how to "maneuver within the system." Suggested information from respondents for navigating the system included the "rules/lingo/services to ask for," "how long waiting lists are," and "explanations of Medicaid programs." Another suggestion was "info on programs and how to apply" since this family "could have saved several thousands a year" if it had been aware of how to access certain services. "Easier ways to cut through the red tape of finding services appropriate to the sibling" was highlighted by one respondent. A suggested method for presenting information was "how-to guides on how to get/maintain services" and to give information so siblings felt "that they do not have to do everything on their own." There is a need for "programs that explain how to get services and what services are provided."

Disability awareness education. Disability awareness was a support need suggested by siblings as a means to educate the public about people with disabilities. Through increased awareness, one sibling hoped she would "see our society more inform[ed]." Suggested methods of educating the public included providing "information about disability issues in schools" and including "more positive things in the media with siblings of disabled people."

Fix the Mess

The overarching theme of "fix the mess" covered three core variables that focus on needs of siblings regarding the formal disability service system including (a) system improvement, (b) funding, and (c) respite.

System improvement. Siblings shared their frustration with the system and the need for great improvement in the system to better support their entire family. Different aspects of the system were mentioned, such as a "better system of checks and balance over group homes," "alternatives to supervised group housing," "better and consistent service coordination for people with disabilities," and "better pay and career advancement for direct care workers." One sibling articulated her needs by writing the following:

> I need support and choices for residential living. As it appears now, I will have to have her live with me, which I don't believe will be the BEST thing for either of us. I would like to live close to her though and see her in a healthy residential group.

Another sibling shared that she felt the service system "doors are not sibling friendly. Service providers discourage, not encourage, involvement."

Funding. The need for funding sources and financial support was indicated by siblings. The current funding is not adequate for all families, and one sibling stated, "SS [Social Security] doesn't go far enough." One sibling articulated the need for the following:

> A LOT more money for individuals on Social Security—at LEAST to the level of poverty; FULL medical care, meaning parity with services for the mentally ill. Caretaker siblings receiving financial compensation when they are caring for a sibling.

Funding is an important source of support for families of people with disabilities so that families "have more options about the care of their child."

Respite. Respite services were needed to give families "a break" and have time apart from the person with a disability to do other tasks and rest. One sibling described respite: "[S]omeone to watch the disabled individual while they go on vacation and small breaks throughout the week for an hour or two to get things done." Respite can be an important service that can help "families to stay together" instead of turning to residential facilities. It can alleviate some of the caregiving of families.

Discussion

The support needs found in this research study highlight the gap in meeting siblings' needs. Three overarching themes for sibling support needs include: (a) getting disability-related information, (b) getting support for their caregiving role, and (c) enhancing the formal support system to address sibling needs.

Information Needs

Siblings need information, just like parents and people with disabilities. Respondents articulated strong needs for education and training opportunities such as conferences, workshops, and seminars. Research that looks at families of people with disabilities shows that the needs of families include information on housing options, financial planning, and guardianship as well as the need for case management, advocacy, and support groups (Heller & Factor, 1994). A model of a future-planning curriculum that includes siblings and has tested outcomes is The Future is Now (Factor et al., 2010; Heller & Caldwell, 2006). Families that participated in a future-planning training intervention took steps to plan for the future such as to develop a special needs trust, complete a letter of intent, and to take action on residential plans for their adult family member with developmental disabilities. Also, the intervention reduced feelings of caregiving burden and increased choice-making opportunities of people with disabilities (Heller & Caldwell, 2006). More future-planning programs should include both the siblings with and without disabilities in the entire process. And, more research needs to be done on the outcomes of future planning and the effectiveness of different training models.

One challenge is getting information to siblings. Although an extensive network of people with disabilities and parents exists through the formal disability support system, information is often not transferred from these established networks to siblings.

Inclusion of Siblings

A concept that resonated throughout the results was that siblings felt that their voices were not being heard and their needs were not being adequately met. The literature on siblings clearly shows how siblings provide critical support to people with developmental disabilities throughout their lifespan. Siblings have the inside story about their siblings' with disabilities habits and preferences, health care history, important relationships, and much more. As the people with the longest lasting relationships, siblings have a wealth of knowledge about their brothers and sisters with disabilities that could be invaluable to professionals and service providers. Therefore, parents and professionals should engage siblings as partners in planning to enhance the support of people with disabilities.

Along with being left out of research and services, siblings are also often left out of the disability advocacy movement. Siblings are an untapped constituency for policy advocacy that can increase the power in the disability advocacy movement. If there are over 3.7 million people with developmental disabilities in the United States (Fujiura, 1998; Larson et al., 2001; U.S. Census Bureau, 2010), and most of these people have at least one sibling, the number of potential advocates grows exponentially. Siblings with and without disabilities can support each other to get involved in advocacy together and learn how to help push the policy system. Also, sibling voices at the policy table may help to ensure more supports are allocated for their unique concerns and needs.

Formal Supports

The highest ranking need in this study, sibling support services, indicated that siblings want ways to connect with each other, share information, and provide support. The present study reinforced the results of the previous study that noted that siblings want support groups, workshops, and trainings for siblings and families (Heller & Kramer, 2009). An important source of information and networking for siblings is the online listserv called SibNet where adults who have a brother or sister with a disability can connect (www.siblingsupport.org/connect/the-sibnet-listserv).

The Sibling Leadership Network (SLN) is a national nonprofit with state chapters created to support siblings of people with disabilities and provide a stronger voice for siblings. The SLN's mission is "to provide siblings of individuals with disabilities the information, support, and tools to advocate with their brothers and sisters and to promote the issues important to them and their entire families" (Heller et al., 2008, p. 4). Siblings want a stronger voice at the policy table to balance the perspective of parents and to walk with their brothers and sisters with disabilities to effect change.

Siblings want to be included in supports that are provided to families. Although many programs and services publicize that they are open to "families," this typically means parents, and they are not always welcoming to siblings. Family support programs often do not consider the perspective of siblings or target siblings in their marketing. Currently, family support policy does not specifically include siblings. The SLN "believe[s] it is time to strengthen family support policy by explicitly including brothers and sisters of people with disabilities in federal family support program guidelines" (Heller et al., 2008, p. 13).

The SLN developed a policy white paper entitled "The Sibling Leadership Network: Recommendations for Research, Advocacy, and Supports Relating to Siblings of People with Developmental Disabilities" (Heller et al., 2008) that had key recommendations that can help address the support needs of siblings in the present research study. These included creating a national clearinghouse for sibling resources and providing information and education to siblings, parents, and professionals. The SLN white paper provides a road map for addressing the support needs of siblings.

Policy Implications

There is a lack of policies that support siblings of people with disabilities in the United States. Kramer's (2008) study of siblings pairs, including siblings with and without disabilities, showed that siblings "believed their efforts to change policy could enhance their support and lead to increased participation with their sibling with [intellectual and developmental disabilities]" (p. 107). As respondents highlighted, the formal disability service system is often difficult for siblings and their families to navigate. Policy advocacy is a key aspect of the SLN and is committed to creating an organization that works with people with disabilities. The SLN has partnered with the national Self Advocates Becoming Empowered (SABE) to ensure the sibling organization is truly advocating with people with disabilities since they are the true experts. This approach models how siblings can learn from each other and work together to improve the system for their entire family.

The Developmental Disabilities Assistance and Bill of Rights Act of 2000 (DD Act) is the legislation that created important programs for people with developmental disabilities and their families. The SLN is advocating for the specific inclusion of siblings in the definition of family on the reauthorization of the DD Act. Also, increased involvement of siblings in the developmental disabilities network programs is recommended such as sibling participation on the sister agencies' advisory councils. Involvement of siblings should be evaluated with specific outcome measures that include siblings in the participation of families (Heller et al., 2008).

With the impending long-term care crisis, policies must take into account the needs of caregivers without forgetting siblings of people with disabilities. Policy for family caregivers is severely lacking and significantly underfunded. There are only two federal programs designed specifically to support family caregivers. The National Family Caregiver Support Program was established in 2000 as the very first national initiative to address family caregivers directly. It was enacted under Title III-E of the Older Americans Act Amendments of 2000. It provides funds to states specifically to serve caregivers of adults age 60 or over and to grandparents providing care to children (Heller, Caldwell, & Factor, 2007; Levine Halper, Peist, & Gould, 2010). The Lifespan Respite Care Act was enacted in 2006 to provide inhome and out-of-home respite for caregivers to get relief to provide quality care to their loved ones. However, it was not funded until 2009, and then it received a minimal appropriation allocating only $2.5 million (Levine et al., 2010) of the total $53.3 million needed to fully fund the program (Heller et al., 2007). This allocation is very small in light of the $375 billion the government is saving because of the work of unpaid family caregivers (Family Caregiver Alliance, 2009). Recommendations for policies include fully funding the Lifespan Respite Care Act and the Family Caregiver Support Program. Along with funding these programs, the government also needs to target the unique needs of siblings. Additional recommendations include providing financial assistance to family caregivers and expanding the Family and Medical Leave Act to provide paid leave time to siblings. Since family caregivers are the bedrock of the long-term care system, with siblings being an especially underserved group, they need to be supported to continue to play an important role and become recognized partners in the solution to the long-term care crisis in the United States.

Limitations

Some limitations exist in this research. The study used a cross-sectional data set from only one point of time. Also, a convenience sample was used, capturing responses from siblings who were already connected to some sibling support, and the results may not be generalizable to siblings who are not connected to SibNet or sibling conferences. This may be a more involved group than is typical and may not represent siblings who are less involved in the lives of their siblings with disabilities and therefore not connected to any sibling support. The majority of the sample included women, yet this reflects the gendered nature of caregiving in the literature (Levine et al., 2010). Also, the sample of respondents was fairly educated, with few minorities. Additionally, the research was limited because it did not include the voice of people with disabilities and relied on self-reported information of siblings. However, this study is one of the first that really looked at the voice of siblings of people with developmental disabilities.

Future Research

Although this research study helps fill a gap in the disability sibling literature, additional research is recommended that includes the siblings with and without disabilities and examines family dynamics beyond just the sibling dyad to see how whole families interact to support each other throughout their lifespans. The sibling experience of people with disabilities is especially important to capture to gain insight into the benefits of supporting people with disabilities. Also, intervention research should examine successful ways to negotiate the transition of caregiving roles from parents to nondisabled siblings to foster positive outcomes for the entire family. Additionally, further research should be done to capture the experiences of siblings who are not already connected to sibling support programs, such as reaching siblings through provider and parent networks, as well as getting the sibling experience in other countries.

Conclusion

The results of this research provided descriptive information about the support needs of adult siblings of people with developmental disabilities. The study helped give voice to the sibling perspective. The hope is that this information will be used by parents, professionals, and policymakers to address these concerns and support needs. These findings have implications for future policy and research. More opportunities are needed for siblings of people with developmental disabilities to connect, network, and share information and resources. Family support services must include siblings so that they are supported to be involved in the care of their brother or sister with disabilities in whatever way they choose. Siblings are an important resource for the disability field as future caregivers and untapped constituents in the disability policy movement. Additional research on siblings is important to increase the understanding of the supports that benefit siblings and their entire families.

References

Braddock, D., Hemp, R., Rizzolo, M. K., Haffer, L., Tanis, E. S., & Wu, J. (2011). *The state of the states in developmental disabilities 2011*. Washington, DC: American Association on Intellectual and Developmental Disabilities.

Celiberti, D. A., & Harris, S. L. (1993). Behavioral intervention for siblings of children with autism: A focus on skills to enhance play. *Behavior Therapy, 24*, 573–599.

Clark, M. L., Cunningham, L. J., & Cunningham, C. E. (1989). Improving the social behavior of siblings of autistic children using a group problem solving approach. *Child Family Behavior Therapy, 11*, 19–33.

Developmental Disabilities Assistance and Bill of Rights Act of 2000, Public Law 106–402, 114 Stat. 1677 (2000).

Evans, J., Jones, J., & Mansell, I. (2001). Supporting siblings: Evaluation of support groups for brothers and sisters of children with learning disabilities and challenging behavior. *Journal of Learning Disabilities, 5*(1), 69–78.

Factor, A., DeBrine, E. J., Caldwell, J., Arnold, K., Kramer, J., Nelis, T., & Heller, T. (2010). *The future is now: A future planning curriculum for families and their adult relative with developmental disabilities* (3rd ed.). Chicago, IL: Rehabilitation Research and Training Center on Aging with Developmental Disabilities, University of Illinois at Chicago.

Family Caregiver Alliance. (2009). *2009 National policy statement*. Available at http://caregiver.org/caregiver/jsp/content_node.jsp?nodeid=2279.

Fujiura, G. T. (1998). Demography of family households. *American Journal on Mental Retardation, 103*, 225–235.

Gallagher, P. A., Powell, T. H., & Rhodes, C. A. (2006). *Brothers and sisters: A special part of exceptional families* (3rd ed.). Baltimore, MD: Paul H. Brookes.

Heller, T., & Arnold, C. K. (2010). Siblings of adults with developmental disabilities: Psychosocial outcomes, relationships, and future planning. *Journal of Policy and Practice in Intellectual Disabilities, 7*(1), 16–25.

Heller, T., & Caldwell, J. (2006). Supporting aging caregivers and adults with developmental disabilities in future planning. *Mental Retardation, 44*(3), 189–202.

Heller, T., Caldwell, J., & Factor, A. (2007). Aging family caregivers: Policies and practices. *Mental Retardation and Developmental Disabilities Research Reviews, 13*, 136–142.

Heller, T., & Factor, A. (1994). Facilitating future planning and transitions out of the home. In M. M. Seltzer, M. W. Krauss, & M. Janicki (Eds.), *Life-course perspectives on adulthood and old age* (pp. 39–50) [Monograph Series]. Washington, DC: American Association on Mental Retardation.

Heller, T., Kaiser, A., Meyer, D., Fish, T., Kramer, J., & Dufresne, D. (2008). *The Sibling Leadership Network: Recommendations for research, advocacy, and supports relating to siblings of people with developmental disabilities* [White paper]. Chicago, IL: Rehabilitation Research and Training Center on Aging with Developmental Disabilities, Lifespan Health and Function, University of Illinois at Chicago.

Heller, T., & Kramer, J. (2009). Involvement of adult siblings of persons with developmental disabilities in future planning. *Intellectual and Developmental Disabilities, 47*(3), 208–219.

Hodapp, R., Glidden, L. M., & Kaiser, A. P. (2005). Siblings of persons with disabilities: Toward a research agenda. *Mental Retardation, 43*(5), 334–338.

Hodapp, R. M., Urbano, R. C., Burke, M. M. (2010). Adult female and male siblings of persons with disabilities: Findings from a national survey. *Intellectual and Developmental Disabilities, 48*(1), 52–62.

James, S. D., & Egel, A. K. (1986). A direct prompting strategy for increasing reciprocal interactions between handicapped and nonhandicapped siblings. *Journal of Applied Behavior Analysis, 19*(2), 173–186.

Johnson, A. B., & Sandall, S. (2005). *Sibshops: A follow-up of participants of a sibling support program*. Seattle, WA: University of Washington.

Kramer, J. C. (2008). *People with disabilities and their siblings: Building concepts of support and transitions* (Unpublished doctoral dissertation). University of Illinois at Chicago, Chicago, IL.

Larson, S. A., Lakin, K. C., Anderson, L., Kwak, N., Lee, J. H., & Anderson, D. (2001). Prevalence of mental retardation and developmental disabilities: Estimates from the 1994/1995 National Health Interview Survey Disability Supplements. *American Journal on Mental Retardation, 106*(3), 231–252.

Levine, C., Halper, D., Peist, A., & Gould, D. A. (2010). Bridging troubled waters: Family caregivers, transitions, and long-term care. *Health Affairs, 29*(1), 116–124.

Lifespan Respite Care Act, P.L. 109–442 (2006).

Meyer, D., & Vadasy, P. (1994). *Sibshops: Workshops for siblings of children with special needs.* Baltimore, MD: Paul H. Brookes.

Older Americans Act Amendments of 2000, Public Law 106–501, 114 Stat. 2226 (2000).

Patton, M. Q. (2002). *Qualitative research and evaluation methods, 3rd edition.* Newbury Park, CA: Sage.

Rawson, H. (2009). "I'm going to be here long after you've gone"— Sibling perspectives of the future. *British Journal of Learning Disabilities, 38,* 225–231.

Sarantakos, S. (1993). *Social research.* South Melbourne, Victoria, Australia: MacMillan Education Australia.

Stoneman, Z. (2005). Siblings of children with disabilities: Research themes. *Mental Retardation, 43*(5), 339–350.

U.S. Census Bureau. (2010). *Data finders: Population clocks.* Available at http://www.census.gov.

Weber, R. P. (1990). *Basic content analysis* (2nd ed.). Newbury Park, CA: Sage.

Critical Thinking

1. If you had a sibling with a developmental disability, what would be your greatest worries or concerns as your parents aged and you became an adult? How do you think having someone with a developmental disability in your family would alter family relationships?

2. What are some challenges and difficulties experienced by adult siblings when their brother or sister has a developmental disability?

3. Using information gained from this article, describe an intervention or support program that could be developed to facilitate positive family relationships, decrease caregiver stress, and aid in transition planning for families where an adult child has a developmental or intellectual disability.

Create Central

www.mhhe.com/createcentral

Internet References

Sibling Support Project
www.siblingsupport.org

Sibs
www.sibs.org.uk

Tufts University Child and Family Webguide
www.cfw.tufts.edu

Arnold, Catherine; Heller, Tamar; Kramer, John. From *Intellectual and Developmental Disabilities,* vol. 50, no. 5, 2012, pp. 373–382. Copyright © 2012 by American Association on Intellectual and Developmental Disabilities AAIDD. Reprinted by permission via Copyright Clearance Center.

Article

Prepared by: Patricia Hrusa Williams,
University of Maine at Farmington

Supporting Siblings of Children with Autism Spectrum Disorders

LING-LING TSAO, RANDY DAVENPORT, AND CYNTHIA SCHMIEGE

Learning Outcomes

After reading this article, you will be able to:

- Understand the characteristics of autism spectrum disorders (ASDs).

- Identify the challenges experienced by siblings when one has an ASD.

- Identity individual and family factors that promote healthy sibling relationships in families where a child has an ASD.

- Recognize supports needed by families when a child has an ASD.

Introduction

Autism is a pervasive developmental disorder. It affects essential human behaviors such as the ability to communicate ideas and feelings, imagination, and the establishment of relationships with others (National Research Council 2001). In a recent report, the Centers for Disease Control and Prevention (2009) estimates an average of 1 in 110 children in the U.S. has an autism spectrum disorder (ASD). Due to these alarming statistics, the topic of ASDs has become a nation-wide concern, prompting discussions among professionals and parents seeking the best possible intervention approaches to support families of children with ASDs (O'Brien and Daggett 2006). There are many unknowns about the most effective treatment strategy for children with ASDs. However, it is generally agreed that early intervention programs are crucial and effective. The National Research Council recommends that educational services begin as soon as a child is suspected of having an autistic spectrum disorder (p. 6, NRC 2001). Given the importance of early intervention for a child with an ASD, much attention is being devoted to the characteristics of effective educational interventions for children with an ASD.

In the family context, attention is typically focused on effective intervention for a child with an ASD. However, many parents, specialists, and researchers have concerns for other children in the family as well (Hastings 2007). Particularly, there is concern about how best to support typically developing siblings of children with an ASD (Kilmer et al. 2008; Lock 2009; Schuntermann 2009). Consequently, the purpose of this paper is to review and synthesize the literature on support for siblings of children with an ASD. With this purpose in mind, this review focuses on approaches for supporting and fostering positive sibling relationships, with consideration of the family system where appropriate.

For the purpose of this paper, we refer to a child with an ASD as *the focal child*, and we refer to a typically developing sibling of a child with a disability or an ASD as *the sibling* or *siblings*. We focused on two basic questions about what it means to be a sibling of a child with an ASD: What is it like to grow up as a sibling of a child with autism? And what can we do to support siblings of children with autism? These questions helped guide us as we reviewed the literature, and we hope to address these questions throughout this review. Before discussing the available support for siblings, it is important to consider what has been researched and what is currently known about sibling relationships.

Sibling Relationships

One special characteristic of sibling relationships is that they share biological and affective ties with parents. Brothers and sisters can be a source of companionship, help, and emotional support. In their interactions with each other, siblings may acquire many social and cognitive skills that are central to healthy social development (Furman and Buhrmester 1985). Travis and Sigman (1998) suggested that siblings may be especially important for children with autism because they provide opportunities to socially interact with other children under maximally supportive conditions (Rivers and Stoneman 2008). Research suggests that children with ASDs need exposure to typically developing children to gain experience and learn about proper social interaction and relationships (Knott et al.1995; Tsao and Odom 2006). Typically developing siblings have great potential to influence children with ASDs, particularly in early development, and in the acquisition of social competencies.

Related to the discussion of sibling relationships is the discussion of what it is like to grow up as a sibling of a child with an ASD. McHale et al. (1986) interviewed 30 siblings of children with autism, 30 siblings of children with cognitive disabilities, and 30 siblings of typically developing children between the ages of 6 and 15. The children were asked questions about their sibling relationships, their attitudes, and their perceptions of their siblings. For both the group with siblings of children with autism and the group with siblings of children with cognitive disabilities, negative sibling relationships were associated with worries about the future of the child with a disability, perceptions of parental favoritism toward the child with a disability, and feelings of rejection toward the child with a disability.

Mascha and Boucher (2006) interviewed 14 siblings of children with autism between the ages of 11 and 18 and identified negative reactions, such as feelings of embarrassment related to the focal child's behavior problems (i.e., aggression or uncontrolled anger). Gold (1993) found siblings of boys with autism scored higher on the depression measure of the Children's Depression Inventory than siblings of typically developing boys. Thereby, siblings of children with autism may have potentially more internalizing symptoms particularly when they are moving into adolescence. (However, the researchers cautioned generalizing the finding due to a disproportionate number of adolescent siblings compared to the control group).

Compared to siblings of typically developing children, higher levels of attentional problems, loneliness, and problems with peers have been found in siblings of children with autism (Bagenholm and Gillberg 1991). Kaminsky and Dewey (2001) also found that in families with a child with an ASD, sibling relationships were characterized by less intimacy, less prosocial behavior, and less nurturance as measured by siblings' perceptions of their relationships on a sibling relationship questionnaire. This is consistent with another study by Knott et al. (1995), who reported that children with autism and their typically developing siblings spent less time together than typically developing sibling dyads.

In contrast to these potentially negative findings concerning sibling relationships, McHale et al. (1986) indicated that siblings with a good understanding of their brother or sister's disability, had positive sibling relationships when they perceived that parents and peers had positive reactions toward their sibling with a disability. Mates (1990) found that siblings of children with autism had high self-concepts, healthy academic performance, and healthy behavioral adjustment as rated by their parents and teachers. These positive findings are also in line with other similar research studies (i.e., Berger 1980; McHale et al. 1986). Although autism has doubtlessly had an impact on the family (e.g., Hastings 2003a; Hastings et al. 2005; Ross and Cuskelly 2006), these positive findings indicate that in some instances, siblings of children with autism seem to adjust well to their family situation, and occasionally perform better in some aspects of their social emotional development (e.g., the development of their mean self concept) than the normative sample (Mates 1990). Other positive impacts related to having a sibling with a disability may involve more acceptance (Roeyers and Mycke 1995), no deficits in social competence (Kaminsky

and Dewey 2002; Rodrigue et al. 1993), and greater admiration and less competition and quarrels (Knott et al. 1995).

Siblings with positive perceptions and experiences related to their sibling with a disability are likely to adapt successfully to the impact of having a disability on the family (Taunt and Hastings 2002). When siblings perceived their parents and peers as reacting positively to the child with a disability, they reported more positive relationships with their sibling (Petalas et al. 2009).

The impact of having a sibling with an ASD may vary among children; as Stoneman (2001) pointed out, the research on sibling relationships is often contradictory and difficult to interpret. Numerous researchers have found that the relationship between children with disabilities and their siblings is usually positive (McHale et al. 1986; Stoneman et al. 1987; Bagenholm and Gillberg 1991; Lobato et al. 1991). However, some negative impacts of ASD on sibling relationships have also been found (e.g., Bagenholm and Gillberg 1991; Kaminsky and Dewey 2001). Certain variables may directly or indirectly affect the adaption of typically developing siblings to their brothers or sisters with disabilities, such as gender, age, information, knowledge about the disability of the child with a disability, or age difference between the typically developing siblings and children with disabilities (Unal and Baran 2011). While there is little or nothing that can be done about the age of children, their ordinal position or the severity of the ASD, there are strategies that can be implemented to promote and facilitate positive relationships between typically developing siblings and their brother or sister with an ASD (Beyer 2009).

Supports and Approaches

Only a limited number of researchers have directly attempted to empirically validate support strategies for siblings that help them develop positive, mutually satisfying relationships with their brothers and sisters (Stoneman 2001). The lack of research on this topic is remarkable because intervention may help ensure that positive rather than negative outcomes of sibling relationship development occur (Mascha and Boucher 2006). Society has no greater task than to provide for the healthy, positive development of children; the ultimate goal is to support children with disabilities and their siblings in ways that enhance their chances of growing into psychologically healthy adults with firmly established positive interpersonal relationships (Stoneman 2005, p. 347).

Parenting

For a variety of reasons, parents may not treat all of their children identically. Not only is each child a unique individual, but parents also experience developmental changes over the course of parenting. This is perhaps particularly an issue for families with a child with a disability. For typically developing children, research has shown that differential parental treatment of siblings is linked to adjustment problems (Feinberg and Hetherington 2001). Many studies have also documented increased differential parenting in families with children with disabilities, generally favoring the child with a disability (Lobato et al. 1991; McHale and Pawletko 1992). Dunn and McGuire (1992) highlight an impressive consensus from the research that maternal differential treatment is linked to the quality of sibling relationships for typically developing children (e.g., Boer 1990; Brody and Stoneman 1987; Bryany and Crockenberg 1980, Dunn and Plomin 1990) and even for siblings of children with disabilities (McHale and Gamble 1989). When siblings are dissatisfied with differential parenting, the quality of the sibling relationship suffers (Rivers and Stoneman 2008). It is not simply a matter of poor sibling relationships and parental favoring that lead to increased psychological difficulties, but it is a more complex issue involving children who are sensitive to changes in the wider sibling context (Richmond et al. 2005; Schuntermann 2007).

Siblings may not always perceive differential parenting as favoritism—siblings' attitudes concerning how they perceive the differential treatment has much to do with their satisfaction with the sibling relationship. Children do not always object to being treated differently from their siblings, as long as they can find meaning in the difference and perceive the difference as being fair (Kowal et al. 2002). Similarly, McHale et al. (2000) found that differential treatment from parents does not always have negative implications for siblings; it is important to consider the subjective evaluation and the legitimacy of the differential treatment of the siblings themselves. Both children who have a sibling with a disability and children who have typically developing siblings experience a full range of feelings related to their brother or sister, their parents, themselves, and other people in general. Many siblings experience similar emotions. Some feel excitement, anger, frustration, and others might feel unfavorable or lonely.

Parenting Strategy: Communication

It is very important to acknowledge the impact of siblings' perceptions about parenting on their sibling relationship before trying to support siblings. Therefore, open communication is one way parents can provide support for siblings of children with autism. Gold (1993) stressed the benefits experienced by siblings when open communication was possible, especially when family members were free to communicate openly about the child with a disability. For more information on specific strategies for facilitating effective family communication (e.g., good listening skills for creating an atmosphere where siblings can feel free to reveal personal thoughts and feelings to parents), see Harris and Glasberg (2003).

In addition to good communication, it may be helpful for siblings to learn to label their emotions. This may help children understand their emotions by linking their own feelings or concerns about their sibling to their perceptions of their parents' emotional state (e.g., stress about care for every family member). Meanwhile, providing age appropriate explanations about what autism is can help siblings understand and manage their perceptions about why their sibling with an ASD receives extra

attention and support (Harris and Glasberg 2003; Gallagher et al. 2006). Parents should do their best to understand what their typically developing children are saying concerning their sibling with an ASD. Furthermore, siblings will feel more supported when parents provide them with clear feedback that what they say has been received and taken into account by their parents. Acknowledgment of siblings' feelings will help them feel respected.

When determining how to best support siblings, it may be beneficial to consider not only good communication in general and education about autism, but also to consider the demands placed upon siblings as a result of having a brother or sister with an ASD. Do typically developing siblings of a brother or sister with an ASD take on more household and care responsibilities than siblings in families without disabilities? Interestingly, Gold (1993) found that siblings of children with autism report doing less domestic work than siblings of typically developing children. Perhaps this is due to parental fears and guilt about potentially burdening siblings by over-relying on them for help with childcare and a desire to not over-burden siblings with extra housework responsibilities.

Parental expectation about sibling responsibilities is one aspect of the parent–child relationship, which illustrates that the relationship between each child and parent can influence the sibling–sibling relationship. Such aspects of the parent–child relationship should be taken into account, and parental awareness of each individual child's needs in a family constellation can reduce sibling rivalry and bring the family members closer together (Cancro 2008). Bryant and Crockenberg (1980) found that parents who are responsive to their children's behavior are likely to foster prosocial behaviors between their children (Furman and Buhrmester 1985).

Support Group

Having a child with an ASD in the family not only has the potential to influence sibling relationships and the emotional well-being of siblings, it can also affect the emotional well-being of the parents. Research has found that parents of children with ASDs have higher rates of depression and stress compared to parents who have children with other disabilities and parents with typically developing children (e.g., Hastings 2003b; Hasting et al., 2005; Ross and Cuskelly 2006). Parents need a good support network. Having access to a support network and receiving specific support related to their child yielded great benefits for parents of children with autism (Guralnick et al. 2008). Parent support groups should involve meeting other parents of children with similar conditions. Such meetings offer parents the knowledge, understanding, and acceptance they seek (Banach et al. 2010). Through programs like a family support group or a parent-to-parent group, families have a place to share their joys and concerns, learn lessons to better support their child's needs, exchange information, and generally support each other.

Family support groups are good for parents and children. There is evidence that social support might moderate the severity of symptoms exhibited by the child with an ASD and might be related to adaptive coping and adjustment of siblings (Banach et al. 2010; Hastings 2003b; Law et al. 2001; Stoneman 2005). Many non-profit organizations provide support group services for families who have a child with autism, such as the Autism Society of America or the ARC of the United States at state and local levels. Some organizations also provide child-care services so that parents can attend without making baby-sitting arrangements—a potential challenge for many families with children who have disabilities. When parents have access to quality emotional and informational resources, they are better positioned to reach out for help and cope more effectively.

Parent Training and Support

Parental attitudes about support for each of their individual children are vital for promoting positive sibling relationships. Parents can act as both support agents and agent trainers; however, before getting to this level, parents need the right information and training themselves. Support groups and community agencies are again likely to be a valuable source for these kinds of resources. A program focused on training parents to teach social skills to young siblings can not only promote positive, adaptive behavior, but can also capitalize on the powerful socialization effects of parents and siblings (i.e., parents and siblings are uniquely situated to make a profound impact on a child's development) (Tiedemann and Johnston 1992).

Parents may need assistance developing strategies to enhance children's social competencies. Programs exist to aid parents with the endeavor of creating their own intervention plan and can help parents create a custom intervention tailored to their families' specific needs. Programs such as these can also help parents understand different intervention approaches, which may help parents overcome the limitations of some existing interventions (e.g., limited ability to generalize from other interventions and maintenance issues; Tiedemann and Johnston, 1992). Parent training is necessary for teaching parents how to appropriately reinforce and maintain sibling efforts to positively interact with their brother or sister with an ASD (Petalas et al. 2009). For example, Lobato and Kao (2002) conducted an integrated sibling–parent group intervention for typically developing siblings of children with a chronic illness or developmental disability and their parents. When parents implemented good reinforcement and maintenance strategies, the authors found improved sibling connectedness and found that siblings had a better knowledge of the child's disorder and behavior problems (Petalas et al. 2009).

Sibling Play Intervention

Play provides the prime social context for children to create reciprocal roles, define power relationships, and facilitate mutual social exchanges (Stoneman 2001). Through trial and error informed by social feedback, typically developing children learn to accommodate their siblings' disabilities and facilitate social interaction (Stoneman 2001). However, the siblings' role as an agent for social skills training is not without challenges. Research indicates that it is more difficult for typically developing siblings to create and lead play behaviors when their brother or sister's disruptive and negative behaviors are more severe (Bagenholm and Gillberg 1991; Knott et al. 1995; Mascha and Boucher 2006; Strain and Danko 1995). Therefore, an individualized play-based social intervention may be an effective strategy for supporting siblings' needs.

Tsao and McCabe (2010) provided a protocol for parents or early intervention specialists to develop a sibling play intervention focused on supporting proper interactions between a child with autism and a typically developing sibling. The intervention begins by observing the children's play and routines. Early intervention specialists and parents then search for opportunities to use the focal child's preferred toys or activities to create play sessions with specific objectives for both children. The key to success for an intervention such as this requires taking the sibling's motivation into consideration (e.g., the specialist and parents should consider whether the sibling enjoys learning new ways of interacting with the focal child). Motivated siblings can be a significant resource for the family, making the situation less difficult and allowing the family to cope more effectively.

Again, siblings can be successful social agents for children with autism. Siblings can facilitate initiations and learn to respond strategically to their siblings (El-Ghoroury and Romanczyk 1999; Tsao and Odom 2006). Siblings adept at selecting activities that actively engage both children will make more effective play partners than children who select activities that exclude one child or the other (Lobato et al. 1991; Stoneman et al. 1987). Through ongoing interactions, siblings with the social skills to appropriately understand and respond to the needs of their brother or sister with a disability can develop high quality sibling relationships (Stoneman 2005). Interaction training for siblings of children with ASDs may prove to be a valuable approach for an intervention. Such training could potentially enhance the social interactions and communication between siblings and thus, reduce conflict. Continuity of training and periodic reassessment will ensure that siblings are provided with the necessary resources to meet the changing demands as the sibling dyad develops and each child grows older (Petalas et al. 2009).

It is possible that skills siblings gain in intervention and sharpened through interactions with their brother or sister can generalize to contexts beyond the sibling–sibling relationship. (Mascha and Boucher 2006). For example, Colletti and Harris (1997) taught siblings of children with ASDs behavior modification techniques—techniques that could potentially be applied to other relationships and conflict management situations (e.g., relationships with friends and other children at school).

A few studies have begun to address the issue of supporting siblings and providing them with the skills and resources they need to be powerful social skill trainers and models for their brother or sister with autism. For example, Celiberti and Harris (1993) taught typically developing siblings behavioral skills to engage their brother or sister in play. Tsao and Odom (2006) taught typically developing siblings how to play more effectively with their brothers (who had an ASD) and found that children with ASDs initiated more interactions with their siblings at the end of the intervention than at the beginning. They also observed more play behaviors between both children suggesting that the children were more socially engaged after the intervention. Parents also mentioned that children played like they were real siblings (e.g., played together and played more often). When siblings see their important role in helping their brother or sister, and see that they are making a positive impact, it is affirming. As a result, showing typically developing siblings how to best enhance their brother or sister's abilities and social skills can potentially boost siblings' self esteem, and help them form stronger relationships with each other (Mascha and Boucher 2006).

Sibling Support Groups

Given the importance of social support from family members, friends, neighbors, professionals, and parent groups, it is possible that social support specifically for siblings may also play an important role in the healthy and adaptive adjustment of siblings (Kaminsky and Dewey 2002). One well-documented program for supporting siblings is Sibshops (Meyer and Vadasy 2007). Sibshops resulted in increased positive feelings about the brother or sister with a disability and siblings acquired useful coping strategies (Johnson and Sandall 2005; Conway and Meyer 2008).

Bagenholm and Gillberg (1991) interviewed 60 children between the ages of 5 and 20 who had a brother or sister with autism, cognitive disabilities, or no apparent physical or cognitive disorders. They found that siblings of children with disabilities talked more about their brothers and sisters than siblings of typically developing children. Children in "ordinary" families do not talk very much about their siblings (p. 304). As a result, Bagenholm and Gillberg (1991) believed that if there is something to talk about—good or bad—it may be a relief for siblings to have the opportunity to talk about their experiences both at home and with friends and other supportive adults. Simply providing opportunities for siblings to express their feelings is a good start, but a more structured and clinical approach may be even better. Mascha and Boucher (2006) indicated that it might be beneficial to work directly with siblings by helping them explore their thoughts and feelings, including reflecting on their experiences with their brother or sister, their understanding of the disability, and the role of each family member within the family system. Therefore, it is often good practice to utilize a professional counselor when possible. Providing resources and appropriate support to siblings is essential, and can potentially have long-term benefits for both siblings. Siblings of persons with disabilities can their brothers and sisters live dignified lives from childhood throughout adulthood (Meyer and Vadasy 1997).

Discussion

The majority of brothers and sisters of children with autism function well (Ferraioli and Harris 2010). Research has shown that relationships between siblings when one child has a disability are not identical to the relationships that exist between typically developing siblings (Stoneman 2001). However, having a brother or sister with a disability does not cause maladaptation or pathology in children (Stoneman 2005; Rodrigue et al. 1993). Instead, siblings of children with disabilities engage in a rich and complex set of roles, such as that of teacher, caregiver, modeler, and confidant, which may promote developmental benefits (Stoneman and Brody 1982). Many siblings of children with disabilities successfully achieve mutually acceptable interactional role relationships, artfully crafted to fit their life contexts (Stoneman 2001, 2005). Certainly, this is in keeping with family theories that suggest that families define situations. The use of available resources and the important aspects of a good intervention, as identified in this review, can assist families to not only cope with a stressor event but also adapt and thrive with their unique challenge.

On the other hand, the behavioral problems frequently associated with an ASD (e.g., aggression or temper issues) can cause a variety of negative emotions for typically developing siblings. Therefore, there is a clear need for proper support of siblings of children with autism (Mascha and Boucher 2006). Siblings are an integrative component of the family system and are key players shaping the experiences and learning opportunities available to children with special needs (Kresak et al. 2009).

It is not always clear what the impact of a disability will be on sibling relationships. There are many factors (e.g., environmental factors) that make studying the effects of an ASD on the sibling relationships difficult (Beyer 2009). Because children on the autism spectrum vary in the severity of their condition, it is difficult to ascertain how the disability impacts a family. The extent of developmental delay could impact how much a family is affected by the disorder. These differences should be taken into account when making decisions about how to support siblings and what kinds of interventions are appropriate for individual families.

The role of siblings who have a brother or sister on the autism spectrum has been underexplored, despite the sibling's potential to significantly enhance family life and foster social skills in children with autism. Efforts should be made to raise parental and professional awareness of the potential issues faced by siblings to promote dialogue in families and between families and professionals. This may prove especially significant later in life, as sibling relationships are often long-lasting relationships. It is recommended that practitioners acknowledge and build on the positive views held by siblings. This may help siblings recognize their personal strengths and abilities, promote positive family relationships characterized by open channels of communication, and provide opportunities for families to bond. Additionally, increasing siblings' access to developmentally appropriate information and support that promotes positive perceptions and experiences may have lasting effects on sibling adjustment and sibling relationships (Petalas et al. 2009). Use of resources (e.g., material, informational, and emotional/social resources, etc.) can impact the dynamic functioning of a whole family, including typically developing siblings. Hence, future autism sibling studies should take a life course approach and consider the context of life stages (Beyer 2009), as well as the impact on the family system as a whole.

Conclusion

Each family member plays an important role in his or her own family system. Siblings are uniquely situated to help children with ASDs and other disabilities. The take-home message of this review is that empowering siblings to be effective intervention partners can potentially yield great benefits for the sibling, the child with a disability, and the greater family constellation. Parents need to utilize the resources and support networks available to them to help them cope with the potential challenges of having a child with a disability. With proper support and resources, parents can ensure the much-needed support of their typically developing children. Parents can also facilitate the training of typically developing siblings, thereby including siblings in the larger intervention plan for the child with an ASD or other disability. Asking what is it like to grow up as a sibling of a child with autism and what can we do to support siblings of children with autism, led to the identification of several important considerations for supporting siblings and designing effective interventions. These considerations included open communication, opportunities for siblings to express their feelings, utilization of support networks, parenting considerations, and training of both parents and siblings. Viewing the sibling in the larger family context and providing siblings with proper support are vital issues—the reward of which is too great to ignore.

References

Bagenholm, A., & Gillberg, C. (1991). Psychosocial effects on siblings of children with autism and mental retardation: A population based study. *Journal of Mental Deficiency Research, 35,* 291–307.

Banach, M., Judice, J., Conway, L., & Couse, L. J. (2010). Family support and empowerment: Post autism diagnosis support group for parents. *Social Work with Groups, 33,* 69–83.

Berger, E. W. (1980). *A study of self concept of siblings of autistic children.* Unpublished Dissertation, University of Cincinnati.

Beyer, J. F. (2009). Autism spectrum disorders and sibling relationships: Research and strategies. *Education and Training in Developmental Disabilities, 44,* 444–452.

Boer, F. (1990). *Sibling relationships in middle childhood: An empirical study.* Leiden: DSWO Press, University of Leiden.

Brody, G. H., & Stoneman, Z. (1987). Sibling conflict: Contributions of the siblings themselves, the parent–sibling relationship, and the broader family system. *Journal of Children in Contemporary Society, 19,* 39–53.

Bryany, B. K., & Crockenberg, S. B. (1980). Correlates and dimensions of prosocial behavior: A study of female siblings with their mothers. *Child Development, 51,* 529–544.

Cancro, R. (2008). Children with autism and their siblings. *Exceptional Parent,* December, 30.

Celiberti, D. A., & Harris, S. L. (1993). Behavioral intervention for siblings of children with autism: A focus on skills to enhance play. *Behavior Therapy, 24,* 573–599.

Centers for Disease Control and Prevention (CDC). (2009). Prevalence of autism spectrum disorders: Autism and developmental disabilities monitoring network, United States, 2006. *Morbidity and Mortality Weekly Report,* December 18, 58 (NoSS-10).

Colletti, G., & Harris, S. L. (1997). Behavior modification in the home: Siblings as behavior modifiers, parents as observers. *Journal of Abnormal Child Psychology, 5,* 21–30.

Conway, S., & Meyer, D. (2008). Developing support for siblings of young people with disabilities. *Support for Learning, 23,* 113–117.

Dunn, J., & McGuire, S. (1992). Sibling and peer relationships in childhood. *Journal of Child Psychology and Psychiatry, 33,* 67–105.

Dunn, J., & Plomin, R. (1990). *Separate lives: Why siblings are so different.* New York: Basic Books.

El-Ghoroury, N. H., & Romanczyk, R. G. (1999). Play interactions of family members towards children with autism. *Journal of Autism and Developmental Disorders, 28,* 249–258.

Feinberg, M., & Hetherington, E. M. (2001). Differential parenting as a within-family variable. *Journal of Family Psychology, 15,* 22–37.

Ferraioli, S. J., & Harris, S. (2010). The impact of autism on siblings. *Social Work in Mental Health, 8,* 41–53.

Furman, W., & Buhrmester, D. (1985). Children's perceptions of the qualities of sibling relationships. *Child Development, 56,* 448–461.

Gallagher, P. A., Powell, T. H., & Rhodes, C. A. (2006). *Brothers and sisters: A special part of exceptional families* (3rd ed.). Baltimore: MD: Brookes.

Gold, N. (1993). Depression and social adjustment in siblings of boys with autism. *Journal of Autism and Developmental Disorders, 23,* 147–163.

Guralnick, M. J., Hammond, M. A., Neville, B., & Connor, R. T. (2008). The relationship between sources and functions of social support and dimensions of child and parent related stress. *Journal of Intellectual Disability Research, 53,* 1138–1154.

Harris, S., & Glasberg, B. (2003). *Siblings of children with autism: A guide for families* (2nd ed.). Bethesda, MD: Woodbine House.

Hastings, R. P. (2003a). Brief report: Behavioral adjustment of siblings of children with autism. *Journal of Autism and Developmental Disorders, 33,* 99–104.

Hastings, R. P. (2003b). Behavioral adjustment of siblings of children with autism engaged in applied behavioral analysis early intervention programs: The moderating role of social support. *Journal of Autism and Developmental Disorders, 33,* 141–150.

Hastings, R. P. (2007). Longitudinal relationships between sibling behavioral adjustment and behavior problems of children with developmental disabilities. *Journal of Autism and Developmental Disorders, 37,* 1485–1492.

Hastings, R., Kovshoff, H., Brown, T., Ward, N., degli Espinosa, F., & Remington, B. (2005). Coping strategies in mothers and fathers of preschool and school-age children with autism. *Autism, 9,* 377–391.

Johnson, A. B., & Sandall, S. (2005). *Sibshops: A follow-up of participants of a sibling support program.* Seattle: University of Washington.

Kaminsky, L., & Dewey, D. (2001). Siblings relationships of children with autism. *Journal of Autism and Developmental Disorders, 31,* 399–410.

Kaminsky, L., & Dewey, D. (2002). Psychosocial adjustment in siblings of children with autism. *Journal of Child Psychology and Psychiatry, 43,* 225–232.

Kilmer, R. P., Cook, J. R., Taylor, C., Kane, S. F., & Clark, L. Y. (2008). Siblings of children with severe emotional disturbances: Risks, resources, and adaptation. *American Journal of Orthopsychiatry, 78,* 1–10.

Knott, F., Lewis, C., & Williams, T. (1995). Sibling interaction of children with learning disabilities: A comparison of autism and Down's syndrome. *Journal of Child Psychiatry, 6*, 965–976.

Kowal, A., Kramer, L., Krull, J. L., & Crick, N. R. (2002). Children's perceptions of the fairness of parental preferential treatment and their socioemotional well being. *Journal of Family Psychology, 16*, 297–306.

Kresak, K., Gallagher, P., & Rhodes, C. (2009). Siblings of infants and toddlers with disabilities in early intervention. *Topics in Early Childhood Special Education, 29*, 143–154.

Law, M., King, S., Stewart, D., & King, G. (2001). The perceived effects of parent-led support groups for parents of children with disabilities. *Physical & Occupational Therapy in Pediatrics, 21*, 29–48.

Lobato, D., & Kao, B. T. (2002). Integrated sibling–parent group intervention to improve sibling knowledge and adjustment to chronic illness and disability. *Journal of Pediatric Psychology, 27*, 711–716.

Lobato, D., Miller, C. T., Barbour, L., Hall, L. J., & Pezzullo, J. (1991). Preschool siblings of handicapped children: Interactions with mothers, brothers, and sisters. *Research in Developmental Disabilities, 12*, 387–399.

Lock, R. H. (2009). Examining the need for autism sibling support groups in rural areas. *Rural Special Education Quarterly, 28*(4), 21–30.

Mascha, K., & Boucher, J. (2006). Preliminary investigation of a qualitative method of examining siblings' experiences of living with a child with ASD. *British Journal of Developmental Disabilities, 52*, 19–28.

Mates, T. E. (1990). Siblings of autistic children: Their adjustment and performance at home and in school. *Journal of Autism and Developmental Disorders, 20*, 545–553.

McHale, S. M., & Gamble, W. C. (1989). Sibling relationships of children with disabled and nondisabled brothers and sisters. *Developmental Psychology, 25*, 421–429.

McHale, S. M., & Pawletko, T. M. (1992). Differential treatment of siblings in two family contexts. *Child Development, 63*, 68–81.

McHale, S. M., Sloan, J., & Simeonsson, R. J. (1986). Sibling relationships of children with autistic, mental retarded, and nonhandicapped brothers and sisters. *Journal of Autism and Developmental Disorders, 16*, 399–413.

McHale, S. M., Updegraff, K. A., Jackson-Newsom, J., Tucker, C. J., & Crouter, A. C. (2000). When does parents' differential treatment have negative implications for siblings? *Social Development, 9*, 149–172.

Meyer, D., & Vadasy, P. (1997). Meeting the unique concerns of brothers and sisters. In B. Carpenter (Ed.), *Family in context: Emerging trends in family support and early intervention.* London: Davis Fulton.

Meyer, D., & Vadasy, P. (2007). *Sibshops: Workshops for siblings of children with special needs* (revised edition ed.). Baltimore, MD: Paul H. Brookes.

National Research Council (2001). Educating Children with Autism. Committee on Educational Interventions for Children with Autism. In C. Lord, & J. P. McGee (Eds.), *Division of Behavioral and Social Sciences and Education.* Washington, DC: National Academy Press.

O'Brien, M., & Daggett, J. (2006). *Beyond the autism diagnosis: A professional's guide to helping families.* Baltimore, MD: Brookes.

Petalas, M. A., Hastings, R. P., Nash, S., Dowey, A., & Reilly, D. (2009). I like that he always shows who he is: The perceptions and experiences of siblings with a brother with autism spectrum disorder. *International Journal of Disability, Development, and Education, 56*, 381–399.

Richmond, M. K., Stocker, C. M., & Rienks, S. L. (2005). Longitudinal associations between sibling relationship quality, parental differential treatment, and children's adjustment. *Journal of Family Psychology, 19*, 550–559.

Rivers, J. W., & Stoneman, Z. (2008). Child temperaments, differential parenting, and the sibling relationships of children with autism spectrum disorder. *Journal of Autism and Developmental Disorders, 38*, 1740–1750.

Rodrigue, J. R., Geffken, G. R., & Morgan, S. B. (1993). Perceived competence and behavioral adjustment of siblings of children with autism. *Journal of Autism and Developmental Disorders, 23*, 665–674.

Roeyers, H., & Mycke, K. (1995). Siblings of children with autism, with mental retardation, and with normal development. *Child: Care, Health and Development, 21*, 305–319.

Ross, P., & Cuskelly, M. (2006). Adjustment, sibling problem and coping strategies of brothers and sisters of children with autistic spectrum disorder. *Journal of Intellectual & Developmental Disability, 31*, 77–86.

Schuntermann, P. (2007). The sibling experience: Growing up with a child who has pervasive developmental disorder or mental retardation. *Harvard Review of Psychiatry, 15*, 93–108.

Schuntermann, P. (2009). Growing up with a developmentally challenged brother or sister: A model for engaging siblings based on mentalizing. *Howard Review of Psychiatry, 17*, 297–314.

Stoneman, Z. (2001). Supporting positive sibling relationships during childhood. *Mental Retardation and Developmental Disabilities Research Review, 7*, 134–142.

Stoneman, Z. (2005). Siblings of children with disabilities: Research themes. *Mental Retardation, 43*, 339–350.

Stoneman, Z., & Brody, G. H. (1982). Strengths in sibling interactions involving a retarded child: A functional role theory approach. In N. Stinnett, B. Chesser, J. DeFrain, & P. Knaub (Eds.), *Family strengths* (pp. 113–129). Lincoln: University of Nebraska Press.

Stoneman, Z., Brody, G. H., Davis, C. H., & Crapps, J. M. (1987). Mentally retarded children and their older siblings: Naturalistic in home observations. *American Journal on Mental Retardation, 92*, 290–298.

Strain, P. S., & Danko, C. D. (1995). Caregivers' encouragement of positive interaction between preschoolers with autism and siblings. *Journal of Emotional and Behavioral Disorders, 3*, 2–12.

Taunt, H. M., & Hastings, R. P. (2002). Positive impact of children with developmental disabilities on their families: A preliminary study. *Education and Training in Mental Retardation and Developmental Disabilities, 37*, 410–420.

Tiedemann, G. L., & Johnston, C. (1992). Evaluation of a parent training program to promote sharing between young siblings. *Behavior Therapy, 23*, 299–318.

Travis, L. L., & Sigman, M. (1998). Social deficits and interpersonal relationships in autism. *Mental Retardation and Developmental Disabilities Research Reviews, 4*, 65–72.

Tsao, L., & McCabe, H. (2010). Why won't he play with me? Facilitating sibling interactions. *Young Exceptional Children, 13*, 24–35.

Tsao, L., & Odom, S. L. (2006). Sibling mediated social interaction intervention for young children with autism. *Topics in Early Childhood Special Education, 26*, 106–123.

Unal, N., & Baran, G. (2011). Behaviors and attitudes of normally developing children toward their intellectually disabled siblings. *Psychological Reports, 108,* 553–562.

Critical Thinking

1. If you had a sibling with an autism spectrum disorder (ASD), what would be your greatest worries or concerns? How do you think having a child in your family with a special need such as an ASD would alter family relationships?

2. What are some challenges and difficulties experienced by a sibling when their brother or sister has an ASD?

3. What are individual and family factors that are important for developing healthy sibling and family relationships when a child in the family has an ASD?

4. How might a typically developing sibling be able to assist in the treatment or education of a child with an ASD?

5. Using information gained from this article, describe an intervention or support program that could be developed to facilitate the positive development of siblings when a child in the family has an ASD.

Create Central

www.mhhe.com/createcentral

Internet References

Sibling Support Project
www.siblingsupport.org

Sibs
www.sibs.org.uk

Tufts University Child and Family Webguide
www.cfw.tufts.edu

Tsao, Ling-Ling; Davenport, Randy; Schmiege, Cynthia. From *Early Childhood Education Journal,* vol. 40, no. 1, January 2011, pp. 47–54. Copyright © 2011 by Springer Science and Business Media. Reprinted by permission via Rightslink.

Prepared by: Patricia Hrusa Williams,
University of Maine at Farmington

Article

The Accordion Family

K ATHERINE S. N EWMAN

Learning Outcomes

After reading this article, you will be able to:

- Identify factors leading adult children to live with their parents.

- Understand challenges for parents and their adult children living together.

Maria Termina and her husband, Alberto, live in the northwestern city of Bra in the Piedmont region of Italy. The people of Bra are traditionalists who struggle to hold the modern world at arm's length. Proud to be the hometown of Carlo Petrini, the founder of the Slow Food Movement, Bra hosts a biennial festival that celebrates artisanal cheeses from around the world.

Alberto, now 67, has lived in Bra almost all his life and worked for the same firm as an engineer for about 40 of those years. Maria is 57. They have three grown children, the youngest of whom, 30-year-old Giovanni, has always lived with his parents and shows no signs of moving out. (All the names in this piece, which is based on interviews, are fictitious to protect privacy.)

Giovanni graduated from the local high school but went no further than that and is content with his steady blue-collar job as an electrician. He works on construction sites and picks up odd jobs on the side. It's a living, barely. His wages are modest, the building trades go up and down, and—in all honesty—his tastes in motorcycles are a bit extravagant. Though he is a skilled worker, Giovanni knows he could not enjoy himself with his friends as he does if he had to support himself entirely on his own earnings. But because he pays no rent and can eat well at his mother's table, his living expenses are low, leaving money for recreation.

Of the three children born to Maria and Alberto, only Giorgio—Giovanni's twin brother—lives on his own. (Laura, divorced, and her 5-year-old daughter recently returned to the nest.) Giorgio completed a degree in economics at a local university and moved to Turin, where he works in marketing and statistics. He is the odd man out, not only in his family but also among many of his family's neighbors. More than a third of Italian men Giovanni's age have never left home; the pattern of "delayed departure" has become the norm in Italy. And while it was common in the past for unmarried men and women to remain with their parents until they wed, the age of marriage has been climbing in the last 30 years, so much so that by the time men like Giovanni cut the apron strings, they are very nearly what we once called "middle-aged." That has made the country an international butt of jokes about the "cult of mammismo," or mama's boys.

It is no laughing matter in Italy, particularly in government circles where the economic consequences are adding up. The former prime minister Silvio Berlusconi came out in support of a campaign against mammismo, having been elected on the promise of doing away with "those hidebound aspects of Italian life which 'inhibit dynamism and growth.'" In January 2010, Renato Brunetta, then a cabinet minister, proposed making it illegal for anyone over 18 to live with his or her parents. He made the suggestion on a radio show where he also admitted that his mother made his bed until he was 30, when he left home.

Why should government officials—including those whose own family lives are hardly worthy of admiration—care one way or the other where adult children make their home? The fact is that those private choices have serious public consequences. The longer aging bambini live with their parents, the fewer new families are formed, and the evaporation of a whole generation of Italian children is knocking the social policies of the country for a loop. Plummeting fertility translates into fewer workers to add fuel to the retirement accounts in an aging society. The private calculations of families like the Terminas, who wonder how long they can support Giovanni, are becoming the public problem of prime ministers.

Does his "delayed departure" worry 30-year-old Giovanni? Not really. Expectations are changing, and there is little pressure on him to be more independent. His family isn't urging him to marry, and he leans back in his chair and opines that "nobody asks you the reason [why you stay] at home with the parents at [my] age . . . nobody obliges me to move away."

Newton, Mass., is famous for its leafy streets, New England-style colonial houses, and well-educated parents who are professionals. The nearby universities—Harvard, MIT, Tufts—and numerous liberal-arts colleges, not to mention the concentration of health-care and computer-related industries, insures a steady influx of middle- and upper-middle-class families. Immigrants—especially high-tech professionals from Israel, India, and Russia—flock to this affluent community in pursuit of opportunity.

Newton boasts first-class schools from top to bottom; graduates of its high schools turn up regularly in the Ivy League. Poor black kids are bused in from inner-city Boston through the Metco integration program to partake of the town's exemplary educational facilities, but few poor families actually live within its boundaries. All but the fairly well heeled are priced out.

William Rollo and his wife arrived in Newton in 1989 after having lived in Seattle, Philadelphia, and Summit, N.J. A Brooklyn native, William married Janet at the age of 22 and set about completing a residency in podiatry. Their elder son, John, grew up in Newton and did well enough in high school to attend Williams College, one of the nation's most selective. Even so, he beat it home after graduating and has lived with his parents for several years while preparing to apply to graduate school. "A lot of my friends are living at home to save money," he explains.

Tight finances are not all that is driving John's living arrangements. The young man had choices and decided he could opt for more of the ones he wanted if he sheltered under his parents' roof. John is saving money from his job at an arts foundation for a three-week trip to Africa, where he hopes to work on a mobile health-care project in a rural region. It's a strategic choice designed to increase his chances of being accepted into Harvard University's competitive graduate program in public health.

John needs to build up his credentials if he wants to enter a program like that. To get from here to there, he needs more experience working with patients in clinics or out in the field. It takes big bucks to travel to exotic locations, and a master's degree will cost him dearly, too. In order to make good on his aspirations, John needs his parents to cover him for the short run.

On his own, John could pay the rent on an apartment, especially if he had roommates. What he can't afford is to pay for it and travel, to support himself and save for his hoped-for future. Autonomy turns out to be the lesser priority, so he has returned to the bedroom he had before he left for college, and there he stays.

John sees few drawbacks to that arrangement. His parents don't nag him or curtail his freedom. Janet wonders if they should ask him to pay rent, to bring him down to earth a bit and teach him some life skills, like budgeting. William is not so sure. He enjoys his son's company and was happy when John moved back into his old bedroom. Having a son around to talk to is a joy, particularly since John's younger brother is out of the house now, studying at the University of Vermont. That empty nest has refilled, and thank goodness, says William, rather quietly.

If John had no goals, no sense of direction, William would not be at ease with this "boomerang arrangement." Hiding in the basement playing video games would not do. Happily, that is not on John's agenda. William is glad to help his son realize his ambitions. He approves of John's career plans and doesn't really care if they don't involve making a handsome living. What really matters is that the work means something. It will help to remake the world, something William has not felt he

could contribute to very directly as a podiatrist. Having a son who can reach a bit higher—if not financially, then morally—is an ambition worth paying for.

And it will cost this family, big time. William and Janet have invested nearly $200,000 in John's education already. They will need to do more if John is going to become a public-health specialist. They are easily looking at another $50,000, even if John attends a local graduate program and continues to live with them. Whatever it costs, they reason, the sacrifice is worth it.

What is newsworthy, throughout the developed world, is that a growing number of young adults in their 20s and 30s have never been independent. In the United States, we tend to see a boomerang pattern in the affluent upper-middle class, with young people leaving for college and then returning home. Among working-class kids, the tendency is to stay put for the duration. Only one-quarter of today's college students are full time, living on campus, and largely supported by their parents. The norm is to live at home, study part time, work to pay your share, and shelter some of the steepest costs of higher education under the parental roof.

And in most countries—outside of the social democracies—there is far less investment in dormitories and other forms of transitional housing, meager government financial aid, and a historical pattern of pursuing university degrees wherever you grew up. With the labor market turning a cold shoulder to new graduates, simply staying at home seems the only option. Hence in Italy today, 37 percent of men age 30 have never lived away from home. Their counterparts in Spain, Japan, and many other developed countries are following a similar path: Millions are staying at the Inn of Mom and Dad for years, sometimes for several decades longer than was true in earlier generations.

In the United States, we have seen a 50-percent increase since the 1970s in the proportion of people age 30 to 34 who live with their parents. As the recession of 2008–9 continued to deepen, this trend became even more entrenched. Kids who cannot find jobs after finishing college, divorced mothers who can't afford to provide a home for their children, unemployed people at their wits' end, the ranks of the foreclosed—all are beating a path back to their parents' homes to take shelter underneath the only reliable roof available.

To some degree, that has always been the way of the private safety net. Families double up when misfortune derails their members, and the generations that have been lucky enough to buy into an affordable housing market, that enjoyed stable jobs for decades, find they must open their arms (and houses) to receive these economic refugees back into the fold. Blue-collar working-class families and the poor have never known anything different: Their kids have no choice but to stay home while they try to outrun a labor market that has become increasingly inhospitable.

Their parents have had it hard as well, as layoffs have spread through the factories of the Midwest and the South; pooling income across the generations is often the only sensible survival strategy, even if the climate becomes testy.

Until relatively recently, the middle class in most prosperous countries did not need to act as an economic shock absorber for such a prolonged period in the lives of their adult children. Their households might have expanded to take in a divorced offspring or support a child who had taken a nonpaying internship, but the norm for most white-collar parents was to send young people out into the world and look on in satisfaction as they took their places in the corporate world or the professions, found their life mates, and established their own nests.

Why, in the world's most affluent societies, are young (and not-so-young) adults unable to stand on their own two feet? Is it because we have raised a "slacker generation" that is unable or unwilling to take the hard knocks that come with striking out on their own? There are questions of taste lurking here: Young people in the middle class want jobs that are meaningful, rather than a means of putting a roof over their heads. They are not as eager as the "60s generation" of yore was to sleep on floors and wear clothes with holes in exchange for their independence.

And it is not especially painful for many of them to stay at home, because they share a lot of interests with Mom and Dad. Parents and their adult children are not staring at one another over the chasm of a "generation gap," but likely share similar tastes in music, movies, and, in many households, politics. That infamous gap was a product of the disjunctures that separated the generation that came of age in World War II from their boomer children, and it loomed large. But it has not emerged in succeeding generations: The Rolling Stones and Bob Dylan perform to sell-out crowds with gray hairs and twenty-somethings in the audience.

Still, we should not overemphasize the role of taste in spurring the trend toward accordion families. There is an unmistakable structural engine at work. International competition is greater than it once was, and many countries, fearful of losing markets for their goods and services, are responding by restructuring the labor market to cut the wage bill. Countries that regulated jobs to ensure they were full time, well paid, and protected from layoffs now permit part-time, poorly paid jobs and let employers fire without restriction. That may serve the interests of businesses—a debatable low-road strategy—but it has destroyed the options for millions of new entrants to the labor market throughout advanced postindustrial societies.

Japanese workers who once looked forward to lifetime employment with a single firm have gone the way of the dinosaur. American workers have seen the emergence of contingent labor (part-time, part-year, and short-term contracts), downsizing, offshoring, and many other responses to globalization that have exposed the American work force to wage stagnation and insecurity. European labor is arguably facing a very rocky future as the global consequences of the current financial crisis weaken the economies of the European Union and threaten the social protections that made them the envy of the developed world.

Eventually, those conditions will envelop the entire work force. For the time being, though, they are most evident in the lives of the least powerful: new entrants to the labor market, immigrants, and low-skilled workers. The generation emerging from college in the first decade of this century has been struggling to find a foothold in a rapidly changing economy

that cannot absorb its members as it once did, while housing prices—foreclosure epidemics notwithstanding—are making it hard for them to stake a claim to residential independence.

They fall back into the family home because, unless they are willing to take a significant cut in their standard of living, they have no other way to manage the life to which they have become accustomed. Moreover, if they aspire to a professional occupation and the income that goes with it, a goal their parents share for them, it is going to take them a long time and a lot of money to acquire the educational credentials needed to grab that brass ring. Sheltering inside an accordion family leaves more money to pay toward those degrees.

So what's the big deal? In earlier eras, people lived at home until they married. Is there anything new here? Yes and no. For several decades now, middle-class people in the United States, at least, expected to see their children live independently for a number of years before they married, and parents expected to have empty nests once their kids passed the magical mark of 18.

That formation was so widespread that it became a national norm, and it was made possible by a rental housing market and patterns of cohabitation (romantic, roommates) that made independence affordable. And for many, it still is. Yet increasingly the forces of labor-market erosion and rising housing and educational costs have combined to put independence out of reach.

Societal norms—the expectations that people bring to the table when social change is in the air—matter for how parents around the world view these new family formations. In Japan, where I found that parents expect discipline and order, this new trajectory is disturbing and tends to be defined as personal failure. Italian families, by contrast, report that they enjoy having their grown children live with them, however vexing it may be for their government.

Spanish parents and their adult children are angry at their government for facilitating lousy labor contracts that have damaged the children's prospects, but they know that it can be a joy to be near the younger generation.

In America, we deploy a familiar cultural arsenal in crafting meaning: the work ethic and the hope of upward mobility. If Joe lives at home because it will help him get somewhere in the long run, that's fine. If he's hiding in the basement playing video games, it's not fine. The accordion family has to be in the service of larger goals or it smacks of deviance.

All of these adaptations are responses to central structural forces beyond the control of any of us. Global competition is taking us into uncharted waters, reshaping the life course in ways that would have been scarcely visible only 30 years ago. It's a brave new world, and the accordion family is absorbing the blows as best it can.

Critical Thinking

1. What does the author mean by the terms "delayed departure," "boomerang arrangement," and "accordion family?"

2. Do you live with your parents now or anticipate moving back home after college? If so, why? What kinds of

problems or challenges come with living with your parents as an adult?

3. List some historical, economic, cultural, and social factors contributing to "accordion families."

4. What are some ground rules that adult children and their parents should set around their living arrangement?

Create Central

www.mhhe.com/createcentral

Internet References

AARP Blog: Boomerang Kids
http://blog.aarp.org/tag/boomerang-kids

National Council on Family Relations
www.ncfr.com

Article

Prepared by: Patricia Hrusa Williams,
University of Maine at Farmington

Daddy Issues

Why Caring For My Aging Father Has Me Wishing He Would Die

Sandra Tsing Loh

Learning Outcomes

After reading this article, you will be able to:

- Identify the financial and emotional burdens adult children face in caring for their aging parents.

- Describe how role reversal in parent–child relationships alters family dynamics.

- Identify supports needed by adult children caring for their aging parents.

Recently, a colleague at my radio station asked me, in the most cursory way, as we were waiting for the coffee to finish brewing, how I was. To my surprise, in a motion as automatic as the reflex of a mussel being poked, my body bent double and I heard myself screaming:

"I WAAAAAAAANT MY FATHERRRRRR TO DIEEEEE!!!"

Startled, and subtly stepping back to put a bit more distance between us, my coworker asked what I meant.

"What I mean, Rob, is that even if, while howling like a banshee, I tore my 91-year-old father limb from limb with my own hands in the town square, I believe no jury of my peers would convict me. Indeed, if they knew all the facts, I believe any group of sensible, sane individuals would actually roll up their shirtsleeves and pitch in."

As I hyperventilated over the coffee-maker, scattering Splenda packets and trying to unclaw my curled fingers, I realized it had finally happened: at 49, I had become a Kafka character. I am thinking of "The Judgment," in which the protagonist's supposedly old and frail father suddenly kicks off his bedclothes with surprisingly energetic—even girlish—legs and, standing ghoulishly tall in the bed, delivers a speech so horrifying, so unexpected, and so perfectly calculated to destroy his son's spirit that his son—who until this point has been having a rather pleasant day writing a letter to a friend, amidst a not unpleasant year marked by continuing financial prosperity and a propitious engagement to a well-placed young woman—immediately *jumps off a bridge.*

Clearly, my nonagenarian father and I have what have come to be known as "issues," which I will enumerate shortly. By way of introduction, however, let us begin by considering *A Bittersweet Season,* by Jane Gross. A journalist for 29 years at *The New York Times* and the founder of a *Times* blog called The New Old Age, Gross is hardly Kafkaesque. An ultra-responsible daughter given to drawing up to-do lists for caregivers and pre-loosening caps on Snapple bottles, Gross undertook the care of her mother in as professional a way as possible. She was on call for emergencies and planned three steps ahead by consulting personally with each medical specialist. Like the typical U.S. family caregiver for an elder (who is, statistics suggest, a woman of about 50), Gross worked full-time, but (atypically) she was unencumbered by spouse or children. She had the help, too, of her child-free brother, a calm, clear-headed sort given to greeting his sister with a quiet, reassuring "The eagle has landed." What could go wrong?

Plenty. As Gross herself flatly describes it, in her introduction:

> In the space of three years . . . my mother's ferocious independence gave way to utter reliance on her two adult children. Garden-variety aches and pains became major health problems; halfhearted attention no longer sufficed, and managing her needs from afar became impossible. . . . We were flattened by the enormous demands on our time, energy, and bank accounts; the disruption to our professional and personal lives; the fear that our time in this parallel universe would never end and the guilt for wishing that it would. . . . We knew nothing about Medicaid spend-downs, in-hospital versus out-of-hospital "do not resuscitate" orders, Hoyer lifts, motorized wheelchairs, or assistive devices for people who can neither speak nor type. We knew nothing about "pre-need consultants," who handle advance payment for the funerals of people who aren't dead yet, or "feeders," whose job it is to spoon pureed food into the mouths of men and women who can no longer hold a utensil.

However ghoulish, it is a world we will all soon get to know well, argues Gross: owing to medical advancements, cancer deaths now peak at age 65 and kill off just 20 percent of older Americans, while deaths due to organ failure peak at about 75 and kill off just another 25 percent, so the norm for seniors is becoming a long, drawn-out death after 85, requiring ever-increasing assistance for such simple daily activities as eating, bathing, and moving.

This is currently the case for approximately 40 percent of Americans older than 85, the country's fastest-growing demographic, which is projected to more than double by 2035, from about 5 million to 11.5 million. And at that point, here comes the next wave—77 million of the youngest Baby Boomers will be turning 70.

Quick back-of-the-envelope calculation, for Baby Boomers currently shepherding the Greatest Generation to their final reward? Hope your aged parents have at least half a million dollars apiece in the bank, because if they are anything like Mama Gross, their care until death will absorb every penny. To which an anxious (let's say 49-year-old) daughter might respond: But what about long-term-care insurance? In fact, Gross's own mother had purchased it, and while it paid for some things, the sum was a pittance compared with a final family outlay of several hundred thousand dollars. But how about what everyone says about "spending down" in order to qualify for Medicare, Medicaid, Medi-Cal, or, ah—which exactly is it?

Unfortunately, those hoping for a kind of *Eldercare for Dummies* will get no easy answers from *A Bittersweet Season.* Chides Gross: "Medicaid is a confusing and potentially boring subject, depending on how you feel about numbers and abstruse government policy, but it's essential for you to understand." Duly noted—so I read the relevant section several times and . . . I still don't understand. All I can tell you is that the Medicaid mess has to do with some leftover historical quirks of the Johnson administration, colliding with today's much longer life expectancies, colliding with a host of federal and state regulations that intertwine with each other in such a calcified snarl that by contrast—in a notion I never thought I'd utter—public education looks hopeful. Think of the Hoyer lift that can be delivered but never repaired, or the feeder who will not push, or the pusher who will not feed.

But it gets worse. Like an unnaturally iridescent convalescent-home maraschino cherry atop this Sisyphean slag heap of woe, what actually appears to take the greatest toll on caregivers is the sheer emotional burden of this (formless, thankless, seemingly endless) project. For one thing, unresolved family dynamics will probably begin to play out: "Every study I have seen on the subject of adult children as caregivers finds the greatest source of stress, by far, to be not the ailing parent but sibling disagreements," Gross writes. Further, experts concur, "the daughter track is, by a wide margin, harder than the mommy track, emotionally and practically, because it has no happy ending and such an erratic and unpredictable course." Gross notes, I think quite rightly, that however put-upon working parents feel (and we do keeningly complain, don't we—oh the baby-proofing! oh the breast-pumping! oh the day care!), we can at least plan employment breaks around such relative foreseeables as pregnancy, the school year, and holidays. By contrast, ailing seniors trigger crises at random—falls in the bathroom, trips to the emergency room, episodes of wandering and forgetting and getting lost. Wearied at times by the loneliness of the daughter track, Gross writes, in a rare moment of black humor:

> I know that at the end of my mother's life I felt isolated in my plight, especially compared to colleagues being feted with showers and welcomed back to work with oohs and aahs at new baby pictures. I was tempted, out of pure small-mindedness, to put on my desk a photo of my mother, slumped in her wheelchair.

Those seeking a more hopeful take on this bittersweet season might turn, for momentary comparison, to *Passages in Caregiving,* by Gail Sheehy. Reading Sheehy is always a boost—even when she's rewriting some Passage she predicted 10 or 20 or 30 years ago, as is necessarily (and, given our ever-increasing life spans, probably will continue to be necessarily) the case. From her intro (as swingingly nostalgic—isn't it, almost?—as Burt Bacharach):

> In my books and speeches since 1995, when I published *New Passages* [the first update of the original *Passages*], I keep predicting liberation ahead—the advent of a Second Adulthood, starting in one's midforties and fifties. At that proud age, having checked off most "shoulds," people generally feel a new sense of mastery. Haven't you done your best to please your parents, your mentor, your boss, and your mate, and now it's time for you? The children are making test flights on their way to piloting solo. Your parents have become giddy globetrotters, piling up frequent-flier miles and e-mailing playful photos of themselves riding camels. . . . Now you can finally earn that degree, start your own business, run for office, master another language, invent something, or write that book you keep mulling.

Ominous new paragraph—to reflect tire-screeching 21st century update:

> Then you get The Call.

In Sheehy's case, The Call was a cancer diagnosis for her husband, Clay Felker, which kicked off an almost two-decade period of medical battles before his death (which was actually not, in the end, from cancer). Although Sheehy offers her book as an umbrella guide for all caregivers, weaving her personal experience together with a demographically wide range of case studies, it strikes this caregiver as less than universal. For one thing—and in fact this is a tribute to how engagingly Sheehy tells her story—even with a tube in his stomach (for which sympathetic chefs blended gourmet food at Paris bistros, whereupon he continued to charm dinner guests as usual in his handsome navy-blue blazer), Clay Felker, on the page anyway, is still pretty great company. And then, to further vanquish the blues, Sheehy and Felker rented a houseboat, spent the summer in France . . . (How is it that, no matter what, Boomers always seem to be having more fun?)

And while there is some aesthetic appeal to Sheehy's mandala-like formulation of the caregiver's journey being not a straight path but a labyrinth (whose eight turnings are Shock and Mobilization, the New Normal, Boomerang, Playing God, "I Can't Do This Anymore!", Coming Back, the In-Between Stage, and the Long Goodbye), this taxonomy feels more descriptive than helpful. Also, her take on what one learns when caring for one's failing loved one is, if not quite a Hallmark card, certainly the best possible case:

> It opens up the greatest possibilities for true intimacy and reconnection at the deepest level. The sharing of strengths and vulnerabilities, without shame, fosters love. And for some caregivers, this role offers a chance in Second Adulthood to compose a more tender sequel to the troubled family drama of our First Adulthood. We can become better than our younger selves.

Jane Gross also believes spiritual growth is possible, but her take, predictably, is far less rosy, even verging on Old Testament:

> Here we are, not just with a herculean job but with a front-row seat for this long, slow dying. We want to do all we realistically can to ease the suffering, smooth the passing, of our loved ones. But we also have the opportunity to watch what happens to our parents, listen to what they have to say to us, and use that information to look squarely at our own mortality and prepare as best we can for the end of our own lives.

For herself, insists Gross: "I can tell you now that it was worth every dreadful minute, a transformative experience." And the inspiring lesson? Here it is, as expressed in a sere opening quotation by May Sarton: "I have seen in you what courage can be when there is no hope."

Clearly, various ruminations on the meaning of the caregiver's "journey" will continue, as ever more literature is added to the caregiving genre, as ever more of us spend ever more of our days belaying loved ones in Hoyer lifts like stricken beef cattle. That said, while I do carry a datebook festooned with soothing nature photography and the proverbs of the Buddhist nun Pema Chödrön (the sort of curious artifact 50-ish women like myself receive as Christmas gifts, along with very tiny—to reduce calories—lavender-and-sea-salt-infused gourmet chocolates), I myself have yet to see any pitch for the spiritual benefit of this grim half-million-dollar odyssey that is remotely inviting. To quote Amy Winehouse, who didn't want to go to rehab: No, no, no!

No . . . No . . . No. What I propose instead is seeking comfort in what I like to call, borrowing in part from Kafka's German, *Elderschadenfreude.* On the one hand, sure, here we stand around the office coffeemaker in middle age, mixing flax into our Greek yogurt and sharing more and more tales about our elderly parents, tales that are dull ("Mom slipped in the shower—at first she said it was nothing"), slow-moving ("And then I took her to the foot doctor, but then, right there in the parking lot, she insisted she had to go to the bathroom—but the door is on the *north* side while we were on the *south*—"), and in the end, well, depressingly predictable (we already know which colleges our wards are getting into—NONE). On the other

hand, I believe it is by enduring this very suffering and tedium that one can eventually tease out a certain dark, autumnal, delightfully-bitter-as-Fernet-Branca enjoyment, best described by some dense and complicated noun-ending German word.

Elderschadenfreude is the subtle frisson of the horror tale that always begins so simply ("Mom slipped in the shower—at first she said it was nothing") but makes listeners raise eyebrows, nod knowingly, begin microwaving popcorn. It is the secret pleasure of hearing about aging parents that are even more impossible than yours. Prepare to enjoy.

My father's old age began so well. Back in his 70s, to prepare for his sunset years, this Chinese widower had taken the precaution of procuring (after some stunning misfires) his retirement plan: an obedient Chinese-immigrant wife, almost 20 years younger than himself, who, in exchange for citizenship, would—unlike American women—accept the distinctly nonfeminist role of cutting up his fruit and massaging his bunions. In addition to doing all that, said Chinese wife, Alice, helped my dad run the informal Craigslist-peopled boarding house he had turned our family home into, for which her reward would be a generous inheritance upon his death, and the right to live in the house until hers. It is a measure of my dad's frugality that he didn't even buy health insurance for Alice until she turned 65—he rolled the statistical dice against the premiums, and won! With $2,000 a month from renters, on top of a Social Security check of $1,500, he and Alice were actually *making* money. What with their habit of taking buses everywhere and a shared love of Dumpster diving, they could star in their own reality show about thrift.

This is not to say my father has been completely "well." After age 78, if you asked him "How are you?" he would exclaim: "I'm dying!" At his 80th-birthday party, when he tremulously lifted his centimeter of red wine while watching my girlfriends dance, I mourned his visible frailty. At 82, he was passing out on bus benches, hitting his head, causing his doctors to insist on a pacemaker (which he refused). By 85, battling Parkinson's, he was still hobbling down to the beach to attempt rickety calisthenics and swimming, but "he's barely *swimming* in those two feet of water," my older sister worried. "It's more like falling." By 89, he was so slowed, like a clock winding down, that, never mind going to the beach, one morning he couldn't even get out of bed.

That was when he called me, in fear and confusion, for help. A pulse-pounding hourlong drive later, arriving at his bedside, I found to my panic that I could not rouse him. He lay in that waxy, inert, folded-up pose that looks unmistakably like death (I had seen it when my mother died, of early Alzheimer's, at 69). "This is it—it's really it—Papa's dead," I wept over the phone, long-distance, to my sister. And I remember, as the dust motes danced in the familiar golden light of our family home, how my sister and I found ourselves spontaneously, tumblingly observing to each other how we were sad . . . and yet oddly at peace.

Yes, my history with this man has been checkered: in my childhood, he had been cruelly cheap (no Christmas, no heat);

in my teens, he had been unforgivably mean to my mother; in my 20s, I rebelled and fled; in my 30s, I softened and we became wry friends—why not, he couldn't harm me now; in my 40s, sensing that these were the last days of a fading elder, the memories of whom I would reflect on with increasing nostalgia, the door opened for real affection, even a kind of gratitude. After all, I had benefited professionally from using him as fodder for my writing (as he had benefited financially for years by forging my signature so I ended up paying his taxes—ah, the great circle of life).

In short, there was real grief now at seeing my father go, but I was a big girl—actually, a middle-aged woman, with some 1,000 hours of therapy behind me—and, chin up, I would get through it. Unlike in the case of my mother, who had left too early, my business here was done. I had successfully completed my Kübler-Ross stages.

The conundrum that morning in the dining room (where my father's bed was), however, was that although my father wasn't rouseable, he wasn't actually dead. (He has a lizard-like resting pulse of 36, so even in his waking state, he's sort of like the undead.) I called the Malibu paramedics, who carted him to the emergency room and stuck an IV in. An hour later, the surprisingly benign diagnosis? Simple dehydration.

With a sudden angry snort, my father woke up. I won't say I wish I had hit him over the head with a frying pan to finish the job when it seemed we were so, so close. But I will say that when my dad woke up that day, my problems really began. Because what this episode made clear was that, while nothing was wrong with my dad, although he was 89—89!—something was wrong with Alice, who was supposed to be taking care of him. Her penchant for gibbering Chinese was not, as we'd imagined, a symptom of her English skills' plateauing after 15 years in America, but of the early or middle stages of dementia. This, I hadn't expected, because, as I remind you, she is much younger than my father. Alice's age is . . . drum-roll . . . 72.

So now, aside from neglecting my elderly father, the formerly mild-mannered Alice is starting to disturb the tenants: waving butcher knives at them, hurling their things into the street. (What a fun life they're having—my father believes some of the more sturdy renters can pitch in and "help shower" him. Best to think twice before renting a room off Craigslist!) Alice is increasingly found wandering at 2 A.M. on freeways in places like Torrance (50 miles away), and is ever more routinely brought home in the dead of night by various police officers and firemen (your tax dollars at work!). And in contrast to her formerly frugal ways, Alice no longer understands money. At one point, my father called the police because she was hitting him—not to have her arrested but, as my dad says, just to "scare" her. To evade capture, she ran away with a duffel bag stuffed with their passports, marriage certificate, immigration papers, and two small, tightly packed envelopes, one with exactly 13 crisp $1 bills inside it and another with a Keystone Kops–type mélange of Chinese money, Turkish money, and . . . as I said, upon discovery, to my sister: "I didn't know Bill Nye the Science Guy *had* his own currency!"

When I gave Alice the bag (returned by the police), she accused me of stealing $2,000 from it. Meanwhile, forensic analysis reveals she had withdrawn $13,000, gone to a bank in Chinatown, and purchased a useless universal life-insurance policy, an event she cannot recall. My father does not want Alice to move to assisted living, however, because he enjoys her cooking. So the solution for Alice is a full-time Mandarin-speaking female companion. At $5,000 a month, this service is a relative bargain if it keeps Alice from withdrawing, and flinging to the winds, her next $50,000. (And who knows *where* all these mysterious accounts are? I'm trying to find out, I'm trying!) Meanwhile, armed with his own capable full-time Filipino male nurse (another $5,000 a month), my father has roared back with formidable energy. As long as he's hydrated, it appears that no bacterium can fell him—remember, he has been eating out of Dumpsters (we're talking expired sushi) for *several decades already.* (Who knows if he hasn't morphed into another life form, possibly amphibian?) Which is to say, now I have a wheelchair-bound but extremely active 91-year-old who greatly enjoys getting bathed and diapered and fed ice cream and crashing UCLA science lectures and, oh, by the way—every day he calls me now: he wants SEX. He proudly needs only 1/16th of a Viagra pill for SEX. Because Alice is no longer complying (she is unfortunately not quite that crazy), and because I have not—yet?—caved (although if one Googles this issue, one will find to one's horror the phrase *healing hands*!), my father has started to proposition Alice's lady nurse, trying to grab her breasts, begging her to touch him. Which he can't do himself, as he can barely clasp his hand around a spoon.

What would Gail Sheehy call this particular new Passage, aside from, peppily, "The New Normal"? Outdoing the "giddy globetrotters" in Sheehy's midlife Boomertopia, my father would park his wheelchair on top of the camel, then get pitched headfirst from the camel, then probably try to molest the camel. Eternally leaping up, like a ghoul, he is the über-Kafka father.

But there's more. My father's care demands an ever-changing flotilla of immigrant caregivers, of whom the chief one is Thomas. Because my father is so difficult, it's not atypical for new caregivers to quit before noon. The miraculously tolerant Thomas is the only nurse who has stuck with my father, which means that my sister, brother, and I basically work for Thomas. We've co-signed on an apartment for him and his wife and four children, who just emigrated from the Philippines; we've fixed up a beater car for him (which I've spent many a weekday smogging, re-smogging, insuring, handicapped-plating). We do all this because Thomas does an excellent job, always trying to raise the standard of my dad's care. Which is a good thing. Or is it?

Thomas is concerned about my dad's regularity. The cranberry pills and stool softeners I regularly deliver from Costco have worked to a point, yes, but now Thomas has hit upon something better: milk of magnesia. Problem is, the product is so effective that when my father is given it before bed, *although* he has finally consented to wearing an adult diaper at night, within four hours he is at capacity and begins fouling his sheets. Hence, Thomas has started finishing his 10-hour day by sleeping in my father's room at night, for which, of course, he must be given a raise, to $6,500 a month.

Thomas is optimistic. He ends conversations about the overflowing diapers with this cheerful reassurance: "I will get your Papa to 100!"

Oh my God—how could he *say* such a horrible thing? I am hyperventilating again. Okay. Never mind the question of whether, given that they have total freedom and no responsibilities, we are indulging our elders in the same way my generation has been famously indulging our overly entitled children. Never mind the question of whether there is a reasonable point at which parents lose their rights, and for the good of society we get to lock them up and medicate them.

The question that really haunts me, and that I feel I must raise now, is: At these prices, exactly how much time do I have to spend *listening to stories about my dad defecating?*

I rant to myself: He is taking everything! He is taking all the money. He's taken years of my life (sitting in doctors' offices, in pharmacies, in waiting rooms). With his horrid, selfish, grotesque behavior, he's chewed through every shred of my sentimental affection for him. He's taken the serenity I fought for—and won—in 1,000 hours of therapy centered on my family. In fact, he's destroyed my belief in "family" as a thing that buoys one up. Quite the opposite: family is like the piano around Holly Hunter's ankle, dragging me implacably down.

I have to ensure Hilton-level care for my barely Motel 6 father, the giant baby, as well as for his caregiver, the big-baby nurse, all caught up with the high-pitched drama of feeding and diapering and massaging. That's right: my family is throwing all our money away on powdering our 91-year-old dad's giant-baby ass, leaving nothing for my sweet little daughters, with their thoughts of unicorns and poetry and dance, my helpless little daughters, who, in the end, represent me! In short, on top of everything else he has taken from me, he has taken away my entire sense of self, because at age almost-50, it appears that I too have become a squalling baby!!!

The other day, my writer friend Laura was doing her own woeful monologue—and how they all just continue, like leaves falling—about her dad.

"He has learned *nothing* in 78 years. He has no wisdom. He has no soul. He insults me. He ignores his grandchildren. How much longer do I need to keep having a relationship with him?"

We were walking in the hills above Griffith Park, which turn into the grassy slopes of Forest Lawn, which put me in mind of the ending of one of the best memoirs I have ever read—and, come to think of it, perhaps the only book one will ever need—about difficult parents, Bernard Cooper's *The Bill From My Father.* The title comes from the day Cooper received a bill from his lawyer father, typed on his customary onionskin paper, demanding immediate reimbursement for parenting outlays (including an entire childhood's worth of groceries and clothing) in the amount of $2 million. Cooper Sr. escalated the pain, upon his other sons' deaths, by not just sending their widows bills but filing actual lawsuits against them.

Still, Cooper continues to have an on-again, off-again relationship with Cooper the Elder (whose history with his sons can be summed up by the progression of painted signs on the front of his law-office door, as telling as a piece of concrete poetry: COOPER; COOPER & COOPER; COOPER, COOPER & COOPER; COOPER, COOPER, COOPER & COOPER; COOPER, COOPER & COOPER; COOPER & COOPER; COOPER). Their relationship eventually drew the interest of a publisher—did Cooper want to write a book about his father? As Cooper recalls:

> It would be foolish to refuse her offer because . . . Well, because money was involved, but also because the rest of my family was gone forever and Dad was all I had left, though I wasn't sure what constituted "all." Or "Dad" for that matter.

He quotes from John Cheever's short story "Reunion": " 'My father,' thinks the son, 'was my future and my doom.' " The memoir concludes with a wonderful Forest Lawn cemetery scene (his father's punchy epitaph: YOU FINALLY GOT ME).

I almost don't know what I envy Bernard Cooper for more—his incomparable literary genius or the fact that his father is *dead.* (Anti-*Elderschadenfreude.*)

The paradox is, I can't miss the good things about my father while he is alive, but I will of course miss him . . . when he is dead. By the same token—and perhaps this is the curious blessing—if my mother were alive today (what would she be, 84?), she would be driving me *insane*!!!

But then, inevitably, comes (at least in my Pema Chödrön calendar) yet another day. And indeed, inspired by my Buddhist stationery, what I decide I will let go of today is any of the previous ideas I had about future planning—the college tuitions, paying off the house, putting together some kind of retirement. . . .

Then again, in the new America, shouldn't the wealth be re-equalized from generation to generation? Is it not somewhat fitting that the Loh family's nest egg should be used to put not our children but Thomas's through college, as Andrew Carnegie advocated? ("I will get your Papa to 100!") Is that really the worst use of this money? Indeed, I muse slyly, perhaps, unlike my own Western daughters, jazz shoes and drawing pads (how useless!) spilling out of their bags, Thomas's children will actually buckle down and get real majors, leading to real jobs—doctor, engineer, or, most lucrative of all . . . *geriatric nurse.*

So I feel a little calmer today, as I deliver my raft of pills. And I find it is a rare calm day at my father's house as well. The various triaging schemes are holding. Thomas has the house smelling soapy, white sheets cover sagging couches, vases hold artificial flowers, medications are arranged on various bureaus in proud and almost spectacular displays. For today, Thomas's beater car runs. For today, Alice is medicated, and therefore pleasant. She serves a mysterious bell-pepper dish that—aside from being wildly spicy—is edible. My father's hair has never been more poofy—or black. He too is vaguely fragrant. Could be his lucky day. SEX.

I have to acknowledge, too, that in traditional China, with its notions of filial responsibility, my elders would be living with me in my home, or I in theirs. So the beautiful oh-so-Western thing is that, for today, I can drive away. And as I drive down PCH—dipping celery into Greek yogurt sprinkled with flax, dropping it all over my sweatpants—I realize that because things are not actually terrible (no cops, no paramedics, no $13,000 bank withdrawals), today qualifies as a fabulous day.

I can no longer think of my dad as my "father." But I recognize in him something as familiar to me as myself. To the end, stubborn, babyish, life-loving, he doesn't want to go to rehab, no, no, no.

Critical Thinking

1. Why does the author sometimes wish her elderly father would die? Is she being selfish in saying this? Why or why not? Do you think other adult children feel this way but do not say anything?

2. What are some of the financial and emotional burdens adult children face in caring for their aging parents?

3. How does the reversal in roles that occurs when children become caregivers for their parents alter family and relationship dynamics?

4. What types of supports do adult children need as they try to meet the needs of their own families and their aging parents?

Create Central

www.mhhe.com/createcentral

Internet References

National Center on Caregiving
www.caregiver.org
National Council on Aging
www.ncoa.org
Alzheimer's Association
www.alz.org

SANDRA TSING LOH is the author, most recently, of *Mother on Fire*.

Article   Prepared by: Patricia Hrusa Williams, *University of Maine at Farmington*

Baby Boomers Care for Grandchildren as Daughters Pursue Careers

Working mothers unanimously agree that raising children is like war. They have to fight for the spare time needed for their children, fight in a workplace inconsiderate of working mothers, and fight against the temptation to give up a career for child raising. The auxiliary troops are their baby boomer parents.

Kim Eun-Ha

Learning Outcomes

After reading this article, you will be able to:

- Identify reasons why grandparents are becoming "second parents."

- Provide examples of the problems experienced in maternity leave policies and in finding high-quality child care for working families.

- Explain some of the pros and cons of grandparents providing care for their grandchildren.

Ms. Lee, 66 years old, seems to be living her life all over again. After raising her two children and seeing them get married, she has been playing the role of a mother again for the past 10 years. Her daughter, Ms. Cho, is a medical doctor at a university hospital in Seoul, and mother of two children, who are fifth and second graders. While Ms. Cho works at the hospital during the day, Ms. Lee takes care of her grandchildren. Ms. Cho leaves home at 7 A.M. and returns home around 8 P.M. at the earliest. She cannot possibly care for her children and prepare their meals. If she works a night shift or an emergency arises, her return home is even later. Her children come home from school between noon and 3 P.M. In place of Ms. Cho, her mother takes care of the children, preparing snacks and coordinating their after-school activities, such as taekwondo and piano lessons.

Learning about Childcare for First Time

Although Ms. Cho has been married 10 years, she still depends heavily on her parents. And Ms. Lee might not have imagined that she would be caring for her grandchildren all this while. She intended to help out until her daughter could place her children in daycare. But her daughter could not find a daycare center that provided extended hours of supervision. So she concluded that moving in with her parents would be the most practical solution. Her mother, understanding the situation, could not refuse. Besides, she enjoyed spending time with her lovely grandchildren.

Ms. Cho's husband, for his part, had to accept living with his parents-in-law for the sake of the children, even if such an arrangement can cause occasional discomfort. In important family matters, such as the children's education and personal pursuits, the mother-in-law's word would often hold absolute sway. The couple, however, believes that they are fortunate. They know many working couples who struggle to take care of their children because none of their parents will help out with the responsibilities.

As ever more young couples rely on their parents to care for their children, an increasing number of men in their 50s and 60s have taken on childcare roles. In Korea's aging society, with improved prospects of living until 100, middle-aged men who are retired find themselves with time on their hands and have thus come to look after their grandchildren.

Retired two years ago, 62-year-old Mr. Kim is now wholly dedicated to raising his two-year-old granddaughter. He agreed to help out because his daughter-in-law needed to work when his son decided to belatedly attend graduate school. The daughter's family lives in the same apartment complex as Mr. Kim and his wife, so the granddaughter is dropped off at their apartment in the morning and picked up in the evening. When the parents come home late, the girl stays with her grandparents overnight. Mr. Kim's wife is not as physically capable, so he takes charge of physical activity with his granddaughter. He also searches the Internet to read up about childcare.

Feeling empty after retiring from his work of 30 years, he says, "I overcame my depression by enjoying my grandchild's lovable antics." He starts and ends each day playing with his granddaughter. Sometimes he goes out to play golf or to hike with friends, but he tries to get back early enough to pick up his granddaughter from the daycare center.

Mr. Kim explains, "I don't have many memories of my own children growing up; from my 30s, I was always so busy." He adds, "I'm learning about childcare for the first time through raising my granddaughter."

New Reality Requires 'Second Parents'

Korean law provides for three months of maternity leave, and up to one year of childcare leave, so a total of 15 months can be used for staying home to care for a new baby. Korea is now facing the demographic dilemma that the world's most economically advanced countries have also experienced. The country's total fertility rate (TFR, the average number of births a woman can expect to have during her child-bearing years), which was over 6.0 in the 1960s, plunged to 1.08, one of the lowest in the world, as of 2006. The Korean government has thus implemented various policy measures to encourage families to have more children. But the changes that make a real difference, particularly in the workplace culture, are always slower to take root than intended.

Most working mothers on maternity leave get a phone call from their workplace, asking when they are coming back, far earlier than the conclusion of their childcare leave. Although companies say that they just want to know how long the position will have to be left open, they often hint that working mothers should return as soon as possible if they don't want to burden their colleagues; the implied message is they should quit if they want to stay away for so long. Undoubtedly, the situation today is far improved from that of just 10 years ago, when no such leave was offered. Few working mothers, however, will dare to use the full period of leave authorized by law, especially if the workplace's prevailing practice is for mothers to return earlier.

But, in order to return to their workplace, they have to find a reliable childcare facility. Ms. Park, a working mother, registered her child at a daycare center near her home immediately after registering the birth itself, but she received number 310 on the waiting list. Ms. Park wants to leave her child in daycare in two years, but she was told that she cannot be assured of her child's admission at that time. Ms. Park says, "If there is a good daycare center that will take my child, I am willing to move near there."

There are 39,842 daycare centers throughout the country, not a small number in light of Korea's low fertility rate (1.24 in 2011), which is far short of the replacement level of 2.01 births per female. But the number of daycare centers that mothers would prefer is far fewer as not all daycare centers provide quality childcare. Every year, accidents from unsafe conditions and child abuse incidents make the news, which make mothers even more selective. The number of reliable public daycare centers operated by the government is only 2,116, less than 5 percent of the total. That is why increasing the number of public daycare centers is one of the basic campaign pledges that politicians emphasize in every election.

The problem of childcare, however, is not entirely solved even if a child is admitted to a reputable daycare facility. Most daycare centers conclude their regular programs at 3 P.M. So for parents who have to pick up their child later in the evening, some facilities provide extended hours, but even those will close by 7 P.M.

The problem is that daycare centers strictly enforce their closing time, while this is not true of workplaces. Officially, the typical workday ends about 6 P.M., but leaving the workplace promptly at that time can be a challenge. Meetings that run late or get-togethers with co-workers can create problems for working mothers as well. A client meeting sometimes extends to dinner. There are very few family-friendly workplaces where a mother can easily call in late or be excused when a child is sick, or leave work to attend a school activity. The Ministry of Gender Equality and Family provides encouragement to such workplaces through the award of "Family-Friendly Enterprise" certificates. The fact that such an award even exists proves that there are not many companies that offer such flexibility.

Working mothers who lack "second parents" ready and able to help out at any time have little choice but to surrender. Statistics starkly show how young Korean women's career aspirations are drastically curtailed around the time they marry and start raising a family. The university entrance rate for girls in Korea is 75 percent, higher than that for boys (70.2 percent). So there is no gender discrimination in getting an education. On the other hand, the economic activity rate of Korean women stands at a mere 49.7 percent, falling far below that of Korean men (73.1 percent), and also lower than the average of OECD countries (61.8 percent). By looking at the statistical trends, you can find the reason for this situation. The economic activity rate of women in their 20s is 71.4 percent, relatively comparable to that of men, but in their 30s, the rate plummets to 55.4 percent. Between their late 20s and mid-30s, a substantial number of women exit the workforce due to marriage and childcare.

Live-in Help Not a Feasible Option

Working mothers who don't give up and keep struggling have to choose between living with parents and hiring a full-time babysitter or live-in nanny. Not all working mothers, however, can seriously consider these options. In order to live with parents, their agreement and support is required, whereas a live-in nanny is beyond the means of most families.

Take the case of 34-year-old Ms. Lee, an office worker. She has two boys, four and two years old. The end of her workday is variable. Even after her regular workday, there are evening get-togethers, and she often has to work on weekends. In her case, she has a live-in babysitter. She had hoped that her parents or her in-laws would help care for her children, but in the end everyone refused to make such a commitment. Her mother-in-law had already told her before the wedding that she doesn't want to sacrifice her mid-life freedom because of grandchildren. Ms. Lee's mother, who had already helped out her two older sisters, adamantly said, "No more sacrifices."

I don't have many memories of my own children growing up; from my 30s, I was always so busy. I'm learning about childcare for the first time through raising my granddaughter.

Ms. Lee pays her Korean-Chinese nanny 1,800,000 won (about $1,700) a month, more than a third of her salary. For a Korean babysitter, she would have to pay at least 20 percent more than that. In the past two years, she changed babysitters three times. She had to terminate the first babysitter for incompetence, while the other two quit because the job was too demanding. Ms. Lee says, "There are few choices, even if you can pay a lot. The key is to maintain a good relationship with the babysitter. Working mothers who have to put their kids in someone else's care are in a weak position."

Even for couples who can leave their children in their parent's care, things don't always go smoothly. When a mother or a mother-in-law assumes responsibility for her grandchildren, she also expects to exercise influence, which can lead to tension and conflict. The authority of the child's parents can be undermined, while placing significant demands on the grandparents. Internet communities that provide forums for working mothers are invariably swamped with complaints about the stress which results from their need for childcare and interference from their otherwise well-meaning parents and in-laws. For some women in their 50s and 60s, taking care of grandchildren can take a toll on their health; they often complain about depression.

According to "Leisure Activities of People in their 50s in Urban Areas," a study published by the Korea Institute for Health and Social Affairs, more than half (52.3 percent) of the survey respondents said they rarely engage in outdoor or sport activities, such as fishing or hiking. Only 22.7 percent have more than one or two outdoor activities every six months; even fewer, a mere 15.2 percent, have one or two activities a month. These statistics are based on a survey of 453 Korean men and women born between 1955 and 1963. The study suggests that because this generation lived their childhood immediately after the Korean War, they not only tend to care less about how to spend leisure time, but they also have little leisure time because they are busy helping to care for their grandchildren.

Return of Extended Families

Raising grandchildren can be a benefit for retired couples because it offers a helpful means to earn pocket money to supplement their income. Young couples who place their child in their parent's care are often generous in paying compensation to their parents, but it's still cheaper than having a babysitter. Many retirees prefer to babysit their grandchildren, as a source of regular income, than having to work as a security guard for an apartment complex or as a cashier at a grocery store. The childcare situation thus has led to a revival of the traditional extended family, which had been, on the whole, displaced by the nuclear family in modern Asian countries. When three or more generations can live together under one roof or close by, the family can share parenting responsibilities so that children can be nurtured in a safe environment, young couples can pursue their careers without undue worry, and elderly couples get financial aid and self-satisfaction.

Even with the government's campaign to boost the number of births, the country's fertility rate in 2011 stood at only 1.24, still at the bottom of OECD countries (a newspaper recently reported that Korea's TFR may have reached 1.3 in 2012). Although the education level and economic activity rate of women have risen dramatically, the rate of social change remains slow. Parents of the baby boomer generation have become the "reserve parents" for their grandchildren, by attending childcare classes offered by district governments and preparing themselves to care for the baby expected by their working daughter. Working mothers, in their endeavors to balance work and family, are helping to revive and redefine the traditional extended family in the 21st century, thanks to their parents' sacrifices.

Critical Thinking

1. While this article was written based on the experience of families in Korea, what are some similarities to experiences of working families here in the United States?

2. What are some challenges of having grandparents provide care for their grandchildren while their parents work?

3. Using information gained from this article, describe an intervention or support program that could be developed to facilitate the positive development of children and families when grandparents provide childcare for their grandchildren.

Create Central

www.mhhe.com/createcentral

Internet References

Alliance for Family, Friend, and Neighbor Care
http://www.familyfriendandneighbor.com/index.html

Families and Work Institute
www.familiesandwork.org

National Council on Aging
www.ncoa.org

Unit 4

UNIT

Prepared by: Patricia Hrusa Williams, *University of Maine at Farmington*

Challenges and Opportunities

Stress is life and life is stress. Sometimes stress in families gives new meaning to this statement. When a stressful event occurs, many processes occur simultaneously as families and their members cope with the stressor and its effects. One thing that can result is a reduction in family members' ability to act as resources for each other. Indeed, a stressor can overwhelm the family system, and family members may be among the least effective people in coping with each other's behavior. In this unit, we consider a wide variety of stressful life events and crises families may experience. Some are normative stressful life events which occur as families evolve and change. Families add and lose members. Family members age and health can fail. Individuals experience changes in employment and the need to balance work–family concerns as families develop and change.

There are also other non-normative stressful life events and crises which many families experience. Marriages can break up.

Divorced spouses remarry and create new families. A person may be called on to serve his or her country and be separated from the family for a period of time. Someone in the family may be diagnosed with a chronic illness or health problem. Personal, economic, relationship, and social strains can result in maladaptive coping strategies such as drug and alcohol use, mental health crises, violence, and infidelity.

The articles in this unit explore a variety of family crises, stresses, and strains. Among them are the impact of family violence, substance abuse, mental health challenges, infidelity, and economic concerns. The nature of stress resulting from a life-threatening and chronic illness, disability, loss, grief, and war are also considered. Family challenges and adaptation for single-parent, divorced, and step-families are also considered. Throughout this unit the focus is not only on understanding the challenges but on how best to support families as they navigate the stresses of life.

Article

Prepared by: Patricia Hrusa Williams,
University of Maine at Farmington

Anguish of the Abandoned Child

CHARLES A. NELSON III; NATHAN A. FOX AND CHARLES H. ZEANAH, JR.

The plight of orphaned Romanian children reveals the psychic and physical scars from first years spent without a loving, responsive caregiver.

Learning Outcomes

After reading this article, you will be able to:

- Understand the political, social, and economic reasons behind the "orphan problem" in Romania.

- Explain reasons why children become orphans worldwide.

- Identify how early experiences of deprivation impact child development and later outcomes.

- Define and explain the term "sensitive period."

In a misguided effort to enhance economic productivity, Nicolae Ceaușescu decreed in 1966 that Romania would develop its "human capital" via a government-enforced mandate to increase the country's population. Ceaușescu, Romania's leader from 1965 to 1989, banned contraception and abortions and imposed a "celibacy tax" on families that had fewer than five children. State doctors—the menstrual police—conducted gynecologic examinations in the workplace of women of child-bearing age to see whether they were producing sufficient offspring. The birth rate initially skyrocketed. Yet because families were too poor to keep their children, they abandoned many of them to large state-run institutions. By 1989 this social experiment led to more than 170,000 children living in these facilities.

The Romanian revolution of 1989 deposed Ceaușescu, and over the next 10 years his successors made a series of halting attempts to undo the damage. The "orphan problem" Ceaușescu left behind was enormous and did not disappear for many years. The country remained impoverished, and the rate of child abandonment did not change appreciably at least through 2005. A decade after Ceaușescu had been removed from power, some government officials could still be heard saying that the state did a better job than families in bringing up abandoned children and that those confined in institutions were, by definition, "defective"—a view grounded in the Soviet-inspired system of educating the disabled, dubbed "defectology."

Even after the 1989 revolution, families still felt free to abandon an unwanted infant to a state-run institution. Social scientists had long suspected that early life in an orphanage could have adverse consequences. A number of mostly small, descriptive studies that lacked control groups were conducted from the 1940s to the 1960s in the West that compared children in orphanages with those in foster care and showed that life in an institution did not come close to matching the care of a parent—even if that parent was not the natural mother or father. One issue with these studies was the possibility of "selection bias": children removed from institutions and placed into adoptive or foster homes might be less impaired, whereas the ones who remained in the institution were more disabled. The only way to counter any bias would require the unprecedented step of randomly placing a group of abandoned children into either an institution or a foster home.

Understanding the effects of life in an institution on children's early development is important because of the immensity of the orphan problem worldwide (an orphan is defined here as an abandoned child or one whose parents have died). War, disease, poverty and sometimes government policies have stranded at least eight million children worldwide in state-run facilities. Often these children live in highly structured but hopelessly bleak environments, where typically one adult oversees 12 to 15 children. Research is still lacking to gain a full understanding of what happens to children who spend their first years in such deprived circumstances.

In 1999, when we approached Cristian Tabacaru, then secretary of state for Romania's National Authority for Child Protection, he encouraged us to conduct a study on institutionalized children because he wanted data to address the question of whether to develop alternative forms of care for the 100,000 Romanian children then living in state institutions. Yet Tabacaru faced stiff resistance from some government officials, who believed for decades that children received a better upbringing in institutions than in foster care. The problem was exacerbated because some government agencies' budgets were funded, in part, by their role in making institutional care arrangements. Faced with these challenges, Tabacaru thought that scientific evidence about putative advantages of foster care for young children over state institutions would make a convincing case for reform, and so he invited us to go ahead with a study.

Infancy in an Institution

With the assistance of some officials within the Romanian government and especially with help from others who worked for SERA Romania (a nongovernmental organization), we implemented a study to ascertain the effects on a child's brain and behavior of living in a state institution and whether foster care could ameliorate the effects of being reared in conditions that run counter to what we know about the needs of young children. The Bucharest Early Intervention Project was launched in 2000, in cooperation with the Romanian government, in part to provide answers that might rectify the aftereffects of previous policies. The unfortunate legacy of Ceauşescu's tenure provided a chance to examine, with greater scientific rigor than any previous study, the effects of institutionalized care on the neurological and emotional development of infants and young children. The study was the first-ever randomized controlled study that compared a group of infants placed in foster care with another raised in institutions, providing a level of experimental precision that had been hitherto unavailable.

We recruited, from all six institutions for infants and young children in Bucharest, a group of 136 whom we considered to be free of neurological, genetic and other birth defects based on pediatric exams conducted by a member of the study team. All had been abandoned to institutions in the first weeks or months of life. When the study began, they were, on average, 22 months old—the range of ages was from six to 31 months.

Immediately after a series of baseline physical and psychological assessments, half the children were randomly assigned to a foster care intervention our team developed, maintained and financed. The other half remained in an institution—what we called the "care as usual" group. We also recruited a third group of typically developing children who lived with their families in Bucharest and had never been institutionalized. These three groups of children have been studied for more than 10 years. Because the children were randomly assigned to foster care or to remain in an institution, unlike previous studies, it was possible to show that any differences in development or behavior between the two groups could be attributed to where they were reared.

Because there was virtually no foster care available for abandoned children in Bucharest when we started, we were in the unique position of having to build our own network. After extensive advertising and background checks, we eventually recruited 53 families to foster 68 children (we kept siblings together).

Of course, many ethical issues were involved in conducting a controlled scientific study of young children, a trial in which only half the participants were initially removed from institutions. The design compared the standard intervention for abandoned children—institutional rearing—with foster care, an intervention that had never been available to these children. Ethical protections put in place included oversight by multiple Romanian- and U.S.-based institutions, implementation of "minimal risk" measures (all used routinely with young children), and noninterference with government decisions about changes in placement when children were adopted, returned to biological parents or later placed in government-sponsored foster care that at the outset did not exist.

No child was moved back from foster care to an institution at the end of the study. As soon as the early results became available, we communicated our findings to the Romanian government at a news conference.

To ensure high-quality foster care, we designed the program to incorporate regular involvement of a social work team and provided modest subsidies to families for child-related expenses. All foster parents had to be licensed, and they were paid a salary as well as a subsidy. They received training and were encouraged to make a full psychological commitment to their foster children.

Sensitive Periods

The study set about to explore the premise that early experience often exerts a particularly strong influence in shaping the immature brain. For some behaviors, neural connections form in early years in response to environmental influences during windows of time, called sensitive periods. A child who listens to spoken language or simply looks around receives aural and visual inputs that shape neural connections during specific periods of development. The results of the study supported this initial premise of a sensitive period: the difference between an early life spent in an institution compared with foster care was dramatic. At 30, 40 and 52 months, the average IQ of the institutionalized group was in the low to middle 70s, whereas it was about 10 points higher for children in foster care. Not surprisingly, IQ was about 100, the standard average, for the group that had never been institutionalized. We also discovered a sensitive period when a child was able to achieve a maximum gain in IQ: a boy or girl placed in a home before roughly two years of age had a significantly higher IQ than one put there after that age.

The findings clearly demonstrate the devastating impact on mind and brain of spending the first two years of life within the impersonal confines of an institution. The Romanian children living in institutions provide the best evidence to date that the initial two years of life constitute a sensitive period in which a child must receive intimate emotional and physical contact or else find personal development stymied.

Infants learn from experience to seek comfort, support and protection from their significant caregivers, whether those individuals are natural or foster parents—and so we decided to measure attachment. Only extreme conditions that limit opportunities for a child to form attachments can interfere with a process that is a foundation for normal social development. When we measured this variable in the institutionalized children, we found that the overwhelming majority displayed incompletely formed and aberrant relationships with their caregivers.

When the children were 42 months of age, we made another assessment and found that the children placed in foster care displayed dramatic improvements in making emotional attachments. Almost half had established secure relationships with another person, whereas only 18 percent of the institutionalized children had done so. In the community children, those never institutionalized, 65 percent were securely attached. Children placed into foster care before the end of the 24-month sensitive period were more likely to form secure attachments compared with children placed there after that threshold.

These numbers are more than just statistical disparities that separate the institutionalized and foster groups. They translate into very real experiences of both anguish and hope. Sebastian (none of the children's names in this article are real), now 12, has spent virtually his entire life in an orphanage and has seen his IQ drop 20 points to a subpar 64 since he was tested during his fifth year. A youth who may have never formed an attachment with anyone, Sebastian drinks alcohol and displays other risk-prone behaviors. During an interview with us, he became irritable and erupted with flashes of anger.

Bogdan, also 12, illustrates the difference that receiving individualized attention from an adult makes. He was abandoned at birth and lived in a maternity ward until two months of age, after which he lived in an institution for nine months. He was then recruited into the project and randomized to the foster care group, where he was placed in the family of a single mother and her adolescent daughter. Bogdan started to catch up quickly and managed to overcome mild developmental delays within months. Although he had some behavioral problems, project staff members worked with the family, and by his fifth birthday the foster mother had decided to adopt him. At age 12, Bogdan's IQ continues to score at an above-average level. He attends one of the best public schools in Bucharest and has the highest grades in his class.

Because children raised in institutions did not appear to receive much personal attention, we were interested in whether a paucity of language exposure would have any effect on them. We observed delays in language development, and if children arrived in foster care before they reached approximately 15 or 16 months, their language was normal, but the later children were placed, the further behind they fell.

We also compared the prevalence of mental health problems among any children who had ever been institutionalized with those who had not. We found that 53 percent of the children who had ever lived in an institution had received a psychiatric diagnosis by the age of four and a half, compared with 20 percent of the group who had never been institutionalized. In fact, 62 percent of the institutionalized children approaching the age of five had diagnoses, ranging from anxiety disorders—44 percent—to attention-deficit hyperactivity disorder (ADHD)—23 percent.

Foster care had a major influence on the level of anxiety and depression—reducing their incidence by half—but did not affect behavioral diagnoses (ADHD and conduct disorder). We could not detect any sensitive period for mental health. Yet relationships were important for assuring good mental health. When we explored the mechanism to explain reduced emotional disorders such as depression, we found that the more secure the attachment between a child and foster parent, the greater probability that the child's symptoms would diminish.

We also wanted to know whether first years in a foster home affected brain development differently than living in an institution. An assessment of brain activity using electroencephalography (EEG)—which records electrical signals—showed that infants living in institutions had significant reductions in one component of EEG activity and a heightened level in another (lower alpha and higher theta waves), a pattern that may reflect delayed brain maturation. When we assessed the children at the eight-year mark, we again recorded EEG scans. We could then see that the pattern of electrical activity in children placed in foster care before two years of age could not be distinguished from that of those who had never passed time in an institution. Children taken out of an orphanage after two years and those who never left showed a less mature pattern of brain activity.

The noticeable decrease in EEG activity among the institutionalized children was perplexing. To interpret this observation, we turned to data from magnetic resonance imaging, which can visualize brain structures. Here we observed that the institutionalized children showed a large reduction in the volume of both gray matter (neurons and other brain cells) and white matter (the insulating substance covering neurons' wire-like extensions).

On the whole, all the children who were institutionalized had smaller brain volumes. Placing children in foster care at any age had no effect on increasing the amount of gray matter—the foster care group showed levels of gray matter comparable to those of the institutionalized children. Yet the foster care children showed more white matter volume than the institutionalized group, which may account for the changes in EEG activity.

To further examine the biological toll of early institutionalization, we focused attention on a crucial area of the genome. Telomeres, regions at the ends of chromosomes that provide protection from the stresses of cell division, are shorter in adults who undergo extreme psychological stresses than those who escape this duress. Shorter telomeres may even be a mark of accelerated cellular aging. When we examined telomere length in the children in our study, we observed that, on the whole, those who had spent any time in an institution had shorter telomeres than those who had not.

Lessons for All

The Bucharest Early Intervention Project has demonstrated the profound effects early experience has on brain development. Foster care did not completely remedy the profound developmental abnormalities linked to institutional rearing, but it did mostly shift a child's development toward a healthier trajectory.

The identification of sensitive periods—in which recovery from deprivation occurs the earlier the child begins to experience a more favorable living environment—may be one of the most significant findings from our project. This observation has implications beyond the millions of children living in institutions, extending to additional millions of maltreated children whose care is being overseen by child-protection authorities. We caution readers, however, not to make unwarranted assumptions that two years can be rigidly defined as a sensitive period for development. Yet the evidence suggests that the earlier children are cared for by stable, emotionally invested parents, the better their chances for a more normal development trajectory.

We are continuing to follow these children into adolescence to see if there are "sleeper effects"—that is, significant behavioral or neurological differences that appear only later in youth or even adulthood. Further, we will determine whether the effects of a sensitive period we observed at younger ages will still be observed as children enter adolescence. If they are, they will reinforce a growing body of literature that speaks to the role of early life experiences in shaping development across one's life span. This insight, in turn, may exert pressure on governments throughout the world to pay more attention to the toll that early adversity and institutionalization take on the capacity of a maturing child to traverse the emotional hazards of adolescence and acquire the needed resiliency to cope with the travails of adult life.

More to Explore

Cognitive Recovery in Socially Deprived Young Children: The Bucharest Early Intervention Project. Charles A. Nelson III et al. in Science, vol. 318, pages 1937–1940; December 21, 2007.

Effects of Early Intervention and the Moderating Effects of Brain Activity on Institutionalized Children's Social Skills at Age 8. Alisa N. Almas et al. in Proceedings of the National Academy of Sciences USA, vol. 109, Supplement no. 2, pages 17, 228–17,231; October 16, 2012.

Scientific American Online

For a video that details more about the importance of early-life caregiving, visit http://ScientificAmerican.com/apr2013/orphans.

Critical Thinking

1. Why did Romania experience an "orphan problem?"
2. Is it possible that children could receive a better upbringing in a state-run institution than they could in foster care or the care of their parents? Why or why not?
3. What do you see as ethical issues in randomly placing children to be cared for either in state-run institutions or foster families?
4. Describe some of the issues experienced by children who spent their early years in a state institution.
5. What is the best strategy to use to provide care for orphans? What should we do in situations when there are not enough foster families available to care for orphans or abused/maltreated children?

Create Central

www.mhhe.com/createcentral

Internet References

Scientific American
http://www.scientificamerican.com/article.cfm?id=orphans-how-adversity-affects-young-children

Child Rights Information Network
www.crin.org

Child Welfare Information Gateway
www.childwelfare.gov

CHARLES A. NELSON III is professor of pediatrics and neuroscience and professor of psychology in psychiatry at Harvard Medical School. He has an honorary doctorate from the University of Bucharest in Romania.

NATHAN A. FOX is Distinguished University Professor in the Department of Human Development and Quantitative Methodology at the University of Maryland, College Park.

CHARLES H. ZEANAH, JR. is professor of psychiatry and clinical pediatrics at Tulane University and executive director of the university's Institute of Infant and Early Childhood Mental Health.

Article

Prepared by: Patricia Hrusa Williams,
University of Maine at Farmington

Terrorism in the Home

Eleven myths and facts about domestic violence

VICTOR M. PARACHIN

Learning Outcomes

After reading this article, you will be able to:

- Identify the signs of domestic violence.

- Understand several causes or factors associated with the occurrence of domestic violence.

- Explain strategies which may be effective in reaching out to and assisting victims.

If anything is truly equal opportunity, it is battering. Domestic violence crosses all socioeconomic, ethnic, racial, educational, age, and religious lines.

— K. J. Wilson, *When Violence Begins At Home*

Sadly, a U.S. Department of Justice study indicates that approximately one million violent crimes are committed by former spouses, boyfriends, or girlfriends each year, with 85 percent of the victims being women. For domestic violence to be defeated, it must begin with information. Here are 11 myths and facts about domestic violence.

Myth 1: Domestic violence is only physical.

Fact: Abusive actions against another person can be verbal, emotional, sexual, and physical.
There are four basic types of domestic violence:
- Physical (shoving, slapping, punching, pushing, hitting, kicking, and restraining)
- Sexual (when one partner forces unwanted, unwelcome, uninvited sexual acts upon another)
- Psychological (verbal and emotional abuse, threats, intimidations, stalking, swearing, insulting, isolation from family and friends, forced financial dependence)
- Attacks against property and pets (breaking household objects, hitting walls, abusing or killing beloved pets)

Myth 2: Domestic violence is not common.

Fact: While precise statistics are difficult to determine, all signs indicate that domestic violence is more common than most people believe or want to believe. Here's one example: due to lack of space, shelters for battered women are able to admit only 10 to 40 percent of women who request admission. Another example is from divorced women. Though they make up less than 8 percent of the U.S. population, they account for 75 percent of all battered women and report being assaulted 14 times more often than women still living with a partner. Whatever statistics are available are believed to be low because domestic violence is often not reported.

Myth 3: Domestic violence affects only women.

Fact: Abuse can happen to anyone! It can be directed at women, men, children, the elderly. It takes place among all social classes and all ethnic groups. However, women are the most targeted victims of domestic violence. Here are some statistics:
- One in four American women report being physically assaulted and/or raped by a current or former spouse, cohabiting partner, or date at some time in their life.
- According to the FBI, a woman is beaten every 15 seconds.
- In 1996, 30 percent of all female murder victims in the United States were slain by their husbands or boyfriends.
- Around the world, at least one in every three women has been beaten, coerced into sex, or otherwise abused in her lifetime.
- While men are victims of domestic abuse, 92 percent of those subjected to violence are women.

Myth 4: Domestic violence occurs only among lower class or minority or rural communities.

Fact: Domestic violence crosses all race and class lines. Similar rates of abuse are reported in cities, suburbs, and rural areas, according to the Bureau of Justice. Abusers can be found living in mansions as well as in mobile homes. Susan Weitzman,

Ph.D., is author of the book *Not to People Like Us: Hidden Abuse in Upscale Marriages*. In her book, Dr. Weitzman presents case-by-case studies of domestic violence in families with higher than average incomes and levels of education.

Myth 5: Battered women can just leave.

Fact: A combination of factors makes it very difficult for the abused to leave. These include: family and social pressure, shame, financial barriers, children, religious beliefs. Up to 50 percent of women with children fleeing domestic violence become homeless because they leave the abuser. Also, many who are abused face psychological ambivalence about leaving. One woman recalls: "My body still ached from being beaten by my husband a day earlier. But he kept pleading through the door. 'I'm sorry. I'll never do that to you again. I know I need help.' I had a 2-week-old baby. I wanted to believe him. I opened the door." Her abuse continued for two more years before she gained the courage to leave.

Myth 6: Abuse takes place because of alcohol or drugs.

Fact: Substance abuse does not cause domestic violence. However, drugs and alcohol do lower inhibitions while increasing the level of violence, often to more dangerous levels. The U.S. Department of Health and Human Services estimates that one-quarter to one-half of abusers have substance abuse issues.

Myth 7: They can just fight back or walk away.

Fact: Dealing with domestic violence is never as simple as fighting back or walking out the door. "Most domestic abusers are men who are physically stronger than the women they abuse," notes Joyce Zoldak in her book *When Danger Hits Home: Survivors of Domestic Violence*. "In the case of elder abuse, the victims' frail condition may limit their being able to defend themselves. When a child is being abused, the adult guardian is far more imposing—both physically and psychologically—than the victim."

Myth 8: The victim provoked the violence.

Fact: The abuser is completely responsible for the abuse. No one can say or do anything which warrants being beaten and battered. Abusers often try to deflect their responsibility by blaming the victim via comments such as: "You made me angry." "You made me jealous." "This would never have happened if you hadn't done that." "I didn't mean to do that, but you were out of control." Victims need to be assured that the abuse is not their fault.

Myth 9: Domestic abuse is a private matter and it's none of my business.

Fact: We all have a responsibility to care for one another. Officials at the National Domestic Violence Hotline offer this advice to people who see or suspect domestic violence: "Yes, it is your business. Maybe he's your friend, your brother-in-law, your cousin, co-worker, gym partner, or fishing buddy. You've noticed that he interrupts her, criticizes her family, yells at her, or scares her. You hope that when they're alone, it isn't worse. The way he treats her makes you uncomfortable, but you don't want to make him mad or lose his friendship. You surely don't want to see him wreck his marriage or have to call the police. What can you do? Say something. If you don't, your silence is the same as saying abuse is OK. He could hurt someone, or end up in jail. Because you care, you need to do something—before it is too late."

Myth 10: Partners need couples counseling.

Fact: It is the abuser alone who needs counseling in order to change behavior. Social Worker Susan Schechter says couples counseling is "an inappropriate intervention that further endangers the woman." Schechter explains her position: "It encourages the abuser to blame the victim by examining her 'role' in his problem. By seeing the couple together, the therapist erroneously suggests that the partner, too, is responsible for the abuser's behavior. Many women have been brutally beaten following couples counseling sessions in which they disclosed violence or coercion. The abuser alone must take responsibility for assaults and understand that family reunification is not his treatment goal: the goal is to stop the violence."

Myth 11: Abusers are evil people.

Fact: "Anyone can find himself or herself in an abusive situation, and most of us could also find ourselves tempted to be abusive to others, no matter how wrong we know it to be," notes Joyce Zoldak. Abusers are people who may be strong and stable in some areas of their lives but weak, unreasonable and out of control in other ways. This does not excuse their behavior, because abuse is always wrong. Abusers need to be held accountable for their actions and encouraged to seek help promptly by meeting with a psychologist, psychiatrist, therapist, or spiritual leader. Abusers can also receive help from The National Domestic Violence Hotline 1-800-799-7233 or via their website: http://www.thehotline.org.

With an informed community, and with the help of family and friends, the cycle of abuse can be broken.

Critical Thinking

1. What are some impediments or reasons why women do not report domestic violence?
2. What are some reasons why domestic violence occurs in couple relationships and in families?
3. Explain why it can be difficult to identify and assist victims.
4. Why do you think some of these myths about domestic violence persist?
5. Given the information in the article, what do you think may be effective strategies which can be used to reach out to and assist victims of domestic violence?

Create Central

www.mhhe.com/createcentral

Internet References

Futures Without Violence
www.futureswithoutviolence.org

National Coalition Against Domestic Violence
www.ncadv.org

National Network to End Domestic Violence
www.nnedv.org

National Resource Center on Domestic Violence
www.nrcdv.org

VICTOR M. PARACHIN writes from Tulsa, Oklahoma.

Prepared by: Patricia Hrusa Williams,
University of Maine at Farmington

Article

We Are Family: When Elder Abuse, Neglect, and Financial Exploitation Hit Home

Jeannie Jennings Beidler

Learning Outcomes

After reading this article, you will be able to:

- Identify the characteristics of elder abuse.
- Explain the practical, legal, financial, and emotional complexities and difficulties encountered in trying to intervene to protect elderly family members.

Research and popular press report alarming instances of familial elder abuse, neglect, and financial exploitation. The House of Representatives Select Committee on Aging found that older adults are at the greatest risk for abuse, and that in more than two-thirds of substantiated cases, the perpetrator is a family member in a caregiving role—usually an adult child (Elder Serve Act of 2009).

Often there are other contributing factors that fuel elder abuse, which include substance abuse (on the part of the abuser or the victim) and diminished capacity of the elder due to conditions such as dementia (Spencer and Smith, 2000). The following true story illustrates what can happen when these factors come into play.

The Visit

In October 2005, police were dispatched to my grandparents' home following a dispute between my parents and my uncle. My uncle, my grandparents' unemployed adult son who was living in the home, became infuriated when my parents arrived for an unscheduled visit and he refused to let them in. Hearing the commotion, my grandmother appeared and insisted that my parents stay, which further exacerbated my uncle's anger. In an effort to keep my grandmother inside, there was a scuffle: several glass panes of a door were broken, and my grandmother and my mother sustained cuts. My father called the police.

When law enforcement arrived, they observed that my grandmother and the home were in poor condition, and that my uncle appeared agitated, inebriated, and unclean. My grandparents were reportedly uncooperative, also unclean, and disoriented. They expressed no concerns about endangerment and declined to press charges.

The exterior of my grandparents' home was in terrible shape, with shattered windows, overgrown landscaping, and broken fencing. Inside, it was filthy and littered with trash. There was little food in the house, but an abundance of alcohol. The police officers insisted this was a case of self-neglect—not of criminal action or intent; they did not create a case or make any further investigation (the only record of the incident was the 911 call that summoned the police). Upon learning that law enforcement would not intervene, my parents, though terrified of my uncle's retribution, reported their concerns to Adult Protective Services (APS).

Soon thereafter, an APS worker made a home visit. Again, my grandparents denied that their welfare was in jeopardy and refused any offers for assistance. The APS worker made the same observations as did the law enforcement officers: My grandparents were clearly oblivious to the dangers of their environment and required immediate medical attention.

After being persuaded by family, law enforcement, and APS, my grandparents were transported to two different local hospitals. My grandfather was treated for various nonlife-threatening conditions and was discharged within a few days, while my grandmother remained hospitalized for nearly three weeks. I visited often and regularly communicated with the hospital staff about her care. Later, I, along with my parents, uncle, and grandfather, attended a "family meeting" in preparation for my grandmother's discharge. During the meeting, it became apparent that my grandfather was confused about his wife's condition and the level of care she would require; he was beginning to show signs of dementia. My uncle agreed to tend to such tasks as transporting his parents to medical appointments, ensuring that prescriptions would be filled in a timely manner, and providing adequate food and water. He also admitted that he had been unemployed for a long time and was working on his sobriety (a glaring "red flag" to me).

Unable to ignore my concerns, I requested a competency evaluation for my grandmother and strongly recommended that she not return home but be assessed for placement in an assisted living facility. I expressed that it was unlikely that my grandparents would receive the care they required should they return home to their son's care. Nonetheless, it was determined that my grandmother would be discharged to home.

The Struggle

I called frequently in the following weeks. Initially, my grandmother would participate in conversations with some degree of awareness, but this capability slowly faded. More often than not, calls placed would go unanswered. Within months, ensuring my grandparents' welfare could only be accomplished by contacting authorities to request a check on their welfare. Ultimately, the rest of my family was forced to trust the APS worker, who had promised to closely monitor the situation.

Over the next four years, my grandparents' home continued to deteriorate. Countless times, concerned neighbors reported suspicious activities to the authorities and APS. My uncle continued to live in the home and, because of unaddressed substance abuse issues, he remained unemployed.

On July 24, 2010, my great-uncle and my husband made an unscheduled visit to my grandparents' home. The house was in deplorable condition. Despite repeated shouts into the house, there was no response. They called 911. The police arrived quickly and confirmed my grandparents and uncle were inside. They warned my great-uncle and husband that they wouldn't "last long" when they went inside the house because of the filth and stench, and suggested they call APS. The police made no attempt to rescue my grandparents or confront my uncle. Stunned, my great-uncle and husband left the premises briefly, returning moments later: they were afraid they would not see my grandparents alive again.

Upon seeing them, my uncle was irate and an explosive dispute ensued. Despite my uncle's unyielding hostility, my great-uncle insisted on seeing my grandparents. He found my grandfather scantily dressed, emaciated and weak, dirty, and lying in his own waste. Down the hall, he found my grandmother, dressed in soiled men's clothing, immobile, and confined to a tattered mattress. My grandparents were oblivious to their circumstances, and responded pleasantly to my great-uncle.

My uncle became increasingly violent toward my great-uncle and husband. Feeling fearful and helpless, with no support from the police, they left. That afternoon, I learned of the situation. Immediately, I made calls to the police, APS, and the crisis hotline. I called for days before a crisis worker agreed to visit my grandparents. To my amazement, the worker believed my grandparents were not in acute danger. Shocked and frustrated, I questioned her perception of acute danger. Couldn't she see that my grandparents were suffering and that they had no food, water, heat, or air-conditioning? The supposed top defenders of the defenseless were now my top source of disappointment.

The Intervention

The following morning, I called the police, APS, the crisis hotline, and miscellaneous advocacy groups. I ended each call saying, "My grandparents are going to die if they aren't helped. What is your name, so I can document that you knew and did nothing!" It was now forty-eight hours since the 911 call on July 24; I feared that my grandparents would die before help reached them. The next day, an APS worker informed me that an intervention was planned for that afternoon and would include her supervisor, paramedics, and the police. I was asked to accompany them, and arrived to find a fleet of ambulances, police cruisers, and official government cars in front of my grandparents' home.

When my great-uncle and husband had described to me the conditions they had found, they had spared me the worst details: black mold covered the walls and ceilings; and it was difficult to breathe due to the intense stench of feces, urine, and rotting trash. The cupboards were bare, the refrigerator inoperative, and there was no running water for drinking, bathing, or cleaning. With no operable HVAC system, the sweltering heat was unbearable. The once-beautiful brick home was now a complete eyesore.

I found my grandparents just as my great-uncle had described. My grandfather was wearing the same undergarment and was sitting in the same urine-saturated chair. Paramedics immediately removed him from the home—against his will—and transported him to the ER. He was in a life-threatening condition and unable to maintain consciousness due to extremely high blood pressure. My grandmother was curled up in the fetal position upon a rotting mattress. Maggots were swarming in the waste that she was forced to lie in. Oblivious to the horror of her environment, my grandmother greeted me with enthusiasm.

For hours, the intervention team and I tried to persuade my grandmother to go to the hospital. She refused, stating there was nothing wrong with her. When the APS workers informed her she could not live in such conditions, my grandmother was grossly offended. She told the worker that she had a beautiful home and scolded her for being so critical. Then, at 5:00 p.m., the APS workers prepared to depart. Panicking, I pleaded with them not to leave, but their day was over. They left. Dismayed, I called the afterhours crisis unit.

The crisis worker was familiar with the case because of my many calls over the past four days. She expressed frustration that APS had made no attempt to get an emergency custody order and had passed the case off. Once at the house, the worker quickly surveyed the premises and looked in on my grandmother. Promising that the "nonsense" would end, within an hour she obtained an emergency custody order and instructed paramedics to remove my grandmother from her home. Though my grandmother was hysterical, I was relieved. Both of my grandparents were finally safe.

In the following days, I acquainted myself with the hospital staff in order to help monitor my grandparents' conditions and to protect them from my uncle. One day, a nurse informed me that my uncle had visited, and it appeared that my grandmother was signing checks for him. While my grandparents were fighting for their lives, my uncle was still using their funds.

The Court Case

I hastened to make a plan for my grandparents' discharge and to institute a measure of protection for them from my uncle. I felt like a sitting duck, appearing calm and cool on the water's surface, but paddling like mad underneath.

Despite making phone calls for a full day, nothing was accomplished. During my final call, I was referred to an Assistant Commonwealth's Attorney (ACA) who was known as a staunch elder advocate. Expecting to reach her voicemail, I was elated when she answered in person. She listened as I explained the situation and my concerns, instructing me to come to the courthouse the next morning and bring any photos and documentation: she would arrange a hearing to request an order of protection for my grandparents. I thanked her and began preparing for the unconventional court appearance (so called because in the eyes of the law, I had no legal authority to request a protective order). Luckily, while at my grandparents' house during the intervention, I had used my cell phone to take photographs and video recordings; and I prepared a succinct presentation of the circumstances.

The next morning, I met briefly with the ACA who helped me muster the courage to go before the judge.

The judge listened to my story, but explained that I could not ask for this kind of protective order against my uncle on behalf of my grandparents. He said that such an order could only be solicited by the person in need of protection, the next of kin (if the person is unable to make such a petition), or the legal guardian. I stated that none of these parties were able to make the request, and that my grandparents were in grave danger. The judge, with some hesitation, granted a temporary protective order and explained that I should return in two weeks for another hearing to determine if a permanent protective order was necessary.

The judge then asked why my uncle had not been arrested. The ACA clarified that my family had been making reports for years, and that APS was involved, but that a case was never created. Dissatisfied with this, the judge directed the ACA to call the police to get a warrant for my uncle's arrest. He also advised that I should take the necessary steps to become the legal guardian and conservator for my grandparents. He allowed that this would cost me thousands of dollars in legal fees and require proving my grandparents' legal incapacity, but would give me the authority to represent my grandparents' best interests. Finally, he informed me that in order to represent my grandparents at the permanent protective order hearing in two weeks, I would have to confirm that I had initiated this complex legal process.

By mid-afternoon, I had been interviewed by several police officers and a warrant against my uncle was obtained. He was arrested and incarcerated. The sergeant in charge apologized that his unit had failed my family and assured me that he would do whatever necessary to be of assistance. Though saddened by the measures taken that day, I felt victorious—and exhausted; I knew this undertaking would be all-consuming. Upon returning home, I contacted my employer to request an extended leave of absence (which later led to my resignation).

My mission was to care for my grandparents. Although I lacked the legal authority to act on their behalf, my family respected my wishes, for no one else was similarly involved. I decided to relocate my grandparents to a nursing home near me and hired legal representation for the guardian/conservatorship proceedings. I worked closely with the ACA and investigators to prosecute my uncle for abusing and neglecting my grandparents. My uncle remained incarcerated, with his requests for bond denied three times.

The Aftermath

Trying to put together the pieces of my grandparent's lives was difficult since both were diagnosed with Alzheimer's-type dementia. I discovered dozens of delinquent accounts that had gone to collection—tens of thousands of dollars in debts. I found out that every day my uncle would persuade my grandmother to write him a check, telling her the money was for household bills. He would cash the check at a convenience store, buy a case of beer, and drink it while sitting in my grandparents' driveway. He also abused a variety of prescription drugs.

Further investigation revealed that the city's building inspector was aware of the situation: the inspector had made multiple visits to the property and had left numerous citations for the hazardous environmental conditions. Unfortunately, no action was taken to report these findings to the authorities, despite the fact that the inspector knew an elderly couple resided in the home with their son. Within two weeks of the intervention, the property was condemned. The home, once valued at $175,000, was reappraised and reassessed. With the permission of the Commissioner of Accounts, I sold the house to an investor for its true value of $32,000, in order to pay my grandparents' debts and mounting medical expenses.

Through numerous court appearances and continuances over an eight-month period, my uncle avoided going to trial. With an overwhelming amount of evidence, he eventually pleaded guilty to two felony charges of the abuse and neglect of an incapacitated adult. He was sentenced to ten years on each charge and mandated to serve three years incarcerated and seventeen on probation.

My grandfather passed away four months after the intervention and my grandmother joined him eleven months later. Though a tragic story, I find great peace in knowing that they were well cared for and happy during their final months of life. This was my life's most challenging and demanding period, but it was also the most meaningful. I will forever cherish my memories of my grandparents.

Conclusion

In retrospect, there were ample opportunities for professionals to intervene. In order to prevent elder abuse and neglect in the future, there must be better inter-agency communication, more personal responsibility taken by agency staff members, collaboration between well-trained professionals, and increased community awareness. Focused research, preventative programs, reformed policies and practices, and increased social awareness of what constitutes elder abuse can help to protect older people and, ultimately, eradicate this heartbreaking problem.

References

Elder Serve Act of 2009, H. R. 973, 111th Cong. (2009). www.gpo .gov/fdsys/pkg/BILLS-111hr973ih/pdf/BILLS-111hr973ih.pdf. Retrieved July 2012.

Spencer, C., and Smith, J. 2000. "Elder Abuse & Substance Abuse: Making the Connection." *Nexus,* a publication for NCPEA affiliates. www.preventelderabuse.org/nexus/spencersmith.html. Retrieved July 2012.

Critical Thinking

1. The article states that two-thirds of cases of elder abuse are perpetrated by family caregivers. Why do you think this is the case?

2. Why can it be so difficult to intervene on behalf of an elderly family member who you suspect may be being abused or taken advantage of?

3. How does elder abuse within a family alter family roles and family dynamics?

4. What can be done to prevent elder abuse?

Create Central

www.mhhe.com/createcentral

Internet References

National Council on Aging
  www.ncoa.org

National Center on Elder Abuse
  www.ncea.aoa.gov

Alzheimer's Association
  www.alz.org

Prepared by: Patricia Hrusa Williams,
University of Maine at Farmington

Article

Alcohol and Drug Misuse: A Family Affair

A shift in the way we understand addiction problems towards a family-inclusive focus has the potential to benefit millions–both those engaging in problematic consumption and those impacted by their behaviour.

ALEX COPELLO

Learning Outcomes

After reading this article, you will be able to:

- Identify the types of harm associated with alcohol and drug misuse.

- Explain the types of supports needed by families affected by substance abuse.

- Describe three different types of family interventions that can be used with individuals and their families affected by addiction.

Alcohol and drug problems tend to be conceptualised as difficulties experienced by an individual, with attention centred on the impact of consumption on the substance user. The predominant focus tends to be either physical symptoms (e.g. signs of tolerance or withdrawal) or psychological factors (motivational, behavioural and/or cognitive). The main belief is that if the therapist or counsellor can make an impact on these factors, it will lead to improvements in the substance-related problem. The resulting help tends to be individually tailored, and occurs within the confines of the treatment or counselling room. While individual work has benefited numerous people experiencing addiction problems, I would like to argue that the adoption of a social focus, involving 'thinking family', can make a significant contribution to the practice and to improved outcomes in this field.

The way in which the concept of harm reduction has been mostly applied is somewhat narrow, stressing mainly the physical aspects of the reduction of harm. Yet the social and family harm that arises when an addiction problem develops is significant, and there is much potential for reducing this harm, even when the substance user is not in contact with services, or has not yet engaged in behaviour change. The facts that engagement in treatment of the substance user can be triggered when working with affected family members, and that substance misuse outcomes are at least as good (and more often superior) when using family-based approaches, strengthen the argument for an increased family focus in services and interventions.

In order to move along the track of family-based approaches, we need to move away from an individualistic view of addiction problems, and to conceive of them instead as problems that have a significant social component—that both impact upon and are to a great extent influenced by the social environment of the substance user. Social interaction can help to shape behaviour, and families and social networks can influence the process of treatment entry as well as addictive behaviour change.

The Impact of Addiction on Families

When an addiction problem develops, those close to the person with the substance problem (mostly family members, but also friends) tend to be significantly affected. Time and again, studies exploring stress in family members living with someone with an addiction problem show high levels of physical and psychological symptoms resulting from this stress, and on a par with those experienced by people approaching mental health services due to anxiety and depression.[1-3] The actual experience of living with and being concerned about someone with an alcohol or drug problem has been described in some detail.[4] It has the nature of severe stress, threat, and abuse, and involves multiple sources of threat to the self and the family—emotional, social, financial, and health and safety-related. Family members also report that it can have a significant impact on children, and that worry is a prominent feature. Attempting to cope creates difficult dilemmas, and there is no guidance on the subject. While social support for the family is needed, it often tends to fail, and professionals who might help are often badly informed at best, and sometimes unhelpfully critical.

When interviewed about their experience of living with someone with a substance misuse problem,[4] family members report two separate, yet related, needs. First, they need to understand the problem they are facing, and to receive support in their own right—which involves receiving accurate information about addiction problems and their effects. Second, they tend to want to contribute to the treatment of their substance-misusing relative if possible, which in some cases may involve helping to promote the substance user's entry into treatment.

Family-Based Interventions: The Research Evidence

A number of intervention approaches have been developed to involve family members in addiction treatment, some of which focus on the family members' own needs.

Two reviews of the academic literature[5,6] have summarised social and family addiction treatments.

These concluded that when all strands of evidence are considered, there is a compelling case to recommend implementation of family intervention approaches in routine clinical practice. Recent NICE guidance on psychosocial interventions for drug misuse has recommended an approach based on working with couples: behavioural couple therapy,[7] and also stresses the need to respond to families in their own right when they approach routine drug services.[8]

Family interventions are of three types:

- those that aim to involve family members in the treatment of the substance user
- those that work with families to promote the entry into treatment of the substance user
- those focused on the needs of family members in their own right.

Involving Family Members in Treating the Substance User

Most interventions that have been reported in the research literature relate to involving family members in the treatment of the substance misuser. This category includes approaches that involve working with the family (and in some cases wider social networks) and substance user together, where the main focus is on the substance user and improvement of the substance user's behaviour. A secondary positive outcome may be a benefit for the family members involved, but, on the whole, the approaches are driven by the aim of reducing substance-related behaviour. Most approaches that have been evaluated are based on cognitive and behavioural models. However, there is some tradition of family therapy, particularly with drug problems. Two examples of evaluated interventions of this type are described below.

Behavioural couple therapy (BCT) is a well established and researched approach to working with couples in which one spouse has an alcohol or drug problem. Recently recommended for implementation by NICE, this approach uses a range of cognitive and behavioural strategies. BCT aims to engage the family's support for the client's efforts to change by working on couple and family interactions in a way that promotes a stable relationship that supports stable abstinence.[7]

Social behaviour and network therapy (SBNT)[9,10] is a family and social network approach that was originally developed for the UK Alcohol Treatment Trial (UKATT). The model drew from a range of evidence-based approaches with a social and family focus. The central idea is that social support is key in facilitating and supporting change in people with alcohol and drug problems. In the language of SBNT, this is called 'social support for a positive change in substance use'. The approach was tested in UKATT,[11] and found to be as effective and as cost-effective as the more established motivational enhancement therapy (MET). Both treatments led to positive outcomes for those receiving them, including significant reductions in alcohol consumption and mental health problems.

SBNT involves a range of different themes and strategies. In the early stages of the intervention, therapists are encouraged to draw a network diagram in order to identify the important people in the problem substance user's social environment. This usually helps both the focal client (a term used in SBNT to denote the person with the alcohol or drug problem) and the therapist to start what we describe as 'thinking network' (i.e. begin understanding the problem as influencing and being influenced by the problem drinker's social environment). At this stage, network members may be invited to join treatment sessions if this is considered appropriate by both client and therapist. Efforts can then focus on strengthening the network, through discussing themes of communication, coping, sharing information, and joint activities. Therapists are trained to work through a coherent set of strategies, driven by the overall aim of developing social support either for a change in substance use or for the maintenance of previous gains. A further important aspect is that the SBNT therapist or counsellor can continue to work with any part of the network that remains engaged in the treatment process. This can help, for example, in cases where the substance user lapses, or has a setback, and temporarily stops attending. Work can continue with network members to support re-engagement of the substance user at this difficult time, as well as to explore the impact of the relapse on network members.

Working with Families to Promote Treatment Entry of the User

Examples of interventions that focus on working with family members as a way of triggering treatment entry include community reinforcement and family training[12] (CRAFT) and the pressures to change (PTC) approach.[13] Both approaches were developed to enable services to respond when family members approach asking for help with a substance misuse situation. Both are structured, and involve some initial exploration of the family member's circumstances, followed by a discussion to explore ways of promoting treatment entry by the user. This can sometimes take place through the family member making a direct request, which can be planned and practised during therapy sessions.

Focusing on the Needs of Family Members

Interventions that involve working directly with family members and seeing them as people with needs in their own right are the least developed in terms of research. The 5-step intervention[14,15] constitutes one example, based on a 'stress-strain-coping-support' model of addiction and the family. An important principle of the

5-step model is that living with a highly stressful experience, such as the impact of an addiction problem in the family, may lead to psychological and physical symptoms of ill-health for family members other than the substance user. Family members in this predicament try to respond to the situation by employing a range of 'coping' behavioural strategies. Coping behaviours, along with available social support, can influence the extent of the stress experienced by family members, as well as the course and development of the addiction problem. As part of the 5-step intervention, family members receive support that is structured around five steps, covering the following specific areas: listening nonjudgmentally; providing relevant information; exploring ways of responding and interacting with the substance misuser; discussing the family member's available and potential social support; and establishing the need for further help. The 5-step intervention has been evaluated in a number of studies in primary care[16,17] and specialist settings,[18] and shown significant promise for reducing physical and psychological stress symptoms. Other approaches focused on family members include programmes for parents of substance misusing adolescents, such as behavioural exchange systems training[19] (BEST); and parent coping skills training.[20] Although the underlying model of the approaches discussed so far is very different, there are some obvious parallels with mutual-aid groups for affected family members, including Al-Anon.[21]

Moving Towards Family-Focused Services

From a research point of view, a number of family interventions have shown enough promise that they can be recommended with confidence for routine service provision. However, beyond the application of specific techniques is the more fundamental issue of impacts on the family and wider social network. Addressing this involves the development of a family-focused way of working and thinking in every case; incorporating a range of strategies to help families dealing with addiction problems; and moving towards the development of family-focused routine addiction services.

In our recent research work with addiction teams,[22] we have found that a combination of the 5-step approach and SBNT can be used flexibly in order to provide a framework for services to increase family-focused and family-inclusive practice into routine, mainstream addiction work. In these studies, whole teams have received training in the 5-step and SBNT methods in workshop format, followed by regular monthly team consultancy and supervision meetings with the researchers over 10–12 months in order to facilitate the development of family-focused practice. Services can then be responsive to family members in their own right, using the 5-step method, or run joint SBNT sessions, including the focal client and their family and network members, if this is considered appropriate and helpful by all involved. Some examples of the type of work conducted by teams as part of this project are summarised in Table 1.

Working in a family-focused way brings challenges to service providers and therapists. The traditional way of thinking about substance-misusing individuals and problems has to give

Table 1 Examples of Family-Focused Work Conducted by Teams

Some examples of the diversity of relationships between the focal client and their family members and wider support network
- Wife
- Husband
- Fiancée
- Mother and father of 18-year-old client
- Wife, sister and brother-in-law
- A friend
- Two neighbours

Some examples of the diversity of therapeutic work with family members
- Focal client and daughter for one session
- Three sessions with a couple, followed by sessions with the client alone
- Client alone, with mother once, then with father once
- One session with the client and their partner, followed by a large family meeting
- Home detoxification, involving five joint sessions with the client's spouse and sometimes other family members

Some examples of the diversity of gains from family/network involvement
- Family members feel calmer
- Conflict handled in the safer environment of the therapy session
- Support for the family after the client has died
- Reassurance after relapse
- Improvement in communication and mutual understanding
- All have a clear goal and plan

way to a broader view of addiction as a family and social problem affecting more than one person. In our experience, this requires a shift in thinking. Existing policies may need to be revised; ways of recording work reviewed; and contracts for services based on individual approaches closely examined.

In introducing the SBNT approach to teams of therapists in our research, we have found that initial concerns regarding the involvement of family members and friends (eg regarding client choice, family members taking over meetings, conflicts arising in sessions, and issues of confidentiality) give way to a more positive view and a problem-solving approach over time. As practitioners gain experience of working in this way, they report developing a clearer picture of the problem through the involvement of concerned and affected others; being able to extend the impact of the work beyond the actual session; and improved relationships between the client with the alcohol or drug problem and affected family members, which can then increase mutual support. Such therapists are better able to see and communicate the benefits of involving families in routine addiction practice, both to clients and their family members, and to the service as a whole.

References

1. Svenson, L., Forster, D., Woodhead, S., Platt, G. *Individuals with a chemical-dependent family member. Does their health care use increase?* Canadian Family Physician. 1995; 41:1488–1493.

2. Ray, G., Mertens J, Weisner C. *The excess medical cost and health problems of family members of persons diagnosed with alcohol or drug problems.* Medical Care. 2007; 45:116–122.

3. Ray, G., Mertens, J., Weisner C. *Family members of people with alcohol or drug dependence: health problems and medical cost compared to family members of people with diabetes and asthma.* Addiction. 2009; 104:203–214.

4. Orford, J., Natera, G., Copello A et al. *Coping with alcohol and drug problems: the experiences of family members in three contrasting cultures.* London; Taylor and Francis; 2005.

5. Copello, A., Velleman, R., Templeton, L. *Family interventions in the treatment of alcohol and drug problems.* Drug and Alcohol Review. 2005; 24:369–385.

6. Copello, A., Templeton, L., Velleman, R. *Family intervention for drug and alcohol misuse: is there a best practice? (invited review).* Current Opinion in Psychiatry. 2006; 19:271–276.

7. O'Farrell, TJ., Fals-Stewart, W. *Behavioral couples therapy for alcoholism and drug abuse.* New York: Guilford Press; 2006.

8. National Collaborating Centre for Mental Health. *Drug misuse: psychosocial interventions. Commissioned by National Institute for Health and Clinical Excellence (NICE). National clinical practice guideline number 51.* London: The British Psychological Society/The Royal College of Psychiatrists; 2008.

9. Copello, A., Orford, J., Hodgson, R., Tober, G., Barrett, C. *On behalf of the UKATT Research Team (2002). Social behaviour and network therapy: basic principles and early experiences.* Addictive Behaviors. 2009; 27:345–366.

10. Copello, A., Orford, .J, Hodgson, R., Tober, G. *Social behaviour and network therapy for alcohol problems.* London: Brunner-Routledge; 2009.

11. UKATT Research Team. *Effectiveness of treatment for alcohol problems: findings of the randomised UK alcohol treatment trial.* British Medical Journal. 2005; 331:541–544.

12. Meyers, R., Miller, W., Hill, D., Tonigan J. *Community reinforcement and family training (CRAFT): engaging unmotivated drug users in treatment.* Journal of Substance Abuse. 1999; 10:291–308.

13. Barber, JG., Crisp, BR. *The 'pressures to change' approach to working with the partners of heavy drinkers.* Addiction. 1995; 90:269–276.

14. Copello, A., Orford, J., Velleman, R., Templeton, L., Krishnan, M. *Methods for reducing alcohol and drug related family norm in non-specialist settings.* Journal of Mental Health. 2000; 9:329–343.

15. Copello, A. *Responding to addiction in the family: natural and assisted change in coping behaviour.* PhD thesis, University of Birmingham; 2003.

16. Copello, A., Templeton, L., Krishnan, M., Orford, J., Velleman, R. *A treatment package to improve primary care services for relatives of people with alcohol and drug problems.* Addiction Research. 2000; 8:471–484.

17. Copello, A., Templeton, L., Velleman, R et al. *The relative efficacy of two primary care brief interventions for family members affected by the addictive problem of a close relative: a randomised trial.* Addiction. 2009; 104:49–58.

18. Templeton, L. *Use of a structured brief intervention in a group setting for family members living with substance misuse.* Journal of Substance Use. 2009; 14:223–232.

19. Toumbourou, J., Blyth, A., Bamberg, J., Forer, D. *Early impact of the BEST intervention for parents stressed by adolescent substance abuse.* Journal of Community and Applied Social Psychology. 2001; 11:291–304.

20. McGillicuddy, NB., Rychtarik, RG., Duquette, JA., Morsheimer ET. *Development of a skill training program for parents of substance-abusing adolescents.* Journal of Substance Abuse Treatment. 2001; 20:59–68.

21. Humphreys, K. *Circles of recovery: self-help organizations for addictions.* Cambridge: Cambridge University Press; 2004.

22. Orford, J., Templeton, L., Copello, A., Velleman, R., Ibanga, A., Binnie C. *Increasing the involvement of family members in alcohol and drug treatment services: the results of an action research project in two specialist agencies.* Drugs: Education, Prevention and Policy. 2009; 16:1–30.

Critical Thinking

1. What is meant by the concept of "harm reduction?" What kinds of harm might alcohol and drug misuse bring to the individual and family?

2. Why is there such an individualistic view of addiction problems?

3. How might the involvement of the family in treatment promote recovery? What problems or issues might arise when families are involved?

Create Central

www.mhhe.com/createcentral

Internet References

Substance Abuse and Mental Health Services Administration
www.samhsa.gov

National Institute of Alcohol Use and Alcoholism
www.niaaa.nih.gov

ALEX COPELLO is Professor of Addiction Research at The School of Psychology, University of Birmingham, and Consultant Clinical Psychologist with the Birmingham and Solihull NHS Foundation Trust addiction services. His career has combined clinical and academic work, and his special areas of interest include the study of the impact of addiction on families, and the development and evaluation of family and social network-based interventions.

Acknowledgements—This article draws on research that I have been involved in, working with close collaborators over the years, in particular Lorna Templeton, Jim Orford, and Richard Velleman.

Article   Prepared by: Patricia Hrusa Williams, *University of Maine at Farmington*

Keeping the Promise: Maintaining the Health of Military and Veteran Families and Children

Colonel Stephen J. Cozza, Ron Haskins, and Richard M. Lerner

Learning Outcomes

After reading this article, you will be able to:

- Identify risks of parental deployment to children and families.

- Describe factors related to the adaptability and resilience of military families.

- Summarize the types of programs and services found to be effective in assisting military families.

. . . More than two million Americans have served in the post-9/11 wars in Iraq and Afghanistan, and nearly 45 percent of them have children. Although polls show that around 90 percent of Americans recognize and appreciate the sacrifice of service members who serve the nation, the public knows little about the actual costs imposed on the health and functioning of families, including children, of service members and veterans. Research on the effects of deployment on families is still in its infancy, but it already shows that deployment leads to distress and mental health problems among parents and that these parental problems are in turn associated with elevated rates of similar social-emotional problems in children. Though military families show remarkable resilience, given the stress most of them face, we argue that the sacrifices they make place a special obligation on the nation to help these distressed families and children. After all, since 9/11, nearly 6,700 service members have died and 50,000 have been physically injured in a combat zone. Hundreds of thousands more suffer from traumatic

brain injury (TBI) and posttraumatic stress disorder (PTSD). After reviewing the evidence on both the elevated levels of emotional and behavioral problems experienced by deployed service members and their families, as well as evidence on their resilience, we discuss a shared national agenda to expand and evaluate the effectiveness of preventive and treatment services for these families.

Deployment and Its Effects

Even routine military life means that families must deal with conditions that, research shows, can cause problems. Members of military families are often separated from one another; children are forced to change schools frequently; and some families, particularly those of lower rank, may face financial problems. Members of the military usually have little choice about where they are stationed, which means that spouses and children cannot decide where to live and when to move. Deployment to a combat zone adds a layer of danger to this already formidable list. The stress that family members feel when their loved one (or loved ones, in the case of families with two military parents) is in harm's way can disrupt family routines, lead to conflict between parents, and cause worry and elevated distress.

Several investigators have surveyed military families and found that combat deployment is associated with higher levels of emotional and behavioral problems in children. Anita Chandra of the RAND Corporation and her colleagues used a computer-assisted telephone interview with more than 1,500 military children aged 11 to 17 and their caretakers. Controlling for family and service member characteristics, they found that older boys and girls of all ages with a deployed parent had significantly more problems with school, family, and peers than do children the same age in the general U.S. population. Longer deployments were associated with more problems. Patricia Lester and her team at UCLA reported similar results among 272 children aged 6 to 12. Importantly, both studies found a strong relationship between the mental health of parents or caretakers and the healthy adaptation of their children to deployment stress.

Alyssa Mansfield of the University of North Carolina and her colleagues also examined how combat deployment affects children's mental health, using outpatient treatment records from 2003 to 2006 of nearly 310,000 children aged 5 to 17 with at least one parent in the Army. They compared the pediatric mental health outpatient visits of children whose parents were deployed longer than 11 months, 1 to 11 months, and not deployed at all. After controlling for children's age, gender, and mental health history, they found that both boys and girls whose parents were deployed received higher-than-normal levels of mental health diagnoses (including acute stress reaction/adjustment, depression, and behavioral disorders). Children of parents deployed more than 11 months had especially high levels of these problems. These results should be interpreted with some caution, because they are based on the procedural diagnostic codes that clinicians must enter in health care records for insurance and other purposes. Although greater use of mental health services likely indicates higher levels of distress in these military children, it should not be equated with mental illness in most of these cases.

Research also identifies an increased risk of child maltreatment among children with a deployed parent. Over the years, rates of child maltreatment in military families have been no greater, and perhaps lower, than among civilian families, and maltreatment rates in military families had been falling continuously until combat operations began in 2001. But at least three studies have now shown that parents are more likely to maltreat children during periods of deployment. A study by Deborah Gibbs of RTI International and her colleagues found that, based on confidential military records from 2001 to 2004, civilian wives of service members were four times as likely to neglect children during their husband's deployment than when he was home, and nearly twice as likely to physically abuse them. Also looking at 2001 to 2004, James McCarroll and his colleagues at the Uniformed Services University of the Health Sciences found rising rates of child maltreatment in military families, following a decline in the 1990s; most of the increase, was in neglect rather than physical abuse. Deployment may contribute to an elevated propensity for child neglect in a number of ways, for example, by temporarily creating the equivalent of a single-parent family, a known risk factor for child neglect.

We can draw two conclusions from these and similar studies on the effects of deployment on families. First, deployment leads to stress that affects both parents and children. Parental absence and parental distress are likely associated with diminished parenting capacity, greater risk for child maltreatment (particularly neglect), and greater parental dysfunction, and these in turn are associated with social-emotional and behavioral problems in children. Second, severity of exposure can make these child and family problems worse. For example, greater cumulative deployment time; a parent suffering from PTSD, as well as TBI or another injury; or a family member's death all increase the risk that a family will encounter trouble. These research findings justify concern and must lead to action by the public, by policy makers, and by senior military and other government officials.

Whatever action we take, however, we should remember that both experience and research show that combat deployment leads to a large range of reactions among military families and children. These reactions fall along a continuum from risk to resilience. Many parents and children handle the stress of deployment well, taking problems in stride and continuing to function normally. At the other end of the continuum, some parents and children struggle significantly with the challenges they face, resulting in dysfunction and risk. Most families are likely to be somewhere in the broad middle, distressed by the hardships but capable of adopting strategies that sustain their health and wellness. This range of responses suggests that we need a broad intervention strategy that supports health, screens for risk, and actively engages those who have the most trouble. To be sure, some children will need behavioral health treatment, although most can be helped with modest and relatively inexpensive interventions. But what is resilience, and do military families possess more of it than do civilian families?

Resilience in Military Families

[. . . M]ost military-connected children and parents have the attributes to be resilient in the face of parental deployment and reunification. One source of resilience is self-regulation, or a person's ability to intentionally alter her behavior, thoughts, attention, and emotions to react to and influence the environment; it is a key strength that helps people adapt and thrive in the face of adversity. A child's self-regulation is enhanced when other family members also possess self-regulation skills. For example, research shows that, when children must adapt to change, their resilience is related to their mother's adjustment and mental health. Therefore, just as in civilian families, positive relationships with close family members can help military children adapt to stress.

Other factors that protect military children and parents from stress include the perception that society appreciates the value of military service, pride in contributing to an important mission, a sense of belonging to a military culture, and awareness that networks of support don't go away when active service ends. In addition to providing a haven of safety and stability in difficult times, family relationships can help military-connected youngsters make meaning of adversity, affirm their strengths, feel connected through mutual support and collaboration, provide models and mentors, offer financial security, and frame the stressful circumstances in the context of family values and spirituality. The culture of the modern military gives families the capacity to help children see their experiences as a badge of honor rather than a burden.

What to Do

Military communities are diverse and rich with cultural heritage and resources that help sustain families and children. As a result, military communities, service members, their families, and, more specifically, their children, possess a capacity for resilience that equals or exceeds that of their civilian counterparts. But when they face deployments or other consequences of war, service members and their families are at risk for higher levels of distress, emotional and behavioral problems, child maltreatment, as well as possible deterioration in parental and family functioning, particularly when parents come home with serious disorders such as PTSD or TBI.

Combat veterans have a significant risk of developing mental disorders as a result of their wartime exposure. However, we must avoid a tendency to employ an "illness" model to understand how military spouses and children respond to wartime deployments. Though some people may develop mental disorders, they are likely to be a minority. Most other affected adults and children will experience distress. Distress is not an illness, but it can still significantly affect individuals, families, and communities. In addition to the anguish it can cause, distress can undermine occupational, social, and emotional functioning. Distressed parents are less likely to be attentive to their children and may lose some of the parenting capacity that they previously possessed. Distressed children may become withdrawn, participate in fewer extracurricular activities, find it difficult to concentrate in school, or demonstrate behavioral symptoms that are unusual or that complicate their normal development.

Interventions for mental illness differ from interventions for distress. The most successful models for helping environmentally stressed, at-risk populations emphasize prevention, particularly when these groups have previously enjoyed health and wellness. In 1994, the Institute of Medicine (IOM) outlined a model of activities that promote and sustain health. It places prevention strategies along a spectrum of intensity: universal (helpful to all), selective (useful to those at higher risk), and indicated (targeted to those who exhibit symptoms of a

disorder). Beyond prevention, the IOM intervention spectrum includes more intensive activities such as case (or illness) identification, traditional treatment, and health maintenance activities. Such a model is an excellent foundation for a national plan to support and sustain military children and families.

[. . .] Universal prevention in military communities is best achieved by programs that ensure social support and make resources readily available. Such programs should also help adults, children, and families develop resilience-enhancing skills—communicating, connecting with others, being flexible, taking on new and appropriate challenges, solving problems, resolving conflicts, and building a core sense of individual and family capacity and wellness. Such skills can prepare individuals, families, and communities and sustain them through challenging times. Universal prevention programs should be available in the many settings where service members, veterans, and their children and families are likely to be found—schools, child-care programs, youth services, faith-based organizations, and health care systems, all of which have the capacity to promote health and wellness. Many such prevention programs are available in military communities, but they are less likely to be found in the civilian communities where National Guard and Reserve families often live, or where veteran families move after their service ends.

In addition to universal prevention, we need programs that target the populations who face the greatest risk, for example, those who experience multiple deployments, PTSD, TBI, or a parent's death. [. . . M]ilitary and veteran families who face long-term disability are more likely to experience disruptions in individual and family functioning. Several new preventive interventions are helping families where deployment, illness, or injury have overwhelmed family resources, disrupted family schedules and routines, or undermined previously normative parenting practices. Though deployment distress may decrease as the wars wind down, military parents' combat-related illnesses and injuries will continue to affect their families and children. Programs designed to help those who are at the most risk or are showing symptoms of distress or dysfunction are at varying stages of development, and they require further refinement and scientific study to better understand which ones are likely to be most effective, and in which circumstances.

One family-focused prevention program shows considerable promise, and it illustrates the kind of programs that should be available to all military and veteran families who need them. FOCUS (Families Overcoming Under Stress) was developed by a UCLA-Harvard team, which based its design on previous research and evaluations of programs developed to help children and families contending with parental depression, a parent's infection with HIV, and military deployment. Based on the previous research and evaluations, the UCLA-Harvard team worked with the Navy and Marine Corps to modify the program's family prevention strategies for use with military families. FOCUS includes these central elements: family education, structured communication through discussing deployment on a personal level, and development of family-level resiliency skills. This multi-session program (typically six sessions, but sometimes more) involves separate meetings with parents and children, followed by sessions with all family members, who participate in structured activities led by skilled family resilience trainers.

FOCUS has been evaluated by checking participants both before and after they took part in the program (this kind of evaluation is called a pretest-posttest design). Data were collected over 20 months from nearly 500 participating families serving at 11 military installations. Before the program began, participating parents scored higher than community norms on measures of posttraumatic stress, depression, and anxiety, and children scored higher for emotional and behavioral problems. After 20 months, parents and children alike who participated in FOCUS showed significant improvement in all these areas. They also showed improvement on measures of family functioning, such as communication, role clarity, and problem solving, all of which were targeted by the FOCUS program. These results suggest that the processes underlying family resilience can be bolstered by family-centered preventive intervention.

Pretest-posttest designs are less than rigorous, however, and evaluations that use such a design cannot be fully trusted. But some of the testing that FOCUS's creators carried out as they designed the program met the highest standard of evaluation design, and the program should continue, although it should undergo more rigorous and better controlled evaluation. Moreover, refining FOCUS specifically for families who are contending with TBI and PTSD would expand its usefulness to those who are likely to experience the highest and longest-term risk. We recommend that federal funding pay to expand, adapt, and refine the program. We also call for funding to rigorously evaluate FOCUS and similar programs, following participants for at least 10 years, to determine whether they make a long-term difference in the lives of adults and children who experience the stress associated with combat deployment and its consequences. Such a plan would require collaboration among the Department of Defense (DoD), the Department of Veterans Affairs, other federal agencies, and universities and other academic or research institutions.

We must also ensure that service members and veterans, as well as their spouses and children, can easily access evidence-based mental health treatments in the communities where they live when formal treatment is required. Since many of the disorders for which veterans are treated are chronic (for example, PTSD, substance use, depression, and TBI), treatment and health maintenance programs that support veterans' functioning and minimize relapses or complications are critical to the

health and wellbeing of military and veteran families and their children. Researchers universally recognize that children's health is related to the health and wellbeing of their parents. Traditional individual treatments of service members and veterans must incorporate family-focused approaches that address the profound impact that diagnoses such as PTSD and TBI can have on families and children. Preliminary evidence suggests that such programs are helpful and well-received.

A national plan to meet the needs of military and veteran children and families will not come cheaply. As the nation debates the size of the national budget and the wars in Iraq and Afghanistan wind down, attention may shift from the needs of military children and families. This is not just an issue for the DoD. Though the DoD has developed many programs to help military children and families, civilian communities—where Guard and Reserve families live and where active-duty families will move when their service ends—remain less well equipped. An effective national plan would require us to expand and integrate systems and resources that exist outside the DoD. Families need access not only to DoD resources, but also to programs provided through other federal agencies (for example, Veterans Affairs and the Substance Abuse and Mental Health Services Administration), other health care systems (for example, TRICARE), and public mental health systems, as well as private providers and community-based programs (for example, public schools, community colleges, child-care programs, and faith-based organizations). Optimally, such a system of care would include programs that coordinate their efforts with one another, that know and respect military culture, and that include the levels of service outlined in the Institute of Medicine spectrum of preventive and treatment interventions.

It is difficult to put a price tag on our recommendations for developing and testing effective prevention and treatment programs, but it will likely be in the tens of millions of dollars. Given the dramatic sacrifices that military families have made to defend the nation, policy makers and taxpayers should honor our promise to these families with the funds necessary to restore and sustain them. To do less would disrespect their service and discredit the nation's commitment to those who serve in harm's way.

Additional Reading

Anita Chandra et al., "Children on the Homefront: The Experience of Children from Military Families," *Pediatrics* 125, no. 1 (2010): 16–25.

Stephen J. Cozza and Richard M. Lerner, eds., "Military Children and Families," special issue, *The Future of Children* 23, no. 2 (2013).

Carol S. Fullerton et al., "Child Neglect in Army Families: A Public Health Perspective," *Military Medicine* 176, no. 12 (2011): 1432–39.

Institute of Medicine, *Returning Home from Iraq and Afghanistan: Assessment of Readjustment Needs of Veterans, Service Members, and Their Families* (Washington: National Academies Press, 2013).

Patricia Lester et al., "Evaluation of a Family-Centered Prevention Intervention for Military Children and Families," *American Journal of Public Health* 102 (2012): S48–54.

Patricia Lester et al., "The Long War and Parental Combat Deployment: Effects on Military Children and Spouses," *Journal of the American Academy of Child and Adolescent Psychiatry* 49 (2010): 310–20.

Ann Masten, "Ordinary Magic: Resilience Processes in Development," *American Psychologist* 56 (2001): 227–38.

James E. McCarroll et al., "Trends in U.S. Army Child Maltreatment Reports: 1990–2004," *Child Abuse Review* 17 (2008): 108–18.

Patricia Beezley Mrazek and Robert J. Haggerty, *Reducing Risks for Mental Disorders: Frontiers for Preventive Intervention Research* (Washington, DC: Institute of Medicine, 1994).

Sean C. Sheppard, Jennifer Weil Malatras, and Allen C. Israel., "The Impact of Deployment on U.S. Military Families," *American Psychologist* 65 (6), 599–609.

Critical Thinking

1. How are challenges faced by children and the non-deployed parent when the other parent is deployed?

2. What are factors that are related to the adaptability and resilience of military families? How can these factors be utilized in interventions and supports to assist military families?

3. What strategies are the most effective in assisting military families?

Create Central

www.mhhe.com/createcentral

Internet References

Military OneSource
www.militaryonesource.mil
National Military Family Association
www.militaryfamily.org
Substance Abuse and Mental Health Services Administration
www.samhsa.gov

STEPHEN J. COZZA's views expressed herein do not necessarily reflect those of the Uniformed Services University of the Health Sciences or the Department of Defense.

Cozza, Colonel Stephen J.; Haskins, Ron; Lerner, Richard. "Policy Brief: Keeping the Promise: Maintaining the Health of Military and Veteran Families and Children." From *The Future of Children*, a collaboration of The Woodrow Wilson School of Public and International Affairs at Princeton University and the Brookings Institution.

Article

Prepared by: Patricia Hrusa Williams,
University of Maine at Farmington

A Guide in the Darkness

When a life starts to unravel, where do you turn for help?

JOHN LELAND

Learning Outcomes

After reading this article, you will be able to:

- Identify the legal, medical, financial, family, and practical challenges faced by families as they navigate the mental health system.

- Explain how having a mentally ill person in the family affects family dynamics.

Melissa Klump began to slip in the eighth grade. She couldn't focus in class, and in a moment of despair she swallowed 60 ibuprofen tablets. She was smart, pretty and ill: depression, attention deficit disorder, obsessive-compulsive disorder, either bipolar disorder or borderline personality disorder.

In her 20s, after a more serious suicide attempt, her parents sent her to a residential psychiatric treatment center, and from there to another. It was the treatment of last resort. When she was discharged from the second center last August after slapping another resident, her mother, Elisa Klump, was beside herself.

"I was banging my head against the wall," the mother said. "What do I do next?" She frantically called support groups, therapy programs, suicide prevention lines, anybody, running down a list of names in a directory of mental health resources. "Finally," she said, "somebody told me, 'The person you need to talk to is Carolyn Wolf.'"

That call, she said, changed her life and her daughter's. "Carolyn has given me hope," she said. "I didn't know there were people like her out there."

Carolyn Reinach Wolf is not a psychiatrist or a mental health professional, but a lawyer who has carved out what she says is a unique niche, working with families like the Klumps.

One in 17 American adults suffers from a severe mental illness, and the systems into which they are plunged—hospitals, insurance companies, courts, social services—can be fragmented and overwhelming for families to manage. The recent shootings in Newtown, Conn., and Aurora, Colo., have brought attention to the need for intervention to prevent such extreme acts of violence, which are rare. But for the great majority of families watching their loved ones suffer, and often suffering themselves, the struggle can be boundless, with little guidance along the way.

"If you Google '*mental health lawyer,*'" said Ms. Wolf, a partner with Abrams & Fensterman, "I'm kinda the only game in town."

On a recent afternoon, she described in her Midtown office the range of her practice.

"We have been known to pull people out of crack dens," she said. "I have chased people around hotels all over the city with the N.Y.P.D. and my team to get them to a hospital. I had a case years ago where the person was on his way back from Europe, and the family was very concerned that he was symptomatic. I had security people meet him at J.F.K."

Many lawyers work with mentally ill people or their families, but Ron Honberg, the national director of policy and legal affairs for the *National Alliance on Mental Illness,* said he did not know of another lawyer who did what Ms. Wolf does: providing families with a team of psychiatrists, social workers, case managers, life coaches, security guards and others, and then coordinating their services. It can be a lifeline—for people who can afford it, Mr. Honberg said. "Otherwise, families have to do this on their own," he said. "It's a 24-hour, 7-day-a-week job, and for some families it never ends."

Many of Ms. Wolf's clients declined to be interviewed for this article, but the few who spoke offered an unusual window on the arcane twists and turns of the mental health care system, even for families with money. Their stories illustrate how fraught and sometimes blind such a journey can be.

One rainy morning last month, Lance Sheena, 29, sat with his mother in the spacious family room of her Long Island home. Mr. Sheena was puffy-eyed and sporadically inattentive; the previous night, at the group home where he has been living since late last summer, another resident had been screaming incoherently and was taken away by the police. His mother, Susan Sheena, eased delicately into the family story.

"I don't talk to a lot of people because they don't get it," Ms. Sheena said. "They mean well, but they don't get it unless they've been through a similar experience. And anytime something comes up, like the shooting in Newtown, right away it goes to the mentally ill. And you think, maybe we shouldn't be so public about this, because people are going to be afraid of us and Lance. It's a big concern."

Her son cut her off. "Are you comparing me to the guy that shot those people?"

"No, I'm saying that anytime there's a shooting, like in Aurora, that's when these things come out in the news."

"Did you really just compare me to that guy?"

"No, I didn't compare you."

"Then what did you say?"

"I said that when things like this happen, one of the first things you hear about is somebody being mentally ill." She added that her son, like most people with mental illness, has never been violent.

Ms. Wolf, a neighbor who attended the same synagogue, was one of the few people Ms. Sheena talked to about her son. Ms. Wolf started her career as a hospital administrator, then after law school represented hospitals in commitment hearings. Families of mentally ill people, she said, heard about her and began to turn to her for help.

A popular, athletic child, Lance started showing signs of obsessive-compulsive disorder at age 11 and began using drugs around the same age.

"I never had trouble buying drugs because I sold drugs," Mr. Sheena recalled. "And when I wasn't buying drugs I got them from the doctor. Valium, Xanax, Adderall, Ritalin, Seroquel. Finished a bottle of Adderall in 12 hours once. That's like 30 pills, 20 mg each. I was lying under the air-conditioner listening to my heart beat. Finally I woke up, took some Xanax."

Eight years ago, after taking "a lot of prescription drugs and Ecstasy," he said, he landed in the psychiatric ward at North Shore Hospital in a state of drug-induced psychosis. It was the first of several such stays, some by his volition, others against his will. Three years ago, Ms. Sheena came home to find him in the woods behind the house, wearing only shorts and a T-shirt in the January cold.

"The level of life I had in me that was productive was so low," he said. "I was almost homeless, I was a complete bum, and I decided to clean the woods. It was the only thing I could do."

Finally, at a psychiatric hospital upstate, he received a diagnosis of schizophrenia.

"It was tearing us apart," Ms. Sheena said. Her son's three younger brothers were angry at him for the turbulence in their home, she said. His youngest brother, who is now in high school, had never known a normal home life. After that hospitalization three years ago Lance Sheena stopped using drugs—for his mother, he said.

Mr. Sheena returned to school and earned an associate's degree. But his illness follows its own agenda. Last summer, he became flooded with thoughts of death and was hospitalized twice in quick succession, the second time against his will. He left his mother angry messages, which she saved.

"Nasty messages," she said. "'I hate you. Get me out of here.' Nasty."

"Why'd you save them?" he asked.

"I don't know."

"No really, why?"

During that time, Ms. Sheena began turning to Ms. Wolf for help. Ms. Wolf said she could petition to have Mr. Sheena released from the hospital and into a different kind of supervised involuntary commitment, known as assisted outpatient treatment, that would be less restrictive. But she also advised the Sheenas not to let their son move back into the family home.

"We were at a breaking point," Ms. Sheena said. "He would come home and we'd be back in the same roles where I'm looking to see if he's going to his meetings, if he's taking his medicine. What is he doing? Is he sleeping? Is he bouncing off the walls all night?"

It was too much, Ms. Wolf said. "I try to get people off of that, because I have found over these 20-plus years that it works better when you put the professionals in place and the family members go back to being the loved ones," she said.

Ms. Wolf helped Mr. Sheena move to a group home, where he has a case manager and social worker and takes the bus to court-mandated therapy appointments and group meetings. Now, when he returns home to visit, "there's a real sense of calmness in the house," his mother said. "It's wonderful, it's peaceful, it's loving, he sleeps home often on Friday night. And he's doing better because he's not as stressed, because we're not watching him like that."

Mr. Sheena said he was unhappy about not being allowed to move back home. But his life is more stable, he said, and he has started to write about his experiences, with help from his mother.

"Now, he's the best he's been in the last 10 years," she said. "He's come to accept that he's mentally ill, that he has an illness and that it needs to be treated. And I hope he can be better than he is now, but who knows?"

Not all of Ms. Wolf's clients can report even that much hope.

In a Midtown financial services office, a consultant whose son suffers from bipolar schizoaffective disorder described an almost unbroken series of setbacks, with his son now living in an efficiency hotel in Georgia, refusing to take medications or acknowledge that he needs care. To avoid causing more pain to family members, the father would be identified only by his first initial, J., and his son by the initial R.

"It tears your heart out as a parent, believe me," J. said.

J. first met Ms. Wolf more than a decade ago at New York-Presbyterian Hospital, where he was visiting his son and she was representing the hospital in commitment hearings. By that time, R., who is now in his early 40s, had been hospitalized involuntarily several times, each time ceasing treatment after he was released. He lost apartment after apartment, sometimes for harassing the owners or other residents.

Then he took a bigger step, going to the home of a film executive and harassing the man's wife. When he was arrested and charged, his father called Ms. Wolf.

"The D.A. wanted to put him in jail for two years," J. said. His son's criminal lawyer was ready to take a plea deal, which would involve prison time, the father said.

Instead, Ms. Wolf negotiated with the prosecution to allow him to be committed involuntarily to Bellevue Hospital Center. When R. petitioned to go home, saying he did not need treatment, Ms. Wolf argued that he was still a danger to himself and others.

"She went to court for us every Tuesday," the father said, "and we were able to show cause why he should be kept there. And the doctors helped us, but only because Carolyn spoke to them and assisted us."

After nine months in Bellevue, R. was finally discharged, against the efforts of Ms. Wolf and his father. Ms. Wolf engaged a psychiatrist, a case manager, and someone to live with R. to make sure he took his medications. But soon he stopped complying again; nothing was different.

Now, J. would like to see his son in a residential psychiatric center or a hospital. But R. will not go voluntarily, and unless he commits a serious crime, the courts will not commit him long-term.

"I've gone through a fortune, and the system stinks," J. said. "It can be shown by some of these recent killings in Sandy Hook and in Aurora. Or Virginia Tech. These are people who are mentally ill and they've proved that they're mentally ill, who the court system fails and the mental health system fails. You can see the glary, starey eyes of this killer from Aurora in court. I've seen that expression from my son when he's been locked up. And it's because he's totally psychotic."

The day Melissa Klump, now 28, tried to kill herself, in April 2011, she woke with a sense of overwhelming serenity, knowing what she wanted to do. She had fought with her brother the day before, when he blamed her for destroying their parents' marriage.

"I was calm," she said. "I went upstairs, I showered, I did my hair, I put on a nice little cute outfit, I wrote a letter to my grandmother apologizing for what I was about to do, and I wrote that I wanted to be cremated. I lined up all my pills and took a picture and sent it to my brother and I said, Happy Easter. And I downed 20 Xanax and 10 Trazodone, and took it all with a warm Corona.

"Just then my dad started pounding on the door. I opened the door and said, 'This is what you guys wanted, so here you go.' I threw my bottles down the stairs."

At a recent appointment in Manhattan, she arrived early, with polished nails and crisp eye makeup, eager to talk—about her suicide attempt, about her future, about her serial medication regimens: Lexapro, Effexor, Cymbalta, Xanax, Trazodone, Prozac, Klonopin, Lamictal, Ativan. She showed the delicate script tattoos on her wrists, reading "Carpe Diem" on one arm and "La Bella Vita" on the other, covering the places where she'd cut herself with a hot safety pin.

After she was sent home from the treatment center for slapping another resident, her mother took her to see Ms. Wolf, who asked her what her goals were.

"I didn't think she would ask me that," Melissa Klump said. "It seemed nice that she was interested in me as a person. She said she had someone who could help. She also said I was one of her few clients who have goals and plans."

Ms. Wolf arranged for a care manager and a life coach to see Ms. Klump several times a week at her grandmother's house.

Christopher Mooney, the care manager, said he was working with her to meet her goals: to pay down her five-figure credit card debt—the result of a few manic sprees—to set a budget, to make a financial plan; then they will start to look for apartments. "She's got the capability, but she needs someone there to help her make it happen," he said.

Mr. Mooney bills $150 an hour for his time. The life coach, who meets with Ms. Klump more regularly, charges $50 an hour. Ms. Wolf would not discuss her fees.

It adds up, Elisa Klump said, especially on top of all the other expenses. "We're coming to the point where there's going to be no more money left," she said. And still she knows that her daughter could slide back, as could any of the others. Their lives remain subject to powerful forces, both internal and external, for which a lawyer can do only so much.

"We're in baby steps," Elisa Klump said. "She's lost many years of her life. Carolyn put her down the right road. We'll see where she goes."

Critical Thinking

1. What do you see as the greatest challenge faced by families where a member has a mental illness? Why?

2. How can we work with families and patients so they feel safe and not stigmatized?

3. How can we best support families struggling with mental health issues? How might the strategy or approach differ by the patient's age, mental health problem, and the characteristics of their family?

4. Using information gained from this article, describe an intervention or support program that could be developed to facilitate the positive development of families struggling with mental illness.

Create Central

www.mhhe.com/createcentral

Internet References

Substance Abuse and Mental Health Services Administration
 www.samhsa.gov

National Alliance on Mental Illness
 www.nami.org

Article   Prepared by: Patricia Hrusa Williams,
                                                University of Maine at Farmington

From Promise to Promiscuity

Hara Estroff Marano

Learning Outcomes

After reading this article, you will be able to:

- Describe how people cheat on their partners.

- Identify why people cheat.

- Explain what happens to a relationship after infidelity.

As devastating experiences go, few events can match the emotional havoc following the discovery that one's partner is having an affair. Atop a suddenly shattered world hover pain and rejection, doubts about one's worth, and, most searingly, the rupture of trust. For Deanna Stahling, discovery struck in a hallucinatory moment that forever fractured time into Before and After. She had just stepped off a plane from the Caribbean after a week's vacation with a family friend and picked up a copy of the city's leading newspaper. There, in the lifestyles section, was a profile of a top woman executive whose name Deanna had heard a lot lately—her husband worked with the woman. Deanna had even met her—introduced by her husband a few weeks earlier at a corporate function. The exec, it was reported, was leaving the company so that she could ethically pursue a relationship with a colleague.

Deanna doesn't remember the trip home from the airport, but the house was empty and her husband's belongings were gone. A denuded bookshelf highlighted now-missing Giants memorabilia. A note on the kitchen table advised her—after 25 years, two newly fledged kids, and the recent purchase of a joint cemetery plot—to refer any questions to his attorney.

The next morning found Deanna sobbing in a therapist's office. Together they began the search for the source of the sudden defection. Like most therapists (and indeed, most everyone else), they subscribed implicitly to a deficit model of affairs: the presumption that there were fatal problems in the relationship.

Over the past several years, however, leading thinkers have begun to abandon such a pathologizing approach. No one doubts that a straying partner is alone responsible for the often disastrous decision to engage in infidelity. But a new, more nuanced perspective that puts far more emphasis on contextual and situational factors has sparked a revolution in understanding and handling affairs. The new approach encourages as a matter of course what happens now only by chance—complete recovery without any feelings being swept under the rug and even fortification of the couple bond.

The Shifting Landscape of Illicit Love

No one knows for sure just how common affairs are. Social desirability and fear of disclosure skew survey responses significantly. In 1994, 77 percent of 3,432 people constituting a representative sample of Americans declared that extramarital sex is always wrong (although the vast majority of people also have fantasies of engaging in an affair). And the number is actually growing. Today, over 90 percent of respondents deem sexual straying unacceptable—and expect sexual monogamy.

Still, decades of studies show that affairs are common, and, at least historically, more so among men than women: Among American couples, 20 to 40 percent of heterosexual married men and 10 to 25 percent of heterosexual married women will have an affair during their lifetime. In any given year, 1.5 to 4 percent of married individuals engage in an affair.

The newest surveys also reveal a very notable shift in the demographics of deception. Among younger cohorts—those under 45—the rates of infidelity among men and women are converging. Psychologists and sociologists attribute the development to huge changes in sheer opportunity, particularly the massive movement of women out of the home and into the workplace; studies show that the majority of individuals engaged in an affair met their lover at work. The rising financial power of women renders them less risk-averse, because they are less dependent on a spouse for support. As for a longstanding belief that men are more instinctually inclined to sexual infidelity than women are? Well, it's now far more of an open question.

That doesn't mean there are no gender differences in affairs. For women, infidelity is thought to be driven more by emotional needs and is most likely when they are not satisfied in their marital relationship, especially when it is not a partnership of equals. For men, infidelity has long been more independent of the state of the marital relationship. The pioneering psychologist Shirley Glass first reported in 1985 that among individuals engaging in infidelity, 56 percent of men and 34 percent of women rate their marriage as "happy" or "very happy." However, some of these differences may be disappearing, too. In 2003, just before she died, Glass reported that 74 percent of men were emotionally (as well as sexually) involved with their affair partner.

While the landscape of illicit love has been shifting, the therapeutic world has remained fairly fixed in the belief that affairs occur because something is radically wrong with the marriage. Make no mistake—most couples stay and want to stay together after a partner has strayed, despite the enormous psychic trauma to the uninvolved spouse. And indeed, 70 percent of couples choose to rebuild the relationship after infidelity, although they may not know how. Even couples for whom the violation is so painful or incomprehensible that divorce seems the only alternative often later regret a decision made in the highly disorienting days after discovery.

Studies indeed show that relationship dissatisfaction is associated with engaging in extramarital sex. But there's evidence that in almost two-thirds of cases, marital problems are the *effect,* not the cause, of extramarital involvements. Further, affairs themselves skew perceptions of the marriage. Once infidelity has occurred, partners tend to look back on their primary relationship and see it as having been flawed all along—an attempt to reduce cognitive dissonance.

Focusing attention exclusively on relationship flaws, say the field's leading thinkers, encourages couples to get psychologically stuck, brooding on the emotional betrayal and assigning blame. There is no statute of limitations on the hurt and anger that follow a partner's affair. But for the sake of dampening emotional volatility, injured partners are often rushed into "moving on," burying distrust and resentments that fester underground, sometimes for decades, forever precluding restoration of closeness.

Context, Context, Context

Affairs, says Washington, D.C., psychologist Barry McCarthy, are "the absolutely best example of behavior being multicausal, multidimensional. There are many contributing factors. Sometimes they have nothing to do with the marriage. The most common reason for an affair is high opportunity. People fall into affairs rather than plan them." Another very common cause of affairs, he observes, is that "people do not feel desired and desirable in their marriage, and they want to see if they can be desired and desirable outside it." For others, he notes, the affair is a symptom of a mental health problem like alcohol abuse or bipolar disorder. But unless all contributing elements are openly discussed and their meaning evaluated by both partners together, injured partners cannot regain the sense of security that allows them to forgive a straying spouse and rebuild trust in their mate. "The reality is that it takes two people to continue a marriage but only one to terminate a marriage," says McCarthy.

By far the biggest predictor of affairs, experts agree, is sheer opportunity—how people vary in access and desirability to others. And the workplace is the great benefactor, providing large numbers of people with constant contact, common interests, an income to camouflage the costs of socializing outside the office, and an ironclad excuse.

In a study of more than 4,000 adults, reported in the *Journal of Family Psychology,* Donald Baucom and colleagues found that both income and employment status are indices of opportunity for affairs. "Income may not be the critical variable in itself," they offer. "Individuals with higher incomes might be considered to have higher status, to travel more, or to interact professionally with more appealing individuals." In their study, those who worked but whose spouses did not were the most likely to report being unfaithful. Opportunity at the office is most ominous when it mixes with a disparity in relationship power at home.

Travel is way up there, researchers find, especially work related travel. "Lots of elements go into that," says Kristina Coop Gordon, professor of psychology at the University of Tennessee. "You're away from your partner, maybe even missing your mate, and you're in situations where you're encountering

---

The Other Woman

She might be history's most reviled female. Or most misunderstood. She isn't all she's cracked up to be. Sex with her is generally no better than sex in the marriage. And she's not likely to be a bombshell. The most you can say for sure is that she's different from the wife, and that may be all some cheaters need. Most male affairs, which is to say most affairs, are excursions of opportunity with little emotional investment. Worth crying over, yes. But not necessarily worth bringing the house down. Fewer than 25 percent of cheaters leave a marriage for an affair partner, and those relationships are statistically extremely unlikely to endure.

However much the mystery woman incites rage and envy and dreams of malevolence, she falls short of the self-destructive comparisons made against her.

Usually, says University of Tennessee psychologist Kristina Coop Gordon, fixation on the other woman and desire for details about her are not what they seem. "It's really a test of the straying spouse by the wounded one: 'Will you be open with me about the affair?' They really don't want to know the gory details; either it will spark a fight or make them feel bad. The wounded spouse just wants proof that she's important enough."

Sometimes, however, the other woman won't let go. She may threaten retaliation or self-harm. On the other hand, the involved spouse may do a miserable job of setting firm boundaries and not make a clean break of it. "Some men are not quite letting go themselves," Gordon finds. "And they're sending mixed messages to the other woman, which both she and the wife pick up on. That may be one reason a wounded wife can become obsessed with the other woman; there's a continuing threat."

—H. E. M.

plenty of people," Gordon explains. "It certainly facilitates one-night stands." Companies that employ large cohorts of young people, especially those who socialize together after work, create an environment for affairs.

No one profession has a lock on infidelity, Gordon maintains. Most relevant is the culture within a company. "Really macho cultures, which often exist in drug enforcement and police work, can involve a 'player' phenomenon where you need to show how virile you are. They are the clearest examples of work environments that foster infidelity that I've seen."

Duplicity also has a downtown address. Living in the midst of a city abets infidelity. Not only is there exposure to large numbers of potential partners, there's more opportunity to escape detection. The larger the city one lives in, researchers have found, the greater the likelihood of an affair.

Attending religious services is generally a deterrent to infidelity, perhaps because it embeds people in a social network that promotes accountability. But it helps only those who are already happy in their relationship. If the primary relationship is less than ideal, then dissatisfaction overrides religious values. Rates of infidelity do not differ by denomination.

Education increases the propensity to infidelity. It may be a marker for more liberal attitudes toward sexuality and permissive attitudes toward adultery. Ditto a history of divorce, or having parents who divorced, especially if either one had an extramarital involvement. Women with more education than their husbands have more affairs, perhaps because they are less dependent on a spouse.

Friendships are a factor in infidelity. Peer groups may sanction or even encourage it, researchers have found. Those who engage in extramarital involvements estimate a higher prevalence of affairs in their community than those who don't and believe their friends would be relatively approving. Separate his and her friendship networks are especially risky. One way of avoiding infidelity is to share a spouse's social network. Befriending a partner's family proves particularly protective. In one study it was linked to a 26 percent decrease in the odds of sexual infidelity.

Personality differences between partners play a role as well. Spouses who are comfortable with conflict and more or less matched on that trait are less likely to have affairs, perhaps because they are most open to airing marital concerns and dissatisfactions with each other.

In general, openness is protective and a characteristic of non-cheaters. Associated with intelligence, creativity, curiosity, and insightfulness, openness makes partners more satisfied with the relationship and better able to express feelings, including love. Some researchers believe that openness is essential to commitment to and enduring satisfaction in a relationship.

Low levels of agreeableness (the tendency to be compassionate and cooperative) bode poorly for monogamy. More important, however, is whether couples are matched on that trait. Spouses who see themselves as more agreeable than their mate believe themselves to be more giving, feel exploited by their partner, and seek reciprocity through outside relationships. Many studies show that a high level of neuroticism also inclines individuals to infidelity, independent of a partner's personality.

Psychological problems factor in, too. Affairs, associated with insecurity and having low self-esteem, can be a way of seeking reassurance of desirability or of combating depression. An affair certainly provides an arousing stimulus that is an antidote, however temporary, to feeling down. Then, too, affairs are also linked to high self-regard, a sense of one's own attractiveness or entitlement, or maybe the accompaniment to narcissism.

Situations that deplete self-control—exposure to alcohol, an exhausting day of travel, doing highly challenging work—raise the risk of infidelity. They disable sexual restraint, psychologists Roy Baumeister and Matthew Gailliot have found. The two manipulated self-control by giving subjects cognitively demanding or simple word puzzles before presenting them with purely hypothetical scenarios testing their willingness to engage in infidelity. The more demanding the tasks, the more depleted self-control, the more subjects were unable to inhibit their inclination to infidelity or to stifle sexual thoughts. Of course, hypothetical infidelity is a long way from landing in bed with someone.

Hypocrisy or Hormones?

The very make-up of the human brain contributes to affairs, too, observes anthropologist Helen Fisher. She has shown in brain-imaging studies that there are separate neural systems for sex drive, romantic love, and attachment, and they can operate independently. "Everyone starts out in marriage believing they will not have an affair. Why do data from around the world consistently show that infidelity occurs even among people who are happy in their marriage? You can feel deep attachment to a partner but also feel intense romantic love for someone else while also feeling a desire for sex with other partners," she observes.

The attachment system, fueled by the neurohormones oxytocin in females and vasopressin in males, drives animals, including humans, to pair-bond to rear their offspring as a team. Both hormones are triggered by orgasm, and both trigger dopamine release in reward regions of the brain. But all animals cheat, even when they form pair bonds.

In most mammals, the bond lasts only as long as it takes to rear the young. Among prairie voles, science's favorite model of monogamy, knocking out the gene that codes for vasopressin receptors abolishes their penchant for pair-bonding. And implanting it in their notoriously promiscuous cousins, the mountain voles, leads the males to fixate on a specific female partner even when alluring others are abundantly available.

More recently, in a study of over 500 men, Swedish researchers found that variations in a gene that codes for vasopressin receptors in humans influences the very ability to form monogamous relationships. Men with two copies of a specific gene variant scored significantly lower on a questionnaire known as the Partner Bonding Scale and reported twice as many marital crises in the past year. Those with two copies of the variant were also twice as likely to be involved in outside relationships and far less likely to have ever been married than those not carrying the allele.

"Monogamy does not mean sexual fidelity. That is a separate issue," says Fisher. In fact, scientists increasingly speak of "social monogamy" to distinguish promise from promiscuity. If we are monogamous, we are also just as predictably adulterous. What's more, people jeopardize their family, their health, their safety, their social standing, their financial well-being for affairs—and violate their own strong beliefs.

Monogamy may be the norm in human culture, but it is only part of the human reproductive repertoire, contends Fisher. "We humans have a dual reproductive strategy," she argues. "We regularly appear to express a combination of lifelong (or serial) social monogamy and, in many cases, clandestine adultery."

Despite its many risks, and sometimes because of them, there are big payoffs for infidelity, Fisher argues. For men especially, genetic variation is the most obvious. But she believes that women benefit, too. Infidelity may provide a "back-up mate" to offer protection and resources when the regular guy is not around. And women may use affairs as away of "trading up" to find a more desirable partner. It's possible, too, that infidelity can serve a positive role in relationships—as a way to gain attention from one's primary partner or to signal that there are problems in the relationship that need attending to.

In a study reported in 2010 in *PLoS One*, Justin Garcia, a postdoctoral fellow at Binghamton University, outlined another payoff—pure, passionate thrill. He found that individuals with a variant of a dopamine receptor gene were more likely than those without it to have a history of "uncommitted sex, one-night stands, and adultery." The motivation, he says, "stems from a system of pleasure and reward." Fisher suspects that's just the tip of the infidelity iceberg, and more biological contributors are likely to be identified in future studies.

From Angry Victim to Proud Survivor

One of the great facts of infidelity is that it has such a wildly different emotional impact on the marital partners. The uninvolved partner is deeply traumatized and emotionally distraught over the betrayal, and desperately trying to piece together what happened. The straying partner, often because of deep shame, may get defensive and shut down or blame the spouse for not moving on, only compounding the hurt. One needs to talk about what happened; the other can't bear to. "It's as if one of them is speaking German, the other is speaking Greek, and they're not speaking English to each other," McCarthy says.

Getting them on the same track of understanding is the key to recovery from affairs, says Gordon, who along with Baucom and Douglas Snyder, professor of psychology at Texas A&M, has sparked the revolution in treating infidelity not only by focusing on the many contributing factors but by developing the first empirically validated model of recovery. As detailed in their book, *Getting Past the Affair,* the first step is for both spouses to recognize the huge emotional impact on the uninvolved partner. Gordon and company have found a powerful device: After encouraging the partners to make no decisions about the future in the immediate aftermath of discovery or disclosure, they ask that the cheated-on partner write a letter to the spouse describing what the hurt feels like.

"The cheating partner must hear, no matter how discomfiting it is," says Gordon. "The experience is very intense and usually a turning point. Partners begin to soften towards each other. It's a demonstration to the injured partner that he or she really matters."

Then together the spouses search for the meaning of the affair by exploring how the choice was made and what contributed to it. Everything is fair game—attitudes and expectations about marriage that each partner has, conflicts and anything else going on in the relationship, hidden desires, personal anxieties and insecurities, needs for excitement, the closeness and distance they feel, job demands, work ambience, flirtations, opportunities, the people and pressures around them at home and outside it. The approach short-circuits the often misguided inclination to focus on The Other Person.

From understanding flows forgiveness, which allows partners to become close again. Wild as the reaction to discovery of a partner's affair can be in the beginning, Gordon welcomes it. "At least it provides the opportunity to interact around the pain. What often happens with the 'nice' couples," she says, "is they stay together but lead parallel lives marked by great distance. There's no bond anymore."

Renewing Romance

Barry McCarthy gives the revolution in recovery from affairs another twist all his own—re-eroticizing the marriage. "A couple has to develop a new sexual style" that facilitates sexual desire both in and out of the bedroom, he says. The point is to abolish the inclination to compare marital sex with affair sex—a hopeless cause as affair partners don't have to contend with sick kids and other realities of life, and the illicitness of the liaison intensifies excitement—but to compare marital sex before the affair and after it.

For the vast majority of American couples today, sexual satisfaction plummets at the birth of the first child and reemerges, if at all, after the last child leaves home. Of course, it doesn't have to be that way. Admittedly, McCarthy says, "it's a balancing act for partners to maintain their sense of who they are as individuals, their sense of being a couple, and being parents and sexual people." But in the long run, it's in everyone's best interest. Most contemporary couples, he laments, treat sexuality with benign neglect—until an affair sets off a crisis.

In healthy marriages, sex plays what he deems "a relatively small part, a 15 to 20 percent part"—but it energizes the whole bond and allows each partner to feel desired and desirable. When couples abandon sex, they wind up draining the entire relationship of its vitality. "You not only lose the marriage connection but your sense of self," McCarthy finds. "An affair can be an attempt to regain a sense of self."

So McCarthy puts great effort into reconnecting partners both emotionally and physically. He focuses on "non-demand pleasure." "We try to reintroduce the idea of touching inside and outside the bedroom, clothed and not clothed, valuing sensual and playful touch. It can be a bridge to intercourse, but there's no demand that it has to go to intercourse." He encourages couples to find a mutually acceptable level of intimacy and come up with their own erotic scenarios.

Pacts of Prevention

Because good intentions do not prove good enough, McCarthy takes post affair repair one step further—asking couples to create an explicit pact to prevent future infidelity by either of them. Together, they lay out the terms for disclosing when their interest is straying. Having painfully reached an understanding of the complex personal, marital, and situational vulnerabilities that led to an affair, couples draft a relapse prevention agreement.

The purpose is to rob any future affair of its spontaneity and its emotional and sexual secrecy. Both partners are encouraged to articulate the types of situation, mood, and person that could draw them into an affair—and to share that information with each other.

Then they commit to alert the spouse if they are in a high-risk situation and to discuss it rather than act on it. As an incentive, the agreement, drawing on recent experience, spells out the emotional costs to both parties of an affair. Because the secrecy and cover-up of infidelity are often more damaging than the defection itself, partners agree that, if there is a sexual incident, they will disclose it within 72 hours. And it works, McCarthy finds.

The pact of prevention embodies a principle Helen Fisher enunciates most succinctly: "Predisposition isn't predestination."

Six years after her disorienting discovery, Deanna is remarried; her new husband shares her taste for travel and adventure. She can talk dispassionately (with close friends) about the thin spots that likely existed all along in her first marriage. She understands how her frequent travels as a consultant, although they never tempted *her* to stray, carried intimations of abandonment for her more anxious ex. And how, under the circumstances, his conversations with an attentive female coworker could have evolved from the collegial to the confidential almost imperceptibly over the course of a year. But there's one question that still nags at her: Why, when their marriage was about to blow apart, did her husband insist that they share eternity by purchasing a joint burial plot? She'll probably never know.

Critical Thinking

1. The article refers to infidelity as a "multicausal, multidimensional behavior." Explain what this means.
2. Who is most likely to cheat in a relationship? Why?
3. What factors contribute to cheating behavior? In what situations is someone more likely to cheat on a spouse and why?
4. What, if anything, can be done to prevent or lessen the likelihood that a spouse will cheat?

Create Central

www.mhhe.com/createcentral

Internet Reference

American Association for Marriage and Family Therapy: Infidelity
www.aamft.org/imis15/content/Consumer_Updates/Infidelity.aspx

Article   Prepared by: Patricia Hrusa Williams, *University of Maine at Farmington*

The State of Extramarital Affairs

Just as the stigma of cheating fades away, opportunities to stray have multiplied—and so have the chances of getting caught.

Melissa Schorr

Learning Outcomes

After reading this article, you will be able to:

- Describe common reactions to a partner's infidelity.

- Recognize how societal changes are contributing to infidelity.

- Explain the reasons why some couples divorce and others don't after infidelity.

"A betrayal can be as simple as a sext," says Sharon-based marriage and family therapist Karen Ruskin. Adultery is still technically a crime in Massachusetts, though a case hasn't been pursued in decades. So perhaps it is fitting that it is in the Reading Police Station where a small cadre of husbands and wives is meeting tonight, to unpack heartache over cheating spouses.

Whom they still love.

Maybe.

About a half-dozen middle-aged men and women trickle into the nondescript room and assemble around a Formica-topped conference table where a jar of colorful hard candy—and a telling box of Kleenex—awaits.

A sandy-haired man who drives down monthly from New Hampshire leans toward the woman sitting across the way. "Did you hear about the woman in Lynn who ran over her ex's girlfriend?" he asks, referencing a story from the day's news. His mouth unexpectedly breaks into a wide smile. "Good for her," he cackles. "Good for her."

Dark humor is not uncommon at the *Beyond Affairs Network,* an international support group founded decades ago solely for those who have been betrayed—cheaters decidedly not welcome. Members come from all over Greater Boston to speak about infidelity's aftershocks: the hurt that still lingers, the anger that still rages, the insecurity, the devastation, and the shame. They cover healing and forgiveness and reconciliation, fear and loneliness and scorn. "I'll never be the same person again," a man in a green shirt with soft brown eyes tells the group. "I'll never be as naïve as I was. It rapes you of your innocence."

Over the two-hour meeting, they speak somberly about the suicide attempts with pills or running engines and jovially about the "infidelity diet," where you shed 51 pounds in two months. They share revenge scenarios, imaginary and ones actually carried out involving strategically placed dog feces. They one-up one another with horror stories—the letter from a spouse's mistress that begins "You and I could have been friends"; the diamond earrings on Valentine's Day that were such an obvious sign, in retrospect; the injustices of making child-support payments for a husband's out-of-wedlock baby and of having to rub elbows with former spouses' paramours at christenings, weddings, and other family occasions. They describe marriages that ended with a bang, on a 30th anniversary, and with a whimper, after indiscretions dating back to the wedding night.

Group members return to meetings year after year because no one else in their life truly understands how they feel—or still has the patience to listen. And their numbers are growing. In 2006, there were 61 Beyond Affairs Network groups in 27 states and 10 countries. Today there are 129 groups in 38 states and 16 countries.

For a long time they wept, but now they can laugh. They are survivors.

On one thing, they agree: There are no consequences for cheating these days. It's accepted. Glorified, almost. And no one cares about it. Until it happens to them.

***

Adultery is as old as the Book of Genesis and as modern as the latest Anthony Weiner revelation. Unlike the more laissez-faire attitude of the French, we Americans are conflicted about infidelity. We denounce it morally—but overlook it politically, time and again. We condemn it in the theoretical—but often quietly forgive it in the personal. It permeates our pop culture, in movies from *The Descendants* to *Blue Jasmine,* reality TV shows from *Cheaters* to *Deadly Affairs,* and dramas like *The Good Wife* and Showtime's upcoming *The Affair.* It fills the airwaves in country ballads and pop anthems. It stays in the shadows, whispered by small-town gossipmongers, until it breaks into the local headlines, such as the Hamilton cop who shot a fellow officer from Beverly last year after accusing him of having an affair with his wife.

"Infidelity is the ultimate crime in a marriage," says Whitman private investigator Mark Chauppetta, author of *Happens All the Time: Cheating in the Good Ol' U.S.A.* "I've had women that want to claw [the other woman's] eyes out. I've had politicians and state troopers crying in my arms."

And yet there are signs everywhere that the shame of stepping out has faded. Politicians bounce back unscathed for another run. The decade-old matchmaking website AshleyMadison.com brazenly hooks up married men and women, promoting extramarital encounters with its motto "Life is short. Have an affair." An infamous 2010 *New York Times* wedding write-up features a couple proudly detailing their "meet-cute"—while married to other people. A Philadelphia man is tagged on Facebook unabashedly bragging in June about an affair to his commuter rail buddies in a picture taken by an outraged female passenger whose "share" went viral.

In a 2013 Gallup Poll that listed behaviors and societal realities that included porn, gambling, abortion, polygamy, and the death penalty, 91 percent of survey respondents flagged adultery as morally reprehensible. It drew a higher rate of disapproval than any issue on the survey. Instinctively, we sense that lying to and betraying the one person we've sworn fealty to is far worse than simply divorcing that person. Condemnation of divorce has decreased since 2001, but disapproval of adultery has held steady.

However, that moral censure doesn't exactly curb the behavior. Nearly 15 percent of wives and 21 percent of husbands reported having an affair in a 2010 poll by the National Opinion Research Center, which has been asking this particular question for two decades.

"Guys do it to get laid, women do it for the emotional connection," Chauppetta says with a shrug, echoing the classic stereotype. Then he stops and amends his thoughts. "Women are starting to dirty up a little bit." Whether their reasons are carnal or emotional, women's infidelity rates are rising. The percentage of wives admitting to cheating has increased in the past two decades from 10.6 percent in 1991, according to the National Opinion Research Center's poll.

"Either you've been cheated on, you are going to be cheated on, you've thought about cheating and shut it down, or you know somebody who has cheated," says Karen Ruskin, a Sharon-based marriage and family therapist. "It's a topic that interests everybody."

From Ruskin's perspective, a number of societal shifts have facilitated a lapse of fidelity, from the growing numbers of women in the workplace to greater acceptance of friendships across gender lines and even our nation's newfound tendency to over-share, whether it be with a co-worker or an online buddy. "The philosophy used to be 'don't air your dirty laundry,'" Ruskin says. "These days we air it at work, on Twitter, Facebook, et cetera," and that kind of sharing can build emotional connections that lead to affairs. What's more, infidelity is in the news. "Affairs are talked about on TV, radio, and in print," Ruskin adds. "The more something is talked about and aired, the more acceptable it becomes."

The relentless media parade of men behaving badly—Weiner, General David Petraeus, Eliot Spitzer, Arnold Schwarzenegger, John Edwards, Mark Sanford, Tiger Woods, David Letterman, Bill Clinton—has only served to accustom us to the behavior. "It's become acceptable," says Ruskin. "It's so prominent we've become desensitized."

And occasionally, although the odds are long, high-profile alliances formed from a dalliance seem to work out—take Brad and Angie. Or onetime GE CEO Jack Welch and former *Harvard Business Review* editor Suzy Wetlaufer, whose affair made headlines a decade ago and who have been together since.

"I think adultery has lost some, but not all, of its stigma," says Quincy divorce attorney Bruce Watson, pointing to changes in the legal system that have greatly lessened the repercussions for cheating. "It's certainly more widespread than it was years ago."

Decades ago, cheating could be cited as the cause in a fault divorce, and the "other party" could even be civilly sued for causing "alienation of affection." Since the advent of no-fault divorce in Massachusetts in 1976, adultery is only rarely brought up as a tactic, sometimes to speed up the process or to affect custody or, occasionally, as a pressure point during settlement negotiations. "People are often trying to vindicate their emotional trauma or to really try to exact some economic reparation," says Boston-based divorce attorney Donald Tye.

More typically it plays no role at all. "Unless the adulterous behavior was objectively harmful to the children or the non-adulterous party, it's not going to have a major impact on the outcome of the divorce," says Watson. "Divorce judges are not all that enthusiastic about seeing adultery as the primary basis for divorce."

***

Modern life has also muddied the waters of what defines an affair, compared with the traditional sex-based rendezvous at the Pierre, a la Don Draper. A once-a-year dalliance at a professional conference? An "office wife" doling out "innocent" back rubs and hugs? An "emo" affair, meaning emotional-only, between two people conducted entirely online?

"We are in a relationship revolution, trying to figure out what even constitutes an affair," says Ruskin. "From a marriage therapist's perspective, it's the secrecy and the intimate connection with another human. A betrayal can be as simple as a sext."

Technology has certainly added a whole new wrinkle, from the start of an affair to its unraveling. Entire books and academic studies have been devoted to Facebook's well-documented role in breaking up marriages. Beyond that, there are apps and devices that can simulate touch, and Snapchat, which allows racy photos to be sent and automatically erased. Savvy cheaters set up secondary, secret e-mail accounts and use disposable cellphones.

"Most of the affairs we deal with have started on classmates .com and Facebook," says Beyond Affairs Network national leader Anne Bercht, author of the book *My Husband's Affair Became the Best Thing That Ever Happened to Me*. "All you need is for some old flame from high school to happen to Facebook you on a day you feel angry with your spouse. It's tempting to have that secret correspondence and create a fantasy—maybe we should have married each other."

A more calculated affair is a click away on AshleyMadison .com, where members post "selfies" more readily than seems wise if they care about getting caught. Within days of signing up to see how it works, I've been barraged by winks, messages, and views from readyornot in Natick, Dirty-GirlSeeker in Minot, and barnside in Chatham, all attached males seeking "fun and lovely times" (discreetly, natch).

But technology is also proving to be an adulterer's Achilles' heel. You may think you're safe because you've cleared your cache—but you may not be. Cheaters have been tripped up by being inadvertently "tagged" on Facebook in an incriminating photo snapped while out with their extramarital partner. Or when a spouse synchs a new device and all those deleted sexts come tumbling out of the cloud. Or even by the digital trail recorded by their car's E-ZPass.

Chauppetta says technology is bad for business, with more men and women catching their own spouses red-handed. But some still hire the PI for incontrovertible proof. "People are just gluttons for punishment," he says. "Sometimes, [they] need to see living, breathing flesh on videotape."

But those visuals come at a cost. Therapists say being confronted with all the dirty details of a conversation thread may be devastating in a way that finding a stray hair or hotel receipt indicating an affair is not. "Long ago, you were not confronted with what actually happens [during an affair]," says Ruskin. "Now it's in your face, and it's hard to get those thoughts out of your head. It's like PTSD. You keep replaying the trauma of what happened."

Once detected, betrayed spouses can find support on websites like SurvivingInfidelity.com—or take their vengeance virtually. CheaterVille.com allows users anonymously to post detailed profiles of cheaters as a warning to potential partners. Wronged spouses have spawned a new genre—the personal revenge blog—where the betrayed spew vitriol upon their spouse's partners on sites like yesthisreallydidhappen or ourjourneyafterhisaffair.

***

Marriages gone stale, sexless marriages, Kardashian-speed marriages. Affairs resulting from those realities are predictable. The stories that keep you up at night are ones like Kristen's.

"We had a fantastic marriage," recalls the 40-year-old mother of three in a MetroWest suburb. Before moving east, she worked in a West Coast clinic testing women for STDs, including wives with cheating husbands. "I remember counseling women like me; nobody ever thinks they're going to be on the other side."

Then, after their youngest child was born, her husband confessed he had gotten involved with a co-worker.

The pain was intense. "We were the last couple anyone would have expected this to happen to," she says. "Not to scare people, but it can happen in absolutely anyone's marriage, not just marriages that are crumbling. Some people within a marriage make poor decisions. Good people get wrapped up in affairs. I do not vilify anyone. Personal vulnerability, plus opportunity, leads to an affair. It's pretty classic."

For many, the journey begins innocuously. A stressful home life. The entrance of someone new who showers you with attention. It starts with just talk. Just lunch. Just dinner. Maybe a trip. "It's this process where you keep moving the moral boundary," Kristen says. "And then one day you've crossed it. There are real feelings involved."

Some ascribe the cheating to a specific flaw in the individual, especially in serial cheaters. Drug addictions or childhood abuse drives their insecurities, their need for the repeated ego boost. But even so, therapists largely call foul on those excuses, saying it is ultimately about deciding to take action.

"I believe people make the choice to cheat," says Ruskin. "The moment we even give ourselves permission to say that 'It just happened,' then we have lost control over who we are." Monica Meehan McNamara, a marriage and family therapist in private practice in the South End, agrees: "Anybody, at any time, could be very drawn to another human being. When that happens, do you take action or not?"

Bruce Elmslie, a professor of economics at the University of New Hampshire, has studied what factors influence the likelihood a spouse will have an affair. Being pious doesn't matter. What does is simple: happiness with the marriage. The chance of a woman having an affair increases about 8.5 percent if she is not very happy in her marriage for whatever reason, while the chance of a man having an affair increases 9.8 percent.

"Keep [your spouse] happy and they won't be as likely to have an affair," Elmslie says. Fail at your own peril. Consider this: AshleyMadison.com claims that the day after Mother's Day brings the highest spike in women signing up for its services.

***

"I thought my life was wonderful," says Kitty, 63, who leads the North of Boston Beyond Affairs Network chapter, recalling the hot July day eight years ago when she stumbled upon her husband's affair. She and her mother-in-law had stopped by his construction site with some bottled water, only to find him leaning against his truck, kissing a co-worker. "That was when the s*** hit the fan. I was in such shock. I threw the water at him and left. I was shaking like I never shook before. Every dream we had was shattered."

They call it D-day: the day an affair is discovered.

It's easy to jump to a conclusion about what you'd do. But this is the moment when our moral certainty runs smack against our pragmatism. We think we'd be like Elin and her window-smashing golf club, kicking Tiger to the curb, but we turn out to be more like Anthony Weiner's wife, Huma, standing by her husband as he campaigned.

"You might not really feel what you think you're going to feel," says Ruskin. "Many people think they would end the marriage; when they find out, more actually stay [than think they will]. A lot of people, as they talk to their spouse, feel they played a role in the cheating."

After discovering her husband's affair in 2000, "I made a decision not to make a decision," recalls Beyond Affairs Network's Bercht. She calls the first three months a period of "craziness" and the second a period of "fighting." "It took two years for me to reach a place where I recommitted myself to my marriage. It's not the affair itself that does the biggest damage; it's the mistakes [people] make after. The person who is unfaithful only tells partial truth; they think the full truth will be too painful. The betrayed spouse can say or do things in anger, make decisions you can't take back."

Your odds of staying together after one partner has had an affair are, essentially, a coin toss. Slightly more than half of men and women who admit they had an affair will end up divorced,

reports a 2012 study in the *Journal of Family Issues*. And those couples who experienced infidelity were more than two times as likely to divorce as those whose partners remained faithful.

That doesn't mean that the affair directly caused the breakup, however. "The affair is typically not just about having sex," says Ruskin. "The theory is that there is an underlying issue that has led to the affair." Those who are successful in attacking the problem may come out on the other side with a sturdier relationship. "Once you start talking, the couple comes to discover other components that were never addressed. People start to feel maybe this can make lemonade, we can grow and recognize our problem and improve."

But for those whose flaws were insurmountable, the marriage may have imploded anyway, affair or no affair.

Kitty is resisting a divorce, though her husband has chosen to move in with his extramarital partner. "I don't feel after 40 years she deserves to take what belongs to me," she says. "What Elizabeth Edwards wrote in her book *Resilience* hit me: What gives this woman the right to come and knock on my door and think what I worked so hard for, she can come in and take it all away?" Kitty finds lack of repercussions from an affair disheartening. "I think no-fault divorce was the worst thing that could happen," she says. "It's so easy. They don't have to answer to anybody if they're cheating."

Despite counseling and attending couples retreats, Kristen's husband was never able to recommit fully to the marriage and she asked for a divorce. "People should invest in fostering their marriage [before infidelity occurs], as opposed to trying to pick up the pieces," she advises others today. "If people aren't growing their marriage, it could lead to openings for third parties."

"I believe that affairs are destroying our country; the core that makes any nation strong is strong families—when children grow up in a stable home environment," says Bercht. She envisions a world where all of us, not just those in a post-affair crisis, would regularly attend couples' counseling to freshen our skills, similar to how we require doctors to enroll in continuing ed. "It's the one area of life that has more potential to make us happy, and we don't bother getting educated; we think we should just know how to do it," she adds. "If someone says, 'We're going to a marriage retreat,' the response would be, 'Are you having problems?' I'd like to see that flipped."

***

Kitty likes to end the Beyond Affairs Network meetings on a positive note, in the same way that she signs all of her e-mails "Keep Smiling." So after two hours of heavy discussion, the meeting wraps up with Kitty passing out slices of white-frosted cake, brought to fete one member's birthday. There's another reason to celebrate tonight. The man with the soft brown eyes and the woman whose husband began cheating on her wedding day are marking their own one-year wedding anniversary tonight, which only goes to show what cheaters know so well: Romance can spring up even under the most unlikely of circumstances.

Kitty wonders aloud whether all that pain was the work of some higher power, designed to bring this new couple together, but the rest of the group looks doubtful. So much anguish, and for what? They can't throw their cheating exes in jail; they can't sue them for breaching their marriage contracts; they can't even shame them socially. There is only one hope, which Kitty voices in a parting shot: "May karma come to them."

To Catch a Sneak

Think you'll get away with it? Think again.

"A lot of cheaters think they're invincible and they're never going to get caught," says private investigator Mark Chauppetta. He rattles off these common mistakes that lead to discovery. "But keep doing it," he urges. "It keeps us in business."

- **Going awol**
  In a world of instantaneous communication, going incommunicado for a few hours.

- **Seeking privacy**
  Taking your phone calls in another room or adding a password to your phone.

- **Stepping up your look**
  Shedding weight, getting pumped at a new gym, or switching to a sexier style of underwear.

- **Changing bedroom habits**
  Trying new techniques, or, conversely, never initiating intimacy.

- **Sneaking a lover into the home**
  "Women are perceptive to a piece of hair or cologne," Chauppetta says. "If a woman is looking, her senses are heightened. They're like superheroes."

- **Leaving a digital trail**
  "If you want to have an affair, you've got to go underground," Chauppetta says. "You've basically got to live in the Stone Age."

- **Charging it**
  Wining and dining your secret partner. Credit card receipts leave a trail of evidence.

- **Confiding in a friend**
  "Eventually, even the coolest person is going to say something that will get back to your spouse." Plus, you never know who could be eavesdropping.

- **Getting sloppy**
  Sooner or later, even the most careful cheater is going to forget something: to delete a text, log off an e-mail account, or get rid of a receipt.

The Cheater Meter

If your partner exhibits any of these signs, it should raise a red flag, says marital therapist Karen Ruskin:

1. Travels often for work
2. Appears to be distancing self from you
3. Doesn't show appreciation, in words or actions
4. Doesn't seem interested in making time for your relationship, emotionally, physically, or sexually
5. Has a disrespectful attitude
6. Consistently reports marital dissatisfaction and then mysteriously stops complaining

Of Note

7
Boston's rank on Ashley Madison's list of cities with the most registered members seeking extramarital encounters. The Back Bay leads the neighborhoods, with highest use.

58
Percent of divorcing clients who reported that infidelity was the main reason for their split (Source: August 2013 survey of Certified Divorce Financial Analysts in North America)

A forthcoming *Journal of Consumer Research* article found women use luxury items such as a Fendi handbag to ward off female romantic rivals by signaling their spouse's devotion.

Critical Thinking

1. Do you think, as the article states, that infidelity and cheating are considered more acceptable in modern society? Why or why not?
2. How would you define what it means to cheat or be unfaithful to a partner?
3. What are some reasons why a spouse or significant other becomes unfaithful?
4. If you learned your spouse or significant other was cheating on you, what would you do?

Create Central

www.mhhe.com/createcentral

Internet References

American Association for Marriage and Family Therapy: Infidelity
www.aamft.org/imis15/content/Consumer_Updates/Infidelity.aspx

Beyond Affairs Network
http://beyondaffairs.com

Dear Peggy: Extramarital Affairs Resource Center
http://www.dearpeggy.com

Prepared by: Patricia Hrusa Williams,
University of Maine at Farmington

Article

International Perspectives on Work-Family Policies: Lessons from the World's Most Competitive Economies

Alison Earle, Zitha Mokomane, and Jody Heymann

Learning Outcomes

After reading this article, you will be able to:

- Identify family-friendly work policies.

- Understand the differences between the United States' and other nations' work-family policies.

- Discuss the challenges parents have in dividing time between work and family.

In the majority of American families with children today, all parents are employed. In 67 percent of families with school-age children, 64 percent of families with preschool-age children, and 60 percent of families with children age three and younger, the parents are working for pay.[1] As a result, the workplace policies that parents face—such as how many hours they need to be away from home, the leave they can take to care for a sick child, and the work schedules that determine whether and when they are able to visit a son's or daughter's school—shape not only their income but also the time they have available for childrearing.

U.S. policies on parental leave, sick leave, vacation days, and days of rest are often in sharp contrast to other developed and developing countries, but those who want to make these policies more supportive of parents and their children face stiff opposition from those who say such policies will harm the United States' ability to compete economically with other countries. This article takes an international perspective to evaluate whether having workplace policies that support parents' ability to be available to meet their children's needs is compatible with economic competitiveness and low unemployment. We analyze a unique global database of labor legislation, focusing specifically on those measures dealing with parental availability in the first year of life, when caregiving needs are particularly intensive; parental availability to meet children's health needs; and their availability to meet their children's developmental needs.

We first review the evidence on the relationship of parental working conditions to children's outcomes. Second, we discuss the claims made in the public debates regarding the potential costs and benefits of family-supportive labor policies to individual employers and national economies, and review the academic literature on this topic. We then use new cross-national data to examine the extent to which highly competitive countries and countries with low unemployment rates do or do not provide these policies. Finally, we summarize the implications of our findings for U.S. policy.

Relationship of Parental Working Conditions to Children's Outcomes

Research in the United States and in other developed as well as developing countries suggests that workplace policies that support parents' ability to be available for their children at crucial periods of their lives have measurable effects on children's outcomes.

Paid Parental Leave

Research shows that the availability of paid leave following childbirth has the potential to improve infant and child health by making it affordable and feasible for parents to stay home and provide the intensive care newborns and infants need, including breast-feeding and a high caregiver-to-infant ratio that most child-care centers are unable to match.[2] Parental leave can have substantial benefits for child health. Christopher Ruhm's examination of more than two decades of data from sixteen European countries found that paid parental leave policies were associated with lower rates of infant and child mortality after taking into account per capita income, the availability of health services and technology, and other factors linked with child health. Ruhm found that a ten-week paid maternity leave was associated with a reduction in infant mortality rates of 1–2 percent; a twenty-week leave, with a 2–4 percent reduction; and a thirty-week leave, with a 7–9 percent reduction.[3]

Sasiko Tanaka reaffirmed these findings in a study that analyzed data from Ruhm's sixteen European countries plus the United States and Japan. The data covered the thirty years between 1969 and 2000 including the period between 1995 and 2000 when several significant changes were made in parental leave policies.[4] Tanaka found that a ten-week extension in paid leave was associated with a 2.6 percent decrease in infant mortality rates and a 3.0 percent decrease in child mortality rates. Maternity leave without pay or a guarantee of a job at the end of the leave had no significant effect on infant or child mortality rates in either study.

One of the most important mechanisms through which paid parental leave can benefit infants is by increasing a mother's ability to initiate and sustain breast-feeding, which a wealth of research has shown to be associated with a markedly lower risk of gastrointestinal, respiratory tract, skin, ear, and other infections; sudden infant death syndrome; and overall mortality.[5] Health benefits of breast-feeding have also been reported for mothers, including reduced risk of premenopausal breast cancer and potentially reduced risks of ovarian cancer and osteoporosis.[6]

Generous maternity leave benefits available across European countries make it possible for mothers to breast-feed their infants for a lengthy period of time without having to supplement feedings with formula. In some cases the leave is long enough that mothers can exclusively breast-feed for at least six months, as recommended by the World Health Organization; and in countries with more than half a year of leave, mothers can continue breast-feeding (while also adding appropriate solid foods).[7] In contrast, in countries with less generous maternity leave, such as the United States, working women are less likely to start breast-feeding their babies, and those who do breast-feed stop sooner, on average, than mothers in countries with these supportive policies.[8] Lacking paid maternity leave, American mothers also return to work earlier than mothers in most other advanced countries, and research has found that early return to work is associated with lower rates of breast-feeding and immunizations.[9]

While far less research has been conducted on the impact of paternity leave policies, there is ample reason to believe that paternal leave can support children's healthy development in ways parallel to maternal leave, with the obvious exception of breast-feeding. Although fathers can take time off under parental leave policies that can be used by one or both parents, they are more likely to stay at home to care for a new child when paternity leave is available.[10]

The longer the period of leave allowed, the more involved with their infants and families fathers are.[11] Moreover, longer leaves increase the probability that fathers will continue their involvement and share in child care even after the leave ends.[12] The benefits of fathers' engagement for children's social, psychological, behavioral, emotional, and cognitive functioning are significant.[13] In short, paternity leave policies are associated with greater gender equity at home and, through fathers' increased involvement with their infants, with positive cognitive and social development of young children.

Leave for Children's Health Needs

Four decades of research have documented that children's health outcomes improve when parents participate in their children's health care, whether it is a treatment for an acute illness or injury or management of a chronic condition.[14] As Mark Schuster, Paul Chung, and Katherine Vestal discuss in this volume, children heal faster and have shorter hospital stays when parents are present and involved during inpatient surgeries and treatments as well as during outpatient medical procedures.[15] Parents' assistance is especially important for children with chronic conditions such as diabetes and asthma, among others.[16] Parents can help improve children's health outcomes in many ways including by maintaining daily medical routines, administering medication, and providing emotional support as children adjust to having a chronic physical or mental health problem.[17]

If children are sick and parents do not have any schedule flexibility or paid leave that can be used to address a family member's health issue, children may be left home alone, unable to get themselves to a doctor or pharmacy for medication or to a hospital if a crisis occurs. Alternatively, parents may have no choice but to send a sick child to school or day care. The contact with other children and teachers contributes to the rapid spread and thus high incidence of infectious diseases in day-care centers, including respiratory infections, otitis media, and gastrointestinal infections.[18]

Research has also documented how significantly parental availability influences the level of preventive care children receive. Getting a child to a clinic or doctor's office for a physical exam or immunizations usually requires parents or other caregivers to take time off work. Working parents in a range of countries have cited schedule conflicts and workplace inflexibility as important obstacles to getting their children immunized against preventable childhood diseases.[19] One study of a large company in the United States found that employees who faced difficulties taking time off from work were far more likely to report that their children were not fully immunized.[20]

In contrast to the vast majority of countries around the globe, the United States has no federal policy requiring employers to provide paid leave for personal illness, let alone to address family members' health issues. (The Family and Medical Leave Act covers only serious health issues of immediate family members and is unpaid.) Only 30 percent of Americans report that their employer voluntarily offers paid sick leave that can be used for family members' care.[21] As a result, many parents are unable to be present to attend to their children's health needs. Parents whose employers provide paid sick days are more than five times as likely to be able to personally provide care to their sick children as parents whose employers do not offer paid sick days.[22] Working adults with no paid leave who take time off to care for ill family members are at risk of losing wages or even their job.[23] The risk of job loss is even greater for parents whose child has a chronic health problem, which typically involves more visits to the doctor or the hospital and more days of illness. In a longitudinal study of working poor families in the United States, we found that having a child with health problems was associated with a 36 percent increase in job loss.[24]

Leave and Availability for Children's Educational and Developmental Needs

When parents are involved in their children's education, whether at the preschool, elementary, or secondary level, children perform better in school.[25] Parental involvement has been linked with children's improved test scores in language and math, fewer emotional and behavioral problems, lower dropout rates, and better planning for and transitions into adulthood.[26] Greater parental involvement in schools appears to improve the quality of the education received by all students in the school.[27] Research has found that fathers' involvement, like that of mothers, is associated with significantly better exam scores, higher educational expectations, and higher grades.[28]

Parental participation and assistance can improve school outcomes for at-risk children.[29] Educational outcomes for children with learning disabilities improve when parents are involved in their education both at school and helping at home with homework in math as well as reading.[30] Low-income children can also benefit markedly when their parents are involved in their classrooms and with their teachers at school.[31] Studies suggest that low-income children benefit as much or more when their parents also spend time assisting their children in learning skills and material outside the classroom; training or instructing parents in providing this assistance further boosts the gains of time spent together.[32]

Parents' working conditions can markedly affect their ability to play an active role in their children's education. Active parental involvement often requires the flexibility to meet with teachers or consult with specialists during the workday. To be able to help with homework, parents need to have a work schedule that allows them time with their children after school and before children go to sleep. Our national research on the availability of paid leave and schedule flexibility among parents of school-age children in the United States shows that parents whose children were struggling academically and most needed parental support were at a significant disadvantage. More than half of parents who had a child scoring in the bottom quartile on math assessments did not have consistent access to any kind of paid leave, and nearly three-fourths could not count on schedule flexibility. One in six of these parents worked during evening hours, and more than one in ten worked nights, making it impossible to help their children routinely. Families in which a child scored in the bottom quartile in reading had equally challenging working conditions.[33]

Economic Feasibility of Workplace Policies Supporting Parents

Despite substantial evidence that children gain when parents have adequate paid leave and work flexibility, the economic costs and benefits of providing this leave and flexibility are still the subject of great contention in the United States. Each time legislation to guarantee parental leave, family medical leave, and related policies has been brought to Congress, the debate has revolved around questions of financial feasibility. In particular, legislators and others have questioned whether the United States can provide these benefits and still remain economically competitive.

For example, the proposed Healthy Families Act would guarantee a minimum of seven paid sick days—a small number by international standards—to American workers so they could stay home when they or family members fall ill. At a hearing in 2007 on the legislation, G. Roger King, a partner at the Jones Day corporate law firm, summarized the general argument raised against the legislation, saying that the Healthy Families Act, or any similar "regulations" to protect employees, would diminish U.S. competitiveness in the global economy. "Employers in this country are already burdened by numerous federal, state and local regulations which result in millions of dollars in compliance costs," King stated in his written testimony. "These mandated and largely unfunded 'cost of doing business' requirements in certain instances not only hinder and impede the creation of new jobs, but also inhibit our nation's employers from competing globally."[34]

We report findings from our recent research that examines the relationship between work-family legislation and national competitiveness and unemployment rates. First, however, we briefly summarize some of the evidence on costs and benefits to employers from policies that support families.

A series of studies including data from the United States, Japan, and the United Kingdom show that women who receive paid maternity leave are significantly more likely to return to the same employer after giving birth.[35] Increased employee retention reduces hiring and training costs, which can be significant (and include the costs of publicizing the job opening, conducting job interviews, training new employees, and suboptimal productivity among newly hired workers during the period just after they start).

There is no research known to us about the costs or benefits to individual American employers related to paid leave for children's health issues, most likely because this type of leave is uncommon in the United States. To the extent that the leave allows parents to ensure their children have time to rest and recuperate and avoid exacerbating health problems that could result in additional lost workdays in the future, parents' productivity could increase and absenteeism be reduced.

Similarly, while we are not aware of any studies that examine the costs and benefits to employers of legislation guaranteeing time off for employees to be with children, recent studies showing that long hours are associated with lower productivity suggest that similar productivity losses may exist for employees who work for long periods of time without a substantial block of time away from work or, in the shorter term, for those who work without a weekly day of rest. A study of eighteen manufacturing industries in the United States over a thirty-five-year period found that for every 10 percent increase in overtime hours, productivity declined 2–4 percent.[36] Although small in absolute size, in the context of a forty-hour workweek, these productivity losses suggest that employers may be able to increase productivity by guaranteeing regular time off.

A study of highly "effective" employers by the Families and Work Institute found that many report a series of economic benefits resulting from their flexibility policies that include paid leave for new mothers and time off for caregiving among other scheduling and training policies.[37] Benefits cited by employers include "increasing employee engagement and retention; reducing turnover; reducing absenteeism and sick days; increasing customer satisfaction; reducing business costs; increasing productivity and profitability; improving staffing coverage to meet business demands; [and] enhancing innovation and creativity."[38]

The centrality of the economic arguments in policy debates calls for further examination of the empirical evidence on workplace policies important to parents and their children. We examine two important indicators of economic performance. The first is a measure of global economic competitiveness, a concept encompassing productivity, a country's capacity for growth, and the level of prosperity or income that can be attained. This indicator is of particular salience to businesses and is used by international organizations such as the World Economic Forum (WEF). The second is the national unemployment rate, the indicator more often cited as being of high concern in the public's mind.

To evaluate the claim that nationally mandating paid leave would cause a reduction in jobs or loss of competitiveness, one ideally would have evidence from a randomized or natural experiment where the policy in place is not associated with other country or state characteristics that could influence the outcome. That approach is not possible, because there have been no such experiments. However, to test whether policies supporting working families inevitably lead countries to be uncompetitive or to have high unemployment, it is sufficient to find counterexamples. To that end, we ask a straightforward question: Are paid leave and other work-family policies that support children's development economically feasible?

To answer this question, we developed a global database of national labor policies and global economic data on competitiveness and unemployment in all countries that belong to the United Nations. The database includes information from original legislation, labor codes, and relevant amendments in 175 countries, as well as summaries of legislation for these and additional countries. The vast majority of the legislation was gathered from NATLEX, the International Labour Organization's (ILO) global database of legislation pertaining to labor, social security, and human rights from 189 countries. Additional sources included global databases that compile and summarize national legislation.[39]

Public Policies Supporting Working Families in Highly Competitive Countries

Using our global labor policy database, we set out to assess whether the countries that have consistently been at the top of the rankings in economic competitiveness provide working conditions that give employed parents the ability to support their children's healthy development. To identify these "highly competitive" countries, we use data from the business-led WEF.[40] Its annual Global Competitiveness Report includes country "competitiveness" rankings based on dozens of indicators of institutions, policies, and other factors that WEF members judge to be the key drivers of economic competitiveness. These factors include, among others, the efficiency of the goods market, efficiency of the labor market, financial market development, technological readiness, market size, business sophistication, innovation, infrastructure, and the macroeconomic environment.[41] We define "highly competitive" countries to be those that were ranked among the top twenty countries in competitiveness in at least eight of the ten years between 1999 and 2008. Fifteen countries meet this definition: Australia, Austria, Canada, Denmark, Finland, Germany, Iceland, Japan, the Netherlands, Norway, Singapore, Sweden, Switzerland, the United Kingdom, and the United States. Although India and China are not among the fifteen, we also present data on their family-supportive policies for two reasons. First, the press and laypersons often single out China and India as U.S. "competitors," and second, they have the two largest labor forces in the world.[42]

Paid Parental Leave

Paid leave for new mothers is guaranteed in all but one of the fifteen most competitive countries (Table 1). The exception is the United States, which has no federal policy providing paid leave for new parents. (As noted, leave provided under the federal Family and Medical Leave Act is unpaid.) Australia's paid leave policy took effect starting in January 2011; under the Paid Parental Leave Act, all workers—full time, part time, or casual—who are primary caregivers and earn $150,000 or less a year are guaranteed eighteen weeks of leave paid at the federal minimum wage. All of the most competitive countries with paid leave for new mothers provide at least fourteen weeks of leave, counting both maternity and parental leave, as recommended by the ILO. The norm of six months or more far exceeds the recommended minimum. China offers eighteen weeks (ninety working days) of leave for new mothers at full pay; India offers twelve weeks.

Table 1 also shows that although the duration of paid leave for new fathers is far less than for mothers, almost all highly competitive countries provide this type of leave. Switzerland is the lone top-ranked nation that provides paid leave to new mothers but not to new fathers. Neither India nor China has paid leave for new fathers.[43]

Breast-Feeding Breaks

Guaranteeing new mothers a breast-feeding break during the workday is the law in about half of the highly competitive countries, including Austria, Germany, Japan, the Netherlands, Norway, Sweden, Switzerland, and the United States (Table 2). India mandates two breaks a day in the child's first fifteen months. China guarantees new mothers breast-feeding breaks totaling an hour a day for the baby's first year.

Leave for Children's Health Needs

Unpaid leave from work to address children's health needs is ensured in every highly competitive nation (see Table 2). All but four of the fifteen most competitive countries provide paid leave for this purpose; the exceptions are Finland, Switzerland, the United Kingdom, and the United States.

Table 1   Parental Leave Policies in Highly Competitive Countries

Country	Paid Leave for Mothers			Paid Leave for Fathers		
	Availability	Duration (Weeks)	Wage Replacement Rate (%)	Availability	Duration (Weeks)	Wage Replacement Rate (%)
Australia	Yes	18	flat rate	Yes	18	flat rate
Austria	Yes	81–146	100, flat rate	Yes	65–130	flat rate
Canada	Yes	50	55	Yes	35	55
Denmark	Yes	50–58	80–100	Yes	34–42	80–100
Finland	Yes	164	25–90	Yes	154	25–70
Germany	Yes	66–118	33–100	Yes	52–104	33–67
Iceland	Yes	26	80	Yes	26	80
Japan	Yes	58	30–60	Yes	44	30–40
Netherlands	Yes	16	100	Yes	0.4	100
Norway	Yes	90–100	80–100, flat rate	Yes	87–97	80–100, flat rate
Singapore	Yes	14	100	Yes	2	100
Sweden	Yes	69*	80, flat rate	Yes	67*	80, flat rate
Switzerland	Yes	14	80	No	n.a.	n.a.
United Kingdom	Yes	39	90	Yes	2	90
United States	No	n.a.	n.a.	No	n.a.	n.a.

Notes: In the database and all tables, data reflect national policy. Coverage conditions such as firm size, sector, and duration of employment vary by country. Paid leave for mothers includes paid leave for women only (maternity leave) and parental leave that is available to women. Paid leave for fathers includes paid leave for men only (paternity leave) and parental leave that is available to men. The table presents data on the maximum amount of leave available to the mother if she takes all of the maternity leave available to mothers and all of the parental leave available to either parent. Parallel data are presented for fathers. The minimum and maximum (as a range) are presented to reflect that country's policy of providing parents with a choice between a shorter leave at a higher benefit level (percentage of wages or flat rate) and a longer leave at a lower benefit.

Source: Based on updated data from Jody Heymann and Alison Earle, *Raising the Global Floor: Dismantling the Myth That We Can't Afford Good Working Conditions for Everyone* (Stanford University Press, 2010).

n.a. = Not applicable.

*Sweden's parental leave policy also allows parents to take part-time leave with partial benefits for a longer duration.

Table 2   Leave Policies to Attend to Children's Health Care in Highly Competitive Countries

Country	Breast-Feeding Breaks	Age of Child When Breast-Feeding Breaks End	Break Time of At Least One Hour a Day	Leave to Care for Children's Health Needs	Leave Is Paid
Australia	No	n.a.	n.a.	Yes	Yes
Austria	Yes	For duration	Yes	Yes	Yes
Canada	No	n.a.	n.a.	Yes	Yes
Denmark	No	n.a.	n.a.	Yes	Yes
Finland	No	n.a.	n.a.	Yes	No
Germany	Yes	For duration	Yes	Yes	Yes
Iceland	No	n.a.	n.a.	Yes	Yes
Japan	Yes	1 year	Yes	Yes	Yes
Netherlands	Yes	9 months	Yes	Yes	Yes
Norway	Yes	For duration	Yes	Yes	Yes
Singapore	No	n.a.	n.a.	Yes	Yes
Sweden	Yes	For duration	Yes	Yes	Yes
Switzerland	Yes	1 year	Yes	Yes	No
United Kingdom	No	n.a.	n.a.	Yes	No
United States	Yes	1 year	Yes	Yes	No

n.a. = Not applicable.

Source: See Table 1.

Leave and Availability for Children's Developmental and Educational Needs

Neither paid vacation leave nor a day off each week is designed specifically for parents; these rest periods benefit all working adults. Yet weekly time off and vacations do provide an important assurance that working parents can spend time with their children and be available to support their educational, social, and emotional development. All of the most highly competitive countries except the United States guarantee paid annual or vacation leave (Table 3). The vast majority of these countries provide generous amounts of leave at full pay. Half provide more than four weeks a year: Austria, Denmark, Finland, Germany, Iceland, Norway, Sweden, and the United Kingdom. China's labor laws guarantee five days of paid leave after one year of service, ten days after ten years on the job, and fifteen days after twenty years. In India workers are provided one day of paid leave for every twenty days worked during the previous year.

Virtually all highly competitive nations also guarantee at least one day of rest a week. The exceptions are the United States and Australia (see Table 3). Both China and India guarantee workers a day of rest a week.

Labor legislation is relatively less common around a small number of issues that are receiving attention as a result of recent economic and technological developments. Countries are still adjusting their labor policies in response to the rise of the "24/7" schedule that has come about as global trade, communications, and sourcing of products have increased. Policies either to restrict or compensate for work at times when school-age children in particular benefit from a parent's presence—evenings and nights—exist in many highly competitive countries. Guaranteeing a wage premium increases the likelihood that a wide range of workers will volunteer for night work and decreases the likelihood that parents will need to work at night merely because of limited seniority. Finland, Norway, and Sweden have passed laws placing broad restrictions on night work for all workers. Germany, Japan, and Switzerland instead guarantee a wage premium for those who are required to work at night. Over half of the highly competitive nations allow night work but restrict or ban it for workers who might be harmed by it: children, pregnant or nursing women, or employees with medical conditions that make them unable to work at night (see Table 3). China bans night work for pregnant women. Although India bans night work for all women, some states have lifted it for women working in information technology and telecommunications.

Not new to parents but to some policy makers is the need for adults to occasionally take time off during the day to address a child's academic, social, or behavioral issue, or to attend a school event. Although leave during the day to meet with a teacher or attend an event typically does not involve a great deal of the employee's time in any given period, only four of the fifteen countries provide leave explicitly for such purposes. Labor laws in Denmark and Sweden require employers to provide leave to attend to "children's needs" including educational issues. Switzerland takes a different approach, requiring

Table 3 Policies on Paid Annual Leave, a Day of Rest, and Night Work in Highly Competitive Countries

Country	Availability of Paid Annual Leave	Duration of Paid Annual Leave (Weeks)	Weekly Day of Rest	Premium for Night Work	Ban or Broad Restrictions on Night Work	Ban or Restriction for Children, Pregnant or Nursing Women, or Medical Reasons
Australia	Yes	4.0	No	No	No	No
Austria	Yes	5.0	Yes	No	No	Yes
Canada	Yes	2.0	Yes	No	No	Yes
Denmark	Yes	5.5	Yes	No	No	Yes
Finland	Yes	4.4	Yes	No	Yes	No
Germany	Yes	4.4	Yes	After 11 P.M.	No	Yes
Iceland	Yes	4.4	Yes	No	No	No
Japan	Yes	1.8	Yes	After 10 P.M.	No	Yes
Netherlands	Yes	4.0	Yes	No	No	Yes
Norway	Yes	4.2	Yes	No	Yes	Yes
Singapore	Yes	1.3	Yes	No	No	No
Sweden	Yes	5.0	Yes	No	Yes	No
Switzerland	Yes	4.0	Yes	After 11 P.M.	No	Yes
United Kingdom	Yes	5.1	Yes	No	No	Yes
United States	No	n.a.	No	No	No	No

n.a. = Not applicable.
Source: See Table 1.

employers to structure work schedules and rest periods keeping in mind employees' family responsibilities including attending to the educational needs of children up to age fifteen. In addition, Switzerland also requires employers to provide a lunch break of at least an hour and a half to parents if requested. Parents in Singapore can take leave for their children's educational needs under the country's family leave law. Neither India nor China provides paid leave for general family needs and issues or for children's education.

Public Policies Supporting Working Families in Low Unemployment Countries

As an additional check, we also examined whether it was possible to have relatively low unemployment rates while guaranteeing a floor of working conditions that help parents care for children. We looked specifically at members of the Organization for Economic Cooperation and Development (OECD). The OECD definition of unemployment is comprehensive, including employment in formal and informal jobs.[44] We defined low unemployment countries as those OECD members ranked in the better half of countries in terms of unemployment at least 80 percent of the time in the decade between 1998 and 2007. Thirteen countries fit these criteria: Austria, Denmark, Iceland, Ireland, Japan, Republic of Korea (South Korea), Luxembourg, Mexico, the Netherlands, Norway, Switzerland, the United Kingdom, and the United States. Overall, do these countries provide working conditions that can help parents support children's healthy development? In short, yes.

Paid Parental Leave

Every low unemployment country but one, the United States, has national legislation guaranteeing paid leave for new mothers. The length of the leaves ranges from twelve weeks in Mexico to more than a year in Austria, Japan, Norway, and South Korea. In the middle are Iceland and Ireland, where new mothers receive six months, and Luxembourg and the United Kingdom, with nine months. All but one of those with paid leave replace 80 percent or more of wages, and seven guarantee 100 percent.

Paid leave for new fathers, whether in the form of leave for fathers only or leave that can be used by either parent, is not universally available but is provided in nine of the thirteen low unemployment countries. Ireland, Mexico, Switzerland, and the United States do not provide this type of leave. New fathers are entitled to take between six months and a year in Denmark, Iceland, Japan, and Luxembourg, and more than a year in Austria, Norway, and South Korea.

Breast-Feeding Breaks

Ten of the thirteen countries ensure that new mothers can continue breast-feeding for at least six months after they return to work, and eight of those ten ensure this right for a year or until the mother chooses to stop.

Leave for Children's Health Needs

Guaranteed leave to address children's health needs is the norm; all but two low unemployment countries—Mexico and South Korea—provide either paid or unpaid leave of this type. The leave is paid in Austria, Denmark, Iceland, Ireland, Japan, Luxembourg, the Netherlands, and Norway and unpaid in Switzerland, the United Kingdom, and the United States.

Leave and Availability for Children's Developmental and Educational Needs

Every low unemployment country except the United States guarantees workers a weekly day of rest and a period of paid vacation leave once a year. Mexico and Japan guarantee from one to two weeks while nine of the thirteen guarantee four weeks or more. As noted earlier, labor laws in Denmark and Switzerland also require employers to provide leave to address "children's needs," which in the Swiss legislation explicitly include educational issues.

These findings show that mandating workplace policies that support parents' ability to ensure their children's healthy development does not inevitably lead to high job loss or high unemployment rates. As this discussion shows, many OECD countries kept unemployment rates relatively low while passing and enforcing legislation that supports parents. In fact, the majority of consistently low unemployment countries have adopted nearly all the policies shown to be important for children's health and well-being. Whether these nations would have had somewhat lower or higher unemployment in the absence of family support policies is not known. But our research clearly shows that it is possible for a nation to guarantee paid leave and other policies that provide parents with time to address their children's needs and at the same time maintain relatively low unemployment.

Summary of Findings

Longitudinal data are not available that would enable researchers to determine conclusively the immediate and long-term impact on national economic outcomes of changing guarantees of parental leave and other family-support policies. However, an examination of the most competitive economies as well as the economies with low unemployment rates makes clear that ensuring that all parents are available to care for their children's healthy development does not preclude a country from being highly competitive economically. Moreover, as noted, evidence from decades of research on parents' roles during children's infancy and in caring for children's health and education makes clear that policies enabling working fathers and mothers to provide that care are likely to have substantial positive effects on the health and developmental outcomes of American children.

Few of the policies that would help working parents raise healthy children are guaranteed in the United States. As noted, the federal Family and Medical Leave Act allows new parents to take unpaid time off without fear of job loss when they adopt or give birth, or to attend to a parent or child suffering from a serious illness. Half of Americans are not covered by the act because of the size of the firms in which they work, the number of hours they have worked, or a recent job change, and many of those who are covered cannot afford to take all the leave they are entitled to because it is unpaid. Only in 2010 did the United States pass federal legislation requiring employers to provide breast-feeding breaks and facilities for breast-feeding (as part of the health care reform bill and without much public awareness). Paid parental leave and child health care leave policies are the norm in the countries that have been highly competitive and those that have maintained low unemployment for a decade. The analysis of global data presented here suggests that guaranteeing paid parental leave as well as paid leave when a child is sick would be feasible for the United States without jeopardizing its highly competitive economy or low unemployment rates in the future.

The overwhelming majority of countries guarantee paid parental leave through a social insurance system. While many countries provide some kind of tax credit or stipend at the birth of a child, next to none rely only on this for paid parental leave. A critical step that European countries have increasingly followed is to guarantee that a percentage of the leave is dedicated to fathers as well as some dedicated solely to mothers. This approach ensures that men have in practice, and not just on paper, an equal chance of using the leave.

The countries that guarantee paid sick leave finance it through a variety of means ranging from requiring employers to pay employees benefits (that is, continue to pay salary or wages during the leave) to establishing a social security system whereby some combination of employees, employers, and government pay into a fund out of which payments are made to individuals while they are unable to work. One two-stage model requires employers to pay wages for short periods of illness but provides benefits from the social insurance system for longer leaves associated with major illnesses. Reasonably short employer liability periods—seven to ten days a year— make it feasible for the employer to reimburse wages at a high rate and keeps administrative costs low, while ensuring that paid leave covers most common illnessess that adults and children suffer. Covering longer illnesses through social insurance ensures that employers will not be overburdened with long-term payments.

The overwhelming majority of countries around the world guarantee all working women and men some paid annual leave and a weekly day of rest. In these nations the right to reasonable work hours is built into employers' labor costs and is often seen as a sensible, basic human right that also enhances productivity.

Considering policy change is always difficult, and recommending programs with public and private sector budgetary implications is particularly difficult when the United States is only now recovering from the Great Recession. That said, many of the country's most important social and labor policies date from the Great Depression. While periods of economic duress raise understandable questions about the feasibility of change, they also naturally focus attention on how critical safety nets are to American of all ages. As articles throughout this issue of the *Future of Children* demonstrate, guaranteeing a floor of decent working conditions and social supports is essential not only to working parents but also to the healthy development of their children. We believe that evidence is equally compelling that such guarantees are economically feasible for the United States.

Notes

1. U.S. Bureau of Labor Statistics, "Employment Characteristics of Families, Table 4: Families with Own Children: Employment Status of Parents by Age of Youngest Child and Family Type, 2008–09 Annual Averages" (www.bls.gov/news.release/archives/famee_05272010.htm); U.S. Bureau of the Census, "Women in the Labor Force: A Databook" (2009 ed.), Table 7, "Employment Status of Women by Presence and Age of Youngest Child" (March) (www.bls.gov/cps/wlftable7.htm).

2. Lawrence Berger, Jennifer Hill, and Jane Waldfogel, "Maternity Leave, Early Maternal Employment and Child Health and Development in the U.S.," *Economic Journal* 115, no. 501 (2005): F29–F47; Sheila B. Kamerman, "Maternity, Paternity, and Parental Leave Policies: The Potential Impacts on Children and Their Families (rev. ed.)," in *Encyclopedia on Early Childhood Development (online),* edited by R. E. Tremlay, R. G. Barr, and R. D. Peters (Montreal: Centre of Excellence for Early Childhood Development, 2005) (www.child-encyclopedia.com/documents/KamermanANGxp_rev-Parental.pdf).

3. Christopher J. Ruhm, "Parental Leave and Child Health," *Journal of Health Economics* 19, no. 6 (2000): 931–60.

4. Sasiko Tanaka, "Parental Leave and Child Health across OECD Countries," *Economic Journal* 115, no. 501 (2005): F7–F28.

5. Richard G. Feachem and Marge A. Koblinsky, "Interventions for the Control of Diarrhoeal Diseases among Young Children: Promotion of Breast-feeding," *Bulletin of World Health Organization* 62, no. 2 (1984): 271–91; Kathryn G. Dewey, M. Jane Heinig, and Laurie A. Nommsen-Rivers, "Differences in Morbidity between Breastfed and Formula-Fed Infants. Part 1," *Journal of Pediatrics* 126, no. 5 (1995): 696–702; Peter W. Howie, and others, "Protective Effect of Breast-feeding against Infection," *British Medical Journal* 300, no. 6716 (1990): 11–16; Philippe Lepage, Christophe Munyakazi, and Philippe Hennart, "Breastfeeding and Hospital Mortality in Children in Rwanda," *Lancet* 319, no. 8268 (1982): 403; M. Cristina Cerqueiro and others, "Epidemiologic Risk Factors for Children with Acute Lower Respiratory Tract Infection in Buenos Aires, Argentina: A Matched Case-Control Study," *Reviews of Infectious Diseases,* suppl. 8, no. 12 (1990): S1021–28; Christopher J. Watkins, Stephen R. Leeder, and Richard T. Corkhill, "The Relationship between Breast and Bottle Feeding and Respiratory Illness in the First Year of Life," *Journal of Epidemiology and Community Health* 33, no. 3 (1979): 180–82; Anne L. Wright and others, "Breast-feeding and Lower Respiratory Tract Illness in the First Year of Life," *British Medical Journal* 299, no. 6705 (1989): 946–49; Michael Gdalevich and others, "Breast-Feeding and the Onset of Atopic Dermatitis in Childhood: A Systematic Review and Meta-Analysis of Prospective Studies," *Journal of American Academy of Dermatology* 45, no. 4 (2001): 487–647; Jennifer Baxter, "Breastfeeding, Employment and Leave: An Analysis of Mothers Growing Up in Australia," *Family Matters* no. 80 (2008): 17–26; Amanda R. Cooklin, Susan M. Donath, and Lisa H. Amir, "Maternal Employment and Breastfeeding:

Results from the Longitudinal Study of Australian Children," *Acta Paediatrica* 97, no. 5 (2008): 620–23; Gustaf Aniansson and others, "A Prospective Cohort Study on Breast-Feeding and Otitis Media in Swedish Infants," *Pediatric Infectious Disease Journal* 13, no. 3 (1994): 183–88; Burris Duncan and others, "Exclusive Breast-Feeding for at Least 4 Months Protects against Otitis Media," *Pediatrics* 91, no. 5 (1993): 867–72; Cody Arnold, Susan Makintube, and Gregory Istre, "Daycare Attendance and Other Risk Factors for Invasive Haemophilus Influenzae Type B Disease," *American Journal of Epidemiology* 138, no. 5 (1993): 333–40; Stanley Ip and others, "Breastfeeding and Maternal and Infant Health Outcomes in Developed Countries," Agency for Healthcare Research and Quality, AHRQ Publication 07-E007 (April 2007).

6. Ip and others. "Breastfeeding and Maternal and Infant Health Outcomes in Developed Countries" (see note 5).

7. Adriano Cattaneo and others, "Protection, Promotion and Support of Breast-Feeding in Europe: Current Situation," *Public Health Nutrition* 8, no. 1 (2005): 39–46.

8. Sylvia Guendelman and others, "Juggling Work and Breastfeeding: Effects of Maternity Leave and Occupational Characteristics," *Pediatrics* 123, no. 1 (2010): e38–46; Baxter, "Breastfeeding, Employment and Leave" (see note 5); Cooklin, Donath, and Amir, "Maternal Employment and Breastfeeding" (see note 5).

9. Berger, Hill, and Waldfogel, "Maternity Leave, Early Maternal Employment and Child Health and Development in the U.S." (see note 2).

10. Berit Brandth and Elin Kvande, "Flexible Work and Flexible Fathers," *Work, Employment and Society* 15 no. 2 (2001): 251–67.

11. Ruth Feldman, Amy L. Sussman, and Edward Zigler, "Parental Leave and Work Adaptation at the Transition to Parenthood: Individual, Marital and Social Correlates," *Applied Developmental Psychology* 25, no. 4 (2004): 459–79; Rudy Ray Seward, Dale E. Yeatts, and Lisa K. Zottarelli, "Parental Leave and Father Involvement in Child Care: Sweden and the United States," *Journal of Comparative Family Studies* 33, no. 3 (2002): 387–99.

12. Linda Haas and Phillip Hwang, "The Impact of Taking Parental Leave on Fathers' Participation in Childcare and Relationships with Children: Lessons from Sweden," *Community, Work and Family* 11, no. 1 (2008): 85–104; Lindy Fursman and Paul Callister, *Men's Participation in Unpaid Care: A Review of the Literature* (Wellington: New Zealand Department of Labour 2009) (www.dol.govt.nz/publication-view.asp?ID=289).

13. According to Catherine S. Tamis-LeMonda and others, "Fathers and Mothers at Play with Their 2- and 3-Year-Olds: Contributions to Language and Cognitive Development," *Child Development* 75, no. 6 (2004): 1806–20, one example is resident fathers who engage their children in more cognitive stimulation have children with higher mental development (that is, memory skills, problem-solving skills, vocalization, language skills) at twenty-four months (as measured by the Bayley Scales of Infant Development, Second Edition Mental Development Index). For a brief summary of this research, see Andrew Kang and Julie Weber, "Opportunities for Policy Leadership on Fathers," Policy Briefing Series 20 (Sloan Work and Family Research Network, Chestnut Hill, Mass., 2009) (www.wfnetwork.bc.edu). See also Ann M. Taubenheim,

"Paternal-Infant Bonding in the First-Time Father," *Journal of Obstetric, Gynecologic, and Neonatal Nursing* 10, no. 4 (1981): 261–64; Per Nettelbladt, "Father/Son Relationship during the Preschool Years: An Integrative Review with Special Reference to Recent Swedish Findings," *Acta Psychiatrica Scandinavica* 68, no. 6 (1983): 399–407. Although the bulk of the literature has focused on the bonds between mothers and infants, no evidence exists to suggest that bonding with fathers is any less significant to children.

14. Inger Kristensson-Hallstrom, Gunnel Elander, and Gerhard Malmfors, "Increased Parental Participation in a Pediatric Surgical Daycare Unit," *Journal of Clinical Nursing* 6, no. 4 (1997): 297–302; Mervyn R. H. Taylor and Peter O'Connor, "Resident Parents and Shorter Hospital Stay," *Archives of Disease in Childhood* 64, no. 2 (1989): 274–76; Patricia A. LaRosa-Nash and Jane M. Murphy, "An Approach to Pediatric Perioperative Care: Parent-Present Induction," *Nursing Clinics of North America* 32, no. 1 (1997): 183–99; Alan George and Janice Hancock, "Reducing Pediatric Burn Pain with Parent Participation," *Journal of Burn Care and Rehabilitation* 14, no. 1 (1993): 104–07; Sarah J. Palmer, "Care of Sick Children by Parents: A Meaningful Role," *Journal of Advanced Nursing* 18, no. 2 (1993): 185; Perry Mahaffy, "The Effects of Hospitalization on Children Admitted for Tonsillectomy and Adenoidectomy," *Nursing Review* 14 (1965): 12–19; John Bowlby, *Child Care and the Growth of Love* (London: Pelican, 1964); James Robertson, *Young Children in Hospital* (London: Tavistock, 1970).

15. See also Taylor and O'Connor, "Resident Parents and Shorter Hospital Stay" (see note 14); Kristensson-Hallstrom, Elander, and Malmfors, "Increased Parental Participation in a Pediatric Surgical Daycare Unit" (see note 14).

16. Annete M. LaGreca and others, "I Get By with a Little Help from My Family and Friends: Adolescents' Support for Diabetes Care," *Journal of Pediatric Psychology* 20, no. 4 (1995): 449–76; Barbara J. Anderson and others, "Family Characteristics of Diabetic Adolescents: Relationship to Metabolic Control," *Diabetes Care* 4, no. 6 (1981): 586–94; Kim W. Hamlett, David S. Pellegrini, and Kathy S. Katz, "Childhood Chronic Illness as a Family Stressor," *Journal of Pediatric Psychology* 17, no. 1 (1992): 33–47; Clara Wolman and others, "Emotional Well-Being among Adolescents with and without Chronic Conditions," *Adolescent Medicine* 15, no. 3 (1994): 199–204; Cindy L. Hanson and others, "Comparing Social Learning and Family Systems Correlates of Adaptation in Youths with IDDM," *Journal of Pediatric Psychology* 17, no. 5 (1992): 555–72.

17. LaGreca and others, "I Get By with a Little Help from My Family and Friends" (see note 16); Wolman and others, "Emotional Well-Being among Adolescents with and without Chronic Conditions" (see note 16); Hamlett, Pellegrini, and Katz, "Childhood Chronic Illness as a Family Stressor" (see note 16); Stuart T. Hauser and others, "Adherence among Children and Adolescents with Insulin-Dependent Diabetes Mellitus over a Four-Year Longitudinal Follow-Up: II. Immediate and Long-Term Linkages with the Family Milieu," *Journal of Pediatric Psychology* 15, no. 4 (1990): 527–42; E. Wayne Holden and others, "Controlling for General and Disease-Specific Effects in Child and Family Adjustment to Chronic Childhood Illness," *Journal of Pediatric Psychology* 22, no. 1 (1997): 15–27; Katrina Johnson, "Children with Special

Health Needs: Ensuring Appropriate Coverage and Care under Health Care Reform," *Health Policy and Child Health* 1, no. 3 (1994): 1–5; Timothy A. Waugh and Diane L. Kjos, "Parental Involvement and the Effectiveness of an Adolescent Day Treatment Program," *Journal of Youth and Adolescence* 21 (1992): 487–97; J. Cleary and others, "Parental Involvement in the Lives of Children in Hospital," *Archives of Disease in Childhood* 61 (1986): 779–87; C. P. Sainsbury and others, "Care by Parents of Their Children in Hospital," *Archives of Disease in Childhood* 61, no. 6 (1986): 612–15; Michael W. L. Gauderer, June L. Lorig, and Douglas W. Eastwood, "Is There a Place for Parents in the Operating Room?" *Journal of Pediatric Surgery* 24, no. 7 (1989): 705–06.

18. Isabelle Diehl, "The Prevalence of Colds in Nursery School Children and Non-Nursery School Children," *Journal of Pediatrics* 34, no. 1 (1949): 52–61; Peggy Sullivan and others, "Longitudinal Study of Occurrence of Diarrheal Disease in Day Care Centers," *American Journal of Public Health* 74, no. 9 (1984): 987–91; Merja Möttönen and Matti Uhari, "Absences for Sickness among Children in Day Care," *Acta Paediatrica* 81, no. 11 (1992): 929. Frank A. Loda, W. Paul Glezen, and Wallace A. Clyde Jr., "Respiratory Disease in Group Day Care," *Pediatrics* 49, no. 3 (1972): 428–37; K. Strangert, "Respiratory Illness in Preschool Children with Different Forms of Day Care," *Pediatrics* 57, no. 2 (1976): 191; Anna-Beth Doyle, "Incidence of Illness in Early Group and Family Day-Care," *Pediatrics* 58, no. 4 (1976): 607; Ron Haskins and Jonathan Kotch, "Day Care and Illness: Evidence, Costs, and Public Policy," *Pediatrics* 77, no. 6, (1986): 951–80; Muriel Oyediran and Anne Bamisaiye, "A Study of the Child-Care Arrangements and the Health Status of Pre-School Children of Employed Women in Lagos," *Public Health* 97, no. 5 (1983): 267; Susan D. Hillis and others, "Day Care Center Attendance and Diarrheal Morbidity in Colombia," *Pediatrics* 90, no. 4 (1992): 582; Centers for Disease Control and Prevention, "National Immunization Program: "Estimated Vaccination Coverage with Individual Vaccines and Selected Vaccination Series among Children Nineteen to Thirty-Five Months-of-Age by State" (Atlanta: 2001); World Health Organization (WHO), *WHO Vaccine Preventable Diseases: Monitoring System* (Geneva: WHO Department of Vaccines and Biologicals, 2000); Kim Streatfield and Masri Singarimbun, "Social Factors Affecting the Use of Immunization in Indonesia," *Social Science and Medicine* 27, no. 11 (1988): 1237–45.

19. Centers for Disease Control and Prevention, "National Immunization Program" (see note 18); World Health Organization, *WHO Vaccine Preventable Diseases* (see note 18).

20. J. E. Fielding, W. G. Cumberland, and L. Pettitt, "Immunization Status of Children of Employees in a Large Corporation," *Journal of the American Medical Association* 271, no. 7 (1994): 525–30.

21. Vicky Lovell. *No Time to Be Sick: Why Everyone Suffers When Workers Don't Have Paid Sick Leave* (Washington: Institute for Women's Policy Research, 2004) (www.iwpr.org/pdf/B242.pdf).

22. S. Jody Heymann, Sara Toomey, and Frank Furstenberg, "Working Parents: What Factors Are Involved in Their Ability to Take Time Off from Work When Their Children Are Sick?" *Archives of Pediatrics and Adolescent Medicine* 153, no. 8 (1999): 870–74; Jody Heymann, *The Widening Gap: Why America's Working Families Are in Jeopardy and What Can Be Done about It* (New York: Basic Books, 2000).

23. National Alliance for Caregiving and American Association of Retired People, "Caregiving in the U.S." (Bethesda: 2004); Heymann, *The Widening Gap* (see note 22).

24. Alison Earle and S. Jody Heymann, "What Causes Job Loss among Former Welfare Recipients? The Role of Family Health Problems," *Journal of the American Medical Women's Association* 57 (2002): 5–10.

25. Charles Desforges and Alberto Abouchaar, "The Impact of Parental Involvement, Parental Support, and Family Education on Pupil Achievement and Adjustment: A Literature Review," *DfES Research Report* 433 (Chelsea: Department for Education and Skills, 2003) (http://publications.dcsf. gov.uk/eOrderingDownload/RR433.pdf); Arthur Reynolds, "Early Schooling of Children at Risk," *American Educational Research Journal* 28, no. 2 (1991): 392–422; Kevin Callahan, Joyce A. Rademacher, and Bertina A. Hildreth, "The Effect of Parent Participation in Strategies to Improve the Homework Performance of Students Who Are at Risk," *Remedial and Special Education* 19, no. 3 (1998): 131–41; Timothy Z. Keith and others, "Does Parental Involvement Affect Eighth-Grade Student Achievement? Structural Analysis of National Data," *School Psychology Review* 22, no. 3 (1993): 474–76; Paul G. Fehrmann, Timothy Z. Keith, and Thomas M. Reimers, "Home Influences on School Learning: Direct and Indirect Effects of Parental Involvement on High School Grades," *Journal of Educational Research* 80, no. 6 (1987): 330–37.

26. Leon Feinstein and James Symons, "Attainment in Secondary School," *Oxford Economics Papers* 51, no. 2 (1999): 300–21. This study found that parental interest had a much stronger effect than either in-school factors such as teacher-student ratios or social factors such as the family's socioeconomic status and parental educational attainment. See also Arthur J. Reynolds, "Comparing Measures of Parental Involvement and Their Effects on Academic Achievement," *Early Childhood Research Quarterly* 7, no. 3 (1992): 441–62; James Griffith, "Relation of Parental Involvement, Empowerment, and School Traits to Student Academic Performance," *Journal of Educational Research* 90, no. 1 (1996): 33–41; Sandra L. Christenson, Theresa Rounds, and Deborah Gorney, "Family Factors and Student Achievement: An Avenue to Increase Students' Success," *School Psychology Quarterly* 7, no. 3 (1992): 178–206; Deborah L. Miller and Mary L. Kelley, "Interventions for Improving Homework Performance: A Critical Review," *School Psychology Quarterly* 6, no. 3 (1991): 174–85; James P. Comer, "Home-School Relationships as They Affect the Academic Success of Children," *Education and Urban Society* 16, no. 3 (1984): 323–37; John W. Fantuzzo, Gwendolyn Y. Davis, and Marika D. Ginsburg, "Effects of Parental Involvement in Isolation or in Combination with Peer Tutoring on Student Self-Concept and Mathematics Achievement," *Journal of Educational Psychology* 87, no. 2 (1995): 272–81; Tracey Frigo and others, "Australian Young People, Their Families, and Post-School Plans" (Melbourne: Australian Council for Educational Research, 2007).

27. James P. Comer and Norris M. Haynes. "Parent Involvement in Schools: An Ecological Approach," *Elementary School Journal* 91, no. 3 (1991): 271–77; Griffith, "Relation of Parental Involvement, Empowerment, and School Traits to Student Academic Performance" (see note 26); Arthur J. Reynolds and others, "Cognitive and Family-Support Mediators of Preschool Effectiveness: A Confirmatory Analysis," *Child Development* 67, no. 3 (1996): 1119–40.

28. National Center for Education Statistics, "Father's Involvement in the Children's Schools," NCES 98-091 (U.S. Department of Education, 1997); Christine Winquist Nord, DeeAnn Brimhall, and Jerry West, "Dads' Involvement in Their Kids' Schools," *Education Digest* 63, no. 7 (March 1998): 29–35; Michael E. Lamb, "The Emergent American Father," in *The Father's Role: Cross-Cultural Perspectives,* edited by Michael E. Lamb (Hillsdale, NY: Lawrence Erlbaum Associates Publishers, 1987); Rebecca Goldman, *Fathers' Involvement in Their Children's Education* (London: National Family and Parenting Institute, 2005).

29. Desforges and Abouchaar, "The Impact of Parental Involvement, Parental Support, and Family Education on Pupil Achievement and Adjustment" (see note 25); Reynolds, "Early Schooling of Children at Risk" (see note 25); Callahan, Rademacher, and Hildreth, "The Effect of Parent Participation in Strategies to Improve the Homework Performance of Students Who Are at Risk" (see note 25).

30. F. Davis, "Understanding Underachievers," *American Education* 20, no. 10 (1984): 12–14; M. Gajria and S. Salend, "Homework Practices of Students with and without Learning Disabilities: A Comparison," *Journal of Learning Disabilities* 28 (1995): 291–96; S. Salend and J. Schliff, "An Examination of the Homework Practices of Teachers of Students with Learning Disabilities," *Journal of Learning Disabilities* 22, no. 10 (1989): 621–23; H. Cooper and B. Nye, "Homework for Students with Learning Disabilities: The Implications of Research for Policy and Practice," *Journal of Learning Disabilities* 27, no. 8 (1994): 470–79; S. Salend and M. Gajria, "Increasing the Homework Completion Rates of Students with Mild Disabilities," *Remedial and Special Education* 16, no. 5 (1995): 271–78.

31. Arthur J. Reynolds, "A Structural Model of First Grade Outcomes for an Urban, Low Socioeconomic Status, Minority Population," *Journal of Educational Psychology* 81, no. 4 (1989): 594–603; C. S. Benson, E. A. Medrich, and S. Buckley, "The New View of School Efficiency: Household Time Contributions to School Achievement," in *School Finance Policies and Practices: 1980's Decade of Conflict,* edited by James W. Guthrie (Cambridge, Mass.: Ballinger Publishers, 2005); Reginald M. Clark, "Why Disadvantaged Students Succeed: What Happens Outside Schools' Critical Period," *Public Welfare* (Spring 1990): 17–23.

32. Joyce L. Epstein, "Parent Involvement: What Research Says to Administrators," *Education in Urban Society* 19, no. 2 (1987): 119–36; Ray T. J. Wilks and Valerie A. Clarke, "Training versus Non-Training of Mothers as Home Reading Tutors," *Perceptual and Motor Skills* 67 (1988): 135–42; United Nations Children's Fund (UNICEF), *The State of the World's Children 2001* (New York: 2001); R. Myers, *The Twelve Who Survive: Strengthening Programmes of Early Childhood Development in the Third World* (London and New York: Routledge in cooperation with UNESCO for the Consultative Group on Early Childhood Care and Development, 1992); Linda P. Thurston and Kathy Dasta, "An Analysis of In-Home Parent Tutoring Procedures: Effects on Children's Academic Behavior at Home and in School and on Parents' Tutoring Behaviors," *Remedial and Special Education* 11, no. 4 (1990): 41–52.

33. Heymann, Toomey, and Furstenberg, "Working Parents" (see note 22); Heymann, *The Widening Gap* (see note 22).

34. G. Roger King, "The Healthy Families Act: Safeguarding Americans' Livelihood, Families and Health with Paid Sick Days," Testimony before the U.S. Senate Committee on Health, Education, Labor, and Pensions, February 13, 2007.

35. Berger, Hill, and Waldfogel, "Maternity Leave, Early Maternal Employment and Child Health and Development in the U.S." (see note 2); Susan Macran, Heather Joshi, and Shirley Dex, "Employment after Childbearing: A Survival Analysis," *Work, Employment, and Society* 10, no. 2 (1996): 273–96.

36. Edward Shepard and Thomas Clifton, "Are Longer Hours Reducing Productivity in Manufacturing?" *International Journal of Manpower* 21, no. 7 (2000): 540–52.

37. Defined as meeting six criteria: job autonomy, learning opportunities, decision making, involvement, coworker/supervisor support, and flexibility.

38. Ellen Galinksy, Sheila Eby, and Shanny Peer, "2008 Guide to Bold New Ideas for Making Work Work from the 2007 Winners of the Alfred P. Sloan Awards for Business Excellence in Workplace Flexibility" (New York: Families and Work Institute, 2008) (http://familiesandwork.org/3w/boldideas.pdf).

39. For a full description of the adult labor database, see Jody Heymann and Alison Earle, *Raising the Global Floor: Dismantling the Myth That We Can't Afford Good Working Conditions for Everyone* (Stanford: Stanford University Press, 2010).

40. The World Economic Forum (WEF) is an international organization made up primarily of business leaders, as well as government officials and academic researchers. Its aims are to be "the foremost organization which builds and energizes leading global communities; the creative force shaping global, regional and industry strategies; [and] the catalyst of choice for its communities when undertaking global initiatives to improve the state the world." WEF primarily gathers together business leaders at summits, conferences, and meetings to discuss and develop solutions to global issues (www.weforum.org).

41. From 1987 to 2005 the WEF published the Growth Competitiveness Index, which ranked each nation according to its score on thirty-five variables that represent three conceptual areas: the macroeconomic environment, the quality of public institutions, and technology. Beginning with the 2006 report, this report was renamed the Global Competitiveness Index. The WEF reported rankings based on each nation's scores on more than ninety competitiveness indicators organized into nine areas: institutions; infrastructure; macroeconomy; health and primary education; higher education and training; market efficiency; technological readiness; business sophistication; and innovation. Many of the data used in the competitiveness reports are obtained through a global network of 104 research institutions and academics that partner and collaborate with WEF, as well as from a survey of 11,000 business leaders in 131 nations. The categories are weighted to account more accurately for levels of development in measuring each indicator's impact on competitiveness.

42. World Bank, World Development Indicators, "Labor Force, Total, 2009" (http://data.worldbank.org/indicator/SL.TLF.TOTL.IN?order=wbapi_data_value_2009+wbapi_data_value+wbapi_data_value-last&sort=asc).

43. China has no national standard, but leave is available in certain circumstances in some provinces.

44. The agreed definition of "unemployed" is working-age individuals who are not working and are available for and actively seeking work. The unemployment rate is then equal to the number of unemployed persons as a percentage of civilian employees, the self-employed, unpaid family workers, and the unemployed. For further information on the selection and development of this unemployment definition, see Eurostat Internet site (http://europa.eu.int/comm/eurostat). The original data from each individual country that are merged to create the OECD unemployment database are either "registered" unemployment from administrative data sources or are from national household surveys (for example, the U.S. Census Bureau's Current Population Survey). In the early 1990s almost all OECD nations agreed to use a common set of criteria for classifying individuals as "unemployed" based on common household survey information. The only variations that still exist are the age group included in the calculation of the unemployment rate and the definition of an "active" job search. Over the past two decades (the time period from which our data come), the consistency, quality, and comparability of the OECD data have increased. In addition to consensus on the definitions, data collection and processing methods have converged.

Critical Thinking

1. Is it incompatible for a country to be economically competitive and family friendly in its workplace and leave policies?

2. How do work-family policies in the United States compare with those in 15 economically competitive nations?

3. What are the two work-family policies that you feel are most important to family well-being? Why are these policies important and needed?

Create Central

www.mhhe.com/createcentral

Internet References

Families and Work Institute
www.familiesandwork.org

Modern Family or Modernized Family Traditionalism?: Master Status and the Gender Order in Switzerland
www.sociology.org/content/vol006.004/lwk.html

Sociological Perspectives of Work and Family
www.scribd.com/doc/24528839

ALISON EARLE is a principal research scientist at Northeastern University. **ZITHA MOKOMANE** is a senior research specialist at the Human Sciences Research Council of South Africa. **JODY HEYMANN** is the founding director of the Institute for Health and Social Policy at McGill University.

Article   Prepared by: Patricia Hrusa Williams,
University of Maine at Farmington

Behind Every Great Woman

Carol Hymowitz

Learning Outcomes

After reading this article, you will be able to:

- Explain why women are becoming primary breadwinners in families.
- Describe the challenges faced by families where mothers are employed outside of the home and fathers assume primary responsibility for childrearing.
- Identify how parents can balance their time spent with their family and their career.

Among the 80 or so customers crammed into Bare Escentuals, it's easy to spot Leslie Blodgett. It's not merely her six-inch platform heels and bright magenta-and-blue dress that set her apart in the Thousand Oaks (Calif.) mall boutique, but her confidence. To the woman concerned she's too old for shimmery eye shadow, Blodgett swoops in and encourages her to wear whatever she wants. With a deft sweep of a brush, she demonstrates a new shade of blush on another customer's cheek. And when she isn't helping anyone, she pivots on her heels for admirers gushing about her dress, made by the breakout designer Erdem.

Blodgett, 49, has spent the past 18 years nurturing Bare Escentuals from a startup into a global cosmetics empire. She sold the company for $1.7 billion to Shiseido in March 2010 but still pitches products in stores around the world and chats incessantly with customers online. Scores of fans post daily messages on Blodgett's Facebook page, confessing details about their personal lives and offering opinions on her additive-free makeup. She only wishes her 19-year-old son, Trent, were in touch with her as frequently as he is with her husband, Keith. In 1995, at 38, Keith quit making television commercials to raise Trent, freeing up Leslie to build her business. She'd do it all again, but she's jealous of her husband's relationship with her son. Trent, a college sophomore, texts his father almost every day; he often goes a week without texting her.

"Once I knew my role was providing for the family, I took that very seriously. But there was envy knowing I wasn't there for our son during the day," says Blodgett. "Keith does everything at home—the cooking, repairs, finances, vacation planning—and I could work long hours and travel a lot, knowing he took such good care of Trent. I love my work, but I would have liked to have a little more balance or even understand what that means."

Blodgett's lament is becoming more familiar as a generation of female breadwinners look back on the sacrifices—some little, some profound—required to have the careers they wanted. Like hundreds of thousands of women who have advanced into management roles in the past two decades—and, in particular, the hundreds who've become senior corporate officers—she figured out early what every man with a corner office has long known: To make it to the top, you need a wife. If that wife happens to be a husband, and increasingly it is, so be it.

When Carly Fiorina became Hewlett-Packard's first female chief executive officer, the existence of her househusband, Frank Fiorina, who had retired early from AT&T to support her career, was a mini-sensation; nine years later, this arrangement isn't at all unusual. Seven of the 18 women who are currently CEOs of Fortune 500 companies—including Xerox's Ursula Burns, PepsiCo's Indra Nooyi, and WellPoint's Angela Braly—have, or at some point have had, a stay-at-home husband. So do scores of female CEOs of smaller companies and women in other senior executive jobs. Others, like IBM's new CEO, Ginni Rometty, have spouses who dialed back their careers to become their powerful wives' chief domestic officers.

This role reversal is occurring more and more as women edge past men at work. Women now fill a majority of jobs in the U.S., including 51.4 percent of managerial and professional positions, according to U.S. Census Bureau data. Some 23 percent of wives now out-earn their husbands, according to a 2010 study by the Pew Research Center. And this earnings trend is more dramatic among younger people. Women 30 and under make more money, on average, than their male counterparts in all but three of the largest cities in the U.S.

During the recent recession, three men lost their jobs for every woman. Many unemployed fathers, casualties of layoffs in manufacturing and finance, have ended up caring for their children full-time while their wives are the primary wage earners. The number of men in the U.S. who regularly care for children under age five increased to 32 percent in 2010 from 19 percent in 1988, according to Census figures. Among those fathers with preschool-age children, one in five served as the main caregiver.

Even as the trend becomes more widespread, stigmas persist. At-home dads are sometimes perceived as freeloaders, even if they've lost jobs. Or they're considered frivolous kept men—gentlemen who golf. The househusbands of highly successful women, after all, live in luxurious homes, take nice vacations, and can afford nannies and housekeepers, which many employ at least part-time. In reaction, at-home dads have launched a spate of support groups and daddy blogs to defend themselves.

"Men are suddenly seeing what it's been like for women throughout history," says Linda R. Hirshman, a lawyer and the author of *Get to Work,* a book that challenges at-home moms to secure paying jobs and insist that their husbands do at least half the housework. Caring for children all day and doing housework is tiring, unappreciated work that few are cut out for—and it leaves men and women alike feeling isolated and diminished.

There's some good news about the at-home dads trend. "By going against the grain, men get to stretch their parenting abilities and women can advance," notes Stephanie Coontz, a family studies professor at Evergreen State College in Olympia, Wash., and author of *Marriage: a History.* And yet the trend underscores something else: When jobs are scarce or one partner is aiming high, a two-career partnership is next to impossible. "Top power jobs are so time-consuming and difficult, you can't have two spouses doing them and maintain a marriage and family," says Coontz. This explains why, even as women make up more of the workforce, they're still a small minority (14 percent, according to New York-based Catalyst) in senior executive jobs. When they reach the always-on, all-consuming executive level, "it's still women who more often put family ahead of their careers," says Ken Matos, a senior director at Families and Work Institute in New York. It may explain, too, why bookstore shelves and e-book catalogs are jammed with self-help books for ambitious women, of which *I'd Rather Be in Charge,* by former Ogilvy-Mather Worldwide CEO Charlotte Beers, is merely the latest. Some, such as Hirshman's top-selling *Get to Work,* recommend that women "marry down"—find husbands who won't mind staying at home—or wed older men who are ready to retire as their careers take off. What's indisputable is that couples increasingly are negotiating whose career will take precedence before they start a family.

"Your wife's career is about to soar, and you need to get out of her way." That's what Ken Gladden says his boss told him shortly before his wife, Dawn Lepore, was named the first female CIO at Charles Schwab in 1994. He was a vice-president at Schwab in computer systems. Lepore's promotion meant she'd become his top boss. "I married above my station," Gladden jokes.

Gladden moved to a job at Visa. When their son, Andrew, was born four years later in 1998, Gladden quit working altogether. He and Lepore had tried for years to have a child and didn't want him raised by a nanny. Being a full-time dad wasn't the biggest adjustment Gladden made for Lepore's career. That came later, when Seattle-based drugstore.com recruited Lepore to become its CEO in 2004.

Gladden had lived in the San Francisco Bay Area for 25 years and wasn't keen to move to a city where it rains a lot and he didn't know anyone. He rejected Lepore's suggestion that she commute between Seattle and San Francisco, and after some long discussions he agreed to relocate—on the condition that they kept their Bay Area home. They still return for holidays and some vacations. "To do what I'm doing, you've got to be able to say 'my wife's the breadwinner, the more powerful one,' and be O.K. with that. But you also need your own interests," says Gladden, who has used his computing skills to launch a home-based business developing software for schools.

The couple's five-bedroom Seattle home overlooks Lake Washington. Gladden, 63, is chief administrator of it and their children, who now are 9 and 13. While they're in school, he works on his software. From 3 P.M. until bedtime, he car-pools to and from sports and music lessons, warms up dinners prepared by a part-time housekeeper, and supervises homework. Lepore, 57, is often out of town. She oversaw the sale of drugstore.com to Walgreens last year, for $429 million. As CEO, she was rarely home before 8 or 9 P.M. and traveled several days a week. Now, as a consultant to several startups and a director at eBay, she still travels frequently. If Gladden envies anything, it's the ease with which his wife can walk into a room filled with well-known executives like Bill Gates and "go right up to them and start talking. I don't feel like I can participate," he says.

Lepore wishes her "biggest supporter" would get more recognition for everything he does at home. When an executive recently told her "having an at-home husband makes it easy for you to be a CEO," she responded, "No, not easy. He makes it possible." Lepore advises younger women to "choose your spouse carefully. If you want a top job, you need a husband who isn't self-involved and will support your success," even if you go further than him. There are tradeoffs, she warns: "I've missed so much with my kids—school plays, recitals, just seeing them every day."

For Lepore and Gladden, the role reversal paid off, and, as one of the few couples willing to go public about their domestic arrangement, they're a rare source of inspiration for those who are still figuring it out. Like Gladden, Matt Schneider, 36, is an

A Changing Landscape

	1970	Now
Percentage of employees who are women	35%	49%
Percentage of college graduates who are women	36%	54%
Share of husbands whose wives' income tops theirs	4%	23%
Contribution of wives' earnings to family income	27%	36%
The number of Fortune 500 CEOs who are women	0	18

at-home dad. A former technology company manager and then a sixth grade teacher, he cares for his sons Max and Sam, 6 and 3, while his wife, Priyanka, also 36, puts in 10-hour days as chief operating officer at a Manhattan real estate management startup. He feels "privileged," he says, to be with his sons full-time "and see them change every day," while allowing that child care and housework can be mind-numbing. He uses every minute of the 2½ hours each weekday when Sam is in preschool to expand the NYC DADS Group he co-founded, 450 members strong. Members meet for play dates with their kids, discuss parenting, and stand up for at-home dads. "We're still portrayed as bumbling idiots," Schneider says. He rails against a prejudice that moms would do a better job—if only they were there. "Everyone is learning from scratch how to change diapers and toilet-train," he says, "and there's no reason to think this is woman's work."

Schneider and his wife, who met as undergraduates at University of Pennsylvania's Wharton School of Business, decided before they wed that she'd have the big career and he'd be the primary parent. "It's her name on the paycheck, and sure, we've thought about the precariousness of having just one breadwinner. But she wouldn't earn what she does if I wasn't doing what I do," he says. Which is not to say that he doesn't wonder "whether I can get back to a career when I want to and build on what I've done before."

At-home moms have snubbed him at arts and crafts classes and on playgrounds. "Men, even those of us pushing strollers, are perceived as dangerous," Schneider says. He was rejected when he wanted to join an at-home neighborhood moms' group, which prompted him to blog more about the similarities among moms and dads. "I've met moms *and* dads who are happy to give a screaming kid a candy bar to get him to settle down, and moms *and* dads who show up at play dates with containers filled with organic fruit," he says. "The differences aren't gender-specific."

It's no different for gay couples. Brad Kleinerman and Flint Gehre have taken turns being at-home dads for their three sons, now 19, 18, and 10. When their sons—biological siblings they adopted through the Los Angeles County foster care system—were young, Kleinerman and Gehre relied first on a weekday nanny and then a live-in one while both worked full-time. Kleinerman, 50, was an executive in human resources at Walt Disney and NASA. Gehre, 46, was a teacher and then director of global learning and communications at Disney. Five years ago, they decided they no longer wanted to outsource parenting. "We always wanted to have dinner together as a family, but by the time we got home, the nanny had fed our kids," says Gehre. "Our kids were at pivotal ages—the two oldest about to go to high school and the youngest to first grade. We wanted to be the ones instilling our values and be there when they needed help with homework or had to get to a doctor."

In 2007 the couple moved from Los Angeles to Avon, Conn., where they were able to get married legally and find better schools for their kids. Kleinerman became the full-time dad and Gehre kept his Disney job, working partly from home and traveling frequently to Los Angeles. A year later they switched: Gehre quit Disney to parent full-time and Kleinerman found a new job as a human resources director at Cigna Healthcare.

Gehre says he's never felt discriminated against as a gay dad or a stay-at-home dad. "No one has ever said to me, 'Why would you stay home with the kids?' Where we're discriminated is when we pay taxes. We don't qualify for the marriage deduction, we have to file as single people," he says. If he has one regret about being at home, it's the lack of adult conversation and stimulation: "I worked in a very high-intensity atmosphere with very intelligent and hard-driving people, and that keeps you sharp." Any dullness doesn't make Gehre doubt his decision. Having consciously chosen to have a family, he and Kleinerman felt they had not only to provide the essentials, but also to be present.

Is there an alternate universe where both parents can pursue careers without outsourcing child care? The five Nordic countries—Iceland, Norway, Sweden, Finland, and Denmark—are noted leaders in keeping moms, in particular, on the job. "These countries have made it possible to have a better division of labor both at work and at home through policies that both encourage the participation of women in the labor force and men in their families," says Saadia Zahidi, co-author of the World Economic Forum's *Global Gender Gap Report*. The policies Zahidi refers to include mandatory paternal leave in combination with maternity leave; generous, federally mandated parental leave benefits; gender-neutral tax incentives; and post-maternity reentry programs.

There were no such programs or precedents for Jennifer Granholm and Dan Mulhern. When the two met at Harvard Law School, she grilled him about what he expected from a wife. Mulhern accepted that Granholm would never be a homemaker like his mother, but he never expected her to run for political office. "When I was young," he says, "I thought *I'd* be the governor"—not married to the governor. Granholm was governor of Michigan from 2003 through 2010, and her election forced Mulhern to walk away from the Detroit-based consulting business he founded, which had numerous contracts with state-licensed health insurance companies, municipalities, and school districts. Once that happened, he felt "in a backroom somewhere" and in a marriage that was "a lot more give than take."

Mulhern understood that his wife faced "extraordinary pressure" during her two terms, including a $1.7 billion budget deficit and the bankruptcies of General Motors and Chrysler. She had limited time for their three children, who were 6, 11, and 14 when she was elected, and even less for him. "I didn't want to say, 'hey, you missed my birthday' or 'you haven't even noticed what happened with the kids,' but I sometimes felt resentful," he says.

Mulhern says he complained to his wife that they spent 95 percent of the little time they had together talking about her work. He missed the attention she used to give him but felt humiliated asking for it. He gradually changed his expectations. He stopped waiting for Granholm to call him in the middle of the day to share what had happened at meetings they'd spent time talking about the prior evening. And he realized he couldn't re-create for her all the memorable or awkward moments he had with their children—like the time he found his daughter and her high school friends in the outdoor shower, "ostensibly with their clothes on. I had to call all the parents and tell them, as a courtesy, 'I want you to know this happened at the Governor's mansion,'" he says. "While my wife was battling the Republican head of the State Senate, I had a teenage daughter who was a more formidable opponent."

When Granholm left office and was asked "what's next?", she said, "it's Dan's turn." As a former governor, though, she's the one with more obvious opportunities. Later this month, Granholm launches a daily political commentary show on Current TV. She's also teaching at the University of California at Berkeley, where Dan has a part-time gig thanks to his wife.

"The employment opportunities that come my way—and my salary potential—aren't what my wife's are now," says Mulhern. He plans to continue to teach, write, and do some consulting, while also taking care of their 14-year-old son. "Someone has to be focused on him every day," he says.

The experiences and reflections of powerful women and their at-home husbands could lead to changes at work so that neither women nor men have to sacrifice their careers or families. "There's no reason women should feel guilty about achieving great success, but there should be a way for success to include professional and personal happiness for everyone," says *Get to Work* author Hirshman. "If you have to kill yourself at work, that's bad for everyone."

Kathleen Christensen agrees. As program director at the Alfred P. Sloan Foundation, she has focused on work and family issues and says we're back to the 1950s, only "instead of Jane at home, it's John. But it's still one person doing 100 percent of work outside the home and the other doing 100 percent at home." Just as we saw the Feminine Mystique in the 1960s among frustrated housewives, Christensen predicts, "we may see the Masculine Mystique in 2020."

The children of couples who have reversed roles know the stakes better than anyone. One morning last year, when Dawn Lepore was packing for a business trip to New York, her nine-year-old daughter burst into tears. "I don't want you to travel so much," Elizabeth told her mother. Lepore hugged her, called

her school, and said her daughter would be staying home that morning. Then she rescheduled her flight until much later that day. "There have been times when what Elizabeth wants most is a mom who stays home and bakes cookies," she says.

Lepore is sometimes concerned that her children won't be ambitious because they've often heard her complain about how exhausted she is after work. But they're much closer to their father than kids whose dads work full-time, and they have a different perspective about men's and women's potential. When a friend of her daughter's said that fathers go to offices every day, Lepore recalls, "Elizabeth replied, 'Don't be silly, dads are at home.'"

Critical Thinking

1. Why are more women becoming the primary breadwinners in their families?

2. What strategies do families use to create work-family balance?

3. When husbands leave their careers to man the home front, what effect does this role reversal have on children, marriages, and families?

4. What types of supports are needed for families where dads serve as primary caregivers?

Create Central

www.mhhe.com/createcentral

Internet References

Families and Work Institute
www.familiesandwork.org

Modern Family or Modernized Family Traditionalism?: Master Status and the Gender Order in Switzerland
www.sociology.org/content/vol006.004/lwk.html

Sociological Perspectives of Work and Family
www.scribd.com/doc/24528839

From *Bloomberg BusinessWeek*, January 9–15, 2012. Copyright © Bloomberg 2012 by Bloomberg BusinessWeek. Reprinted by permission of Bloomberg LP via YGS Group.

Article   Prepared by: Patricia Hrusa Williams, *University of Maine at Farmington*

Exploring the Lived Experiences of Homeless Families with Young Children

STEPHANIE HINTON AND DARLINDA CASSEL

Learning Outcomes

After reading this article, you will be able to:

- Explain the reasons families are homeless.

- Describe how homelessness affects parenting and young children.

- Understand supports needed to assist homeless families and prevent homelessness.

Homelessness is a reality in the United States for many families with young children. Though accurate and thorough accounts of the homeless population are difficult to assemble there are several telling statistics on homeless families with young children. The U.S. Conference of Mayors reported in 2008, "At least 3.5 million people are likely to experience homelessness during a year . . . more than half of this group is women and children," and 42 % of this population is reported to be under the age of 5 by the National Law Center on Homelessness and Poverty (2012, p. 1). Only a year later, U.S. cities saw "the sharpest increase in the demand for hunger assistance since 1991 and an increase in homeless families" (The U.S. Conference of Mayors 2009, p. 1). In 2011 U.S. cities saw, on average, a 6 % increase in homelessness and a 16 % increase among families with children experiencing homelessness (The U.S. Conference of Mayors 2011, p. 3). Young children subjected to experiencing homelessness are "twice as likely to experience learning disabilities and three times as likely to experience an emotional disturbance" compared to housed children (Shaw and Goode 2008, p. 6). The injustice of this life situation on our youngest, most vulnerable citizens was addressed by President Obama in his First Presidential Press Conference. President Obama stated: "It is not acceptable for children and families to be without a roof over their heads in a country as wealthy as ours" (Obama 2009).

In a review of the current literature on the issue of homeless families with young children, much of the research compiled sought to understand homelessness through the parents' perspectives and attempted to provide ideas for resources and solutions to assist families of homelessness. "Housing only addresses the structural needs . . . which does not completely alleviate the often complex stresses associated" with being homeless (Karim et al. 2006, p. 455). Families living homeless are under overwhelming amounts of stress. Homelessness, by itself, is considered a powerful source of stress on parents with young children; however, two common themes throughout current research suggest that the major causes of stress within families of homelessness are chemical dependency and family violence (Swick and Williams 2006). These two factors were not only noted as a cause of homelessness but also a reason for chronic homelessness (Vostains et al. 2001). Swick (2008) reported that homeless children and families experience a great deal of violence; while witnessing a violent act still produces negative effects on young children, creating an atmosphere of "high anxiety, distrust, and chaos within family dynamics" (p. 81).

Homeless families reported not feeling as "safe and secure" in their environment as compared to housed families (Swick 2005, p. 195). Living in shelters can cause families with young children to feel insecure and vulnerable. Shelter conditions can also hinder parents' feelings of control and independence over one's own life. Parents also reported a lack of enabling resources within shelters. Many resources that were supposed to help parents often prevented their ability to gain independence (Swick 2005). Other peripheral themes that emerged from the research included unstable relationships within the family and an abdication of parental responsibility (Morris and Butt 2003). Torquati (2002) also suggested that during "periods of stress, parents may be able to maintain some warmth and support in their relationships with their children, but they may be at higher risk for irritable parenting" (p. 481).

Early childhood educators hold a position in which they can encourage and support homeless parents and young children; however, schools are often "ill equipped to combat the multifaceted problems associated with homelessness" (Gargiulo 2006, p. 360). Through authentic communication, early childhood educators can gather information about "families' perceptions of needs, resources, and strengths," build trusting relationships with homeless families, and connect parents to key supports for food and clothing (Swick and Bailey 2004, p. 212). It is important that homeless parents with young children are heard; homeless mothers "experience the needs of their children every minute of the day" (Swick 2010, p. 299). Swick found many parents wanted "to do a good job in parenting and family life . . . because of their problems, they often want to compensate by increasing their focus on their children" (2010, p. 301). In the same study, the clear and essential needs of most homeless mothers and fathers were listed by parents as supportive help, adequate and affordable housing, high quality child care so they can work or receive training, and education opportunities especially in parenting (Swick 2010). Early childhood educators can begin by "developing an awareness of the challenges and situations experienced by homeless children and families" (Powers-Costello and Swick 2008, p. 243). Educators can also engage "in service-learning roles with shelters and other groups that serve" homeless children and families, through mentoring and tutoring opportunities educators can use their "liaison roles to weave together more supportive school and community settings," and involve "community experts on various issues connected to homelessness" (Powers-Costello and Swick 2008, p. 244). Swick and Williams listed key strategies on how early childhood educators can build relationships and effectively support homeless families. These strategies include: (1) encouraging the family to access education and counseling to address the challenges of their situation; (2) support the family with resources and help that empowers them; and (3) involve family in learning ways to promote healthy life styles (2006). In a later study, Swick and Williams (2010) also pointed out that; since "single parent homeless mothers develop adaptive parenting strategies to accommodate the various contexts they experience . . . early childhood professionals need to better understand the problems faced by single parent homeless mothers" (p. 53). Their research concluded that early childhood educators and shelters serving homeless families needed to: (a) involve "faith-based groups more effectively in supporting and empowering homeless families, (b) seek to dispel the many negative and incorrect stereotypes about homeless mothers and

their children, and (c) interact more with homeless mothers in supportive ways such as mentoring and one-on-one counseling" (Swick and Williams 2010, p. 54).

The research available on homeless families with young children lacks information on how young children experience homelessness and the importance of early childhood educators understanding the homeless experience and effectively providing care to families with young children through that experience. If early childhood educators are going to effectively serve homeless families with young children, research is needed that brings understanding to their life situation through their perspectives. The purpose of this qualitative phenomenological research study is to explore the lived experiences of young children, ages four to eight, and their families who have experienced or are currently experiencing living in [a] fixed, non-transient, homeless situation. Research will seek to understand common themes of the family dynamics and the development of young children who are homeless to help early childhood educators relate to these families and to support their children's learning. The basis for conducting this research study is: (1) to understand reasons families with young children become homeless; (2) become aware of beneficial resources available to families and their perceptions of the resources; (3) and [understand] the developmental effects that homeless living situations can have on young children.

Methodology

Context for the Study

Participants in this study were homeless parents with young children living in a fixed, non-transient, urban downtown shelter in the southwestern United States. This shelter was selected for this study because the mission of the shelter complied with the research of Swick and Williams (2010) on meeting the needs of homeless families. The shelter is a faith-based program that seeks to dispel the many negative and incorrect stereotypes about homeless mothers and their children while interacting with homeless families in supportive ways. All the participants in this study were involved in a faith-based program provided by the shelter. On entering the shelter, any homeless individuals or families are limited to a 30 days stay. Within that 30 days time frame, the individual or family has the option of entering the program the shelter provides. The program offers a variety of classes for individuals and families and is specific to the needs of each individual or family. The classes offered to the residents include Bible study, parenting, marriage, job or skill related education, and GED test preparation. If a resident is married upon entering the shelter he or she is required to attend marriage classes. Likewise, if a resident is a parent, she or he is required to attend parenting classes. Family units lived together in apartment-like housing, fathers were permitted to live in family units if the father was a single parent or was married to the mother. With this exception to fathers, all other women and men were kept separate inside the shelter.

The program has four steps: anger management, spirituality, addiction control, and transition to life outside the shelter. The program's main goal is to educate and equip homeless individuals to be successful after leaving the shelter. Residents can move to a new step after receiving a counselor's approval. The majority of residents completed the entire program within 10 months to 1 year, yet some residents stayed in the program for multiple years. The residents of the shelter agreed to adhere to a specific schedule on entrance into the program. The schedule consisted of a morning wake-up call, periods of free time, three meals, devotions and church services, and work shifts. The shelter consists of common areas and private living areas for the families and individuals. The common areas include the lobby, gym, and dining hall. The living areas are separated according to families with children, individual men, and individual women.

The role of the researcher was that of a participant-observer. The researcher had participated in volunteer work with the children of the families living at the shelter before the research began. The researcher voluntarily participated with children in their activities. These activities were educational and engaging for the children. As a volunteer in the program, the researcher had built relationships with the children and their parents through these interactions prior to the research.

Participants

Eight families who reside at the homeless shelter participated in the study. All parents and children involved in the study volunteered to participate. Each family participating had at least one child between the ages of four and eight. The average age of child participants was 5.4 years. The average number of children living with these families at the shelter was 2.8. All the participants in this study were jobless; four participants were working on completing their GED, three had received their GED, one had a few years of college work completed, and one was seeking a degree in higher education at the time of the study. At the time of the interview, the families had spent an average of 5.5 months at the shelter. The parents' ages ranged from 22 to 38 years old with the average age being 30.3 years old. The families were 25 % white, 50 % African American, and 25 % Hispanic. Only the mother was interviewed due to the fact that only three were married.

Procedures

The research study was a qualitative phenomenological study that was carried out from October 2011 until March 2012.

Weekly interviews occurred in an office at the shelter on Friday after dinner, and observations occurred throughout the week at the shelter in the common areas of the foyer and the dining hall. Interviews lasted approximately 1 h for each family and observations occurred weekly until the completion of the study. After each interview, field notes were written on the details of the interviews.

The interviewer asked parents about their own childhood and what brought their family to living in the shelter, their child(ren)'s strengths and interests, their support system as a homeless family, the impact homelessness has had on their family, and their views on parenting. The children's interview questions focused on the children's favorite activity for fun and play, who they like to play with, their favorite thing about school, and what makes them happy and scared. An audiotape was used to help accurately record interviews; without the use of the audiotape important details of the participants' responses might have been missed. Families were observed interacting twice per week.

While conducting observations, the researcher focused on parent and child interactions and types of communication between the child(ren) and parent. During the observations the researcher observed from the common areas during the residents' dinner time and their 2 h of free time in the evening. During free time the families were observed in the foyer, the dining hall, and the apartments. The researcher interacted with the participants while observing only when participants initiated an interaction with the researcher.

Data Collection

Reasons for Homelessness

Data were gathered into three themes: (1) reasons families with young children become homeless, (2) beneficial resources available to families and their perceptions of those resources, and (3) effects of homeless living situations on young children's development. The first category indicates reasons for homelessness. Table 1 details the reasons participants cited for being homeless.

During the interview, each participant explained multiple reasons for homelessness. An unhappy childhood was a common theme. They described growing up in poverty, stating that their basic needs were met, even though their childhood felt unstable. One of the participants talked about alcohol usage of caretakers, another participant described the early death of her parents, and seven participants discussed parental fights or the abandonment of parents. While an unhappy childhood was considered by seven participants as a reason for homelessness, these seven mothers further described their unhappy childhoods

Table 1   Reasons for homelessness as stated by homeless parents

Participant in study	Reason for homelessness						
	Unhappy childhood	Teenage pregnancy	Multiple children	High school drop out	Drug use	Spouse (father) abandonment	Jobless
1	X	X	X	X			X
2	X	X	X	X		X	X
3	X	X	X	X		X	X
4	X	X	X	X	X		X
5	X		X	X	X	X	X
6			X	X	X	X	X
7	X		X	X	X	X	X
8	X	X	X			X	X

as being the source of their lack of resources and support system as an adult.

Teenage pregnancies were common with five participants. All of the participants in the study had at least two children. Teenage pregnancies and multiple children were cited as reasons for homelessness because it led many of the participants to dropping out of high school. The participants who became pregnant as teenagers felt they could not juggle the responsibilities of a baby with the demands of high school. These parents also found it difficult to find affordable housing with minimum wage jobs. Five of the families who participated in the study also cited a lack of paternal involvement as a source of their homelessness, stating the difficulties of being a single mother. Multiple children increased the chances of a homeless lifestyle because of the increased financial responsibility.

All but two of the participants in the study dropped out of high school. At the time of the interviews three of the participants had obtained their GED and the other three were working to obtain their GED through courses the shelter provided. All participants were jobless before coming to the shelter. Thus a cycle formed; dropping out of high school causes a lack of job opportunities which in turn caused financial problems leading to homelessness.

Four of the participants cited that joblessness and the stress of having multiple children led to their drug usage. One participant explained that she had started using drugs at the age of 17 which led to her [to] (1) drop out, (2) multiple children, and (3) [a] jobless condition. Drugs were explained as being a reason for homelessness by participants because they could not leave their addiction without support. The shelter is a drug rehabilitation center; therefore, participants were able to receive the interventions needed to quit using drugs without the concern that their children might be taken from them.

Individuals participating in the shelter's rehabilitation process are encouraged to take responsibility for life decisions that led to their current situation. The interviews with homeless parents revealed similar themes among each family's reasons for being homeless. These factors included unhappy childhoods, young pregnancies, multiple children, failure to complete schooling, drug or substance abuse, paternal abandonment, and unemployment.

Resources and Perceptions of Resources

The second category analyzed participants' comments about available resources. The shelter provides clients with a four-step process to recovery from homelessness; these steps are anger management, spirituality, addiction control, and transition to life outside of the shelter. At each step a variety of resources are provided to the families. Resources that were used by the participating families include: mentoring, family and marriage counseling, drug rehabilitation, parenting classes, GED preparation courses, Bible study classes, and classes on finding and maintaining a job. Counselors at the shelter are responsible for evaluating clients and, together with the client, deciding what resources to use. Participants interviewed discussed which resources they used, which ones were most effective for their families, and ideas for resources that would potentially benefit them and their family.

Support from others; including counselors, mentors, or other homeless families, was viewed by seven of the participants as an important resource. Having these supports in place led participants to feel successful in the program. Seven of the participants were positive about life at the shelter. Some of the participants with a positive view of life at the shelter cited that other families living in the shelter were part of the needed support system. Participants also explained their positive experience came from the staff and the program itself. These parents explained the positive effect that the mandatory regular and predictable schedule had on their young children, as well as how this aspect of shelter life taught them how to maintain a normalcy in their family that they did not have before.

As a part of the shelter's program, clients are encouraged to plan for the future when they leave the shelter. Two of the participants discussed job plans. One participant wanted to be a nurse and was enrolled in college courses. Many participants explained how they would like to give back to the homeless community by becoming a resource to other homeless families. All of the participants expressed a desire to be stable and independent. The goal of the resources was to ensure their success in this area. Because of the shelter's decision to constantly discuss life beyond the shelter, participants were able to look ahead and plan for their next step; the resources that the shelter provides gave participants the opportunity to make their goals a reality.

The shelter provided tutoring and after school activities for school aged children. However, children up to age five, who were not in an outside program such as a child care facility, were required to stay with their parents. Children in prekindergarten, kindergarten, or Head Start were not engaged in any tutoring or after school activities. One parent described a need for more opportunities for the younger children, she stated the shelter needs to get ". . . . a class together for the kids" with more opportunities to learn. This resource could have the potential to use developmentally appropriate practices, such as engaging children in play with materials like water, sand, while also giving children early literacy opportunities. There is also a need for parenting classes to include what parents should expect at different developmental stages as well as ways that parents can promote learning in the home for their young child.

The interviews revealed that the parents felt positively about the resources provided by the shelter. The shelter provides individualized, specific resources matched to each client's needs and goals. However, there is a need to develop more engaging resources for the young children, resources that engage and promote learning.

Effects on Young Children

Data placed into the third category revealed information about the effects on young children. Parents were asked to describe how their child(ren)'s behavior had changed since moving to the shelter. Many parents who had described a positive experience also described their young child(ren) as being angry and emotional since arriving at the shelter. One parent described her 6-year-old as "getting more emotional and he has more issues

going on with him cause he's able to see and know what's going on around him." Another parent stated "they like that there's a lot of other kids," while still another parent explained that; "sometimes it's rough on my kids" having other people around all the time. One parent felt that due to the stability and constant routine her children were "a lot happier" since moving into the shelter than when they were living on the streets. Each child reacted to the experience of moving to the shelter differently, but each of the participants stated that they saw a change in their child(ren).

In observations of parent and child interactions, behaviors of educational support, such as reading and completing homework, were not observed at any time. One parent did discuss listening to her child read. Four parents were active in their young child's play or engaged in play with the child; four parents were not observed playing with their child(ren) nor was there parental supervision of the child when playing was observed. At times when parents were required to be supervising their children, children were observed to be running around the common area, going in and out, and climbing on tables and chairs. During these observations children were seen interacting freely with others in the shelter. Lack of supervision had effects on the young child(ren)'s behavior; which led to negative behaviors displayed by the children throughout the shelter.

Families were required to eat meals together while the children were not in school. Regular observations were made of seven of the families eating dinner together. Observations included family communication and affection, especially between parent and child. Three of the parents spent time having conversations with their child(ren); while five of the parents communicated through short verbal directions or did not communicate with their child(ren). Parents were also observed yelling and making negative comments towards the young child(ren). Affection, such as hugs and kisses, was observed frequently in three of the families. Restrictions, harsh tones, and general disapproval were observed with five of the families. Verbal and nonverbal communication affected the young children living in the shelter. When interviewing the young children, single word responses to questions were common with all but two of the children. During observations, single word responses were also common from child to parent. In interviews with the young children, all the children stated an interest in learning. Nine children were interviewed. Three of the nine attended school, another three participated in an early childhood program, and the last three children stayed at the shelter. All of the children exhibited an inability to engage in conversation during the interview questions and they all were easily distracted.

Through interviews and observations, research verified that moving into the homeless shelter affected the young children participating in this study. Parents interviewed described behavioral changes that occurred with their children; issues of anger and anxiety were raised as a result of being homeless. A behavior change was noticed by all participating parents. Observations and interviews on parent–child interactions and communication revealed effects on homeless children's behavior and vocabulary.

Conclusion

The basis for conducting this study was: (1) to understand reasons families with young children become homeless; (2) become aware of beneficial resources available to families and their perceptions of the resources; (3) and the developmental effects that homeless living situations can have on young children. Conclusions were assembled based on themes that emerged from the observations and the interviews conducted for the research study. Reasons for homelessness that emerged from the parent interviews; themes included: unhappy childhoods, young pregnancies, multiple children, failure to complete schooling, drug or substance abuse, paternal abandonment, and unemployment. These factors were considered to be the cause of homelessness and reasons for continual homelessness resulting in an inability to leave a homeless lifestyle. These factors are consistent with research conducted by Swick (2008).

By interviewing the parents and observing the family interactions it became apparent that particular resources were beneficial to the families with young children. Overall the interviews revealed that the parents felt positively about the resources the shelter provided. The shelter provided very individual and specific resources to the clients thus ensuring their clients' needs and goals were met. However, there were some resources lacking. There is a need to develop more resources that engage young children in learning. Another needed resource is educational support for parents with young children.

Interviews with the parents and children as well as observations of family interactions and their ways of communicating revealed that moving into the homeless shelter affected the young children. Parents described behavioral changes in their children; such as anger and anxiety. Observations and interviews also revealed that homeless children's vocabulary is underdeveloped. Living in the shelter affected the development of the young children.

In conclusion, common themes emerged from the families that participated in this study, participants shared similarities in understanding the circumstances that led to homelessness and to the shelter as well as expressing responsibility for the actions that led them to homelessness. Other similarities involved setting goals and reporting a strong support system. However, observations proved that families still struggled in understanding the basic needs of their children. It also seemed that parents

did not fully understand the importance of early education and intervention. The study validates the importance of educating families of young children who are homeless as well as the importance of early childhood educators developing an awareness of ways to support children in a homeless situation (Powers-Costello and Swick 2008).

Implications

Research suggested that parents and young children were affected by homelessness and found common themes which occurred throughout the parents' reasons for being homeless, their perception of resources, and their perceptions of themselves and their children. Early childhood educators know the value of understanding the young child's background story and know the importance of providing care and support to the entire family. By knowing why families with young children become homeless, the early childhood educator becomes aware of the families circumstances. This information can only help the early childhood educator in supporting the family as well as educating the whole child while meeting his or her needs.

Not all homeless families are part of a working program. Many homeless families with young children are unaccounted for and available resources are limited. Swick and Williams suggested three key strategies for early childhood educators to remember when working with homeless families, no matter their current location: (1) encourage the family to access education and counseling to address the challenges of their situation; (2) support the family with resources and help empower them; and (3) involve the family in learning ways to promote healthy lifestyles (2006). Any early childhood educator who is aware of the family with young children's situation can be essential in ensuring that the family feels supported and empowered.

It is vital that early childhood educators are aware that homelessness affects young children and their development. Developmental delays, such as below average vocabulary, an inability to focus, or issues of anger and resentment towards life may be present. Early childhood educators can play a crucial role in providing support to these young children as they transition into a public school environment. Therefore, it is important for early childhood educators to be unbiasedly aware of the reasons families with young children become homeless, the resources that are available to these families as well as ways that an educator can be a liaison to resources, and understand the effects that homelessness can have on young children.

Further research should consider looking into the family structures of homelessness and the benefits of engaging activities for young children who are homeless. Research should look into the differences between families with young children who are transient and ones who are not and are living [in] a fixed location, such as a shelter. Early childhood educators also need to be informed on the dynamics of life that lead homeless families into their current predicament, as well as the developmental needs of young children. This information is valuable to help families navigate their own way back out of their homelessness.

References

Gargiulo, R. M. (2006). Homeless and disabled: Rights, responsibilities, and recommendations for serving young children with special needs. *Early Childhood Education Journal, 33* (5), 357–362. doi:10.1007/s10643-006-0067-1.

Karim, K., Tishcler, V., Gregory, P., & Vostanis, P. (2006). Homeless children and parents: Short-term mental health outcome. *International Journal of Social Psychiatry, 52* (5), 447–458. doi: 10.1177/0020764006066830.

Morris, R. I., & Butt, R. A. (2003). Parents' perspectives on homelessness and its effects on the educational development of their children. *The Journal of School Nursing, 19* (1), 43–50. doi: 10.1177/10598405030190010701.

National Law Center on Homelessness and Poverty. (2012). *Some facts on homelessness, housing, and violence against women.* Retrieved from www.nlchp.org.

Obama, B. (2009). *First Presidential press conference.* The East Room: The White House Washington D.C.

Powers-Costello, E., & Swick, K. J. (2008). Exploring the dynamics of teacher perceptions of homeless children and families during the early years. *Early Childhood Education Journal, 36,* 241–245. doi:10.1007/s10643-008-0249-0.

Shaw, E., & Goode, S. (2008). Fact sheet: Vulnerable young children. *The National Early Childhood Technical Assistance Center.* Retrieved from http://www.nectac.org/~pdfs/pubs/nectacfact sheet_vulnerableyoungchildren.pdf.

Swick, K. J. (2005). Helping homeless families overcome barriers to successful functioning. *Early Childhood Education Journal, 33* (3), 195–199. doi:10:1007/s10643-005-0044-0.

Swick, K. J. (2008). The dynamics of violence and homelessness among young families. *Early Childhood Education Journal, 36,* 81–85. doi:10.1007/s10643-007-0220-5.

Swick, K. J. (2010). Responding to the voices of homeless preschool children and their families. *Early Childhood Education Journal, 38,* 299–304. doi:10.1007/s10643-010-0404-2.

Swick, K. J., & Bailey, L. B. (2004). Working with families: Communicating effectively with parents and families who are homeless. *Early Childhood Education Journal, 32* (3), 211–214.

Swick, K. J., & Williams, R. D. (2006). An analysis of Bronfenbrenner's bio-ecological perspective for early childhood educators: Implications for working with families experiencing stress. *Early Childhood Education Journal, 33* (5), 371–378. doi:10.1007/s10643-006-0078-y.

Swick, K. J., & Williams, R. (2010). The voices of single parent mothers who are homeless: Implications for early childhood professionals. *Early Childhood Education Journal, 38,* 49–55. doi:10.1007/s10643-010-0378-0.

The United States Conference of Mayors. (2008). *Hunger and homelessness survey: A status report on hunger and homelessness in America's cities.* Retrieved from http://www.usmayors.org/pressreleases/ documentshungerhomelessnessreport_121208.pdf.

The United States Conference of Mayors. (2009). *U.S. cities see sharp increases in the need for food assistance; decreases in individual homelessness: Mayors issue annual report on hunger, homelessness in cities.* Retrieved from: http://www.usmayors.org/ pressreleases/uploads/RELEASEHUNGERHOMELESSNESS 2009FINALRevised.pdf.

The United States Conference of Mayors. (2011). *Hunger and homelessness survey: A status report of hunger and homelessness in America's cities.* Retrieved from: http:// usmayors.org/pressreleases/uploads/2011-hhreport.pdf.

Torquati, J. C. (2002). Personal and social resources as predictors of parenting in homeless families. *Journal of Family Issues, 23* (4), 463–485. doi:10.177/0192513X02023004001.

Vostains, P., Tischler, V., Cumella, S., & Bellerby, T. (2001). Mental health problems and social supports among homeless mothers and children victims of domestic and community violence. *International Journal of Social Psychiatry, 47* (4), 30–40. doi:10.1177/002076400104700403.

Critical Thinking

1. What factors are contributing to an increase in homeless families in the United States?
2. What are challenges for children, parents, and families in adapting in the face of residential instability and homelessness?
3. What supports are needed by families to prevent homelessness?
4. What supports are needed to ensure child and family wellbeing while homeless?

Create Central

www.mhhe.com/createcentral

Internet References

National Alliance to End Homelessness
www.endhomelessness.org/pages/families

The National Center on Family Homelessness
www.familyhomelessness.org

Article

Prepared by: Patricia Hrusa Williams,
University of Maine at Farmington

The Coming Special Needs Care Crisis

MICHELLE COTTLE

Learning Outcomes

After reading this article, you will be able to:

- Identify the daily challenges experienced by families raising special needs children.

- Explain the concerns and needs of families with special needs children as they become adults.

Eli Toucey has seizures and social issues that make it all but impossible to leave him with a random babysitter. What could really save Hillary Toucey's life is a personal-care attendant to help with her 7-year-old son, Eli. Dark-haired, fair-skinned, and fragile, Eli suffers from a raft of health problems: cerebral palsy, celiac disease, epilepsy, asthma, and what his mom calls "pretty severe" autism.

His speech is "kind of garbled"; he has leg braces and a wheelchair; seizures render him incontinent at night; and he has acute sensory sensitivities. He cannot bear to touch Styrofoam or the paper wrappings on crayons. Loud music sends him into a panic. When his first-grade class took a field trip this Christmas to see The Cajun Nutcracker, "we lasted three minutes," says Toucey.

Eli is extremely attached to his mother. Toucey spends as much time with him as possible, but since her divorce, the 32-year-old Louisianan has been attending nursing school in the hopes of escaping her hand-to-mouth existence. When her husband left in November 2009 (two weeks before their 10th anniversary and four days after Toucey had surgery for a thyroid tumor), he took the car with him. Toucey isn't sure when she'll be able to afford another one.

Eli's seizures and social issues make it all but impossible to leave him with a random babysitter. "There's only a handful of people he can be with," says Toucey. Having one of the state's personal-care attendants (PCAs) come in for 30 hours a week would make a world of difference: the attendant could take him to therapy, help him practice life skills like brushing his teeth and showering, watch him while Toucey studied. Maybe then she could give more attention to her other kids: 11-year-old Jonah, himself diagnosed with Asperger's, who cries easily and doesn't have many friends; and Charlotte, "a perfectly healthy, wonderful, brilliant" 9-year-old who her mom fears will fall through the cracks. "I feel horrible," says Toucey. "I really have to carve out time for her." Toucey has been told that the PCA bureaucracy can take "forever," and she calls the agency constantly to make sure the process hasn't stalled. Taking care of the essentials is pretty much all she can handle these days. Says Toucey matter-of-factly, "I have no life."

Now and again, the spotlight falls on the challenges of raising special-needs children. In 2008 Sarah Palin captured public attention with her son Trig, who has Down syndrome. This election cycle, Rick Santorum did so with heartbreaking stories about 3-year-old Bella, who suffers from Trisomy 18. Dramatic parenting moments often take the spotlight: stories of diagnosis, acute health crises, surprise breakthroughs.

But for most parents, it's the day-to-day stuff that consumes them: the hours of therapy, the doctor visits, the financial pressures, and the grinding anxiety that comes with it all. It is a rough, often isolating road. And one that promises to become even more challenging as our society enters a new, more complicated era of caregiving. That era is coming in part because many of the medical and social advances that have improved the lives of special-needs individuals have also increased the burden of caring for them. For instance, people with Down syndrome were once lucky to survive to age 30; today, the average lifespan is 55. This presents parents (and society more broadly) with the challenge of somehow providing for an adult child decades after their own deaths, a situation complicated by the fact that the Down population develops Alzheimer's at a rate of 100 percent, typically in their 40s or 50s.

Then there is the 800-pound gorilla in the room: autism. In late March, the Centers for Disease Control issued an estimate that 1 in 88 children now fall on the autism spectrum. While debate rages over the roots of the "epidemic," this swelling population is placing increasing strains on our health-care, education, and social-services systems. A study released last month put the annual cost of autism in the U.S. at $126 billion, more than triple what it was in 2006. The bulk of those expenses are for adult care. Geraldine Dawson, chief science officer for the advocacy group Autism Speaks, calls the situation "a public-health emergency." And if you think things are tough now, she cautions, just wait until autistic teens start aging out of the education system over the next few years. "We as a nation are not prepared."

Saya Barkdoll doesn't remember much about the meeting at which a grim-faced neurosurgeon told her that the kindest thing to do was to let her newborn daughter die. The baby, Taylor, had been born with multiple malformations, and her prognosis was grim. "They took us into this room—it was really intense, with about 20 doctors and nurses—to show us the result of this MRI," recalls the 32-year-old massage therapist. "It was not good. They sat us down and drew us pictures. They were basically saying Taylor had little to no brain mass."

"I didn't believe them," says Barkdoll. "I had not even held her yet, but I could see life in her." Her girlish voice takes on a hard edge: "We fired that neurosurgeon."

Seven years later, Taylor is an outgoing first-grader thriving at her local public school in Silver Springs, Md. She's big into dress-up, Monster High dolls, and Taylor Swift. And though the little girl's health remains delicate and she can neither run nor write clearly, Taylor suffers no cognitive delays. "She's totally there," Barkdoll beams.

Getting Taylor this far, however, has exacted a steep toll on her mom. For the first few years, Barkdoll did nothing but tend to her daughter as Taylor underwent multiple surgeries and extensive therapy. Barkdoll and Taylor's dad, Kevin, originally opted not to marry so as not to risk a combined household income that could jeopardize their daughter's government benefits. By the time Taylor was 3, the relationship had crumbled under the strain of constant caregiving. "We lost sight of each other," says Barkdoll sadly.

It is perhaps unsurprising that the pressures of parenting special-needs children prove too much for many couples. There is a commonly cited statistic that the divorce rate among the parents of autistic children is 80 percent. (Toucey mentioned it during our talk.) Recent studies have debunked this figure, yet it persists among parents because it feels so true. "Based on my and my friends' experience, that stat makes complete sense," asserts journalist Hannah Brown, the mom of a teenage boy with autism and the author of a new novel, *If I Could Tell You*, about the challenges of parenting autistic children. Of her son's condition, she says, "I tried to fight it, but it completely took over my life." Brown recalls that when she and her husband split up, she was initially embarrassed to tell the staff at her son's school. As it turned out, she chuckles, "they were really good at dealing with it because they deal with it all the time!"

Even when marriages survive, such long-term caregiving can have a corrosive impact on parents' well-being. Research indicates that the mothers of special-needs children have higher stress levels and poorer health than other parents. One 2009 study found that the mothers of older autistic children had levels of the stress-related hormone cortisol similar to those found in combat soldiers and sufferers of post-traumatic stress disorder.

Part of the problem is that the experience is so isolating. Not only are parents overwhelmed by the practical matters of caregiving, they often have a tough time relating to people with "normal" children. "When people call you and are like, 'Oh, I'm so stressed out, my plans for Disney are falling through, blah blah blah,' I can't relate to that," says Toucey. "I'm like, 'My kid stopped eating three weeks ago and is on a liquid diet, and we're wondering if we're going to have to put a feeding tube in him.'"

For parents whose children have behavioral problems, the situation can be even trickier. "When my son was younger and his behavior less manageable, people didn't invite us over that much," says Brown. "And I can't really blame them."

The arrival of a special-needs child brings an onslaught of warnings about risks and limitations rather than the usual fantasies of a baby's limitless promise. "You receive an overwhelming amount of information, and most of it is talking about everything that may go wrong," says Rep. Cathy McMorris Rodgers, whose 4-year-old son, Cole, has Down syndrome. Soon after Cole's delivery, the doctor briefed the Washington state congresswoman and her husband on Cole's increased risk for leukemia, hearing difficulties, vision problems, and thyroid issues. "It was a long list," she says, and more than a little dispiriting.

Rodgers colleague, Mississippi Rep. Gregg Harper, faced a similar litany when his 22-year-old son, Livingston, was diagnosed at age 4 with Fragile X syndrome, the most common inherited mental disability. But the couple pushed on. "We threw away a lot of the stuff and said, 'We're not going to accept that,'" says Harper's wife, Sidney.

Like many parents of special-needs children, Sidney found herself swallowed up by her child's condition. "Your whole life revolves around figuring out what to do to help him," she says. Quitting her nursing job, Sidney drove Livingston to endless therapy sessions (with his infant sister, Maggie, in tow), enrolled him in an early-intervention program, and put him in a mothers-day-out class to help his socialization. Told that Livingston would never swim or ride a bike, his mom signed him up for swim lessons and literally strapped him to a specially outfitted bicycle until he could ride like a pro. "The more they told me he wouldn't do something, the more I took him to do it," she says.

Both Harpers get misty-eyed talking about their son's achievement. "Our goal was to have him graduate from high school," says Sidney. "That was it: get him through the 12th grade." Today, Livingston is enrolled in a pilot program at Mississippi State University designed for students with intellectual disabilities. Gushes the congressman: "He's living in a dorm, eating in the cafeteria, going to classes. He's living the life!"

And yet . . . for all Livingston's progress, his future remains a question mark. The hope is that after two or three years at college, he can find some sort of job (he has experience working at a family friend's restaurant) and, with a little luck and more oversight, live basically on his own. But as his father softly acknowledges, "We don't know what the long term is."

Part of what makes special-needs parenting so daunting is that the load often does not lighten with time—that golden day when one's child is more or less self-sufficient never arrives. In fact, many parents report that the school years are by far the easiest. Autism Speaks' Dawson says she frequently hears the shift out of school described as "falling off a cliff, because so few services are available after you exit high school." In the wake of high school, she says, about 40 percent of these young adults have no activity outside the home, and the same percentage have no social activity.

Finding appropriate housing for an adult child with special needs is one of the biggest challenges. Residential facilities are in short supply, even for the well off and well connected. Just ask Rep. Pete Sessions. The Texas Republican has an 18-year-old son, Alex, with Down syndrome, who attends 10th grade at a special school in Dallas. Alex will never be able to live on his own, says Sessions, and the programs for young adults with Alex's needs tend to be full and/or prohibitively expensive. Instead, the congressman hopes to "cobble together" an unofficial group home with a few other families—an increasingly popular choice. "Generally what happens is a group of parents who all have the same needs get together and buy a community house or find an apartment," Sessions explains. "Alex can have a bright, bright future," he says hopefully.

For her part, Hillary Toucey assumes she will be Eli's caregiver for the rest of her life—and she hates to think about what will happen when she's gone. "It's very scary what the future holds," she says. "Right now my plan is to be around as long as possible and to save as much money as possible."

Maybe a little later, when she's not "struggling just to make ends meet," she will be able to focus more on long-term planning. But for now, she has more pressing concerns, like getting Eli to therapy, keeping an eye on his schooling, trying not to flunk her classes, and, of course, calling to find out when that PCA might arrive. And so she waits—and tries to keep her head above water.

Critical Thinking

1. Why does the author of the article believe there is a special needs care crisis on the horizon?

2. What do you think is the hardest part of having a child with special needs when they are young? How might the challenges be different as children grow older and enter adulthood?

3. What types of supports are needed for families with special needs children across the lifespan?

Create Central

www.mhhe.com/createcentral

Internet References

Federation for Children with Special Needs
www.fcsn.org

Family Caregiver Alliance National Center on Caregiving
http://caregiver.org

Article

Prepared by: Patricia Hrusa Williams,
University of Maine at Farmington

Family Members' Informal Roles in End-of-Life Decision Making in Adult Intensive Care Units

JILL R. QUINN, RN, PhD, CS-ANP ET AL.

Learning Outcomes

After reading this article, you will be able to:

- Understand the types of decisions that need to be made when a family member is critically ill.

- Identify the different formal and informal roles family members take in the decision making process.

- Explain how family dynamics are influenced when someone is critically ill.

Background To support the process of effective family decision making, it is important to recognize and understand informal roles that various family members may play in the end-of-life decision making process.

Objective To describe some informal roles consistently enacted by family members involved in the process of end-of-life decision making in intensive care units.

Methods Ethnographic study. Data were collected via participant observation with field notes and semistructured interviews on 4 intensive care units in an academic health center in the mid-Atlantic United States from 2001 to 2004. The units studied were a medical, a surgical, a burn and trauma, and a cardiovascular intensive care unit.

Participants Health care clinicians, patients, and family members.

Results Informal roles for family members consistently observed were primary caregiver, primary decision maker, family spokesperson, out-of-towner, patient's wishes expert, protector, vulnerable member, and health care expert. The identified informal roles were part of families' decision making processes, and each role was part of a potentially complicated family dynamic for end-of-life decision making within the family system and between the family and health care domains.

Conclusions These informal roles reflect the diverse responses to demands for family decision making in what is usually a novel and stressful situation. Identification and description of these informal roles of family members can help clinicians recognize and understand the functions of these roles in families' decision making at the end of life and guide development of strategies to support and facilitate increased effectiveness of family discussions and decision making processes.

Health care clinicians in settings such as intensive care units (ICUs) are part of an institutional social system and are linked through a variety of relationships. They fill formal roles (eg, nurse, physician), exercise rights and privileges, and are expected to discharge obligations and responsibilities in conformity with established values, norms, and rules for behavior.[1] Similarly, persons in a family comprise a small social system; they function in a different sociocultural domain. They occupy formal roles (eg, mother, son), exercise rights and privileges, and discharge obligations and responsibilities in conformity with established family values, norms, and rules for behavior. When a member of a family becomes a patient in the ICU, members of these 2 domains come into dynamic interaction with each other. Family members are often involved in decision making for withdrawal of life-sustaining treatment.[2]

Sometimes a family member has been named the legally designated surrogate end-of-life decision maker (health care proxy or agent) for an ICU patient who has lost capacity; this formal role has been studied extensively.[3–8] Although 1 family member is asked or expected to be the "voice" for the patient by clinicians involved with the patient's care, often several family members become involved in the process of end-of-life decision making. Under these circumstances, the complexity of the end-of-life decision making process can escalate. This increased complexity not only affects the level of tension associated with end-of-life decision making, but also the satisfaction of family members involved.[9,10] To understand and support the process of effective family decision making, it is important to understand the informal roles that various family members may play in the end-of-life decision making process.

The findings reported here are part of a larger study of the sociocultural contexts for end-of-life decision making in ICUs.[11] In an earlier article,[11] we focused on variation in cultures of different ICUs related to end-of-life decision making; the focus of this article, that emerged from the data, is on the various informal family roles that are expected of and engaged in by family members during end-of-life decision making in an ICU.

Formal family roles are not culturally defined to address every circumstance, or to accommodate the personal characteristics of families and their individual members. Families functioning in an ICU context are not in a usual setting for family life. Informal roles emerge in the context of situational demands and describe how people actually behave in particular situations, rather than how they are expected to behave.[12] Informal roles can reflect responses to the common situational demands of any small system, including families, and a number of these roles have been previously identified. They include the scapegoat, who may be seen as the problem when negative emotions threaten the system, and the deviant, whose behavior helps clarify system boundaries by challenging norms.[13] The emergence of informal roles of clinicians specific to the developing small system of the health care team also has been studied.[14]

Study of informal role behavior is particularly useful in the situation of family members in the ICU because family members have no agreed-upon normative "script" for their behavior. Informal roles emerge in this context to help fill the gaps in how family members respond to the novel challenge of end-of-life decision making.[15–18] Recognizing and understanding the informal roles that family members may play in this setting can help guide clinicians in their strategies for working with family members in end-of-life decision making.

Design and Methods

This ethnographic study was prospective. Data were collected on 4 ICUs in an academic health center in the mid-Atlantic United States from 2001 to 2004. The units studied were a medical ICU, a surgical ICU, a burn and trauma ICU, and a cardiovascular ICU.

The university institutional review board for human subjects protection approved the study. All interviewed participants signed informed consent forms. A full description of the study design has already been published.[11]

Participants

Participants included health care clinicians, patients, and patients' family members interviewed in relation to specific cases or in general on end-of-life decision making. When possible, we interviewed clinicians and patients or family members involved in the same situation. If decision making continued for several days, participants were approached for another interview to assess changes and explore questions raised by field observations and earlier interviews. The total number of interviews conducted was 157, with 130 participants. The interviews were with the following categories of

participants: 46 interviews with 30 physicians; 60 interviews with 48 nurses; 13 interviews with 10 other providers such as clergy, social worker, ethicist, and pharmacist; 4 interviews with 4 patients; and 34 interviews with 38 family members. Field notes were included in the analysis, along with recordings from 22 family meetings.[11]

Methods

A 6-member research team used participant observation, field notes, and semistructured interviews to examine the end-of-life decision making process from different participants' perspectives. The semistructured interviews were audiotaped and lasted from 15 to 60 minutes. For this analysis, we focused on interview questions specific to the participation of family members, including questions related to their relationships with the patient, with other family members, and with health care clinicians; their involvement in the decision making; and problems or disagreements related to the decision making process. Information from the medical record was used to identify some circumstances of decision making, for example, the patient's condition and availability of advance directives.

Procedure

Data were collected for approximately 5 hours a day, 5 to 7 days a week for 7 months on each unit sequentially (>700 hours per unit). Once a potential end-of-life decision making situation was identified, the attending physician was asked for permission for a research team member to contact the patient and/or the patient's family. Data collection began as soon as possible. Patients were followed up by the research team until the patient's death or discharge from the ICU.

Data Analysis

All the tapes were transcribed verbatim and reviewed for accuracy. Transcribed corrected interviews, family meetings, field notes, and chart data were dated and entered into the ATLAS.ti program.[19] Analysis, using an ethnographic approach,[20,21] began at the time of the first observation and continued throughout the study.

Small group and family dynamics theories[12,13,14] informed the understanding of family members' informal roles in end-of-life decision making in ICUs that were identified in data analysis. In the analysis for this article, we used data coded as "Roles-Family," which was defined as various key roles that family members played in end-of-life decision making. This general code was generated in our early analysis and subsequently was divided into subcodes for the specific informal roles of family members in end-of-life decision making that consistently emerged as data analysis progressed.

Results

Eight informal roles that family members engaged in during the end-of-life decision making process in these ICU settings were identified: primary caregiver, primary decision maker, family spokesperson, out-of-towner, patient's wishes expert, protector, vulnerable member, and health care expert.

The Primary Caregiver

If family caregiving was involved before ICU admission, the primary caregiver was a role of the family member who had spent the most time caring for the patient before hospitalization. One spouse said:

> After she had the stroke I took care of her naturally. I'm her husband. I did everything for her or whatever. I made sure that she's had therapy . . . I mean, I've looked out for her best care the best I could. I don't know . . .

When a loved one was admitted to the ICU, the primary caregiver was confronted with the reality that it was no longer possible for him or her to care for the ill family member. This previously important role was relinquished in the hospital setting. The same spouse explained:

> "I'm using his [doctor's] judgment [now]. That's why I brought her. I can't take care of her. I can't— I've gotta use their judgment . . ."

The primary caregiver often experienced great angst over relinquishing this role to hospital personnel. Often clinicians expected a quick shift of the primary caregiver into the role of primary decision maker for treatment decisions in the ICU. A family member of another patient stated:

> He [doctor] did say go with the way you feel but he also said if that was my wife or my daughter, I would remove life support, and I said but I can't do that. Something in my heart is saying we've got to give her more time.

The Primary Decision Maker

As others[3,7,22] have described, the role of the primary decision maker emerges in families as a response to the demands for surrogate end-of-life decision making. Sometimes a family member fulfilling this role was formally designated (eg, in the patient's advance directive). Whether this had occurred or not, ICU clinicians sought 1 individual to become the primary decision maker, a family role viewed by clinicians as central to the end-of-life decision making task when the patient was incapacitated. As 1 social worker described this role:

> Probably the people I work with the most in these situations are the decision makers, you know, the primary people in the family that are there the most and taking the lead and initiative to make the decisions that provide the care. Often families had multiple decision makers rather than 1 primary decision maker as preferred by the clinicians.

The primary decision maker frequently conversed with other family members in the decision making process, and the burden of decision making could be shared informally among family members. Family language around decision making often contained "we" as the referent, reflecting this shared decision making process. A striking example from the field notes illustrates this process of sharing in the decision making and in the decision itself. The family acted in concert to support the primary decision maker.

> [The physician] gets the DNR [do not resuscitate] order sheet out and goes over the entire form with the family. He then asks which one is the proxy. [A daughter] says she is; he asks her to sign. [Another daughter] says, "We all want to sign, we don't want only [named proxy] to feel like she's the one who did this." [Two sons] immediately agree; and [one daughter] hugs [the other daughter] who is teary. [The physician] says there is room for everyone to sign. They all sign the form.

If multiple decision makers were not acceptable to clinicians or family members, either 1 clear primary decision maker emerged or the primary decision maker's role was contested.

On the other hand, discussion could become too inclusive, as shown in the following example from a family meeting, where family friends exerted their own opinion in the decision making process.

> [Friend of family]: Maybe he [patient] won't do it [recover] as quickly as a 20-year-old. But they want their father, and she wants her husband. And that's what we should be focusing on, rehabilitation, getting him up and getting him going.
>
> Physician: Well, I think it's always important and the thing I was asking [his wife] about. I think there's nobody in the whole world better able to speak to the desire of her husband than she. And I think sometimes families forget that what they really want is what's best for their loved one.

Family Spokesperson

One informal family role, family spokesperson, was encouraged by clinicians because of the clinician's wish to address families' needs for information efficiently and to facilitate the decision making processes. Despite the complexity of many families' internal decision making processes, many clinicians preferred to deal with 1 family spokesperson, as reflected in the following staff quotation: "The problem often is that we do not have a family spokesperson but a spokesgroup." The nurse manager of 1 ICU spoke of the formal process expected on their unit to be followed to identify the family spokesperson.

> What we ask is . . . there be a family spokesperson that we can give information to, and we ask that that family spokesperson disseminate the information to the other family members . . . if somebody calls in, it needs to be the spokesperson. . . .

At least 3 ICUs had this role formally identified in the visitor brochure they provided, which included visitation policy and asked for an individual name with contact information to be placed in the medical record and care plan. Some units were inconsistent with identifying and documenting an individual family member for this role. Further, although this was constructed on several units as a formal role for 1 family member, we found that some families would informally evolve this role to include other members. Although the tendency was for the hospital staff to combine the roles of spokesperson and primary decision maker, it was observed that a family member who acted as a spokesperson with hospital staff was not necessarily the primary decision maker (eg, an adult child as spokesperson for a parent who was making final decisions).

Families, especially when there was disagreement among members, often were reluctant to identify just 1 member as the sole spokesperson. Regardless of whether the unit had a formal process of identifying the spokesperson, clinicians and staff tried to seek one out when a problem arose. However, at times, we observed that any family member who was convenient, at the bedside or in a visitor waiting area, was approached by a clinician and offered information or asked questions about the patient. This clinician's behavior conveyed a message that any family member present could be a spokesperson, but this was also seen as contrary to the formal rule regarding identification of 1 family spokesperson. One nurse expressed this situation well:

> Some nurses will talk to all—a lot of different family members about what's going on. That makes it very, very difficult. I think . . . that it's very important to have it be [the] family spokesperson. Just 1 person should be the proxy to whom that information is going. . . .

The Out-of-Towner

Complex family dynamics of decision making were apparent through other informal roles of family members that were identified. One such role was the out-of-towner, a family member who had not been involved in the daily care giving and may not have been engaged during the early ICU stay and, therefore, often brought a different perspective to the in-town family's end-of-life decision making discussions. End-of-life decisions often were put on hold until in-town family members could communicate with out-of-town relatives and they could be part of the discussion about the patient's condition and the status of decision making thus far. Because they were from out of town, they often also had time limits on their ability to be physically present in the situation and, if present, might be eager to have a firm decision made before their departure. Consequently, their involvement added complexity to the decision making process and could create conflict within the patient's family and with clinicians. An example of this is a brother who described his perspective on his out-of-town sister's role in decision making about their father:

> My sister was—you have to take a lot of things into consideration. She is the child from out of town. She is the one that feels that she has to have this whole thing fixed before she can go home. She is the one that doesn't have the time to wait it out. This illness is a wait out. . . . She is trying to get this whole thing fixed before she goes home. She has to go home and I understand that. She just has to leave and trust that it's gonna happen correctly. . . .

> Especially where family members may not all be in the same city. So, they have not seen mom or dad, [and] you will be in a family meeting and, the one [local] daughter will say, "Look, I'm with Mom all the time; I know what she wants. You see her twice a year. How do you know what she wants?"

This example illustrates another emergent family informal role related to decision making, when the family had not achieved consensus about what the dying family member's wishes might have been as a guide to that decision making.

The Patient's Wishes Expert

Being primary decision maker was difficult, but family members were much more likely to come together in support of a primary decision maker and collectively to feel confident they were following the patient's wishes in the context of known preferences of the patient. In the context of unknown preferences, decision making was often much more difficult for the primary decision maker, and other family members were much more open to differing interpretations of what the patient would have wanted. The patient's wishes experts were family members who claimed that their interpretations of the patients' wishes were the correct interpretations.

> [Son]: You have to listen to everything my father says . . . it's like his living will. I read it, and I know what my mother and sister said, and I said wait a minute, my father doesn't want to be intubated, I understand that. Okay, if he is brain dead, he doesn't want to be intubated; but he is alive, he can get better. My father wants to live; he is afraid to die. This is something that has been on his mind for 10 years.

When this role was enacted by several family members with different interpretations of the patient's wishes, end-of-life decision making was often prolonged and inconclusive.

The Protector and the Vulnerable Family Member

In this situation, a family member who might typically be expected to be the primary decision maker was viewed as vulnerable for some reason, and another family member asserted family decision making authority to protect the vulnerable family member. Commonly, these paired roles emerged when adult children believed they needed to protect an older parent (eg, spouse of the ill family member) from the stress of end-of-life decision making. An example was a daughter who was concerned about her mother being expected to decide about withdrawal of mechanical ventilation from her husband, resulting in end of life too quickly for the mother to handle emotionally. The daughter stated, "Taking him off the respirator is only going to change things by hours, and I think that that would be way too painful for my mom given the rapidity of this event." If the vulnerable member did not accept that role, it caused family conflict that made the decision making process more difficult and delayed the decision making process.

Occasionally, patients had at least some capacity for decision making. However, in such circumstances they could be identified by family members as the vulnerable member. The quotation below is about a dying woman who was intubated but aware. Her husband had been very involved in the decision making and wanted her included in any decision about reintubation if extubation failed. However, some negative information about her condition, known to her husband, had been withheld from her at the husband's request. He questioned whether she would be able to make a decision about reintubation, especially when she did not have all of the relevant clinical information.

> [Husband]: I'm trying to—I'm trying to think if her choice would be a real choice, to her. Because I would be okay with whatever her choice was, so I'm trying to think, would it be a real choice? Would she know that that's a real choice and her deciding, and it might be . . . because she doesn't like that and maybe she had enough of it and she doesn't want it. Or maybe she'd say, "Yup, if I start to lose it, put it back in."

Even though in this rare ICU situation, the patient had the capacity to participate, her protector family member saw her as vulnerable, remained in charge of the family end-of-life decision making process, and asked clinicians to withhold some information about her condition from her.

Another field note observation illustrates the patient's wishes expert and the paired set of family informal roles of protector and vulnerable member roles occurring in the context of a clinician looking for consent to perform a procedure. He said:

> They [mother and father, father is the patient] have been married for 52 years. He [father] never let her [mother] make a decision in 52 years. You are gonna let her [mother] cut her teeth on this one? No, she is not cutting her teeth on life or death. I'll do that. I will give mom my feelings on that and I'm not gonna subject her [mother] to making that decision. I think I know what he [father] wants, so that's what I told her [mother].

In this example, the son claims his own expertise in knowing his father's preferences (or wishes). He also was prepared to protect his mother from having to make a life and death decision about her husband. He saw his mother as vulnerable because, in his view, she had never made decisions during 52 years of marriage.

The Health Care Expert

The health care expert was a family member who could influence decision making in the family system through a claim of clinical expertise by virtue of some connection to the health care domain (eg, nurses, physicians). Family members and sometimes clinicians viewed this role as one that had the potential to facilitate the decision making process. The health care expert might use resources to bridge the gap between the 2 domains, whereas family members who lacked this expertise struggled more with the

situation and with end-of-life decision making. Family members often relied heavily on the family health care expert for direction in the end-of-life decision making process. The quotation that follows illustrates the role of the health care expert, in this case a daughter who was a licensed practical nurse:

> [Daughter]: My brothers and sisters never thought of the antibiotics and you know, I think sometimes you have a little more knowledge. Whether you understand things better, which is why they [my family members] put me down as the spokesperson. Which is why she put me down as her [proxy]. . . .

Clinicians' reactions to family health care experts could be mixed: on the one hand, sometimes they were viewed as able to understand medical situations and expected to be "reasonable" about the treatment decisions or more in line with the clinicians' way of thinking. An example of this is expressed by a registered nurse:

> I think her mother deferred to her [daughter] the physician. . . . It is definitely nice when the family is so knowledgeable about what is going on that, you know, they realize as you realize, at almost the same time, that this is . . . that CPR would be futile.

Other family health care experts challenged the thinking and recommendations of the ICU clinicians, as well as the quality of care that their family members were receiving, stimulating conflict between the family and clinicians. A good example of this from the field notes is when a group of nurses talked one day about a patient's son-in-law, who was a physician. On the phone he had yelled at one of the nurses and then had hung up. From the nurse's perspective, he had conveyed that the nurses were all incompetent. When family health care experts did not agree with the clinicians, there was an element of surprise and frustration expressed, as this resident physician viewed it: "Granted that her son-in-law is a physician, but we are still not getting through."

The situation got even more complicated when more than 1 family member could claim a role as health care expert, and the different "experts" were not in agreement. Family members could also "call in" friends who were health care clinicians to play the role of health care expert for the family or some subgroup of the family; again, calling in multiple experts could complicate the decision making process.

Discussion

As illustrated in these results, the identified informal roles were intricately tied to the family's decision making process, and each helped to create a potentially complicated family dynamic for end-of-life decision making within the family system, and between the family and health care domains. In their expectations for end-of-life decision making, clinicians, on the other hand, often pushed for 1 family member to be both primary decision maker and family spokesperson to facilitate communication and decision making. However, our findings suggest that this often did not happen and made the process more complicated than desired by clinicians.

These 8 informal roles did not all emerge in every family. More than 1 role might be assumed by a single family member (eg, the out-of-towner could also be the health care expert) or the informal roles might be shared among multiple family members. Whether these informal roles facilitated decision making or escalated family conflict or family/clinician conflict depended on the family context (ie, family history and culture around difficult decision making).

In situations where other family members interacted to support a single member both as primary decision maker and family spokesperson, consensus within families was more easily achieved. In other families where there was less cohesion, as more family members became involved there was a greater proliferation of informal roles in the decision making process, potentially more conflict and disagreement, and a more difficult time with making end-of-life decisions. When no consensus was reached among family members around end-of-life decision making, informal roles might be used to leverage a decision in a way that advanced the role of the person in the family system, for example by claiming to be a protector or health care expert.

Jockeying for position in the family system can be viewed as a consequence of the removal, by life-threatening illness, of a member of the system and a scramble for a new status in that altered system. Thus, for example, with the removal of an ill parent, adult children might move to claim status and authority in the system previously held by that parent.

In either circumstance of cohesive or conflict-prone family decision making processes, ICU clinicians who attempted direct communication through identification of a family spokesperson often found that there was a "spokesgroup" of family members playing differing informal roles but all wanting input into the decision making process either directly or indirectly. As others who have studied family involvement with end-of-life decision making have found, the decision to withdraw or withhold treatment generally includes multiple family members,[23] and communication needs for families often go unmet.[9,24,25]

Recognizing and understanding the roles that family members play within the family unit during critical decision making is important in facilitating more effective interaction and consensus among family members and reducing conflict among family and clinicians. Interventions limiting conflict and strengthening family supports should be a major goal, but the manner in which this is done needs to incorporate the cultural differences of families and the expertise of clinicians. Family meetings with clinicians, when held, can make these complex roles involved in family end-of-life decision making visible.

Family meetings can also reduce conflict between clinicians and family members regarding frustration with not having 1 person as family spokesperson and/or primary decision maker.[25] More recently, emphasis has increased on conducting effective family meetings within critical care as well as use of other services, such as palliative care services, that may be called to consult if the process of decision making becomes problematic.[26] Awareness of the potentially complicated dynamics associated with some of these family informal role processes may assist clinicians to seek earlier consultation.

Limitations

Although the purpose of qualitative research is not to make broad generalizations but to examine the depth of individual experience in a phenomenon such as end-of-life decision making, this study had some limitations. First the study was conducted in 1 setting, a university medical center, although different types of ICUs were included to capture cultural differences regarding end-of-life decision making among the units.[11] The data were collected some time ago; however, the nature of the data and analyses reported here, as well as the results, concerning informal roles in family decision making processes in critical care situations, are not likely to "age" quickly, as family systems processes such as the decision making processes identified are fundamental to family life. The approach taken to analysis is theoretically informed, drawing on a rich body of theoretical literature related to informal roles in family systems, family crisis responses, and small group functioning, which became relevant as we explored the data.

The presence of the researchers and the process of audiotaping during family meetings and interviews could have influenced the responses. We describe the results only of participants who agreed to participate, although few potential participants who were approached refused to participate. Finally, we do not claim to have exhausted potentially identifiable informal family roles. There may be other informal roles that did not emerge in these data either because we missed them in our analyses, they are infrequent, or they do not play as prominent a role in the end-of-life decision making process.

Conclusions

End-of-life decision making for patients in ICUs involves an intersection of both the health care domain and the family domain. Promoting family responses to end-of-life questions that honor the wishes of the patient requires an understanding of informal family roles such as those observed and described, as well as an awareness of how these roles may be enacted. Strategies should be developed to facilitate smooth resolution of conflicting views and decisions among family members and between clinicians and family members that foster effective decision making processes. Potentially fruitful areas for further exploration include the identification of other important informal family roles that may be less prominent or less frequently portrayed but may be equally important in some end-of-life decision making, and the role of advance directives in family end-of-life decision making processes. A closer examination of family meetings as a way to foster effective family end-of-life decision making and the role of hospital-based palliative care services in supporting effective family end-of-life decision making processes are vital areas for further study.[27]

Notes

Financial Disclosures
1. This study was supported by grants from the National Institutes of Health/National Institute of Nursing Research (RO1NR04940 and 1R15NR012147).

References

1. Breitborde LB. *Rebuttal Essay. Int J Soc Lang.* 1983;39: 161–177.

2. Search Google Scholar Kirchhoff KT, Kowalkowski JA *Current practices for withdrawal of life support in intensive care units. Am J Crit Care.* 2010;19:532–541.

3. Abstract/FREE Full Text Tilden VP, Tolle SW, Nelson CA, et al. *Family decision making to withdraw life-sustaining treatments from hospitalized patients. Nurs Res.* 2001;50:105–115.

4. CrossRefMedline Arnold RM, Kellum J. *Moral justifications for surrogate decision making in the intensive care unit: implications and limitations. Crit Care Med.* 2003;31:S347–S353.

5. CrossRefMedline Berger JT, DeRenzo EG, and Schwartz J. *Surrogate decision making: reconciling ethical theory and clinical practice. Ann Intern Med.* 2008;149:48–53.

6. Medline Evans LR, Boyd EA, Malvar G, et al. *Surrogate decision makers' perspectives on discussing prognosis in the face of uncertainty. Am J Respir Crit Care Med.* 2009;179:48–53.

7. Abstract/FREE Full Text Heyland DK, Cook DJ, Rocker GM, et al. *Decision making in the ICU: perspectives of the substitute decision-maker. Intensive Care Med.* 2003;29:75–82.

8. Medline Luce JM *End-of-life decision making in the intensive care unit. Am J Respir Crit Care Med.* 2010;182:6–11.

9. Abstract/FREE Full Text Radwany S, Albanese T, Clough L, et al. *End-of-life decision making and emotional burden: placing family meetings in context. Am J Hosp Palliat Care.* 2009;26:376–383.

10. Abstract/FREE Full Text Westphal DM, McKee SA. *End-of-life decision making in the intensive care unit: physician and nurse perspectives. Am J Med Qual.* 2009;24:222–228.

11. Abstract/FREE Full Text Baggs JG, Norton SA, Schmitt MH, et al. *Intensive care unit cultures and end-of-life decision making. J Crit Care.* 2007;22:159–168.

12. CrossRefMedline Dunphey DC. *The Primary Group: A Handbook for Analysis and Field Research.* New York, NY: Appleton-Century-Crofts; 1972.

13. Search Google Scholar Mills TM. *The Sociology of Small Groups.* Englewood Cliffs, NJ: Prentice-Hall; 1984.

14. Search Google Scholar Farrell MP, Schmitt MH, and Heinemann GD. *Informal roles and the stages of interdisciplinary team development. J Interprof Care.* 2001;15:281–295.

15. CrossRefMedline Abbott KH, Sago JG, Breen CM, et al. *Families looking back: one year after discussion of withdrawal or withholding of life-sustaining support. Crit Care Med.* 2001;29:197–201.

16. CrossRefMedline Bartels DM, Faber-Langendoen K. *Caring in crisis: family perspectives on ventilator withdrawal at the end of life. Fam Syst Health.* 2001;19:169–176.

17. CrossRef Johnson N, Cook D, Giacomini M, et al. *Towards a "good" death: end-of-life narratives constructed in an intensive care unit. Cult Med Psychiatry.* 2000;24:275–295.

18. CrossRefMedline Norton SA, Tilden VP, Tolle SW, et al. *Life support withdrawal: communication and conflict. Am J Crit Care.* 2003; 12:548–555.

19. Abstract/FREE Full Text *ATLAS.ti: The Knowledge Workbench* [computer program]. Version 5.0. Berlin, Germany: Atlas.ti; 2004.

20. Munhall PL, Boyd CP, and Germain CP. *Ethnography: the method.* In: Munhall PL, Boyd CP, eds. *Nursing Research: A Qualitative Perspective.* New York, NY: National League for Nursing; 1993:237–268.

21. Search Google Scholar Morse JM, Field PA. *Qualitative Research Methods for Health Professionals.* Thousand Oaks, CA: Sage; 1995.

22. Search Google Scholar White DB, Malvar G, Karr J, et al. *Expanding the paradigm of the physician's role in surrogate decision making: an empirically derived framework. Crit Care Med.* 2010;38:743–750.

23. CrossRefMedline Wiegand D. *In their own time: the family experience during the process of withdrawal of life-sustaining therapy. J Palliat Med.* 2008;11:1115–1121.

24. CrossRefMedline Hsieh HF, Shannon SE, Curtis JR. *Contradictions and communication strategies during end-of-life decision making in the intensive care unit. J Crit Care.* 2006;21: 294–304.

25. CrossRefMedline Norton SA, Bowers BJ. *Working toward consensus: providers' strategies to shift patients from curative to palliative treatment choices. Res Nurs Health.* 2001;24:258–269.

26. CrossRefMedline Norton SA, Hogan LA, Holloway RG, et al. *Proactive palliative care in the medical intensive care unit: effects on length of stay for selected high-risk patients. Crit Care Med.* 2007; 35:1530–1535.

27. CrossRefMedline Daly BJ, Douglas SL, O'Toole E, et al. *Effectiveness trial of an intensive communication structure for families of longstay ICU patients. Chest.* 2010;138:1340–1348.

Critical Thinking

1. What are some formal roles that family members take when making decisions about someone who is critically ill? How do you think the decision is made regarding who will formally represent the family?

2. Do you agree with the statement made in the article that health care providers often feel that they "do not have a spokesperson but a spokesgroup?"

3. The study identified a variety of different, informal roles that family members may take on when someone is critically ill. Have you witnessed anyone in your family take on these types of roles or responsibilities?

4. What can be done to support families as they are making important decisions about a critically ill family member?

Create Central

www.mhhe.com/createcentral

Internet References

Family Caregiver Alliance National Center on Caregiving
http://caregiver.org

Hospice Foundation of America
www.hospicefoundation.org

JILL R. QUINN is an associate professor, MADELINE SCHMITT is a professor emerita, SALLY A. NORTON is an associate professor, MARY T. DOMBECK is a professor, and CRAIG R. SELLERS is an associate professor of clinical nursing at the University of Rochester School of Nursing in Rochester, New York. JUDITH GEDNEY BAGGS is a distinguished professor at Oregon Health & Science University School of Nursing in Portland.

Corresponding author: Jill R. Quinn, RN, PhD, CS-ANP, University of Rochester School of Nursing, 601 Elmwood Avenue, Box SON, Rochester, NY 14642 (e-mail: jill_quinn@urmc.rochester.edu).

Acknowledgments—We thank the patients, families, and clinicians who made this study possible. We also thank Dr. Nancy Press for her review of this manuscript.

Article

Prepared by: Patricia Hrusa Williams,
University of Maine at Farmington

Why Do Marriages Fail?

JOSEPH N. DUCANTO

Learning Outcomes

After reading this article, you will be able to:

- Identify some common reasons why couples divorce.
- Consider strategies to decrease the frequency of divorce in the United States.

After 56 years as a divorce lawyer, people may assume that I know a lot about marriage and, therefore, can easily answer the inevitable question "why do marriages fail?" Indeed, a divorce lawyer can relate much about his/her personal observation respecting this issue, anticipating that many will take exception to at least one or more of the following views.

Increased Life Span

I blame medical science for a significantly large percentage of failed marriages! During the past 100 years, the average life span of humans in the Western world has increased nearly 60 percent from the start of the 20th century (average 49 years) to 2010 (average 78 years). This increase alone has had an overpowering impact upon marriage, which is a static institution remaining unchanged from the dawn of time. It remains to be seen what civil union marriage will do to both the state of marriage (now at an all-time low) and the absolute numbers of divorce (without reference to customary marriages—as opposed to civil unions), which have fallen in recent years because of increasing disinterest by the young to legally engage in such relationships.

In past centuries, the young married very young, parallel-ing the onset of puberty, produced numerous children (many of whom died during their infancy), and departed life in their 30's and 40's. Perhaps the greatest love story of all time, Romeo and Juliet, exemplifies this phenomenon with Juliet 14, and Romeo 16, yearning for the nuptial couch. They clearly were not unique in their era, and in many places throughout the world, such early teenage marriages continue as acceptable and are endorsed by cultural principals and religious adherence.

Quite clearly, a marriage duly made "until death do us part," that could be reasonably expected to endure 20 to 25 years at most, is a far different commitment made today, where joint lifespan can see marriages endure for 50, 60, and even 70 years! Clearly, then, medical science, which has so effectively increased the lifespan of people, must bear some responsibility for the proven fact that marriages of long duration enlarge inordinately the number of prospective clients who ultimately find their way to a divorce lawyer's office. Divorce among the "Metamucil Generation" is no longer an unusual event.

Individual Changes Over the Years

Accompanying the incredibly long duration of marriages today is the unhappy fact that married people do not always mature and grow at the same rate and quality over the longer period of years people are married today. She is involved in her career and he is consumed by his occupation. Inevitably—particularly as the kids age and leave home—the parties metamorphose in their interest, attitudes, and aspiration in ways that do not necessarily correlate with the essential unity of the original underlying basis of the marriage. For example, her involvement with professional requirements could create conflicts with the lifestyle adopted over time by him and his colleagues as sports become a passion. Conflict here is inevitable and divorce often a certainty, as neither can abandon the pillars of support each has erected in terms of his or her own individual desires and concerns.

Exacerbation of Pre-Existing Strains

Kids are beautiful and, for many, life would not be worth living without them. Little is said, however, of the disruptive problems that the appearance of children may inflict upon a marriage already experiencing some irritation and doubts. Over my years of practice, I have observed that pre-existing strains in a marriage are strongly exacerbated by additional adverse events which, surprisingly, can often be the appearance of a newborn or, worse, the death of a child, the loss of a job or a business, or the purchase of a new home. Any existing cracks in an otherwise placid marriage will often produce significant fractures when such events occur, thus leading to divorce. These customary strains upon a marriage are intensified when one or both of the parents begin to indulge in escape from drudgery by excessive use of alcohol or drugs, or seek out others to escape from marital unhappiness.

Boredom

Boredom in a relationship is often insidious and corrosive of the marriage bonds. Repetitive behavior, even if initially enjoyed, can soon pale and become irritating. Think, I tell my friends, of eating oatmeal every morning for 40 years and tell me what you believe your reaction would be? Indeed, many marriages are destroyed by boredom and the need or necessity by one of the parties to exit the doldrums of their life for some excitement—any excitement—good or bad—known or unknown.

Life Changes

Virtually nothing has been written relating to the role that menopause plays in leading ultimately to a divorce. Much is known and published that describes the onset and symptoms of menopause in women, which appears around the age of 50 in normal development. With menopause there are numerous psychological and emotional symptoms that present themselves, which can include rapid mood shifts, irritability, and loss of libido.

Many men find these newly-emerging symptoms difficult, and their presence in a wife of many years may lead to emotional and physical withdrawal by both parties. From the female's point of view, many former "quirks" possessed by her husband or supposed personal strengths and long-held opinions may become intolerable during this period, leading to increasing tension and endless arguments between the parties. The husband, if experiencing his wife's coldness or withdrawal altogether from sex, could find easy excuses for infidelity with younger women who "understand and appreciate me" when his wife has failed to do so.

Any meaningful change in the marital relationship coincidentally occurring with the arrival of menopause, such as becoming "empty nesters," a change of occupation or retirement, unemployment, financial instability, plus the unavoidable onset of old age may tip the marital scales toward separation and, inevitably, a mid-life divorce.

Another Man or Woman

The often-supposed "reason" for divorce attributed to the appearance or presence of the other man or woman in the life of one of the partners is simply a symptom of a pre-existing desire to escape the malaise of a moribund relationship. One may seek solace in the other man/woman relationship with the prime purpose of re-injecting life or purpose in an existence that may seem to have become barren. It is not uncommon in my experience that one of the parties to a meretricious relationship will operate with a certainty of detection by the other party, thus motivating the otherwise "innocent" spouse to move for the courthouse door!

Personality Changes

As life goes on, we all undergo personality changes. None of us by age 50 can truthfully believe we are the same person we were at 25. We learn, educate, grow, and change at uneven rates that are heavily dependent upon many variables—including intelligence, receptivity, and intensity of experiences. Uneven growth between spouses is common, and unless great pain is taken to assure continuing effective communication, the marriage can fail. A mother with a high-school education who is housebound for 20 years talking to three-foot-high people over those years may not be expected to maintain a close communion and relationship with an ever-working husband who has acquired several advanced degrees, travels the world over in his occupation, and consorts with the intellectual opinion makers of the world.

Limited Marriage Contract

I have in the past, partially in jest, suggested that there actually be a "marriage contract"—as opposed to a prenuptial one—in which the marriage has a finite term; say five years. At or near the end of that time, the parties are called upon to renew or rewrite their agreement or proceed to divorce. Such a shocking requirement requires a balancing of what is good in the relationship as opposed to that which is destructive. A "time out" to reconstitute the ongoing basis of the marriage is clearly preferable to an inevitable drift toward ending the relationship. Remember, a "civil union" complete written contract is not limited to homosexual relationships, but can be extended to a man/woman relationship that falls outside of the usual bounds of matrimony.

It is imperative, if the marriage is to continue, that both parties commit themselves to a course of re-bonding and enhancement of communication with each other. With kids, it is often difficult but essential that there be frequent "time outs" where a couple can recommit to one another, compare notes so to speak, and plan for their future as a couple in addition to that as a family. A failure to work on the changing nature of a relationship over time is to be confronted by the inescapable fact that the marriage may be dead and, unfortunately, in need of a decent burial!

Critical Thinking

1. With our increased life spans, is it realistic to think that marriages will last "until death do us part?"
2. Of the factors listed as contributing to divorce, which do you see as more important? Why?

3. Given the list of factors that the author states contribute to divorce, what can be done to help couples sustain marriages?

4. What can be done as couples enter marriage to better prepare them for the challenges ahead?

Create Central

www.mhhe.com/createcentral

Internet References

HelpGuide: Children and Divorce
www.helpguide.org/mental/children_divorce.htm

HelpGuide: Divorce and Remarriage
www.helpguide.org/topics/breakup_divorce.htm

Article

Prepared by: Patricia Hrusa Williams,
University of Maine at Farmington

Helping Children Endure Divorce

MARLENE ESKIND MOSES

When in the midst of a divorce, it is understandable for a party to become entrenched in what is felt to be a personal battle and preoccupied with details such as where to live, how to maximize the financial settlement, and how to pay the legal fees. Sometimes, this preoccupation leads to losing sight of what is going on with one's children, who are unquestionably also directly affected by that parent's decision to divorce.

Learning Outcomes

After reading this article, you will be able to:

- Describe the impact of divorce on children.

- Summarize how the parent–child relationship survives divorce.

- Explain how divorce can happen without devastating the children involved.

If the divorce practitioner receives little feedback from a client about the children, it is all too easy to focus exclusively on meeting the client's personal goals with minimal awareness of how doing so will truly affect the client's children. However, it is up to us to actively solicit feedback from our clients about their children and educate our clients about how to help their children navigate the transition. We should remain mindful that our clients' children are "shadow clients,"[1] and we should strive to fine-tune our advice and strategies accordingly.

The Effects of Divorce on Children

There has been an abundance of research concluding that growing up in a single-parent household is less than ideal and can be detrimental to a child's well-being. Even in low-conflict divorces, children can suffer in a myriad of ways. The obvious immediate repercussion is the disruption of life as they have known it. Children not living with both biological parents are more likely to experience psychological struggles and academic problems.[2] Long-term effects of divorce on children can include increased susceptibility to substance abuse. Teenagers with divorced parents are 50 percent more likely to drink alcohol than those with married parents.[3] Children of divorce also are more likely to experience divorces of their own down the road.[4]

Research shows that the effects of divorce on a child depend to some extent on the age of the child at the time of divorce, the child's gender and personality, and the degree of conflict between the parents. Infants may react to changes in parents' energy level and mood by losing their appetite or spitting up more. Preschool-aged children often blame themselves for their parent's divorce, viewing it as the consequence of their own misbehavior. They may regress and exhibit behavior such as bedwetting and may become uncooperative or aggressive. School-aged children are old enough to understand that they are hurting because of their parents' separation. They may feel rejected by the parent who left. It is not uncommon for children in this age group to exhibit psychosomatic symptoms such as headaches or stomachaches. Adolescents may become excessively moody, withdrawn, depressed or anxious. They may favor one parent, blaming the other for the divorce.[5]

Some research even suggests gender differences. Certain studies have found that children raised primarily by a parent of the same sex tend to have greater success adjusting to the divorce than those who are raised primarily by a parent of the opposite sex.[6] Although there is little correlation between the sheer amount of time that divorced fathers spend with their children and those children's overall adjustment, children of divorce whose fathers spend quality time actively engaged in their lives and activities tend to perform better in school and exhibit fewer behavioral problems.[7] Father involvement has been linked to children feeling less at the mercy of the world and more willing to behave responsibly.[8]

The quality of a child's relationship with the primary parent is a particularly strong indicator of the child's successful adjustment following a divorce. It also goes without saying that day-to-day involvement of both parents lets a child know that he or she is loved. This does not mean, however, that an equal or near-equal division of parenting time is necessarily the best option. For instance, preschool-aged children may feel they are being punished when they are moved from one household to another. Older children, too, may dislike this type of arrangement if it intrudes on their daily lives. Some parents with equal or near-equal division of time, or who engage in multiple transfers of the children back and forth in a short period of time, fight more often because they are in constant contact, which in turn causes the children to suffer.[9] A child's well-being is particularly affected by the amount and intensity of conflict between the parents. Marital conflict is associated with increased anxiety and depression, and poorer overall social and academic adjustment in children.[10]

So, how can we use this research to educate our clients with the goal of helping ensure that their children adjust with minimal side-effects to the divorce?

Guidelines for Helping Children

1. *Telling children about the divorce:*

   Ideally, children should be told about the divorce as soon as a definite decision has been made to get divorced. Children need to be told before any changes occur, and they should be informed of the changes to expect, such as moving to a new house or school, or beginning a parenting schedule. If possible, both parents should tell the children together, with the parents agreeing on the details of the explanation ahead of time. It is important to present a united front as much as possible.[11]

   Children are entitled to know why their parents are divorcing, and the reasons given should be simple and honest. Telling children that it is too complicated to explain or that they would never understand the reasons could leave them wondering whether they might be able to change their parents' plans. Blanket reassurances do not always work, and children will likely need an opportunity to talk about why they feel at fault for the divorce, oftentimes on more than one occasion. Parents need to acknowledge the reasons for the child's concerns, such as "Yes, you are right that your father and I do argue about how much time we each feel you should spend on the computer or with friends or watching television, and I can see why this makes you worried that the divorce is your fault." Then, words of reassurance need to follow immediately, such as: ". . . but you didn't cause the breakup . . ." If a child's concerns are not cavalierly dismissed but are instead truly heard and discussed, without the parents becoming defensive or dismissive, the child is more likely to feel assured that indeed he or she was not the cause of the parents' divorce. The child who feels at fault could also feel responsible for fixing the problem. Therefore, children need a clear statement from each parent that they cannot prevent or reverse the divorce.[12] They also need to be reassured that while parents and their children do not always get along, they do not stop loving each other and do not get divorced from each other.[13]

   Finally, it may be tempting to place blame on the other parent for the divorce, but such defensiveness sends a message that the children need to take sides, which only serves to increase their anxiety, guilt and stress.[14]

2. *Encouraging a relationship with the other parent:*

   Because of the inherently adversarial nature of divorce, it may seem counter-intuitive to a litigant not to seek to limit the other parent's time with the children. The "winner" gets the kids, and the "loser" does not. In fact, a better legal strategy may be to encourage and facilitate time and a continuing relationship with the other parent. Tennessee's custody statute requires the court to consider, in making a custody determination, "each parent's past and potential . . . willingness and ability . . . to facilitate and encourage a close and continuing parent–child relationship between the child and both of the child's parents, consistent with the best interest of the child. In determining the willingness of each of the parents . . . to facilitate and encourage a close and continuing parent–child relationship between the child and both of the child's parents, the court shall consider the likelihood of each parent . . . to honor and facilitate court ordered parenting arrangements and rights, and the court shall further consider any history of either parent or any caregiver denying parenting time to either parent in violation of a court order."[15]

   In addition to what the law tells us, social research tells us that children are better off with the influence and presence of both parents in their lives, absent extraordinary circumstances. It is important for both parents to be mindful of this and to strive to create a parenting plan that provides this for their children.

   Hand-in-hand with encouraging and facilitating a meaningful relationship with the other parent is showing respect for the other parent. It is harmful to a child for either parent to make derogatory remarks about the other parent. The child can be made to feel as if he or she is expected to take the side of the parent who is disparaging the other parent. This behavior by a parent violates the statutory standard parenting rights set forth in all Tennessee parenting plans. Such rights include "the right to be free of unwarranted derogatory remarks made about the parent or his or her family by the other parent to the child or in the presence of the child."[16] Acting contrary to this mandate can lead to a finding of contempt and sometimes even a change of custody in extreme circumstances.

3. *The parenting schedule.*

   It is usually best for each parent's time with the children to be scheduled at regular and predictable times.[17] Once the schedule is created, it is important that it be honored. Children may see missed visits, especially without notification, as rejection.[18] Children crave consistency, and routines provide a sense of security and may help ease fears of abandonment. If possible, the parents should work together to ensure that the same routines and rules are followed at each home. It is important to resist the temptation to spoil the children during or following a divorce by not enforcing limits or allowing children to break rules.[19]

   Handovers between the two households can be particularly stressful for children, let alone parents. Children often feel guilty and are reluctant to admit to one parent that they are thinking about or missing the other parent. As a result, children are often anticipating the emotional turmoil of the handover back to the other parent instead of enjoying the time remaining before the transfer.[20] The divorce practitioner can counsel clients to minimize the number of handovers each week. Furthermore, it may help for the handovers to occur at a neutral location such as the child's school, as this is likely to cause less stress than handovers occurring on either parent's home turf. The parents will need to commit to making handovers free of arguments and hostility.

Although the typical parenting plan mentions only in passing that each parent has the statutory "right to unimpeded telephone conversations with the child at least twice a week at reasonable times and for reasonable durations,"[21] it may be worthwhile to be proactive and help clients work through the logistics. For instance, it can be wise to avoid phone calls at emotionally charged and more intrusive times such as meal time or bedtime.[22] It is not uncommon for a parent to feel that the ex-spouse is interfering with the phone calls in a multitude of ways, so a word to the wise: address these potential issues before they arise.

Finally, in crafting the parenting schedule, thinking outside the box can make for much more meaningful periods of parenting time. When children have been asked what they would change about their scheduled times with each parent, some have responded that they do not necessarily care to be shuffled back and forth with their siblings as a group. Children enjoy and benefit from one-on-one time with each parent. However, frequently, for the purposes of organizing the schedule, children are indeed "lumped together as a homogenous group, irrespective of their ages and needs."[23] Tennessee's standard parenting plan form treats the children as a group, so we lawyers need to be more proactive and consider suggesting to our clients that separate parenting times for each child be carved out if feasible for the family.

Conclusion

Given the proof that parents have the power to affect their children's reactions to divorce, it is necessary that parents put their children's welfare ahead of their own conflict with their spouse or former spouse. We as divorce practitioners also have the power to influence our clients' behavior by educating them and helping them craft parenting plans that minimize as much as possible the negative effects of divorce on our clients' children.

Notes

1. Sammons, William A.H., and Lewis, Jennifer M. (1999), *Don't Divorce Your Children.*

2. Pendergrast, Val (1997), "Sheathing Solomon's Sword," http://www.weeklywire.com/ww/08-04-97/knox_feat.html.

3. *Family Matters: Substance Abuse and the American Family,* The National Center on Addiction and Substance Abuse at Columbia University (March 2005), http://www.casacolumbia.org/articlefiles/380-Family percent20Matters.pdf.

4. Nuri, Banister, "Children of Divorced Parents Are More Likely to Themselves Divorce," *Journal of Young Investigators,* vol. 23, issue 3, March 2012, http://www.jyi.org/news/nb.php?id=352.

5. Temke, Mary (1998), "The Effects of Divorce on Children," University of New Hampshire, Cooperative Extension, http://extension.unh.edu/Family/Documents/divorce.pdf.

6. *Id.*

7. Nowinski, Joseph (2011), "The New Grief: Helping Children Survive Divorce: Three Critical Factors," http://www.psychologytoday.com/blog/the-new-grief/201110/helping-children-survive-divorce-three-critical-factors.

8. Biller H., Solomon R.S. (1986), *Child Maltreatment and Paternal Deprivation: A Manifesto for Research, Treatment, and Prevention.*

9. Temke, *supra.*

10. Nowinski, *supra.*

11. Ferrer, Millie and McCrea, Sara (2002), *Talking to Children about Divorce,* University of Florida, IFAS Extension.

12. Sammons, *supra.*

13. Block, Jocelyn; Kemp, Gina; Smith, Melinda; Segal, Jeanne (2012), "Children and Divorce: Helping Kids Cope with Separation and Divorce," http://www.helpguide.org/mental/children_divorce.htm.

14. Sammons, *supra.*

15. *Tenn. Code Ann.* § 36-6-106(a)(10).

16. *Tenn. Code Ann.* § 36-6-101(a)(3)(A).

17. Sammons, *supra.*

18. Gold-Bikin, Lynne Z. and Kolodny, Stephen (2003), *The Divorce Trial Manual: From Initial Interview to Closing Argument.*

19. Block, *supra.*

20. Sammons, *supra.*

21. *Tenn. Code Ann.* § 36-6-101(a)(3)(A).

22. Sammons, *supra.*

23. *Id.*

Critical Thinking

1. Do you think divorce is always something children merely endure? What do you think they are aware of during the process?

2. Can divorce ever be beneficial or helpful to children? Are the results always negative?

3. The author makes several recommendations regarding how parents can help their children through a divorce. Do you agree with them? Why or why not?

4. Using information gained from this article, describe an intervention or support program that could be developed to facilitate the positive development of children from families where parents are divorcing.

Create Central

www.mhhe.com/createcentral

Internet References

HelpGuide: Children and Divorce
www.helpguide.org/mental/children_divorce.htm
HelpGuide: Divorce and Remarriage
www.helpguide.org/topics/breakup_divorce.htm

MARLENE ESKIND MOSES is the principal and manager of MTR Family Law PLLC, a family and divorce law firm in Nashville.

She is currently serving as a vice president of the International Academy of Matrimonial Lawyers. She has held prior presidencies with the American Academy of Matrimonial Lawyers, Tennessee Board of Law Examiners, Lawyer's Association for Women, and the Tennessee Supreme Court Historical Society. She has also served as vice president for the United States Chapter of the International Academy of Matrimonial Lawyers and first vice president of the Nashville Bar Association. Selected as a Diplomate in the American College of Family Trial Lawyers, she is the only one in the College from Tennessee. The Tennessee Commission on Continuing Legal & Specialization has designated Moses as a Family Law Specialist; she is board certified as a Family Law Trial Specialist in addition to holding certifications in mediation, arbitration, and collaborative law.

Article   Prepared by: Patricia Hrusa Williams, *University of Maine at Farmington*

The Effects of Co-Parenting Relationships with Ex-Spouses on Couples in Step-Families

CLAIRE CARTWRIGHT AND KERRY GIBSON

Learning Outcomes

After reading this article, you will be able to:

- Identify stresses experienced in families when a divorced spouse remarries.

- Evaluate the strengths and weaknesses in a study examining step-families.

- Utilize research findings in developing ideas about needed interventions and supports for step-families.

According to the Australian Bureau of Statistics (ABS, 2007) approximately one in ten couple families contain resident step-children. In Wave 3 of the Household, Income and Labour Dynamics in Australia (HILDA) survey, 13% of households had either residential or non-residential step-children, or both (Qu & Weston, 2005). In the United States, approximately 9% of married couple households, and 12% of cohabiting households contain resident step-children (Teachman & Tedrow, 2008). Step-family data are not collected in the New Zealand Census. However, 19% of the 1,265 child participants in the longitudinal Christchurch Health and Development Study had lived in a step-family between the ages of 6 and 16 years (Nicholson, Fergusson, & Horwood, 1999).

The majority of step-families are formed after divorce through the repartnering or remarriage of a parent (Pryor & Rodgers, 2001). As newly formed step-couples begin to live together, they must manage a complex family transition through which they establish a new household and bring together a number of adults and children, some of whom are unrelated (step-parents, step-children and step-siblings). Unlike first-marriage couples, newly repartnered couples do not have the luxury of getting to know each other before becoming parents and step-parents. Instead, they begin life together facing the challenges associated with developing their new couple's relationship and new step-relationships, at the same time as having to deal with multiple changes in their lives and those of their children.

Step-families are also closely linked to other households because of children's relationships with parents in other residences. When parents repartner, former spouses must continue to deal with each other over issues to do with child care, including parenting arrangements and financial support of children (Braithwaite, McBride, & Schrodt, 2003). How well parents manage these co-parenting issues affects both the step-couple and the children (Braithwaite et al., 2003).

This paper comes from the Couples in Repartnered (Step-) Families study, conducted in New Zealand (Cartwright, 2010). The study consisted of an online questionnaire completed by 99 adults living in step-families; and interviews, both individual and joint, with 16 step-couples. The step-couples reflected back on the processes associated with repartnering and establishing a step-family. The effects of co-parenting issues with former spouses emerged as a source of stress for many step-couples, so the decision was made by the authors to examine this area of step-family life. The results present a thematic analysis of the qualitative data from the interviews that are relevant to ongoing co-parenting relationships and interactions with former spouses and the effects of these on the step-couple.

Co-parenting Relationships Following Separation and the Effect on Step-Couples

In a review of the step-family research conducted in the previous decade, Coleman, and Fine (2000) talked about the importance of extending step-family research beyond the step-family household. However, few researchers have since made this move. As Schrodt (2011) noted, co-parenting has been investigated in first-marriage families and divorced families, but researchers have generally neglected the investigation of co-parenting relationships and their effects in the step-family context.

To do so is important, as the remarriage of one parent brings about another family transition and its associated stressors (Coleman et al., 2000). As Christensen & Rettig (1996) noted, systems theory suggests that co-parenting relationships established between parents following divorce are likely to be disrupted with the addition of a new parental partner, and require adjustments to accommodate the presence of the step-parent. There is evidence that some former spouses struggle to accept the development of new relationships, and the arrival of new parental partners is a common stressor for divorced individuals (Hetherington & Kelly, 2002). This may be particularly difficult, for example, for those who did not want to divorce and have remained single, and those who have settled into a comfortable co-parenting arrangement. American clinicians (e.g., Papernow, 2006) and researchers (e.g., Hetherington & Kelly, 2002) have noted that some former spouses feel threatened by new partners. For example, in an interview study with 35 divorced adults, the men and women talked about feeling that they were being replaced, both as a partner and a parent (Miller, 2009). Hence, having one's former spouse repartner may lead to feelings of insecurity and either disrupt settled arrangements or exacerbate ongoing difficulties.

There is evidence from studies in the United States that co-parenting relationships can deteriorate after the addition of a step-parent to the family, leading to increased stress for all family members (Coleman, Fine, Ganong, Downs, & Pauk, 2001). Christensen & Rettig (1996) examined the effects of remarriage on co-parenting relationships in a sample of 372 women and 277 men contacted three years after their divorce. The researchers found that both the women and men in the study reported having less frequent co-parental interaction, less parenting support from former spouses, and more negative attitudes towards their former spouses. Further, in a study of 327 divorced adults' attitudes to co-parenting, Ganong, Coleman, Markham, and Rothrauff (2011) found that repartnered mothers reported a lower level of intention to co-parent in the future compared to mothers who remained single. The authors suggested that

repartnered women may have seen their new partners as being potential father replacements and that this may have affected their attitudes to co-parenting with their former spouses. Alternatively, the authors posited that the change in attitude could be as a result of increased conflict that occurred following remarriage.

On the other hand, a recent study of the interactions of 22 parenting teams including both of the former spouses and a step-parent, found that the participants expressed moderate satisfaction with their interactions with the other household, and interactions were generally not conflicted (Braithwaite et al., 2003). Interactions were mainly child-focused, were between parents, and were rarely initiated by a step-parent. The researchers concluded that this group of volunteer participants, who had been together on average 6 years, had reached a position of equilibrium. This suggests that given time a number of former spouses and their new partners can develop functional ways of interacting around the children that are satisfactory to them. There is also some evidence that contact with a former spouse who is supportive and engages in cooperative co-parenting can have a positive effect on the repartnered parent in the step-family (Weston & Macklin, 1990).

It is also important to note that some researchers believe that fathers whose children are primarily in the care of mothers can lose further contact with their children when the father remarries. However, Ganong and Coleman (2004) concluded in their review of the step-family literature that the small number of studies on the effects of remarriage on father–child contact have shown mixed results. Some studies have found no change in contact between children and fathers (Stephen, Freedman, & Hess, 1994) while other studies have found a decrease in contact (McKenry, McKelvey, Leigh, & Wark, 1996). Given the evidence of the disruption to co-parenting relationships caused by repartnering, it seems likely, as Smyth (2004) concluded, that some children will have less contact with parents who remarry or repartner, but it [is] also possible that some children will have increased contact, and contact for others will remain unchanged.

Finally, some of the problems that arise between divorced co-parents after remarriage relate to financial issues, including support of the children. Just as men fare better economically after divorce than women, women fare relatively better economically after remarriage than men (Ozawa & Yoon, 2002). Fathers who remarry are potentially placed under greater financial stress due to expectations that they will support children from the previous union, step-children, and children born to the new partnership (Hans & Coleman, 2009). Following remarriage, a father's income may thus be further stretched while a mother's is potentially added to. Further, in Hans' (2009) study of social beliefs around child support modification following remarriage, the majority of their sample of 407 people believed that it was appropriate to modify child support following remarriage to maintain an equitable agreement. It seems likely therefore that in such circumstances disagreements over child care payments may re-emerge or, if disagreements are ongoing, be exacerbated following remarriage as there is potentially more competition for economic resources.

Ganong and Coleman (2004) pointed out that many step-couples come together with "an audience of interested and powerful third parties" (p. 76), some of whom (such as former spouses and, in some instances, children) may have an investment in the relationship not succeeding. As discussed, researchers (e.g., Hetherington & Kelly, 2002) and step-family therapists (e.g., Papernow, 2006) have found that some former spouses engage in behaviours that have a negative effect on step-couples. Papernow observed that resentful or jealous former spouses can make managing child care issues difficult for parents and step-parents. Some former spouses also respond to the repartnering as a competition over the children's affection (Ganong & Coleman, 2004), fearing that they might lose their children. This potentially increases the emotional distress associated with child care arrangements; hence, former spouses who are struggling themselves can have a significant psychological presence in the step-family (Ganong & Coleman, 2004), which in turn is likely to affect the step-couple's relationship.

Method

Participants

Participants were recruited from among 99 participants who had taken part in the study's online survey. At the completion of the online questionnaire, participants could volunteer to take part in a couple's interview. Sixteen couples (32 participants) were recruited in this manner. All couples were living in Auckland. Two participants were in the 30–34 age range; 16 were 35–39; 13 were 40–44; and one was over 50 years.

The couples had been living in a step-family household for between one and nine years, with a mean of 3.9 years. Ten of the couples had remarried, the remainder were cohabiting with new partners. They had between one and four children from previous unions living in their households, with a mean of 2.5 children. All the couples had children with them at least one-third of the time, and the majority had step-children in the household for at least two-thirds of the time. Four couples had children born to their relationship and one was expecting. The children from previous unions ranged in age between 4 and 14 years, with a mean of approximately 10 years.

In the group of participants, there were 12 mothers, 12 fathers, and 9 adults who did not have children from a previous marriage. Between them, they had 25 former spouses. Five of these families were step-father families, five were step-mother families, and six were complex step-families in which both adults had children of their own. However, two of the complex step-families were living mainly as step-father families due to them having irregular contact with the step-fathers' children.

Interviews

The couples were interviewed together and then separately. The joint interviews lasted between an hour and an hour and a half, and the individual interviews each lasted around 20 minutes. In the joint interviews, the couples were asked for the story of their relationship and how it began and developed. They were then asked to talk about their children's experiences and how they had responded to the formation of the new relationship and step-family living. The couples were asked to talk about how they had worked out the care arrangements for the children; what they agreed and disagreed about; how they looked after their own relationship; what worked and what did not. They were asked to talk about the positive aspects of their relationship, and any recommendations they would give to couples considering repartnering.

In the individual interviews, the participants were asked if there was anything else that was important to them that they would like to talk about. They were also asked to talk about the greatest challenges they had experienced in their family situation, and the most positive aspects of their experiences.

Data Analysis

The interviews were transcribed and a number of datasets were created to allow for further analysis. These included the challenges internal to the couple's relationship, the responses of children, influences external to the step-family household, positive experiences, and the parenting of children. This paper presents the analysis of the body of data taken from the interviews in regard to ongoing contact with former spouses that was in the dataset relating to influences from outside the step-family. A thematic analysis was conducted on the data using the methods described by Braun and Clarke (2006). This included the process of re-reading the data, and recording a summary of the comments made by participants in regard to interactions with former spouses and the effects of these. These comments were then examined and grouped into sets of related data. From this process, a number of themes were proposed. These proposed themes were then checked against the data to see if they fit and represented the main ideas that were present. The themes were further examined by the second author for their fit to the data and the final themes were defined. These themes are presented in the next section.

Before presenting the themes, it is important to acknowledge that this analysis is based on the step-couples' interviews. The former spouses' stories of their experiences are not included. It is also important to note that the majority of the data is about negative experiences with former spouses. Eight of the 25 parents in the group did not talk about relationships with former spouses in any significant way and four step-couples' experiences did not include issues with spouses. Hence, 12 couples (17 parents) were negatively affected by the nature of the co-parenting relationship and the data presented in the results come from these participants.

Results of the Thematic Analysis

The results section presents four themes that were established from the data analysis process described above. These include: battles over children's residence and financial matters; not pulling their weight; lack of cooperation; and the other parent's negativity towards the step-parent or the new step-family. The effects that these areas had on the step-couples will be examined throughout each theme.

Battles over Children's Residence and Financial Matters

As has been well documented by previous research (Amato, 2000; Pryor & Rodgers, 2001), separated and divorced parents often continue to engage conflictually as they deal with each other over issues concerning their shared children and shared property. In this group of participants, six step-couples described conflict with former spouses over child care and support and/or joint property, which was associated with high levels of stress or distress. For five of the six couples, the discord was between fathers and their ex-wives. For some participants, the conflict with former spouses had mostly resolved at the time of the interviews, for others it was current and ongoing. Participants described a range of feelings they experienced during periods of conflict with former spouses, including feeling frustrated, anxious and exhausted, and sometimes hopeless or desperate. They also described a range of effects on the couple's own relationship. Some couples had conflict between themselves over how to handle difficulties with former spouses, others became united, and one couple considered separating. As might be expected, some also disagreed some of the time and were supportive and felt united at other times.

Three fathers who repartnered quickly after separating, including one whose new relationship pre-dated the separation from his spouse, experienced severe levels of stress that involved legal "battles" over children's residence and financial arrangements. The couples' stories of the beginning of their relationships were dominated by descriptions of these problems. As one step-mother said about the effects of the conflict

between her partner and his ex-wife over joint property and, to a lesser extent, contact with the children:

> The fact that for the first two years it was a battleground. And just constantly in your face everyday. . . . You never had the courting and the dating type scenario. You just go, bang, and you're straight in and we had two and a half, three years of just absolute battle and grief.

The father talked about his experiences in similar terms, describing "a lot of nasty conflict and a lot of expensive lawyers" and two years of "war". He also talked about his perception that his ex-wife was driven by a desire for revenge, as the quote below suggests:

> I guess some of it was, I know the whole of that thing was she was out to sort of ruin me personally and there was no way that was going to happen. . . . For the first two years she was just irrational. Her actions were just irrational and it was driven by vengeance and anger, and trying to rationalise that with someone just doesn't work.

Another father, who had repartnered within six months of separating, had lost regular contact with his pre-adolescent and adolescent children at the time of the interviews. He moved towns and hoped that his ex-spouse would cooperate with transporting the children, but this had not happened. For this couple, the first half of the interview was dominated by the story of his attempts to see his children, his ex-wife's unwillingness to assist with travel, and their contact through lawyers. They talked about trying to "be united as a couple as you have so many things against you". However, the relationship came under pressure over time, as the father missed his children more. The step-mother talked about her frustration, how she tried to assist by talking to the children's mother, and also her annoyance at times with her partner. She had difficulty understanding why it was so difficult, given that her interactions with her own former spouse were uncomplicated:

> I guess the longer it went on, the harder it became. . . . I'd get wound up or I'd have a knot in my stomach. I think the stress side of things came more from frustration. . . . I have such a simple arrang[e]ment with my son's dad . . . and I couldn't understand why we couldn't have that with their mother, because I knew it could be simple. Then I'd say, you know, they're your kids, you can sort it out because she [mother] is not listening to me.

Another couple, who repartnered shortly after their former relationships had ended, had three ex-partners between them, and they experienced difficulties with all of them when they repartnered. While none of the situations were as difficult as the ones described above, the effect of having three ex-partners made their first two years together stressful. The father talked about the challenges of this over the first year, which illustrates the complexity of the issues that some step-couples face:

> When we first met, the children only went to their mother's on a Saturday night, every fortnight. . . . Then she [ex-wife] split up from her husband and then after that she didn't want to work, so went for custody—shared care of the boys—so she could get the benefit. And we fought it for a year, but in the end it was too stressful, and the kids wanted to go to their mother half the time.
>
> . . . Just creating your own family unit to fit in with them [his ex-partners] as well, and then we had to do it with my wife's daughter and iron that side out as well!

Two couples talked about their experiences of mothers who complained that the step-mothers were mistreating their children and how these claims were linked with attempting to have increased time with the children. As an example, one of the fathers told the story of his former spouse, who left to live overseas when the children were preschoolers. As the children grew older, they visited their mother occasionally. After the father and the step-mother married some years later, the mother accused the step-mother of mistreating the children. The step-mother talked about the effects on her at the time and how she coped with it:

> I wanted out. I thought, I am not going to do this. We'd only just got married, and then I was worried because she'd sent us a copy, she'd sent the school a copy, she's sent the courts a copy. . . . I raised above it. I knew it wasn't true. The kids knew it wasn't true and denied it. . . . She was just jealous and she still is jealous because I'm bringing up her biological kids.

Finally, one mother was frightened about the welfare of her infant son. The mother separated from her ex-husband when their child was a baby, because of her concern for their physical safety, but the father attempted to gain shared care of the young child. As she said, talking about her ex-husband:

> He's got a hatred for me, has a total hatred for me. . . . He hates the fact that [step-father] is in [son's] life.

The step-father also talked about the effects of this and his caution about getting involved:

> Yeah, whether I really wanted to get myself tangled up in what was happening, a custody dispute, taking on a toddler. . . . So whether I was willing to adjust to that, whether I wanted to get involved in all of that and the baggage, I suppose you would call it.

This custody dispute continued for four years and was coming to an end at the time of the interviews. The mother commented, "It's gone on for four years. So now that's dealt with, I am finding it a bit hard to believe that this is it". The step-father also spoke about his approach over the recent years and how he tried to be supportive:

> [Partner] was pretty highly strung there for a while. And I just had to keep telling myself I know what's causing this mess. I couldn't possibly understand how she feels, going through a custody battle, and just had to wait for it all to finish really, so at times it was pretty hard.

Hence, these couples came under what could be considered severe levels of stress, often during the early stages of their relationships, because of conflict with former spouses over children's residence and/or financial arrangements. The parents in this group appeared to feel threatened by the former spouses' attitudes towards them, the potential loss of custody of the children, or issues related to joint property. The conflict between the former spouses, including the ongoing legal "battles", sometimes affected the step-couples' relationships, becoming a source of disagreement for some of them, and making it harder for them to develop their relationship and the step-family while they were feeling under a state of "siege".

Not Pulling Their Weight!

Another experience that some participants talked about were the ongoing feelings of frustration or sense of unfairness that arose when some former spouses' demands or lack of contribution led to a sense of increased pressure for the step-couple. These experiences were less severe than those in the previous theme, but were an ongoing source of stress. A number of participants felt that the other parent was not pulling their weight, whether financially, in provision of child care, or both. One mother talked about her frustration at her child's father and her concern for her child that her father was not meeting his parenting responsibilities:

> There's this person who's never grown up and they're not going to. . . . And it frustrates me, for [daughter's] sake as well. It's just that kind of responsibility thing when somebody just doesn't fundamentally get that as a parent they have a responsibility. He's never organised a holiday. He's never paid me a cent of maintenance. He's never been to any of [daughter's] important dates at school!

Couples also talked about the financial pressures they were under, and perceived that these were exacerbated by the demands of former spouses. One couple talked about the stress associated with each of them having an ex-spouse whom they perceived placed a financial burden on their household. They reported that one of the former spouses, a father, contributed nothing financially for his child; and the other former spouse, a mother, made ongoing requests for financial support for her child over and above the monthly support payment. As the couple said about the woman's former spouse:

> We won't go into character assassination, but his father basically told [son], you know, he was not his responsibility. He was entirely my responsibility and not to expect anything from him. (Step-father)

> He's the type of parent who won't go out and get a job to support his other two children and his [new] partner because it means paying me more child support. (Mother)

This couple also felt that the mother of his child, who was on a benefit, was also demanding. He talked about the pressure he was under and his guilt about his daughter, and appeared to feel torn between his former spouse, daughter and wife:

> It was like I was paying out this money [child support], and she would say, "Our child wants to go on a schoo[l] trip". I can't afford to do it and I'd be like, "What do I do now?", because I don't want any more money going out, but its affecting my child and it would really become difficult. And then I would have my wife saying, "We can't afford to do much" . . . and I would think, "I know, but my daugher is missing out", and I used to feel like I was in the middle of everything.

Another father talked about feeling similarly torn and resentful towards his ex-wife for not working and not contributing more to the financial support of their sons:

> I feel resentful sometimes about forking out, because she treats us like the bank. But I don't want the children to go without. Don't get me wrong, but it does piss me off, excuse my language.

Finally, one couple talked about a mother who had given up much of the responsibility for her children, both in terms of child care and economic support, because of her changed personal circumstances. As a result, the step-mother, who was at home with her young children born to her new marriage, had become, by default, the main caregiver for her step-children, and talked about the difficulties of fulfilling a parenting role for them:

> I'm not saying that [father] doesn't take responsibility, but at the moment because of what's been going on, it's just even more highlighted the fact that I'm actually the primary caregiver and making these decisions [about the step-children] and trying to feel my way through this. . . . I find it hard to actually understand and believe that she's just about dropped them like hot potatoes.

While this step-mother appeared to be managing well with her step-children and the couple reported the children were happy in their home, for her it came as an unexpected shock

that she should become the primary caregiver for the step-children, and this was also a source of tension between the couple.

Lack of Cooperation

A number of participants talked about their disappointment or frustration at what they perceived to be an ongoing lack of cooperation from the other parent, usually over care of the children. This lack of cooperation took many forms. It included an unwillingness of some spouses to allow some flexibility in care arrangements to fit in with contingencies, to communicate or negotiate, and/or to cooperate with a step-parent, when this was required. For some participants, this lack of cooperation began or was exacerbated when the parent repartnered.

One father, for example, described how he and his ex-spouse had developed a workable routine for handing over the children from one home to the other and how this had changed since he repartnered:

> It'd gone from being businesslike, where we would occasionally, at hand-over time, meet in a café and have a morning tea together with the children and try to normalise things. The kids would say goodbye to me, kiss and cuddle, and off they'd go. . . . [Now] we'll meet outside Burger King. You park on one side of the place, I'll park on the other, and the kids can walk over the carpark. And, you know, back to deep freeze, sort of frosty. We are back to that.

Another couple talked about problems with former partners on both sides. The father had child care issues with an ex-wife and the couple also perceived a lack of cooperation from her ex-husband (as each is both a parent and step-parent, they are referred to by gender):

> *Female:* But then we had other issues on the other side, just trying to make everything fit, and that person [ex-husband], I don't know why, being difficult!

> *Male:* Her dad being difficult!

> *Female:* Just over school holidays really.

> *Male:* Yeah, and other stuff. When he's got one person to think about, we don't understand why he was difficult.

> *Female:* He doesn't care!

> *Male:* Doesn't care what we do!

> *Female:* As far as he's concerned, our family unit is none of his business.

One couple with parents living overseas had difficulty gaining permission from the children's mother to allow the children to visit their grandparents. As the step-mother said:

> When we wanted to go on a holiday, and she had agreed to it, and then she withdrew her agreement. And we'd already

bought the overseas tickets and the kids thought they were going. And then she's saying they th[at] couldn't go, or it had to go through the court for the court to say, "Yes, they could go to see their grandparents". And I just hate that!

Another couple also experienced a lack of cooperation from the children's step-mother. This couple had moved house in the early stages of repartnering, and the oldest child, who normally got on well with his step-father, was objecting to the new living situation. The couple told the story of what happened when the mother rang the children's father to ask for support while they worked through the issues with the teenager:

Mother: I asked for the dad's support, which he gave me, but the woman that he's married used the opportunity to undermine us. . . .

Step-father: They went to their dad's that night, so we weren't there to talk about it that evening. Then the following night they came back with these questionnaires that the step-mum had written out, like, what do they feel about living here?

Mother: And using the same questionnaire to ask the children about what it was like at their place as well. Yeah, that wasn't useful.

Another mother talked about her frustration and disappointment with her daughter's father and his unwillingness to help out, especially during the school holidays. This couple did not have any extended family support:

For us as a family, we don't have people that help us with our kids. . . . There's just us, so that really is where it kind of bites. You get six weeks of summer holidays and you're both working and there's this other person who's just gone. They're not there for six weeks every summer.

Hence, some of the participants talked about their disappointment and frustration at the lack of cooperation that they experienced with the other parent, or in one case, step-parent. This added to their stresses and appeared to put pressure on them as a couple. Over time, some also appeared to learn to live with the lack of cooperation and were less frustrated by it. As one mother said, referring to the decrease in the effects of problems with the former spouse, "Once it was an elephant in the room, now it's a little mouse in the field".

The Other Parent's Negativity towards the Step-Parent or the New Step-Family

A number of parents and step-parents talked about their concerns or worries that the former parents' negativity towards the step-parent or step-family situation might adversely affect the children and the children's attitude towards the step-parent or living in a step-family, thereby undermining the efforts they were making to build the step-family and care for the children.

One mother did not allow the children to visit the new step-family household for the first few months. Over time, the step-mother became involved in picking the children up from school, assisting them with homework, helping to make lunches for them, and found the mother's treatment of her difficult to accept. This situation came to a head and improved after the step-mother stood up for herself. Following a call where the mother had spoken rudely to her, she said:

I'm not the nanny. I'm not the receptionist. I'm bringing your children up whether you like it or not. They're with us nearly 50% of the time. . . . You can't even have the decency to be civil to me when I ring up or to acknowledge that fact that I'm picking them up from school! . . . I said I spend my good earned money on them buying them clothes and food, and you've got the nerve to treat me like this! . . . And I said we have the decency to treat [your new partner] with respect and talk to him directly!!

While this type of response might have been followed by ongoing conflict or difficulty between the mother and the step-mother, in this instance, the mother apologised and the relationship became more civil. It is also important to note that in this instance, the young children did not appear to develop any negative attitutides towards their step-mother and were reported to be moving between houses quite happily.

Another couple talked about their worries about the mother's negative attitude towards the step-mother and their concerns about how this affected the children. This couple had a relatively smooth transition into step-family life, and the greatest challenge was the ex-wife's response to the remarriage. The father talked about his ex-wife's reaction to his new partner and his concerns about this:

My ex-wife hasn't reacted at all well to [step-mother] being on the scene, and insinuated in the early part of our relationship that the girls completely disliked [step-mother]. . . . She wrote this vitriolic email saying about how insensitive it was for me considering marrying someone who the girls obviously disliked so much. . . . The data didn't match what I was seeing. . . . I'm not paranoid about it, but I still worry to an extent what she will feed the girls about us.

A step-father also spoke about what he perceived as interference from the step-mother in the children's other home. He talked about his perceptions that the step-mother acted as if she was the mother of the children but failed to accept his role as a step-father:

> I've met her a few times and she blanked me completely. . . . There's a couple of things she has done that I've felt have been against me . . . Her interference seems to be a lot, and thinking she's the mother, whereas although I've been around less time, I don't think I'm the dad. That's been difficult.

Finally, a mother's story of her preschool child's experience provides some insight into how loyalty issues affect children. She talked about the effects on her son of the non-residential father's attempts, as she perceived it, to turn the child against his step-father. The mother talked about her concerns for her partner's feelings and for the wellbeing of her son:

> The only time we've really had difficulties with [step-father] and [son] is when he's come back from his father's and, "Me and my dad hate you", this sort of stuff. . . . I said to [step-father] at the time, "You need to remember that this is [my ex-] talking. That is not my son because he absolutely idolises [his step-father]". [Later] I said to [my son], "Why did you say that about [step-dad]? You don't hate him", and he said, "Because my dad said". And he was so young!

Hence, some parents and step-parents experienced the other parent(s) as competing for the children, and attempting to turn the children against them or to win the children over to their side. In only one instance, a step-mother was seen as the main instigator of the difficulties. The other instances concerned former spouses' lack of acceptance and angry responses to the step-parent or the new step-family situation.

Discussion

Previous research suggests that co-parenting relationships can deteriorate when a former spouse repartners (Christensen & Rettig, 1996; Coleman et al., 2001). This study provides insights into how this can occur and the effects it has on step-couples. A number of the parents observed an increase after they repartnered in the conflict they experienced with former spouses over the children's residence, child support and/or joint property. This appeared to be heightened for couples where one of them had repartnered early during the post-separation period, when issues around child contact and joint property were not yet resolved, and feelings on both sides were still running high. On the other hand, disturbance in some co-parenting relationships also occurred after repartnering when the divorce had taken place some years earlier. A small number of parents

perceived that former spouses were being deliberately difficult in response to their repartnering.

For some parents, the conflict over child contact and financial issues was associated with high levels of stress and added a great deal to the pressure that couples were experiencing as part of their adjustment to step-family living. It also placed stress on their relationships with each other, and this was exacerbated if they disagreed over how to manage the issues with the former spouse. It was also difficult at times for the step-parents to accept and deal with the stress associated with the conflict between their partners and former spouses. On the other hand, it is important to note that around a third of the parents who participated in the study did not talk about experiencing problems in their co-parenting relationships with former spouses as part of their adjustment to step-family living.

These results support the notion discussed earlier that remarriage and the entrance of new parental partners can destabilise family systems (Christensen & Rettig, 1996), either by exacerbating difficulties that exist or leading to new problems that need to be resolved. It also provides indirect support for previous evidence that the entrance of a new parental partner into the extended family system can lead to feelings of insecurity and a fear that the parent is not only being replaced as partner but also being replaced as a parent (Miller, 2009). This may be particularly difficult for former spouses who observe step-couple closeness and attractive step-parent qualities. It may also be difficult for individuals who are struggling emotionally. This appeared to be so in a small number of instances discussed in the thematic analysis, in which the participants talked about the attitude of the former spouse to the step-parent and had a sense that their ex-partner was attempting to turn the children against the step-parent and perhaps the remarriage. This supports Papernow's (2006) conclusion that some former spouses engage in jealous behaviour that makes co-parenting difficult and places stress on the step-couple. In a small number of instances, couples perceived that the former spouse's negativity was directed at the step-parent. In some instances, this lead to increased tensions between the step-couple and/or feelings of insecurity for the step-parent.

As found previously (Braithwaite et al., 2003), however, step-parents did not appear to deal with or negotiate with former spouses on anything but an occasional basis. This was left mainly to parents. An exception to this was a wife of a former spouse who was seen as interfering directly with the management of the children, and one step-mother who attempted to assist with resolving disagreements. She stepped back from this, however, when it was unsuccessful.

It is also important to note that some of the stressors associated with former spouses were not severe, but were an ongoing source of stress or irritation that made life more difficult for the couples at times. Some former spouses were experienced as being inflexible or refusing to negotiate special requests or one-off changes to routines to allow for special arrangements or events. Some ex-spouses were experienced as not meeting their responsibilities, either through child care (such as assisting with holidays), or in providing financial support of the children. Some parents thought that the other parent was not pulling his or her weight financially and found this added to the financial stessors they were already experiencing. There was also some evidence to support previous finding[s] that some fathers in step-family situations feel torn between former spouses, their children and current partners, in regard to financial support (Hans & Coleman, 2009).

As researchers, we were surprised to note that five of the six co-parenting relationships that we considered came under severe levels of stress, were between repartnered fathers and their ex-wives. On the other hand, it has been found consistently that men tend to repartner more quickly than women (Cartwright, 2010) and some men in this study repartnered within six months of separating, at a time when issues around child care and finances were still under negotiation and the relationship between the two former spouses was still emotionally fraught. Early repartnering is likely to lead to heightened distress for former spouses, especially when they have not wanted to divorce.

American researchers (e.g., Hetherington & Kelly, 2002) and step-family therapists (e.g., Papernow, 2006) have observed that repartnering parents often have unrealistally positive expectations of step-family life, believing, for example, that step-children will love their new partners as much as they do. Some step-couples in this study also appeared surprised or taken aback by their former spouses' responses to them or their new partner following repartnering, including those who repartnered quickly. It may be that some step-couples are not cognisant of the problems that can arise with former spouses if repartnering occurs quickly after a separation, before the necessary period of adjustment has taken place. The likelihood of step-couples having realistic expectations may also be affected by the lack of research in the area of co-parenting following remarriage, and also the lack of norms to guide parents and step-parents in how to relate to each other (Weston & Macklin, 1990). It might be helpful for those considering repartnering to understand that relating to former spouses can become an obstacle course if the former spouse feels threatened or believes that they have not been treated fairly. It may also be helpful for former spouses to be aware of the strong emotions that are evoked by their exes repartnering, and to have guidance about how to manage themselves during this stressful period.

It is important to acknowledge the limitations of this study and briefly discuss future research directions. First, this sample of participants volunteered to be interviewed and may not be representative of step-couples generally. The sample may have included a greater proportion of people who had experienced considerable difficulty and wanted to talk about this to a researcher. Second, the views of former spouses were not included in this study and hence their experiences and viewpoints are missing. Research that includes all the adults involved is likely to provide greater insights into the dynamics of co-parenting within step-family situations. Third, because of the nature of the interviews, participants who told the story of the development of their relationships tended to talk only about the problems and challenges they experienced with former spouses. Hence, this study is informative about the types of problems that step-couples experience, but not of positive co-parenting relationships following repartnering. Around a third of the participants appeared to have non-problematic relationships with former spouses, but little data were collected about these relationships because of the focus on the step-couples' challenges and the experiences they regarded as important to them.

In terms of future research, it is important that family transition researchers in Australia and New Zealand focus more on the areas of co-parenting following remarriage, and the relationships between former spouses, parents and step-parents. No previous research has been conducted in either country in this area. The lack of research in this area may also exacerbate a lack of norms to guide repartnering parents and former spouses. In line with this, in order to better understand how co-parenting relationships work, it is also important to study well-functioning co-parenting relationships and how these develop or are maintained following the repartnering of at least one former spouse. Finally, given that the majority of separated parents will eventually repartner, and some will do so quickly, it may be desirable for educational programs and literature aimed at separated couples to include information about the stressors associated with the transition into step-family life and their potential effects on co-parenting relationships between former spouses.

References

Amato, P. (2000). The consequences of divorce for adults and children. *Journal of Marriage and the Family, 62* (4), 1269–1287.

Australian Bureau of Statistics. (2007). *2006 Census of Population and Housing* (Cat. No. 2008.0). Canberra: ABS.

Braithwaite, D. O., McBride, M. C., & Schrodt, P. (2003). Parent teams and the everyday interactions of co-parenting in stepfamilies. *Communication Reports, 16* (2), 93–111.

Braun, V., & Clarke, V. (2006). Using thematic analysis in psychology. *Qualitative research in psychology, 3,* 77–101.

Cartwright, C. (2010). Preparing to repartner and live in a stepfamily: An exploratory investigation. *Journal of Family Studies, 16* (3), 237–250.

Christensen, D. H., & Rettig, K. D. (1996). The relationship of remarriage to post-divorce co-parenting. *Journal of Divorce & Remarriage, 24* (1–2), 73–88.

Coleman, M., Fine, M. A., Ganong, L. H., Downs, K. J. M., & Pauk, N. (2001). When you're not the Brady Bunch: Identifying perceived conflicts and resolution strategies in stepfamilies. *Personal Relationships, 8* (1), 55–73.

Coleman, M., Ganong, L., & Fine, M. A. (2000). Reinvestigating remarriage: Another decade of progress. *Journal of Marriage and the Family, 62* (4), 1288–1307.

Ganong, L., & Coleman, M. (2004). *Stepfamily relationships: Development, dynamics and interventions.* New York: Kluwer Academic/Plenum Publishers.

Ganong, L. H., Coleman, M., Markham, M., & Rothrauff, T. (2011). Predicting postdivorce co-parental communication. *Journal of Divorce & Remarriage, 52* (1), 1–18.

Hans, J. D. (2009). Beliefs about child support modification following remarriage and subsequent childbirth. *Family Relations, 58* (1), 65–78.

Hans, J. D., & Coleman, M. (2009). The experiences of remarried stepfathers who pay child support. *Personal Relationships, 16* (4), 597–618.

Hetherington, E. M., & Kelly, J. (2002). *For better or for worse: Divorce reconsidered.* New York: W. W. Norton and Company.

McKenry, P. C., McKelvey, M. W., Leigh, D., & Wark, L. (1996). Nonresidential father involvement. *Journal of Divorce & Remarriage, 25* (3–4), 1–14.

Miller, A. E. (2009). Face concerns and facework strategies in maintaining postdivorce co-parenting and dating relationships. *Southern Communication Journal, 74* (2), 157–173.

Nicholson, J. M., Fergusson, D. M., & Horwood, L. J. (1999). Effects on later adjustment of living in a step-family during childhood and adolescence. *Journal of Child Psychology and Psychiatry, 40*, 405–416.

Ozawa, M. N., & Yoon, H.-S. (2002). The economic benefit of remarriage. *Journal of Divorce & Remarriage, 36* (3–4), 21–39.

Papernow, P. (2006). Blended family relationships: Helping people who live in stepfamilies. *Family Therapy Magazine*, May, 34–42.

Pryor, J., & Rodgers, B. (2001). *Children in changing families: Life after parental separation* (Understanding Children' Worlds). Oxford, UK: Blackwell.

Qu, L., & Weston, R. (2005). Snapshot of couple families with stepparent–child relationships. *Family Matters, 70,* 36–37.

Smyth, B. (2004). Postseparation fathering: What does Australian research tell us? *Journal of Family Studies, 10* (1), 20–49.

Stephen, E. H., Freedman, V. A., & Hess, J. (1994). Near and far. *Journal of Divorce & Remarriage, 20* (3–4), 171–191.

Teachman, J., & Tedrow, L. (2008). The demography of step-families in the United States. In J. Pryor (Ed.), *The international handbook of step-families: Policy and practice in legal, research, and clinical environments* (pp. 3–29). Hoboken, NJ: John Wiley.

Weston, C. A., & Macklin, E. D. (1990). The relationship between former-spousal contact and remarital satisfaction in stepfather families. *Journal of Divorce & Remarriage, 14* (2), 25–48.

Critical Thinking

1. What do you see as the biggest challenges faced when a step-family is formed?
2. If this study were conducted in the United States, do you think the findings would be the same and why? Are there things about this study that could be strengthened or which limit the generalizability of its findings about step-families?
3. How could the findings of this study be used in developing interventions and supports designed for step-families?

Create Central

www.mhhe.com/createcentral

Internet References

HelpGuide: Children and Divorce
www.helpguide.org/mental/children_divorce.htm

HelpGuide: Divorce and Remarriage
www.helpguide.org/topics/breakup_divorce.htm

National Stepfamily Resource Center
http://www.stepfamilies.info

Stepfamilies Australia
http:// www.stepfamily.org.au

CLAIRE CARTWRIGHT and KERRY GIBSON are both at the Doctor of Clinical Psychology Programme, School of Psychology, the University of Auckland, New Zealand. This paper is based on a presentation made at the 12th Australian Institute of Family Studies Conference, 25 July 2012, Melbourne.

Unit 5

UNIT

Prepared by: Patricia Hrusa Williams, *University of Maine at Farmington*

Families, Now and into the Future

What is the future of the family? Does the family even have a future? These questions and others like them are being asked. Many people fear for the future of the family. As previous units of this volume have shown, the family is an institution which continues to evolve and change. Still, certain elements of family appear to be constant. The family is and will remain a powerful influence in the lives of its members. This is because we all begin life in some type of family, and this early exposure carries a great deal of weight in forming our social selves—who we are and how we relate to others. From our biological families, we are given our basic genetic makeup. In the context of daily routines and rituals we also learn how to care for ourselves and attend to our health. In families, we are given our first exposure to values, and it is through families that we most actively influence others. Our sense of commitment and obligation begins within the family as well as our sense of what we can expect of others.

Much that has been written about families has been less than hopeful, focusing on ways of avoiding or correcting "maladaptive"; behaviors and patterns. The articles in this unit take a positive view of family and how it influences its members. Through its diversity, rituals, traditions, history, and new ways of establishing connections, the family still remains a vital and important structure in which we work, play, love, and adapt.

The articles in this unit explore the different shapes and forms families come in and the rituals and celebrations that link them. Articles also consider how technology and changes in societal norms and values are altering how we procreate, relate, marry, and parent the next generation. A goal is to explore the family now and as it might be as we venture into the future, considering its role as a healthy, supportive place for personal growth.

Article   Prepared by: Patricia Hrusa Williams, *University of Maine at Farmington*

The Changing American Family

Natalie Angier

Learning Outcomes

After reading this article, you will be able to:

- Describe shifts in family characteristics and structure in the United States.

- Explain how demographic, social, political, and economic forces have contributed to changes in the family in the United States.

Kristi and Michael Burns have a lot in common. They love crossword puzzles, football, going to museums and reading five or six books at a time. They describe themselves as mild-mannered introverts who suffer from an array of chronic medical problems. The two share similar marital résumés, too. On their wedding day in 2011, the groom was 43 years old and the bride 39, yet it was marriage No. 3 for both.

Today, their blended family is a sprawling, sometimes uneasy ensemble of two sharp-eyed sons from her two previous husbands, a daughter and son from his second marriage, ex-spouses of varying degrees of involvement, the partners of ex-spouses, the bemused in-laws and a kitten named Agnes that likes to sleep on computer keyboards.

If the Burnses seem atypical as an American nuclear family, how about the Schulte-Waysers, a merry band of two married dads, six kids and two dogs? Or the Indrakrishnans, a successful immigrant couple in Atlanta whose teenage daughter divides her time between prosaic homework and the precision footwork of ancient Hindu dance; the Glusacs of Los Angeles, with their two nearly grown children and their litany of middle-class challenges that seem like minor sagas; Ana Perez and Julian Hill of Harlem, unmarried and just getting by, but with Warren Buffett-size dreams for their three young children; and the alarming number of families with incarcerated parents, a sorry byproduct of America's status as the world's leading jailer.

The typical American family, if it ever lived anywhere but on Norman Rockwell's Thanksgiving canvas, has become as multilayered and full of surprises as a holiday turducken—the all-American seasonal portmanteau of deboned turkey, duck and chicken.

Researchers who study the structure and evolution of the American family express unsullied astonishment at how rapidly the family has changed in recent years, the transformations often exceeding or capsizing those same experts' predictions of just a few journal articles ago.

"This churning, this turnover in our intimate partnerships is creating complex families on a scale we've not seen before," said Andrew J. Cherlin, a professor of public policy at Johns Hopkins University. "It's a mistake to think this is the endpoint of enormous change. We are still very much in the midst of it."

Yet for all the restless shape-shifting of the American family, researchers who comb through census, survey and historical data and conduct field studies of ordinary home life have identified a number of key emerging themes.

Families, they say, are becoming more socially egalitarian over all, even as economic disparities widen. Families are more ethnically, racially, religiously and stylistically diverse than half a generation ago—than even half a year ago.

In increasing numbers, blacks marry whites, atheists marry Baptists, men marry men and women women, Democrats marry Republicans and start talk shows. Good friends join forces as part of the "voluntary kin" movement, sharing medical directives, wills, even adopting one another legally.

Single people live alone and proudly consider themselves families of one—more generous and civic-minded than so-called "greedy marrieds."

"There are really good studies showing that single people are more likely than married couples to be in touch with friends, neighbors, siblings and parents," said Bella DePaulo, author of *Singled Out* and a visiting professor of psychology at the University of California, Santa Barbara.

But that doesn't mean they'll be single forever. "There are not just more types of families and living arrangements than there used to be," said Stephanie Coontz, author of the coming book *Intimate Revolutions,* and a social historian at Evergreen State College in Olympia, Wash. "Most people will move through several different types over the course of their lives."

At the same time, the old-fashioned family plan of stably married parents residing with their children remains a source of considerable power in America—but one that is increasingly seen as out of reach to all but the educated elite.

"We're seeing a class divide not only between the haves and the have-nots, but between the I do's and the I do nots," Dr. Coontz said. Those who are enjoying the perks of a good marriage "wouldn't stand for any other kind," she said, while those who would benefit most from marital stability "are the ones least likely to have the resources to sustain it."

Yet across the divide runs a white picket fence, our unshakable star-spangled belief in the value of marriage and family. We marry, divorce and remarry at rates not seen anywhere else in the developed world. We lavish $70 billion a year on weddings, more than we spend on pets, coffee, toothpaste and toilet paper combined.

We're sappy family romantics. When an informal sample of 52 Americans of different ages, professions and hometowns were asked the first thought that came to mind on hearing the word "family," the answers varied hardly at all. Love! Kids! Mom! Dinner!

"It's the backbone of how we live," said David Anderson, 52, an insurance claims adjuster from Chicago. "It means everything," said Linda McAdam, 28, who is in human resources on Long Island.

Yes, everything, and sometimes too many things. "It's almost like a weight," said Rob Fee, 26, a financial analyst in San Francisco, "a heavy weight." Or as the comedian George Burns said, "Happiness is having a large, loving, caring, close-knit family in another city."

In charting the differences between today's families and those of the past, demographers start with the kids—or rather the lack of them.

The nation's birthrate today is half what it was in 1960, and last year hit its lowest point ever. At the end of the baby boom, in 1964, 36 percent of all Americans were under 18 years old; last year, children accounted for just 23.5 percent of the population, and the proportion is dropping, to a projected 21 percent by 2050. Fewer women are becoming mothers—about 80 percent of those of childbearing age today versus 90 percent in the 1970s—and those who reproduce do so more sparingly, averaging two children apiece now, compared with three in the 1970s.

One big reason is the soaring cost of ushering offspring to functional independence. According to the Department of Agriculture, the average middle-class couple will spend $241,080

to raise a child to age 18. Factor in four years of college and maybe graduate school, or a parentally subsidized internship with the local theater company, and say hello to your million-dollar bundle of oh joy.

As steep as the fertility decline has been, the marriage rate has fallen more sharply, particularly among young women, who do most of the nation's childbearing. As a result, 41 percent of babies are now born out of wedlock, a fourfold increase since 1970.

The trend is not demographically uniform, instead tracking the nation's widening gap in income and opportunity. Among women with a bachelor's degree or higher, 90 percent adhere to the old playground song and put marriage before a baby carriage. For everybody else, maternity is often decoupled from matrimony: 40 percent of women with some college but no degree, and 57 percent of women with high school diplomas or less, are unmarried when they give birth to their first child.

More than one-quarter of these unwed mothers are living with a partner who may or may not be their child's biological father. The rise of the cohabiting couple is another striking feature of the evolving American family: From 1996 to 2012, the number jumped almost 170 percent, to 7.8 million from 2.9 million.

Nor are unmarried mothers typically in their teens; contrary to all the talk of an epidemic of teenage motherhood, the birthrate among adolescent girls has dropped by nearly half since 1991 and last year hit an all-time low, a public health triumph that experts attribute to better sex education and birth-control methods. Most unmarried mothers today, demographers say, are in their 20s and early 30s.

Also démodé is the old debate over whether mothers of dependent children should work outside the home. The facts have voted, the issue is settled, and Paycheck Mommy is now a central organizing principle of the modern American family.

The share of mothers employed full or part time has quadrupled since the 1950s and today accounts for nearly three-quarters of women with children at home. The number of women who are their families' sole or primary breadwinner also has soared, to 40 percent today from 11 percent in 1960.

"Yes, I wear the pants in the family," said Ana Perez, 35, a mother of three and a vice president at a financial services company in New York, who was, indeed, wearing pants. "I can say it brings me joy to know I can take care of my family."

Cultural attitudes are adapting accordingly. Sixty-two percent of the public, and 72 percent of adults under 30, view the ideal marriage as one in which husband and wife both work and share child care and household duties; back when Jimmy Carter was president, less than half of the population approved of the dual-income family, and less than half of 1 percent of husbands knew how to operate a sponge mop.

Mothers are bringing home more of the bacon, and of the mortarboards, too. While most couples are an even match scholastically, 28 percent of married women are better educated than their mates; that is true of just 19 percent of married men. Forty years ago, the asymmetry went the other way.

Some experts argue that the growing legion of mothers with advanced degrees has helped sharpen the already brutal competition for admission to the nation's elite universities, which stress the importance of extracurricular activities. Nothing predicts the breadth and busyness of a child's after-school schedule better, it turns out, than the mother's level of education.

One change that caught many family researchers by surprise was the recent dip in the divorce rate. After many decades of upward march, followed by a long, stubborn stay at the familiar 50 percent mark that made every nuptial feel like a coin flip, the rate began falling in 1996 and is now just above 40 percent for first-time marriages.

The decline has been even more striking among middle- and upper-middle-income couples with college degrees. For them, fewer than one in three marriages is expected to end in divorce, a degree of stability that allows elite couples to merge their resources with confidence, maximally invest in their children and otherwise widen the gap between themselves and the struggling masses.

There are exceptions, of course. Among baby boomers, the rate of marriage failure has surged 50 percent in the past 20 years—perhaps out of an irritable nostalgia, researchers said, for the days of free love, better love, anything but this love. Nor do divorce rates appear to have fallen among those who take the old Samuel Johnson quip as a prescription, allowing hope to triumph over experience, and marrying again and again.

For both Mike and Kristi Burns, now in their 40s, the first marriage came young and left early, and the second stuck around for more than a dozen years.

Kristi was 19, living in South Carolina, and her Marine boyfriend was about to be shipped to Japan. "I wasn't attached to him, really," she said, "but for some reason I felt this might be my only chance at marriage."

In Japan, Kristi gave birth to her son Brandon, realized she was lonely and miserable, and left the marriage seven weeks after their first anniversary. Back in the States, Kristi studied to be a travel agent, moved to Michigan and married her second husband at age 23.

He was an electrician. He adopted Brandon, and the couple had a son, Griffin. The marriage lasted 13 years.

"We were really great friends, but we weren't a great husband and wife," Kristi said. "Our parenting styles were too different."

Besides, she went on, "he didn't verbalize a lot, but he was mad a lot, and I was tired of walking around on eggshells."

After the divorce, friends persuaded her to try the online dating service Match.com, and just as her free trial week was about to expire, she noticed a new profile in the mix.

"Kristi was one of the first people to ping me," said Mike Burns, an engineer for an e-commerce company. "This was at 3 in the morning."

They started chatting. Mike told Kristi how he'd married his first wife while he was still in college—"definitely too young," he said—and divorced her two years later. He met his second wife through mutual friends, they had a big church wedding, started a software publishing company together, sold it and had two children, Brianna and Alec.

When the marriage started going downhill, Mike ignored signs of trouble, like the comments from neighbors who noticed his wife was never around on weekends.

"I was delusional, I was depressed," he said. "I still had the attitude that divorce wasn't something you did."

After 15 years of marriage, his wife did it for him, and kicked him out of the house. His divorce papers hadn't yet been finalized, he told Kristi that first chat night. I'll help you get through it, she replied.

Mike and Kristi admit their own three-year-old marriage isn't perfect. The kids are still adjusting to one another. Sometimes Kristi, a homemaker, feels jealous of how much attention her husband showers on his daughter Brianna, 13.

Sometimes Mike retreats into his computer. Yet they are determined to stay together.

"I know everyone thinks this marriage is a joke and people expect it to fail," said Kristi. "But that just makes me work harder at it."

"I'd say our chances of success are better than average," her husband added.

In America, family is at once about home and the next great frontier.

Critical Thinking

1. Would you say you grew up in a typical American family? What does the typical American family look like today?
2. Consider three ways families are different than they were 50 years ago. Why have these changes occurred? How have they served to change American society in both positive and negative ways?
3. Where do you see the future of the family in America going? What trends and changes in families do you anticipate seeing in the next 50 years?

Create Central

www.mhhe.com/createcentral

Internet References

Kearl's Guide to the Sociology of the Family
www.trinity.edu/MKEARL/family.html

U.S. Census: Families and Living Arrangements
http://www.census.gov/hhes/families

U.S. Department of Health and Human Services: Families
http://www.hhs.gov/children/index.html

World Family Map
http://worldfamilymap.org/2014/about

Article   Prepared by: Patricia Hrusa Williams, *University of Maine at Farmington*

A Million First Dates

How Online Romance Is Threatening Monogamy

DAN SLATER

Learning Outcomes

After reading this article, you will be able to:

- Recognize the positive and negative aspects of online dating.
- Understand how technology and changes in ideas about pre-marital sex, marriage, and commitment are changing dating and relationship formation.
- Describe factors important to relationship commitment.

After going to college on the East Coast and spending a few years bouncing around, Jacob moved back to his native Oregon, settling in Portland. Almost immediately, he was surprised by the difficulty he had meeting women. Having lived in New York and the Boston area, he was accustomed to ready-made social scenes. In Portland, by contrast, most of his friends were in long-term relationships with people they'd met in college, and were contemplating marriage.

Jacob was single for two years and then, at 26, began dating a slightly older woman who soon moved in with him. She seemed independent and low-maintenance, important traits for Jacob. Past girlfriends had complained about his lifestyle, which emphasized watching sports and going to concerts and bars. He'd been called lazy, aimless, and irresponsible with money.

Before long, his new relationship fell into that familiar pattern. "I've never been able to make a girl feel like she was the most important thing in my life," he says. "It's always 'I wish I was as important as the basketball game or the concert.'" An only child, Jacob tended to make plans by negotiation: if his girlfriend would watch the game with him, he'd go hiking with her. He was passive in their arguments, hoping to avoid confrontation. Whatever the flaws in their relationship, he told

himself, being with her was better than being single in Portland again.

After five years, she left.

Now in his early 30s, Jacob felt he had no idea how to make a relationship work. Was compatibility something that could be learned? Would permanence simply happen, or would he have to choose it? Around this time, he signed up for two online dating sites: Match.com, a paid site, because he'd seen the TV ads; and Plenty of Fish, a free site he'd heard about around town.

"It was fairly incredible," Jacob remembers. "I'm an average-looking guy. All of a sudden I was going out with one or two very pretty, ambitious women a week. At first I just thought it was some kind of weird lucky streak."

After six weeks, Jacob met a 22-year-old named Rachel, whose youth and good looks he says reinvigorated him. His friends were jealous. Was this The One? They dated for a few months, and then she moved in. (Both names have been changed for anonymity.)

Rachel didn't mind Jacob's sports addiction, and enjoyed going to concerts with him. But there were other issues. She was from a blue-collar military background; he came from doctors. She placed a high value on things he didn't think much about: a solid credit score, a 40-hour workweek. Jacob also felt pressure from his parents, who were getting anxious to see him paired off for good. Although a younger girlfriend bought him some time, biologically speaking, it also alienated him from his friends, who could understand the physical attraction but couldn't really relate to Rachel.

In the past, Jacob had always been the kind of guy who didn't break up well. His relationships tended to drag on. His desire to be with someone, to not have to go looking again, had always trumped whatever doubts he'd had about the person he was with. But something was different this time. "I feel like I underwent a fairly radical change thanks to online dating,"

Jacob says. "I went from being someone who thought of finding someone as this monumental challenge, to being much more relaxed and confident about it. Rachel was young and beautiful, and I'd found her after signing up on a couple dating sites and dating just a few people." Having met Rachel so easily online, he felt confident that, if he became single again, he could always meet someone else.

After two years, when Rachel informed Jacob that she was moving out, he logged on to Match.com the same day. His old profile was still up. Messages had even come in from people who couldn't tell he was no longer active. The site had improved in the two years he'd been away. It was sleeker, faster, more efficient. And the population of online daters in Portland seemed to have tripled. He'd never imagined that so many single people were out there.

"I'm about 95 percent certain," he says, "that if I'd met Rachel offline, and if I'd never done online dating, I would've married her. At that point in my life, I would've overlooked everything else and done whatever it took to make things work. Did online dating change my perception of permanence? No doubt. When I sensed the breakup coming, I was okay with it. It didn't seem like there was going to be much of a mourning period, where you stare at your wall thinking you're destined to be alone and all that. I was eager to see what else was out there."

The positive aspects of online dating are clear: the Internet makes it easier for single people to meet other single people with whom they might be compatible, raising the bar for what they consider a good relationship. But what if online dating makes it *too* easy to meet someone new? What if it raises the bar for a good relationship *too* high? What if the prospect of finding an ever-more-compatible mate with the click of a mouse means a future of relationship instability, in which we keep chasing the elusive rabbit around the dating track?

Of course, no one knows exactly how many partnerships are undermined by the allure of the Internet dating pool. But most of the online-dating-company executives I interviewed while writing my new book, *Love in the Time of Algorithms,* agreed with what research appears to suggest: the rise of online dating will mean an overall decrease in commitment.

"The future will see better relationships but more divorce," predicts Dan Winchester, the founder of a free dating site based in the U.K. "The older you get as a man, the more experienced you get. You know what to do with women, how to treat them and talk to them. Add to that the effect of online dating." He continued, "I often wonder whether matching you up with great people is getting so efficient, and the process so enjoyable, that marriage will become obsolete."

"Historically," says Greg Blatt, the CEO of Match.com's parent company, "relationships have been billed as 'hard' because, historically, commitment has been the goal. You could say online dating is simply changing people's ideas about whether commitment itself is a life value." Mate scarcity also plays an important role in people's relationship decisions. "Look, if I lived in Iowa, I'd be married with four children by now," says Blatt, a 40-something bachelor in Manhattan. "That's just how it is."

"As we become more secure in our ability to find someone else . . . the old thinking about commitment will be challenged very harshly."

Another online-dating exec hypothesized an inverse correlation between commitment and the efficiency of technology. "I think divorce rates will increase as life in general becomes more real-time," says Niccolò Formai, the head of social-media marketing at Badoo, a meeting-and-dating app with about 25 million active users worldwide. "Think about the evolution of other kinds of content on the Web—stock quotes, news. The goal has always been to make it faster. The same thing will happen with meeting. It's exhilarating to connect with new people, not to mention beneficial for reasons having nothing to do with romance. You network for a job. You find a flatmate. Over time you'll expect that constant flow. People always said that the need for stability would keep commitment alive. But that thinking was based on a world in which you didn't meet that many people."

"Societal values always lose out," says Noel Biderman, the founder of Ashley Madison, which calls itself "the world's leading married dating service for discreet encounters"— that is, cheating. "Premarital sex used to be taboo," explains Biderman. "So women would become miserable in marriages, because they wouldn't know any better. But today, more people have had failed relationships, recovered, moved on, and found happiness. They realize that that happiness, in many ways, depends on having had the failures. As we become more secure and confident in our ability to find someone else, usually someone better, monogamy and the old thinking about commitment will be challenged very harshly."

Even at eHarmony—one of the most conservative sites, where marriage and commitment seem to be the only acceptable goals of dating—Gian Gonzaga, the site's relationship psychologist, acknowledges that commitment is at odds with technology. "You could say online dating allows people to get into relationships, learn things, and ultimately make a better selection," says Gonzaga. "But you could also easily see a world in which online dating leads to people leaving relationships the moment they're not working—an overall weakening of commitment."

Indeed, the profit models of many online-dating sites are at cross-purposes with clients who are trying to develop long-term commitments. A permanently paired-off dater, after all, means a lost revenue stream. Explaining the mentality of a typical dating-site executive, Justin Parfitt, a dating entrepreneur based in San Francisco, puts the matter bluntly: "They're thinking, *Let's keep this fucker coming back to the site as often as we can.*" For instance, long after their accounts become inactive on Match.com and some other sites, lapsed users receive notifications informing them that wonderful people are browsing their profiles and are eager to chat. "Most of our users are return customers," says Match.com's Blatt.

In 2011, Mark Brooks, a consultant to online-dating companies, published the results of an industry survey titled "How Has Internet Dating Changed Society?" The survey responses, from 39 executives, produced the following conclusions:

"Internet dating has made people more disposable."

"Internet dating may be partly responsible for a rise in the divorce rates."

"Low quality, unhappy and unsatisfying marriages are being destroyed as people drift to Internet dating sites."

"The market is hugely more efficient. . . . People expect to—and this will be increasingly the case over time—access people anywhere, anytime, based on complex search requests. . . . Such a feeling of access affects our pursuit of love . . . the whole world (versus, say, the city we live in) will, increasingly, feel like the market for our partner(s). Our pickiness will probably increase."

"Above all, Internet dating has helped people of all ages realize that there's no need to settle for a mediocre relationship."

Alex Mehr, a co-founder of the dating site Zoosk, is the only executive I interviewed who disagrees with the prevailing view. "Online dating does nothing more than remove a barrier to meeting," says Mehr. "Online dating doesn't change my taste, or how I behave on a first date, or whether I'm going to be a good partner. It only changes the process of discovery. As for whether you're the type of person who wants to commit to a long-term monogamous relationship or the type of person who wants to play the field, online dating has nothing to do with that. That's a personality thing."

Surely personality will play a role in the way anyone behaves in the realm of online dating, particularly when it comes to commitment and promiscuity. (Gender, too, may play a role. Researchers are divided on the question of whether men pursue more "short-term mates" than women do.) At the same time, however, the reality that having too many options makes us less content with whatever option we choose is a well-documented phenomenon. In his 2004 book, *The Paradox of Choice,* the psychologist Barry Schwartz indicts a society that "sanctifies freedom of choice so profoundly that the benefits of infinite options seem self-evident." On the contrary, he argues, "a large array of options may diminish the attractiveness of what people *actually* choose, the reason being that thinking about the attractions of some of the unchosen options detracts from the pleasure derived from the chosen one."

Psychologists who study relationships say that three ingredients generally determine the strength of commitment: overall satisfaction with the relationship; the investment one has put into it (time and effort, shared experiences and emotions, etc.); and the quality of perceived alternatives. Two of the three—satisfaction and quality of alternatives—could be directly affected by the larger mating pool that the Internet offers.

At the selection stage, researchers have seen that as the range of options grows larger, mate-seekers are liable to become "cognitively overwhelmed," and deal with the overload by adopting lazy comparison strategies and examining fewer cues. As a result, they are more likely to make careless decisions than they would be if they had fewer options, and this potentially leads to less compatible matches. Moreover, the mere fact of having chosen someone from such a large set of options can lead to doubts about whether the choice was the "right" one. No studies in the romantic sphere have looked at precisely how the range of choices affects overall satisfaction. But research elsewhere has found that people are less satisfied when choosing from a larger group: in one study, for example, subjects who selected a chocolate from an array of six options believed it tasted better than those who selected the same chocolate from an array of 30.

On that other determinant of commitment, the quality of perceived alternatives, the Internet's potential effect is clearer still. Online dating is, at its core, a litany of alternatives. And evidence shows that the perception that one has appealing alternatives to a current romantic partner is a strong predictor of low commitment to that partner.

"You can say three things," says Eli Finkel, a professor of social psychology at Northwestern University who studies how online dating affects relationships. "First, the best marriages are probably unaffected. Happy couples won't be hanging out on dating sites. Second, people who are in marriages that are either bad or average might be at increased risk of divorce, because of increased access to new partners. Third, it's unknown whether that's good or bad for society. On one hand, it's good if fewer people feel like they're stuck in relationships. On the other, evidence is pretty solid that having a stable romantic partner means all kinds of health and wellness benefits." And that's even before one takes into account the ancillary effects of such a decrease in commitment—on children, for example, or even society more broadly.

Gilbert Feibleman, a divorce attorney and member of the American Academy of Matrimonial Lawyers, argues that the phenomenon extends beyond dating sites to the Internet more generally. "I've seen a dramatic increase in cases where something on the computer triggered the breakup," he says. "People are more likely to leave relationships, because they're emboldened by the knowledge that it's no longer as hard as it was to meet new people. But whether it's dating sites, social media, e-mail—it's all related to the fact that the Internet has made it possible for people to communicate and connect, anywhere in the world, in ways that have never before been seen."

Since Rachel left him, Jacob has met lots of women online. Some like going to basketball games and concerts with him. Others enjoy barhopping. Jacob's favorite football team is the Green Bay Packers, and when I last spoke to him, he told me he'd had success using Packers fandom as a search criterion on OkCupid, another (free) dating site he's been trying out.

Many of Jacob's relationships become physical very early. At one point he's seeing a paralegal and a lawyer who work at the same law firm, a naturopath, a pharmacist, and a chef. He slept with three of them on the first or second date. His relationships with the other two are headed toward physical intimacy.

He likes the pharmacist most. She's a girlfriend prospect. The problem is that she wants to take things slow on the physical side. He worries that, with so many alternatives available, he won't be willing to wait.

One night the paralegal confides in him: her prior relationships haven't gone well, but Jacob gives her hope; all she needs in a relationship is honesty. And he thinks, *Oh my God*. He wants to be a nice guy, but he knows that sooner or later he's going to start coming across as a serious asshole. While out with one woman, he has to silence text messages coming in from others. He needs to start paring down the number of women he's seeing.

People seeking commitment—particularly women—have developed strategies to detect deception and guard against it. A woman might withhold sex so she can assess a man's intentions. Theoretically, her withholding sends a message: *I'm not just going to sleep with any guy that comes along.* Theoretically, his willingness to wait sends a message back: *I'm interested in more than sex.*

But the pace of technology is upending these rules and assumptions. Relationships that begin online, Jacob finds, move quickly. He chalks this up to a few things. First, familiarity is established during the messaging process, which also often involves a phone call. By the time two people meet face-to-face, they already have a level of intimacy. Second, if the woman is on a dating site, there's a good chance she's eager to connect. But for Jacob, the most crucial difference between online dating and meeting people in the "real" world is the sense of urgency. Occasionally, he has an acquaintance in common with a woman he meets online, but by and large she comes from a different social pool. "It's not like we're just going to run into each other again," he says. "So you can't afford to be too casual. It's either 'Let's explore this' or 'See you later.'"

> ## "The Internet has made it possible for people to communicate and connect . . . in ways that have never before been seen."

Social scientists say that all sexual strategies carry costs, whether risk to reputation (promiscuity) or foreclosed alternatives (commitment). As online dating becomes increasingly pervasive, the old costs of a short-term mating strategy will give way to new ones. Jacob, for instance, notices he's seeing his friends less often. Their wives get tired of befriending his

latest girlfriend only to see her go when he moves on to someone else. Also, Jacob has noticed that, over time, he feels less excitement before each new date. "Is that about getting older," he muses, "or about dating online?" How much of the enchantment associated with romantic love has to do with scarcity (*this person is exclusively for me*), and how will that enchantment hold up in a marketplace of abundance (*this person could be exclusively for me, but so could the other two people I'm meeting this week*)?

Using OkCupid's Locals app, Jacob can now advertise his location and desired activity and meet women on the fly. Out alone for a beer one night, he responds to the broadcast of a woman who's at the bar across the street, looking for a karaoke partner. He joins her. They spend the evening together, and never speak again.

"Each relationship is its own little education," Jacob says. "You learn more about what works and what doesn't, what you really need and what you can go without. That feels like a useful process. I'm not jumping into something with the wrong person, or committing to something too early, as I've done in the past." But he does wonder: When does it end? At what point does this learning curve become an excuse for not putting in the effort to make a relationship last? "Maybe I have the confidence now to go after the person I really want," he says. "But I'm worried that I'm making it so I can't fall in love."

Critical Thinking

1. What are some advantages and disadvantages of online dating to relationship formation?

2. This article suggests that online dating is contributing to less commitment among singles and higher divorce rates. Do you agree or disagree? Why?

3. List factors important to relationship commitment. Describe how online dating may serve to strengthen or weaken commitment in relationships.

4. How do you see technology changing dating, mate selection, and relationship formation in the future?

Create Central

www.mhhe.com/createcentral

Internet References

Helpguide: How to Find Lasting Love
http://www.helpguide.org/mental/how_to_dating_find_love.htm

Love Is Respect
www.loveisrespect.org

Relationships Australia
www.relationships.org.au

Article

Prepared by: Patricia Hrusa Williams,
University of Maine at Farmington

Goy Meets Girl

Anna Weaver

Learning Outcomes

After reading this article, you will be able to:

- Define interfaith and interchurch marriages.

- Discuss the challenges faced by couples who do not share the same religious faith experience.

- Describe some ways interfaith and interchurch couples negotiate religious differences and conflicts.

Before Juliann Richards met Neal Levy, she didn't doubt that she'd marry a fellow Catholic someday. After all, Richards was raised Catholic, attended Catholic school, grew up mostly around fellow Catholics, and knew she wanted her children raised with the same faith.

"For many years, I told myself (and others) that I was going to the nearby Catholic college so I could meet a nice Catholic boy and get married," Richards recalls.

But when she met Levy—who is Jewish—the two quickly became friends and eventually started dating. Fast-forward several years: Richards and Levy, both 27, are newlyweds who married in a Jewish-Catholic ceremony.

Such marriages—interfaith (between a Catholic and a non-Christian) and interchurch (between a Catholic and another Christian)—have been on the rise for the past 30 years.

In fact, a 2007 survey on marriage by the Center for Applied Research in the Apostolate (CARA) revealed that marrying another Catholic is a low priority for young Catholics. Of never-married Catholics, only 7 percent said it was "very important" to marry someone of the same faith.

"We realize that this is a major pastoral issue," says Sheila Garcia, associate director of the U.S. Conference of Catholic Bishops' Secretariat on Laity, Marriage, Family Life, and Youth.

Good Foundation

Garcia says that while supporting these couples pastorally, the church also is concerned with making sure the Catholic in a mixed-religion marriage continues to practice his or her faith and that the couple takes seriously the Catholic party's pledge to raise their children Catholic.

Despite these challenges, Garcia believes that mixed marriages offer an opportunity for "peace and understanding, and, where possible, unity."

"The Catholic Church is moving towards how to support the interchurch/interfaith couple," Garcia says. "Mixed religion couples can live out Christ's call to be one."

One of the landmark changes in how the church approaches interfaith and interchurch engaged couples came with the 1983 revision to the Code of Canon Law, around the same time many of the millennials getting married today were born. Before the revision, the non-Catholic party had to sign a document saying they agreed that their children would be raised Catholic. Post-revision, the Catholic spouse pledges to maintain his or her faith and "to do all in her or his power so that all off-spring are baptized and brought up in the Catholic Church." The non-Catholic is informed of that pledge.

"We've changed quite a bit of stuff since Vatican II," says Claretian Father Greg Kenny. "I don't think allegiance to one church or one faith should keep you from the most basic command, that you should love one another."

Kenny says the way the Catholic Church should deal with the growing number of interfaith marriages is on a grassroots level, one couple at a time, with parish and diocesan programs.

"If we can get across to people that religion is not getting in the way, that religion is there to help, that makes so much more sense to me," he says. "Marriage preparation becomes a possible moment of grace."

A Nice Catholic Boy

Despite the rise in interfaith and interchurch marriages, they're not at an all-time high. According to CARA, the highest rate of interfaith marriages took place in the 1970s and 1980s, when young Catholics dispersed from East Coast and Midwestern cities into areas of the country where there were fewer Catholic enclaves.

But as Ohio couple Richards and Levy illustrate, attraction and love can trump proximity to potential partners of the same faith. While Richards' Ohio hometown has three Catholic churches and a majority Christian populace, once she met Levy all her plans for a "nice Catholic boy" disappeared.

As they dated, the two made sure big issues like how their children would be raised or what religious traditions were important to them were discussed respectfully and resolved early on without either forgoing their faith.

When the two decided to get married, the prospect of planning for a Jewish-Catholic ceremony and, more importantly, a marriage got easier when they found an understanding priest, Father David Bline, pastor of St. Francis de Sales Parish in Akron, Ohio. Bline had worked with Rabbi Susan Stone on another interfaith marriage and put the couple in touch with her.

Richards and Levy went through both Catholic and Jewish pre-marital counseling and were surprised at how "refreshingly similar" the advice they received from both sides was. "It was good to know that the same things were being asked of us," Richards says.

They plan to raise their children Catholic, but they both say their kids will be well aware of their Jewish heritage, and they were encouraged to raise them as such by Bline.

Respect for both of their beliefs extended into their wedding ceremony, which was led by both the priest and the rabbi. There were readings from the Hebrew scriptures and the New Testament, signing of an interfaith *ketubah* (a Jewish marriage contract), drinking from a *kiddush* cup, and the couple stood under a *chuppah,* or canopy during the ceremony. All the ceremony components were explained to guests in an extensive program.

Richards and Levy say being rasised in "very open and accepting families," has helped support them throughout their relationship.

Family Conflict

Things went differently for Midwesterners Sarah and Mike Miles (not their real names), who were surprised at just how much tension their own Jewish-Catholic union churned up in Mike's family.

This is Sarah's second marriage. In her first, which lasted about three years, she married a fellow Jew. "It was important for me to marry someone Jewish at that time," she says, adding that her mother was also a big advocate of marrying someone of the same faith.

Mike was raised Catholic, in what he calls a "very religious family." He went to a Catholic school and attends Mass regularly.

"When I started dating and when I met Sarah, religion wasn't a factor," he says. "I wasn't marrying someone because of her religion. I was marrying Sarah because she was who she was."

I wasn't marrying someone because of her religion. I was marrying Sarah because she was who she was.

When they got engaged, both Sarah and Mike took interfaith marriage preparation classes, which helped with tough discussions they had about raising kids, celebrating holidays, and dealing with family dynamics.

The classes suggested they pick one religion for their future children. "We chose Judaism early on because it was the root of all Christianity, and there was nothing in my religion that Mike couldn't understand," Sarah says.

It wasn't until after they were married and the topic of children came up that Mike's parents voiced their disagreement with how their grandchildren would be raised. They also complained that the Jewish traditions had overshadowed the Catholic traditions at the Miles' wedding.

Sarah and Mike decided to go to an interfaith marriage counselor and tried to talk with Mike's parents. But face-to-face conversations, letters, and phone calls didn't seem to help.

Several years later, Sarah and Mike have a distant relationship with Mike's parents. But the difficulties have only brought them closer, they say.

"We'd like [his parents] to be a part of [our lives], and we welcome that opportunity, but only if we can get these issues resolved."

Ecumenical Glue

Even with a common Christian background, interchurch couples have issues to resolve in order to make their marriages work. For Lena and Luke Glover, the bond that holds their marriage together goes beyond Sunday church services. Lena, 35, is Catholic, and Luke, 34, is a nondenominational Christian.

When the two were first married there were tensions, such as when they would attend Mass together and Luke couldn't receive communion, including at their own nuptial Mass. "It highlights our divisions," Luke says.

What helped the Glovers find common ground was the ecumenical charismatic group People of Praise. "It's kind of the glue for our marriage," Luke says. "It focuses on the similarities of our life together."

"It gives us something to do together as a family and as a couple that's kind of bigger than church," Lena says. "If we went round and round about our differences we would spend all our time arguing!"

The couple believes that the differences they have in faith aren't major but that the things they do hold in common, such as their belief in Christ and the gospel, are.

"Now I wouldn't want to change [our religions] for the world," Lena says. "It doesn't bother me anymore because I feel like we experience a level of ecumenism more acutely than those couples that are of the same denomination, and I'm so grateful for that."

The couple now lives in Portland, Oregon and has four children, ages 11, 9, 6, and 5, all of whom are being raised Catholic. For a while the Glovers would attend both a Catholic and a Protestant service on Sundays plus the People of Praise community meetings. But being in church all day was difficult with young kids. Luke decided he'd choose going to Mass with the family.

"We do raise them Catholic, but we give that a little caveat and say we are raising them in a very ecumenical home," Lena says.

Their older two kids are asking more questions now, like why Luke doesn't take communion—he receives a blessing—or why some people pray the rosary. "We teach that there are Christians that emphasize different things," Lena says.

She's proud that her children are learning about different denominations. . . .

The USCCB's Sheila Garcia says that ecumenical and interfaith couples are the grassroots version of what the Catholic Church hopes to accomplish in its ecumenical and interfaith statements, dialogues, conferences, and outreach.

"What these couples are living out in their own lives is what these dialogues are trying to accomplish," Garcia says.

One Family Table

No matter how much interchurch couples such as the Glovers work toward unity, there's a clear and highly visible sign of their disunity—communion.

Bonnie Mack, who works for the Archdiocese of Cincinnati's Marriage and Family Life Office, says, "For nearly every Catholic-Protestant couple that I've talked to, there is pain from not receiving communion together.

"There are some who would say, 'I don't think Jesus would do that. I think he'd call anyone forward.'"

And in fact she has seen some young couples from the marriage preparation classes she teaches go up and receive communion together despite one not being Catholic. "Their way of handling church teachings is much different today," she says. "It's no big deal to them."

Over the years she's seen pastors try to balance the pastoral side and the church-teaching side of the issue. One pastor who has long dealt with the issue is Claretian Father Kenny. He has worked with interfaith and interchurch couples in the Northeast and now at his present assignment in the South as pastor emeritus of Corpus Christi Parish in Stone Mountain, Georgia.

Kenny says that in his area interchurch marriages are very common since Catholics are only the third largest denomination in the region, outnumbered by Baptists and Methodists.

"What I now explain is why the church is so stringent on that issue. There needs to be unity of worship, unity of belief, of dogma, and unity of conduct and morality to receive communion."

But he adds, "If you could say that this was the only way to get the spiritual nourishment you seek, follow your conscience. I can't tell you not to follow your conscience."

Sometimes what begins as an interchurch relationship ends with one person joining the Catholic Church. Matt and Jessica Williams are one such couple who found their faith backgrounds coming together even before they were married. Jessica, 32, was baptized Lutheran but was not raised practicing that faith.

Jessica first met Matt, 43, through a mutual friend. About three or four months into their relationship, Matt, a cradle Catholic, invited Jessica to attend Mass with him at his parish, St. Margaret Mary in Winter Park, Florida.

"It really helped strengthen our relationship . . . to go to church together," Matt says. "It was just a very important part of the week for us."

He also recalls being surprised when, a few months into going to church together, Jessica turned to him and said, "All you have to do is ask me to convert."

Matt says he'd been careful not to put any pressure on her, but was delighted. Jessica enrolled in RCIA, where the director, Dominican Sister Rosemary Finnegan, double-checked that, as Jessica puts it, "Your heart was in it, and that you were not just converting because it was 'the right thing to do.'"

When the pair married in 2010, two months after Jessica became Catholic, it was at a Mass at St. Margaret Mary. The Williamses say that a mutual Catholic faith has served as a strong base when they face challenges.

"It's nice to have that extra support system in place," Jessica says. And as they look into the future at having kids, she says she's happy that they won't be one of those families she'd observed at church with an absentee or non-Catholic parent.

"I wanted our kids to grow up being raised in the faith, praying with them, and trying to educate them on the faith wherever we can," Jessica says.

Matt says he never felt "locked into" the idea of marrying another Catholic. "But now that it's a reality, it's very important to me," he says. "And looking back, maybe it's more important than I realized."

Belief Differences

It's one thing for a couple to come from a common Christian background, or to at least share a religious foundation, but Bonnie Mack says it's another thing when one person has no faith.

"One, you can't draw on commonalities, and two, those couples tend to drift away from church altogether," she says.

Christie and Peter Wood disagree. The 27-year-old couple met while attending the University of Maryland. They dated for four years before Peter proposed while stargazing in Christie's backyard. They married in 2010, at Peter's home parish, St. Paul in Damascus, Maryland.

Christie was raised Methodist but now considers herself an agnostic. Peter describes himself as a "pretty hard-core" Catholic.

The newlyweds' marriage parallels Peter's parents' relationship. Peter's dad was raised Methodist but didn't practice his faith as an adult, and Peter's mom is Catholic. His father was active in helping out with church and community projects and never converted to Catholicism.

"My dad showed me that it really matters more that you walk the walk as opposed to talk the talk," Peter says. "I was able to see that a marriage like that could work. I have a good model and good support in my parents."

Christie says that when they began dating, she found Peter's faith appealing. "I kind of admired it actually. I felt it was a lot of who he is," she says. "It was that level of dedication [to his faith] that was impressive, and it was also obvious to me that his faith is what made him such a good person. I could see that reflected in his everyday actions.

"We have the same morals. We still agree on most issues and how we run our life," Christie adds.

The Woods admit that it will be more difficult once they have kids and want to send a consistent message to them about religion.

On the Web

For more tips on how to prepare for an interfaith or interchurch marriage, visit *uscatholic.org*.

"The most difficult thing will probably be when our [child] starts asking questions, but before they're old enough to understand that Peter and I have different views," she says. "For example, I'm sure the question of, 'Why doesn't mommy go to church?' will come up. It's a complicated answer that Peter and I understand, but one that will be trickier to explain to a little child."

However, Peter adds, "I feel like it would be a lot more challenging if we had different religious perspectives that were competing with one another or trying to steal time from each other."

Sheila Garcia notes that even Catholics who marry Catholics often have faith differences. A regular Mass-goer in a relationship with a twice-a-year Catholic is "practically a mixed marriage in and of itself," she says.

What's key, Garcia believes, is that every couple has to address and explore the differences in their religious beliefs because the issues won't resolve themselves. And diocesan and parish programs should support them in their faith explorations.

Critical Thinking

1. What is the difference between an interfaith marriage and an interchurch marriage?
2. How much does a potential partner's religion factor into mate selection and marriage decisions?
3. What challenges are faced by couples who are part of interfaith and interchurch marriages?
4. This article explores the challenges of unions between Catholics and non-Catholics. Do you think interfaith or interchurch marriages between different groups are more or less challenging?
5. What supports are needed for couples contemplating interfaith and interchurch marriages?

Create Central

www.mhhe.com/createcentral

Internet References

Combined Jewish Philanthropies: Interfaith Couples and Families
www.cjp.org/interfaith-couples-and-families.aspx

Families Forever: Strengthening Interfaith Marriages
http://foreverfamilies.byu.edu/Article.aspx?a=146

ANNA WEAVER is a Hawaii-born writer now living in Washington, D.C.

Article

Prepared by: Patricia Hrusa Williams,
University of Maine at Farmington

The Child's Advocate in Donor Conceptions: The Telling of the Story

KRIS A. PROBASCO

Learning Outcomes

After reading this article, you will be able to:

- Define the term "donor conception."

- Understand the ethical and personal dilemmas faced by parents who conceive via donor conception.

- Recognize how issues about family, adoption, and biological heritage can be addressed with children in a developmentally appropriate way.

Traditionally, to create a child, there is a joining of a woman's egg and a man's sperm via sexual intercourse. When, by choice or by happenstance, this process is not available, modern persons have access to additional methods. These methods stem from the donation of materials originating in others, a donated egg, donated sperm, or more recently, a donated fertilized frozen embryo. The donations range from easily obtained material (sperm) to complexly obtained material (eggs) to material created via a large sum of money and effort by the donors (embryo) (see Figure 1). As in traditional adoption, the donor procedure of creating a child involves a minimum of two parties, one in whom the gamete material was created and one who accepts this material to obtain a child.

> **Donated Egg:** Transfer of preovulatory oocytes from voluntary donor to a suitable host. Oocytes are collected through an invasive procedure, fertilized in vitro, and transferred to the host.
>
> **Donated Sperm:** Collection of ejaculated sperm from voluntary donor used to fertilize egg in human host or in vitro.
>
> **Donated Embryo:** Embryo that has been created through in vitro fertilization in excess of what was used by the gestating woman. Often frozen for further use, recent trend to donate for adoption by others.

Figure 1. Definitions

The history of donor conception dates back to 1884, when the first case of donor insemination was documented. At that time, physicians were using their own sperm for conception (Snowden, 1983). The first documented case of egg donation was in 1983 (Buster et al., 1983), and embryo placement and adoption began in 1997 ("Embryo adoption becoming the rage," 2009). Donor conceptions are provided for couples with male or female infertility, individuals who have a genetic disorder they do not want to pass on to a child, second marriages where there was a vasectomy in the first marriage, single women, and the lesbian and gay population. Estimates are that thousands of children are born by donor conception each year in the United States, more than the number of infants placed in traditional adoptions.

This article suggests the assistance families will need in sharing the stories of their children's beginnings with them. This author believes that keeping origins secret can be detrimental to a child's mental health, and that open donation, similar to open adoption, is most helpful in the healthy family system.

Preparing for Parenthood

Unlike the traditional method of pregnancy in which one-third of all pregnancies are unplanned, using donor material takes some intention. An essential step in the process is coming to terms with the choice to use donor material. Parents must accept that this chosen alternative is different. Grieving the loss of personal ability to create the genetic offspring, the loss of the biological child or a marriage or relationship that would create a genetic child is an important factor in being prepared to parent children through a donor conception. Mental health therapists have found through experience as counselors to families that without preparation of the parents through education and courses, the losses tend to become the responsibility and burden of the child. Mental health therapists believe a child should be born into a family without having to cure the situation that brought donor conception to the family. For many, a history of infertility has preceded the decision for a donor conception. Acknowledgement and acceptance of all losses connected to the infertility struggle is a part of parenting preparation.

Young Children (Ages 3 to 10)

How I Began: The Story of Donor Insemination, by N.S.W
Infertility Social Workers Group, J. Paul, (Ed.), 1988, Port
Melbourne, Australia: The Fertility Society of Australia.

Let Me Explain: A Story About Donor Insemination, by J. Schnitter,
1995, Indianapolis, IN: Perspectives Press.

*Mommy, Did I Grow in Your Tummy? Where Some Babies Come
From,* by E. Gordon, 1992, California: E.M. Greenberg
Press, Inc.

My Story/Our Story, by Donor Conception Network, 2002, London:
Donor Conception Network.

Phoebe's Family: A Story about Egg Donation, by L. Stamm, 2010,
Niskayuna, NY: Graphite Press.

*Sometimes It Takes 3 to Make a Baby: Explaining Egg Donation to
Young Children,* by K. Bourne, 2002, Melbourne, Australia:
Melbourne IVF.

The Family Book, by T. Parr, 2003, New York: Little, Brown & Co.

Before You Were Born, Our Wish for a Baby, by J. Grimes, 2004,
Webster, IA: X, Y, and Me.

Older Children (12 and Older)

Behind Closed Doors: Moving Beyond Secrecy and Shame, by
M. Marrissette, 2006, New York: Be-Mondo Publishing Inc.

Who Am I? Experiences of Donor Conception, by A. McWhinnie,
2006, Warwickshire, UK: Idreos Education Trust.

Nurses and Parents

Building a Family with the Assistance of Donor Insemination, by
K. Daniels, 2004, Wellington, New Zealand: Dunmore Press.

*Choosing to be Open about Donor Conception: Experiences of
Parents,* by S. Pettle and J. Burns, 2002, London Donor
Conception Network.

*Experience of Donor Conception: Parents, Offspring & Donors
through the Years,* by C. Lorbach, 2003, London: Jessica
Kingsley Publishers.

*Families Following Assisted Conception: What Do We Tell Our
Child?* by A. McWhinnie, 1996, Dundee, UK: University of
Dundee.

Telling and Talking about Donor Conception: A Guide for Parents,
by Donor Conception Network, 2006. London: Donor
Conception Network.

*Third Party Assisted Conception Across Cultures: Social, Legal
& Ethical Perspectives,* by E. Blyth and R. Landau, 2003,
London: Jessica Kingsley Publishers.

*Truth & the Child 10 Years On: Information Exchange in Donor
Assisted Conception,* edited by E. Blyth, M. Crawshaw, and
J. Speirs, 1998, Birmingham, UK: British Association of
Social Workers.

*Lethal Secrets, The Psychology of Donor Insemination Problems
and Solutions,* by A. Baron and R. Pannor, 2008, Las Vegas,
NV: Triadoption Publications.

*Mommies, Daddies, Donors, Surrogates: Answering Tough
Questions and Building Strong Families,* by D. Ehrensaft,
2005, New York: Guilford Press.

Figure 2.   Readings

Note: Many of these publications are available through the Infertility Network
(www.InfertilityNetwork.org).

The Donor Sibling Registry
www.donorsiblingregistry.com
Infertility Network
www.InfertilityNetwork.org
Embryo Adoption Awareness Center
www.embryoadoption.org
Adoptive Families (magazine)
www.adoptivefamilies.com
American Society for Reproductive Medicine
www.asrm.org

Figure 3.   Websites of Interest

For couples planning to parent a child by donor conception,
it is vital that both individuals emotionally accept the decision
for a donor. The infertile couple needs assistance from others
to make the conception medically possible. The nature vs. nurture debate has been illuminated by years of adoption research
(Bouchard, Lykken, McGue, Segal, & Tellegan, 1989) that who
we become is approximately 50% nature and 50% nurture.
Those who choose sperm or egg donation must accept the sig-
nificance of the genetic component in their child's life. For an
embryo placement, the child's complete genetics are connected
to another family. Thus, it is important that parents learn as
much as they can about the donors they are 'inviting into their
home,' accept that another person or family is helping to conceive the child, and that the child may have life-long genetic,
social, and emotional connections to that family.

Earlier in my career as a social worker in the infertility and
donor world, there was very little information, if any, provided
regarding the anonymous donors. Sperm and eggs came privately or with very basic medical information. This has now
changed. Resources are now available to select a donor's
genetic material based on social, psychological, and medical
information, including pictures, videos, and audio tapes, and
identified donors who can be available for medical emergency
and as social contacts at a later date. In embryo placement,
there are open arrangements so the genetic family and prospective adoptive family know about each other and continue to be a
resource for both families as their children grow in understanding their particular stories.

Education

Whether traditional adoption, donor conception, or embryo placement, education of prospective parents is mandatory. Educational
resources are increasingly available, including books, children's
books, the Infertility Network from Canada, and the Donor Sibling Registry (see Figures 2 and 3). All of these resources have
Internet connections for those in the decision-making process
and families who are parenting children, and also include messages from those who came to a family by donor conception. It
is important to learn from those who have come before us so parents can become effective advocates for their children.

In adoption, it is positive for families to announce their decision to their family and friends to gain their support. Because a donor conception includes a pregnancy in the family, the question of whether to go public is more difficult. While families deserve some privacy regarding personal decisions, it is well known from family systems theory that secrets cause problems. From my clinical experience, it is generally best that couples who are successful with a donor conception share with family and friends. It benefits the family to celebrate the unique arrival of this child and to share in the celebration because this will be a very important part in the child's story.

Legal Issues

Legal issues with donor conception are evolving. Many states have legislation regarding sperm donor insemination, few states have legislation regarding egg donation, and only one state has legislation regarding embryo placement. In the Kansas City area, both Kansas and Missouri have legislation for sperm donation. There is no legislation for egg donation or embryo placement. In my practice, we recommend a stepparent adoption in egg donation and a full adoption for embryo placement with an adoption decree. Recognizing what legal liabilities are present for a child born by donor conception in the state of residency provides for the child's security.

The Child's Story
Beginning the Story

The basic need of a child brought to any family is a positive attitude about his or her conception, birth, and family. Accepting the child as an individual with a unique, genetic history is a crucial factor for donor conceptions. The parents' decision to bring a child into their family by donor represents the first step for creating a positive story. As in traditional adoption, it is the parents' job to tell all they know regarding their donor conception to help the child understand. There is an attachment process during the child's growing years, which is enhanced by honest stories about how the child came to be. We want a child/adult to say they do not remember being told because they always knew how they came into the family.

Infancy

During the child's infancy is a time for parents to practice talking to their child with positive language and feelings. "We so wanted to be parents. We were meant to be your parents. We are so happy that we got help. Many people assisted us in your coming to our family, especially our donor." Tone of voice communicates pride, love, and celebration, explaining, "We have so much to tell you and we are so excited for you to understand how you came into our family." Continue the positive language and talk basically throughout the child's growing years.

Early Childhood

Some details can be helpful in the understanding process for the child in early childhood. Children in this stage are more aware of the world around them and basically understand the concept of "family." By this age, children will be able to tell you who their family members are and how they are related to each other. They do this by family experiences and being exposed to different families.

This is a great time to start reading storybooks, and many are available. The Web site www.XYandMe.com contains a series of 16 books that begin and end the same, with not being able to have a biological child, to the joy of having a child. The middle section describes the child's particular reproduction method for coming to the family.

It is also a good idea to put a beginning book together of pictures of the child coming home. These pictures should include parents wanting a child, waiting for a positive pregnancy test, the clinic where the parents received assistance or picture of the sperm bank and/or egg facility, the doctor's office, pictures of the donor and/or genetic family, and pictures throughout the pregnancy and birth. This book will start the child from his or her beginning, which includes the parents' decision, individuals from whom they received assistance, and the helper/donor who gave his or her genetics for the child's life. For a known donor situation, actual pictures of the family member, friend, or extended family can also be provided in the book. The message is clear, that "we wanted to have children in our family, we worked really hard for our children to arrive, and we accepted and celebrated the assistance of many people."

This is also a time to look for opportunities to point things out to children as they learn about the world around them. For example, "This is a fire station, where firemen help people when they are in an emergency." "This is where we went when we needed help for you to come into our family." "This is the hospital where you were born." Showing the child these places provides images and concrete facts along the way. This is also an excellent time to be talking to the child about the many ways that children come into a family. Todd Parr (2003) has authored many books about families and the importance of the love they share with each other.

Middle Childhood

During the middle years, as in adoptions, children have many questions. These can occur when driving the car, seeing a pregnant woman, or standing in line at a grocery store. Parents are wise to "go with the flow" in terms of these questions. Parents do well to keep the conversations active in bringing up the subject from time to time. The healthy message is that this is a comfortable subject to talk about, and it is okay to ask questions. Girls tend to ask questions earlier than boys. As children move into the questions of how babies are made, more factual information can be shared. Generally during this time, the "ah-ha" moments will occur, and children will figure out what "donor" actually means and then understand this genetic connection to another.

Sex education received from parents and schools is now starting to make more sense: They have inherited genes from the donor and may now begin to question who their "real" parent(s) are. The questions "What is real?" and "Who is real?" come into their thoughts. The realization of who they are and who their identity is to become is not a shock because of all the early telling. However, there is some sadness when children actually understand that one or both of their parents is not genetically connected to them.

During this time, the child will ask lots of questions, and the parents will provide them with information. It is best to share most of this information before the adolescent years. In this way, children can put the puzzle pieces together as they work on identity formation. In our experience, girls are more likely to ask lots of questions; boys tend not to want to be different and may not display curiosity. All extremes are possible from not wanting to talk about it to talking about it frequently.

The best parental stance is to keep the communication lines open and answer questions with as much factual information as possible. If the child asks a question about the donor, and the parent does not have the information, it is best to have empathy for the child and say, "I wish I could answer that question. If I were you, I would want to know, too." In an open, identified donor or a known donor situation, it may be helpful to write the questions down so the value of the child's curiosity is validated. The parent can assure the children these questions can be asked of the donor.

Adolescence

As children move into their teenage years, they will learn about science, reproduction, and deoxyribonucleic acid (DNA) in school. For some children, this will simply be academic information. However, donor children will identify these scientific concepts with themselves. In teenage years, everything is fair game for challenges and questions. Most adults remember when, as adolescents, they thought, "Parents don't really know anything. I am so different from them." The psychological task in adolescent years, as discussed by Erikson (1968), is to individuate, to become a person with individualized needs, tasks, and freedoms. Teens want to find out how they are similar and different from their parents and how they became a unique individual. Donor-conceived children also have to figure out how they are similar and different from the genetic donor. These questions will often challenge the non-genetic parents' authority, which may produce anxiety for parents. The adolescent may say things like "You are not my real parents." It is best for parents to understand the teenager's quest for identity without becoming defensive. Parents need to continue to distinguish between the facts of the teen's conception from the normal responsibilities of parenting.

A teenager who now chooses to share information with his or her peers may cause concern for parents because not everyone will understand (or approve of) how the child came to their family. This is a very fine detail because parents want to ensure their teen has pride in him or herself. Some parents might have chosen to maintain more privacy about the methods used for conception. The child, however, is really in charge of who is told, and there may be some surprises along the way.

Summary

Parents who use donor gametes should feel firm and entitled to say they are this child's parents. Health care providers (doctors, nurses, and social workers) must help these parents. Their decision to bring a child into the world creates continuous consequences for the whole family. The parents' responsibility is to attach, parent, and educate, and the child's responsibility is to ask questions to form an identity and find ways to feel secure about the individual he or she is becoming. Participating as the child's advocate presents many joys and celebrations, as well as many challenges. Pediatric nurses can help families resolve infertility issues and obtain education about donor conception. This advocacy provides the freedom for parents to be proud of their decision, attach to the process, and rejoice for the child who comes to their family. This is a true blessing for everyone.

References

Bouchard, T.J., Jr., Lykken, D.T., McGue, M., Segal, N.L., & Tellegan, A. (1990). Sources of human psychological differences: The Minnesota Study of Twins Reared Apart. *Science* 250(4978), 223–228.

Buster, J.E., Bustillo, M., Thorneycroft, I.H., Simon, J.A., Boyers, S.P., Marshall, J.R., . . . Louw, J.A. (1983) Non-surgical transfer of an invivo fertilized donated ovum to an infertility patient. *The Lancet, 1*(8328), 816–817.

"Embryo adoption becoming the rage." (2009, April 19). *The Washington Times*. Retrieved from http://www.washingtontimes.com/news/2009/apr/19/embryo-adoption-becoming-rage.

Erikson, E. (1968). *The stages of psychosocial development*. New York: Norton.

Parr, T. (2003). *The family book*. New York: Little, Brown & Co.

Snowden, R., Mitchell, G.D., & Snowden, E.M. (1983). *Artificial reproduction: A social investigation*. London: George Allen & Unwin.

Critical Thinking

1. If you were conceived via donor conception, what questions would you have about your donor biological parent, if any? How would it feel if there was no way to have your questions answered?

2. The article suggests that parents who conceive through donor conception share this information with family and friends. Do you agree or disagree with this piece of advice? Why or why not?

3. Explain how children's questions or concerns about their biological heritage may change as they grow up.

4. The article provides advice for parents about how to address issues related to donor conception with children at different ages. Do you agree with the article's advice? Why or why not?

Create Central

www.mhhe.com/createcentral

Internet References

Adoptive Families
www.adoptivefamilies.com

American Society for Reproductive Medicine
www.asrm.org

Society for Assisted Reproductive Technology
www.sart.org

Adelaide Center for Bioethics and Culture
www.bioethics.org.au

KRIS A. PROBASCO, LSCSW, LCSW, is Executive Director, Adoption & Fertility Resources, A Division of Clinical Counseling Associates, Inc., Liberty, MO, and Overland Park, KS.

Author's Note: *I would like to dedicate this article to my mentors, Annette Baron (author of* The Adoption Triangle *and* Lethal Secrets*) and Sharon Kaplan Rozia (author of* The Open Adoption Experience*). Annette and Sharon have taught me to speak the truth and to encourage parents to speak the truth to their children for the benefit of their children.*

Reprinted from *Pediatric Nursing*, 2012, vol. 38, no. 3, pp 179–182. Reprinted with permission of the publisher, Jannetti Publications, Inc., East Holly Avenue/Box 56, Pitman, NJ 08071-0056; (856) 256-2300; FAX (856) 589-7463; Web site: www.pediatricnursing.net. For a sample copy of the journal, please contact the publisher.

Article   Prepared by: Patricia Hrusa Williams, *University of Maine at Farmington*

What Kids Learn from Hearing Family Stories

Elaine Reese

Learning Outcomes

After reading this article, you will be able to:

- Define what a personal narrative is.

- Recognize reasons why some parents may not read to their children.

- Identify the benefits of telling family stories and personal narratives to children.

"Dad, tell me a story from when you were little. Tell me the story about the time you met your best friend Chris at school." Six-year-old Alex, who has just started school himself, snuggles into his pillow and catches his dad's hand in the dark. They have finished the nightly reading of *Tin Tin* and now it's time for "just one more story" before Alex goes to sleep.

Most parents know about the benefits of reading stories from books with their young children. Parents are blasted with this message in pediatricians' offices, at preschool, on TV, even with billboards on the city bus. Reading books with children on a daily basis advances their language skills, extends their learning about the world, and helps their own reading later in school. Reading with your child from a young age can instill a lifelong love of books. A new study published in *Science* even shows that reading literary fiction improves adults' ability to understand other people's emotions.

Reading books with your children is clearly a good idea.

The cozy image of cuddling up with your young child while poring over a book, however, doesn't fit with reality for some parents and children. Parents from some cultures are not as comfortable reading with their children because books were not part of their everyday lives growing up. For other parents,

reading with children is a fraught activity because of their own negative experiences learning to read. And for some highly active children, sitting down with a book is a punishment, not a reward. Fortunately, parents can learn new ways of reading books with their children to engage even the most irascible customer—and to engage themselves.

Yet what most parents don't know is that everyday family stories, like the one that Alex's dad spun out that night, confer many of the same benefits of reading—and even some new ones.

Over the last 25 years, a small canon of research on family storytelling shows that when parents share more family stories with their children—especially when they tell those stories in a detailed and responsive way—their children benefit in a host of ways. For instance, experimental studies show that when parents learn to reminisce about everyday events with their preschool children in more detailed ways, their children tell richer, more complete narratives to other adults one to two years later compared to children whose parents didn't learn the new reminiscing techniques. Children of the parents who learned new ways to reminisce also demonstrate better understanding of other people's thoughts and emotions. These advanced narrative and emotional skills serve children well in the school years when reading complex material and learning to get along with others. In the preteen years, children whose families collaboratively discuss everyday events and family history more often have higher self-esteem and stronger self-concepts. And adolescents with a stronger knowledge of family history have more robust identities, better coping skills, and lower rates of depression and anxiety. Family storytelling can help a child grow into a teen who feels connected to the important people in her life.

Best of all, unlike stories from books, family stories are always free and completely portable. You don't even need to have the lights on to share with your child a story about your day, about their day, about your childhood or their grandma's. In the research on family storytelling, all of these kinds of stories are linked to benefits for your child. Family stories can continue to be part of a parent's daily interactions with their children into adolescence, long past the age of the bedtime story.

All families have stories to tell, regardless of their culture or their circumstances. Of course, not all of these stories are idyllic ones. Research shows that children and adolescents can learn a great deal from stories of life's more difficult moments—as long as those stories are told in a way that is sensitive to the child's level of understanding, and as long as something good is gleaned from the experience.

Telling the story about the time the Christmas tree ignited because of faulty wiring and burned up the presents is fine, as long as you can find a tinsel lining. For example: Luckily you were able to save some favorite ornaments from the blaze, and your family ended up at a soup kitchen for Christmas dinner where you met Marion, who would become a treasured family friend.

Books contain narratives, but only family stories contain your family's *personal* narratives. Fortunate children get both. They hear and read stories from books to become part of other people's worlds, and they hear and tell stories of their family to understand who they are and from whence they came.

As Ursula LeGuin said, "There have been great societies that did not use the wheel, but there have been no societies that did not tell stories." Oral storytelling has been part of human existence for millennia. Toddlers start telling primitive stories from nearly as soon as they can speak, beginning with simple sentences about past experiences such as "Cookie allgone." Adults quickly build on these baby stories, "What happened to your cookie? You ate it!" so that by age three or four, most children can tell a relatively sensible story of a past experience that a naïve listener will (mostly) understand. By the time they are in school, children will regale a sympathetic adult with highly detailed stories about events of great importance to them, such as scoring a goal at a soccer game, but they may fail to mention the bigger picture that their team still lost. In the preteen and early adolescent years, children tell highly proficient stories about events in their lives, but they still need help understanding difficult events, such as the time their best friend dumped

them for someone else. It is not until mid-adolescence that teens can understand the impact of events on their lives and on who they are becoming. Even older adolescents still benefit from their parents' help in understanding life's curveballs.

The holidays are prime time for family storytelling. When you're putting up the tree or having your holiday meal, share a story with your children about past holidays. Leave in the funny bits, the sad bits, the gory and smelly bits—kids can tell when a story has been sanitized for their protection. Then invite everyone else to tell a story too. Don't forget the youngest and the oldest storytellers in the group. Their stories may not be as coherent, but they can be the truest, and the most revealing.

Family stories can be told nearly anywhere. They cost us only our time, our memories, our creativity. They can inspire us, protect us, and bind us to others. So be generous with your stories, and be generous *in* your stories. Remember that your children may have them for a lifetime.

Critical Thinking

1. How is the experience of hearing family stories different from the experience of being read books by parents?

2. What are some of the benefits for children of hearing family stories?

3. What is a favorite family story you remember being told as a child? How and why is the story important to you, even now?

Create Central

www.mhhe.com/createcentral

Internet References

Family Narratives Lab, Emory University
http://www.psychology.emory.edu/cognition/fivush/lab/FivushLabWebsite/index.html

Family History and Genealogy
http://www.usa.gov/Citizen/Topics/History-Family.shtml

Storytelling for Parents
http://storytellingforparents.com

Article   Prepared by: Patricia Hrusa Williams,
University of Maine at Farmington

Family Unplugged

SHAWN BEAN

Learning Outcomes

After reading this article, you will be able to:

- Identify some different ways that parents, children, and families utilize technology.

- Explain how technology use influences family interaction.

- Describe some benefits of families taking a "digital sabbatical."

For five days, I broke up with my BlackBerry. And my iPad. Oh yeah, my computer, too. I even ditched my TV (it isn't you, it's me). Perhaps not so surprisingly, I discovered that disconnecting my family is actually the best way to make a connection.

Red. It's the color of love, of passion. It's also the color of the little blinking light on my BlackBerry.

Oh, blinky red light. Your allure is so magnetic. It doesn't matter if I'm at a traffic light, with my firstborn, Jackson, at the playground, or watching Tanner sing at his preschool graduation. That red light (paired with the titillating purr of a couple of vibrations) draws me in. Technology is my mistress.

Technology is also the medicine, the babysitter, the emergency contact. On numerous occasions, I've calmed a sibling squabble with a 50-milligram dose of *Supah Ninjas. He-Man* clips on YouTube have bought me extra minutes to meet a deadline. Then, of course, there was the time I got lost in the spaghetti-loop vortex of Disney World's highway system. There I was, an iPad open on my lap, stealing glances at MapQuest as I navigated through the Mouse Trap.

1 in 4 people would consider a completely tech-free day for their family.

It's not only me, of course. Our collective whatever-ness about technology has become a smidge scary. Roughly one in five adults admits to poor mobile etiquette but continues the behavior because everyone else is doing it. Forty-two percent of children think their parents need to disconnect when they're at home. "iParents" (digitally connected moms and dads) are twice as likely as regular parents to neglect their responsibilities because they're on Facebook and Twitter, according to a study by Retrevo. And it's not just that we've all been there. We *are* there.

59 percent of kids have seen their parent use a mobile device while driving.

The Disney World moment was a real wakeup call. I'm sure I would have made a smarter decision had the boys been in the car. (Right?) I need to rediscover undivided attention, eye contact, stillness, the nothings that happen between the somethings.

My whatever-ness is officially over. It's time to break up with the blinky red light.

Shawn Bean Just Met a Modern Dad Who Checks His E-mail at the Public Library

William Powers's version of whatever-ness ended just before Labor Day 2007. At his family's home in Cape Cod, there were three sets of eyes, and three screens: His then 9-year-old son, William, was playing a game online, his wife, Martha Sherrill, was on a laptop doing research, and Powers was on his own computer. "We were exchanging silent glances," recalls Powers. "That's when I realized something, anything, had to be done."

That something, anything, was the Internet Sabbath: From bedtime on Friday to sunrise on Monday, all plugged-in devices (laptops, smartphones, etc.) were off-limits. If someone absolutely, positively had to get online, they could use one of the computers at the public library. It was this experience—and the lessons learned—that inform his book, *Hamlet's BlackBerry: A Practical Philosophy for Building a Good Life in the Digital Age.*

I tell Powers about my plan: I'm taking my boys on a digital sabbatical. For five days, we'd forgo all technology. No *Supah Ninjas.* No YouTube. No MapQuest. No more trysts with the blinky red light.

"Expect that your house will feel slightly different," he says. "You won't know exactly what to do. We also had to relearn the art of sustained conversation with eye contact." (An interesting point. See how long your next parent–child conversation goes before a device interrupts. Technology has a wicked case of attention deficit disorder.)

One more thing: "You'll be shocked at the tics you've developed. You'll realize how often you reach for a tech fix." Powers says the first two months "were a real struggle. There was unbelievable withdrawal. I can't lie—there were tears."

Shawn Bean Is Off the Grid, and Has No Idea What He Will Do to Fill the Time

Before unplugging on Day One, I put a status update on Facebook about my experiment: "About to embark on a digital sabbatical with the boys. See you on the other side!" Comments included "Good luck!" and "Emme would die without her *Phineas and Ferb* fix."

I did not forewarn the boys that we were doing this, nor did I plan anything. It's easy to unplug when you've got a dozen distractions lined up. I want to face the analog world unarmed. Surprisingly, Jackson is on board from the get go, and wonders why we are only doing it for five days. I write up a contract: "Daddy, Jackson, and Tanner will not watch TV or play on the computer." I sign my name, Jackson writes "Jackson B," and Tanner squiggles a line resembling a seismograph reading.

Without a plan of attack, we quickly find ourselves doing, well, everything. Fishing poles come out of the garage, and we dig for earthworms in the front yard. We break out a bubble machine, left unopened from a recent birthday. We remix boring items into something new, from tinfoil (police badges) to plastic bottles in the recycling bin (test tubes). But I realize I'm going about this all wrong. I'm making our activities fast-paced, high-energy, and visually stimulating. Why am I re-creating television?

I also notice tingling in my phantom limb. More than twice, I mindlessly feel my pants pocket for my BlackBerry. Each time I pass the nightstand, I look for the blinky red light. There it is, blinking. Sweet, beautiful blinking. *Don't worry, baby. We'll be together again soon.*

---

42 percent of kids think their parents need to disconnect more at home.

Shawn Bean just Scared a Woman in Portland with Talk of Cell Phones Causing Cancer

Even with newborn Casey in her arms, Ellen Currey-Wilson was momentarily distracted by something else she loved: *The Price Is Right*. As she was rolled through the maternity ward,

---

Tech-Free Fun

A list of the unplugged activities my boys and I created out of thin air.

1. Built a ninja obstacle course using sofa cushions and pillows.
2. Repurposed empty plastic bottles in the recycling bin as test tubes. We filled them with water and added food coloring.
3. Created a mosaic sidewalk by coloring in the bricks with chalk.
4. Invented a "mocktail" using the fruit juices and drinks we already had in the refrigerator.
5. Played "airport." I gave them plane tickets and empty suitcases to pack. I also played the security agent who screened their luggage.

---

she caught Bob Barker on a wall-mounted screen, then quickly returned to her son's gaze.

"Television was my other parent," says Currey-Wilson. "I grew up with a single mom." B.C. (Before Casey), television was "a companion, an escape, a drug, a procrastinator's dream." Life was a series of sitcoms and game shows (creating a bridal registry, for example, reminded her of *Let's Make a Deal*). But A.D. (After Delivery), it was an obsession she did not want to pass on to her child. So she went cold turkey, to mixed results. She details her journey in *The Big Turnoff: Confessions of a TV-Addicted Mom Trying to Raise a TV-Free Kid*. Like Powers, she had a tough transition. She hid a television in the storage room upstairs and snuck in viewings of *Three's Company* while her baby napped.

During my funny and insightful conversation with Currey-Wilson, I catch glimpses of the nervous, hyper-analyzing mother from *The Big Turnoff*: the mom who acted as a human shield to block *Sesame Street* during a playdate, the mom who worried that her son would be ostracized at school for not knowing the theme song to *SpongeBob SquarePants*. After a quick introduction, we discuss the ways technology affects our kids. (Currey-Wilson conducted an informal survey of the students in her fourth-grade class and discovered that those who watched the most TV were the least focused.) We then chat about recent findings connecting cell-phone use to cancer. How ironic, I say: Here we are, both on cell phones, discussing cell-phone use and cancer. The line goes quiet. She politely asks if I can call her back on the landline.

For so many new moms, who feel isolated by their new 24-hour job, technology is a way to connect. Roughly 35 percent of moms consider a mother they met on a message board a friend, according to a *Parenting*-BlogHer survey. Seventy-three percent talk about sensitive issues like their children's behavior and development on message boards; about 43 percent do the same on Facebook.

"With technology, you can instantly interact with real people," Currey-Wilson explains. "Even watching a TV show made me feel like I was part of the conversation. I was lonely without it."

How did she change after breaking up with the boob tube? "I learned to face my problems more quickly, skipping over the hours of TV I usually needed to watch before attempting to deal with anything challenging or unpleasant," she says. "I also became closer to my husband. We fought more, too, much to his dismay. It was a big adjustment for him to learn to deal with a wife who wasn't zoned out anymore."

49 percent of parents prohibit their kids from having a computer in their bedroom.

"To have a deep relationship, you have to spend time and focus," Powers explains. "It's hard to be present when one part of your mind is wondering what's happening out in the world."

At the end of Day Three, my wife, Brandy, and I tuck the boys into bed and head out to the porch. The stars are out—faint, winking gemstones—but tonight I don't use *Star Walk* on my iPad to discover what corner of the sky is getting filleted by Orion's Sword. A few minutes later, Jackson walks out and curls up on my lap. We sit quietly. Across the lake, milky blue light flickers inside a living room. "They're watching TV," Jackson says.

Shawn Bean is Watching His Son Catch His First Wave

Four years later; Powers and his family still observe their Internet Sabbath. "When I come back to the digital world on Monday morning, I'm reminded of how great it is," he says. "I love it more because I've had a break." He adds that his son, William, has a huge fort at the back of the property. "He convinces his friends to leave their phones in the house."

By Day Five, Jackson had not only caught an earthworm and a smallmouth bass, but his first wave on a longboard during a trip to the beach. He yells like a banshee as I push him into the swirling meringue of the breaking wave. He falls. He bobs to the surface. He wants to do it again.

Of course, these activities are not exclusive to the analog world. But we know that in the digital world, children 6 and under spend two hours a day using screen media, and adults spend more than five hours a day online. That's two days every week without sustained eye contact or conversation. The digital sabbatical gives us that time back. It's no longer the blinky red light versus your son's question about the food on Mars. As it should be, a ridiculous debate about lunch in outer space wins every time.

"It's not about turning against technology," Powers notes, "but designing our lives the way we want them."

I open Microsoft Word to begin writing this story, and there it is: the cursor. It's blinking impatiently, waiting to move forward, like a runner jogging in place at a red light. That's when it hits me: Technology is about next. Family is about now.

Critical Thinking

1. What are some challenges for families as technology becomes an ever-present force in our lives?

2. What are some benefits of unplugging and giving our family a "digital sabbatical?"

3. What guidelines can you develop for families regarding computer and cell-phone use?

Create Central

www.mhhe.com/createcentral

Internet References

Family Online Safety Institute
www.fosi.org

Pew Internet and American Life Project: Networked Families
www.pewinternet.org/Reports/2008/Networked-Families.aspx